THE PROTESTANT PULPIT

The
PROTESTANT PULPIT

*An Anthology of Master Sermons
from the Reformation to Our Own Day*

Compiled by
ANDREW WATTERSON BLACKWOOD

ABINGDON PRESS
NEW YORK ● NASHVILLE

THE PROTESTANT PULPIT

Copyright MCMXLVII by Stone & Pierce

Library of Congress Catalog Card Number: 47-12188

F

SET UP, PRINTED, AND BOUND BY THE
PARTHENON PRESS, AT NASHVILLE,
TENNESSEE, UNITED STATES OF AMERICA

Foreword

Our age calls for a revival of preaching. Many voices unite in the appeal. At the 1946 meeting of the Federal Council of Churches President Truman pleaded for "a moral and spiritual awakening in the life of the individual and in the councils of the world. . . . There is no problem on this earth tough enough to withstand the flame of a genuine revival of religious faith. . . . The church must provide the shock forces to accomplish this moral and spiritual awakening. Oh, for an Isaiah or a St. Paul to awaken this sick world to its moral and spiritual responsibility!" [1]

Mr. Truman spoke as a Protestant, but not against any other faith. In much the same spirit this book brings sermons by Protestant leaders of yesterday and today. Such a book might well exhibit messages from other masters, including prophets and apostles, as well as Chrysostom, Bossuet, and Dr. Fulton J. Sheen. But a compiler must remember the limit of space. So this work includes only Protestant sermons.

The book has grown out of long experience as a teacher of ministerial students and as an adviser of parish ministers. Thirty years of study about preaching seem to show that the best approach is through history, and that the best way to improve one's pulpit work is through the study of sermons. At some early stage almost every master preacher has made a study of printed sermons by former divines. In the classroom I have felt the need of some one volume of sermons for use in "laboratory work." In replying to letters, also, I have wished to recommend such a collection as a help to friends out on the field. Hence I have prepared this volume.

The work should help readers of three sorts. First, students in seminaries. These ministers of tomorrow will use the book under the eye of an expert teacher. They will stress the facts about any given sermon, and not details of biography. They might entertain each other by telling about the number of children in the home of John Wesley's parents, or the possible reasons why Phillips Brooks remained a bachelor. But men will learn more about preaching if they dig down into each sermon and discover the secrets of its effectiveness. Such "laboratory work" may grow monotonous, but in years to come it will bear fruit. Much of the value depends on the skill of the teacher. Let him encourage the student to deal with each sermon according to its purpose and tone color. Who could devise a uniform way of approaching two different pieces of art?

For encouragement the professor will turn to lectures by the masters. Often he will look to Henry Ward Beecher. For a few years after young Henry left the seminary he floundered in the pulpit. Then he determined that

---

[1] *New York Times*, March 7, 1946, report on the address of the preceding day before the meeting at Columbus, Ohio.

he would master his craft. He did so partly through study of printed sermons from other days. At the height of his renown in Brooklyn he spoke to the divinity students at Yale: "You have got to learn your business. It will take years and years before you are expert preachers. . . . You are not practiced workmen until you understand human nature, and how to touch it with the divine truth. . . . That is the study. You have not begun your education yet. You are but getting ready to study when you begin to preach." [2]

This advice should also help the second group of readers—parish ministers. In our needy age what local interpreter feels content with his pulpit work? Like the physician next door, the pastor may wish to hie away and take a "refresher course." In lieu of that, why not study homiletics at home? Devote a year or more to "laboratory work" among sermons like those that follow. Then single out a master preacher and make a special study of his handiwork. Instead of admiring sweeping surveys by distant critics, why not get down and dig? The clergyman of a liberal turn may derive much help from a study of Spurgeon and Maclaren. The minister of a conservative type can learn much from Robertson or Bushnell. Why not study what you do not know?

Laymen also, I hope, will find these sermons helpful. Since the outbreak of World War II many lay people have become concerned about the meaning of Christianity. They wish to learn the facts about the Protestant church. They have neither the time nor the desire for hard study, but they are willing and anxious to read. In this volume laymen will find a path of approach to Protestantism as it appears in sermons. Here they will see how closely some of the ablest interpreters have held to the "faith of our fathers," and how largely the message of the Protestant pulpit has come from the Scriptures, especially the New Testament.

Now and again some reader may shake his head in dissent. He may ask why an evangelical compiler should include certain sermons. The query seems fair; let the reply be frank. I hold to the old-fashioned faith known as evangelical. But a teacher of homiletics may learn much from preachers with whom he does not agree about doctrine. In the present book I serve as a reporter, not as an advocate. After a lifelong study of preaching in the light of its history, how could one pass by Channing, the Unitarian, and others not "orthodox"? Must a compiler always agree with a preacher of yesterday or today in order to look upon him as a pulpit master? Likewise one need not regard "Billy" Sunday and Frank W. Boreham as exemplars of our art at its best. Still one must remember that in an earlier day each of them appealed to a host of Protestant hearers and readers.

As for the choice of the remaining sermons, I have kept away from those that appear in other collections. However, there are a few exceptions, such as the masterpiece by Thomas Chalmers, "The Expulsive Power of a New Affection." Among the discourses by men now living, in a number of cases the wishes of the preachers have prevailed. More than one has asked to

---

[2] *Yale Lectures on Preaching*, first series (New York: J. B. Ford & Co., 1872), p. 61.

be heard through a message written and spoken after the end of World War II.

Conscience troubles me more because of omissions. Why pass by such giants as John Calvin and George Fox, Alexander Campbell and John Knox? Because even with the help of experts I have not found sermons worthy to represent those men of might. Why not include messages from Richard Baxter, Lyman Beecher, John A. Broadus, Charles R. Brown, Robert William Dale, John Donne, Ralph Waldo Emerson, George A. Gordon, Robert Hall, Charles E. Jefferson, Henry P. Liddon, G. Campbell Morgan, Francis L. Patton, Friedrich E. D. Schleiermacher, Matthew Simpson, Robert South, Jeremy Taylor, John Tillotson, Henry van Dyke, Alexander Whyte, and other men of renown? In response I can only plead lack of space.

As for ministers now at work, one could present discourses by forty or fifty divines. One could make a book out of sermons by leaders in any large denomination. Once again, space forbids. But let there be no repining. Let there be thanksgiving because of deepening friendships with all sorts of good sermons, and gratitude to ministers who have gone far out of their way to make this book a reality. Let there be credit also to librarians and publishers and counselors whose kindnesses I can never repay.

One question remains: How many of these sermons can qualify as "great"? Who knows? Who can judge, save God? He appears to think of pulpit work in terms of goodness rather than "greatness." According to the Scriptures, "greatness" in preaching seems to be a menace.[3] If the Lord had His way, we seminary teachers might put the term "great sermons" on an *index expurgatorius*. At any rate, Christendom has produced few "great" preachers, or "great" scholars. Instead of styling every hilltop "great," why not keep that term for the Alps? Why not insist that sermons be good? According to a master of the art, a good sermon means one that does good. From this point of view the level of pulpit work has been rising in recent years. Let us hope that the upward trend will continue. Good sermons abound, but not everywhere. Let there be far more pulpit work that the Lord will call good.

The sermons appear practically word for word. With a single exception—that from *Pilgrim's Progress*—the plan calls for no abridgment. In each case the selection comes from what seems to be an authentic edition. In Part I, "Sermons by Masters in Other Days," the men appear chronologically, according to the years of birth. In Part II, "Sermons by Masters in Our Own Day," the names come alphabetically. The small superior number at the beginning of each paragraph will facilitate work in study or classroom. So will the first appendix, "A Work Sheet: How to Study a Sermon"; and the second appendix, a representative bibliography, "Books in This Field." The short biographical sketches at the end of the volume ought to interest every lover of good preaching.

May these sermons bring many a reader the sort of food and light they have brought me. May the reader note "the continuity of Christian thought,"

[3] Ezek. 33:30-33, Mark 10:35-45, I Cor. 2:1-5, I Pet. 5:1-4, et al.

and look on the pulpit as the crowning glory of the Protestant church. May he think of the sermon as Christian truth and duty "drawn out in living characters," and on the local interpreter as the key man in the work of the Kingdom here below. Through the blessing of the Triune God may the future of the Protestant pulpit be more than worthy of its past.

As the father of young ministers and the teacher of countless others, I feel a special concern about the coming leaders of Protestantism. I pray that the mantle of some good preacher may fall on every young pastor, with a double portion of the master's loyalty to Christ and the Church. How else can the Protestant pulpit meet the needs of today and tomorrow? Not by great sermons, but by good servants of the great God. "Not by arms, nor by force, but by my Spirit, saith the Lord of hosts." [4]

ANDREW WATTERSON BLACKWOOD

The Theological Seminary
Princeton, New Jersey

[4] Zech. 4:6b (American Translation).

8

Contents

Part I

Sermons by Masters in Other Days

1. MARTIN LUTHER: Justification by Faith 13
2. JOHN BUNYAN: From *The Pilgrim's Progress* 21
3. JOHN WESLEY: The Scripture Way of Salvation 23
4. GEORGE WHITEFIELD: The Burning Bush 32
5. JONATHAN EDWARDS: The Christian Pilgrim 40
6. THOMAS CHALMERS: The Expulsive Power of a New Affection . . . 50
7. WILLIAM ELLERY CHANNING: The Character of Christ 63
8. HORACE BUSHNELL: Every Man's Life a Plan of God 75
9. HENRY WARD BEECHER: The God of Comfort 86
10. FREDERICK WILLIAM ROBERTSON: The Loneliness of Christ 99
11. ALEXANDER MACLAREN: Love and Forgiveness 107
12. CHARLES HADDON SPURGEON: Songs in the Night 114
13. PHILLIPS BROOKS: The Fire and the Calf 129
14. DWIGHT LYMAN MOODY: What Think Ye of Christ? 138
15. WILLIAM ASHLEY SUNDAY: Heaven 144
16. JOHN HENRY JOWETT: The Magnetism of the Uplifted Lord 147
17. WILLIAM McCALLUM CLOW: The Cross and the Memory of Sin . . . 152
18. GEORGE WASHINGTON TRUETT: The Conquest of Fear 158
19. FRANK WILLIAM BOREHAM: David Livingstone's Text 164

Part II

Sermons by Masters in Our Own Day

20. KARL BARTH: Repentance 173
21. GEORGE ARTHUR BUTTRICK: The Sound of Silence 180
22. CLOVIS GILLHAM CHAPPELL: The Forks of the Road—Moses 185
23. HARRY EMERSON FOSDICK: Forgiveness of Sins 191

24. ARTHUR JOHN GOSSIP: But When Life Tumbles In, What Then? . . . 198

25. DOUGLAS HORTON: Taking a City 205

26. EDGAR DEWITT JONES: The Light on the Lord's Face 211

27. RUFUS MATTHEW JONES: The Heart of Christianity 218

28. CLARENCE EDWARD MACARTNEY: Your Unknown Self 224

29. WALTER ARTHUR MAIER: Thanks Be Unto God for His Unspeakable Gift! 231

30. JOSEPH FORT NEWTON: Reconciliation 238

31. MARTIN NIEMÖLLER: Maundy Thursday 244

32. HAROLD COOKE PHILLIPS: An Angel in the Sun 249

33. EDWIN MCNEILL POTEAT: Vandalism or Faith? 256

34. JAMES REID: The Victory of God in the Disasters of Life 264

35. PAUL EHRMAN SCHERER: Protestantism: Its Liabilities and Assets . . . 270

36. JOSEPH RICHARD SIZOO: The Way of Faith 277

37. RALPH WASHINGTON SOCKMAN: Through Jesus Christ Our Lord . . . 283

38. JAMES STUART STEWART: The Lord God Omnipotent Reigneth . . . 288

39. LESLIE DIXON WEATHERHEAD: Why People Do Go to Church 295

Appendices

A. A Work Sheet: How to Study a Sermon 305

B. Bibliography: Books for Study in This Field 307

Biographical Index of Authors 310

Part 1

SERMONS BY MASTERS
in Other Days

Justification by Faith

Ninth Sunday After Trinity

Luke 16:1-9

ALTHOUGH in my Postils hitherto, and in my little book, *Christian Liberty and Good Works*, I have taught very extensively how faith alone without work justifies, and good works are done first after we believe, that it seems I should henceforth politely keep quiet, and give every mind and heart an opportunity to understand and explain all the Gospel lessons for themselves; yet I perceive that the Gospel abides and prospers only among the few; the people are constantly dispirited and terrified by the passages that treat of good works; so that I see plainly how necessary it is, either to write Postils on each Gospel lesson, or to appoint sensible ministers in all places who can orally explain and teach these things.

² If this Gospel be considered without the Spirit, by mere reason, it truly favors the priests and monks, and could be made to serve covetousness and to establish one's own works. For when Christ says: "Make to yourselves friends by means of the mammon of unrighteousness; that, when it shall fail, they may receive you into the eternal tabernacles"; they force from it three points against our doctrine of faith, namely: first, against that we teach faith alone justifies and saves from sin; second, that all good works ought to be gratuitously done to our neighbors out of free love; third, that we should not put any value in the merits of saints or of others.

³ Against our first proposition they claim that the Lord says here: "Make to yourselves friends by means of the mammon of unrighteousness," just as though works should make us friends, who previously were enemies. Against the second, is what He says: "That they may receive you into the eternal tabernacles"; just as though we should do the work for our own sakes and benefit. And against the third they quote: "The friends may receive us into the eternal tabernacles"; just as though we should serve the saints and trust in them to get to heaven. For the sake of the weak we reply to these:

I. *Faith alone makes us good, and friends of God.*

⁴ The foundation must be maintained without wavering, that faith without any works, without any merit, reconciles man to God and makes him good,

---

From *The Precious and Sacred Writings of Martin Luther*, ed. John Nicholas Lenker Minneapolis: (Lutherans in All Lands Co., 1904), Vol. IV. Sermon title supplied.

as Paul says to the Romans: "But now apart from the law a righteousness of God hath been manifested, being witnessed by the law and the prophets; even the righteousness of God through faith in Jesus Christ unto all them that believe." Paul at another place says: "To Abraham, his faith was reckoned for righteousness"; so also with us. Again: "Being therefore justified by faith, we have peace with God through our Lord Jesus Christ." Again: "For with the heart man believeth unto righteousness; and with the mouth confession is made unto salvation." These, and many more similar passages, we must firmly hold and trust in them immovably, so that to faith alone without any assistance of works, is attributed the forgiveness of sins and our justification.

⁵ Take for an illustration the parable of Christ: "Even so every good tree bringeth forth good fruit; but the corrupt tree bringeth forth evil fruit." Here you see that the fruit does not make the tree good, but without any fruit and before any fruit the tree must be first good, or made good, before it can bear good fruit. As He also says: "Either make the tree good, and its fruit good; or make the tree corrupt, and its fruit corrupt: for the tree is known by its fruit. Ye offspring of vipers, how can ye, being evil, speak good things?" Thus it is the naked truth, that a man must be good without good works, and before he does any good works. And it is clear how impossible it is that a man should become good by works, when he is not good before he does the good works. For Christ stands firm when He says: "How can ye, being evil, speak good things?" And hence follows: How can ye, being evil, do good things?

⁶ Therefore the powerful conclusion follows, there must be something far greater and more precious than all good works, by which a man becomes pious and good, before he does good; just as he must first be in bodily health before he can labor and do hard work. This great and precious something is the noble Word of God, which offers us in the Gospel the grace of God in Christ. He who hears and believes this, thereby becomes good and righteous. Wherefore it is called the Word of Life, a Word of Grace, a Word of Forgiveness. But he who neither hears nor believes it, can in no way become good. For St. Peter says in the Acts: "And he made no distinction between us and them, cleansing their hearts by faith." For as the Word is, so will the heart be, which believes and cleaves firmly to it. The Word is a living, righteous, truthful, pure and good Word, so also the heart which cleaves to it, must be living, just, truthful, pure and good.

⁷ What now shall we say of those passages which so strongly insist on good works, as when the Lord says: "Make to yourselves friends by means of the mammon of unrighteousness"? And in Matthew: "For I was hungry, and ye did not give me to eat." And many other similar passages, which sound altogether as though we had become good by works. We answer thus:

⁸ There are some who hear and read the Gospel and what is said by faith, and immediately conclude they have formed a correct notion of what faith is. They do not think that faith is anything else than something which is altogether in their own power to have or not to have, as any other natural

14

human work. Hence, when in their hearts they begin to think and say: "Verily, the doctrine is right, and I believe it is true," then they immediately think faith is present. But as soon as they see and feel in themselves and others that no change has taken place, and that the works do not follow and they remain as before in their old ways, then they conclude that faith is not sufficient, that they must have something more and greater than faith.

9 Behold, how they then seize the opportunity, and cry and say: Oh, faith alone does not do it. Why? Oh, because there are so many who believe, and are no better than before, and have not changed their minds at all. Such people are those whom Jude in his Epistle calls dreamers who deceive themselves with their own dreams. For what are such thoughts of theirs which they call faith, but a dream, a dark shadow of faith, which they themselves have created in their own thoughts, by their own strength without the grace of God? They become worse than they were before. For it happens with them as the Lord says: "Neither do men put new wine into old wine-skins; else the skins burst, and the wine is spilled." That is, they hear God's Word and do not lay hold of it, therefore they burst and become worse.

10 But true faith, of which we speak, cannot be manufactured by our own thoughts, for it is solely a work of God in us, without any assistance on our part. As Paul says to the Romans, it is God's gift and grace, obtained by one man, Christ. Therefore, faith is something very powerful, active, restless, effective, which at once renews a person and again regenerates him, and leads him altogether into a new manner and character of life, so that it is impossible not to do good without ceasing.

11 For just as natural as it is for the tree to produce fruit, so natural is it for faith to produce good works. And just as it is quite unnecessary to command the tree to bear fruit, so there is no command given to the believer, as Paul says, nor is urging necessary for him to do good, for he does it of himself, freely and unconstrained; just as he of himself without command sleeps, eats, drinks, puts on his clothes, hears, speaks, goes and comes.

12 Whoever has not this faith talks but vainly about faith and works, and does not himself know what he says or whither it tends. For he has not received it; he juggles with lies and applies the Scriptures where they speak of faith and works to his own dreams and false thoughts, which is purely a human work. Whereas the Scriptures attribute both faith and good works not to ourselves, but to God alone.

13 Is not this a perverted and blind people? They teach we cannot do a good deed of ourselves, and then in their presumption go to work and arrogate to themselves the highest of all the works of God, namely faith, to manufacture it themselves out of their own perverted thoughts. Wherefore I have said that we should despair of ourselves and pray to God for faith as the Apostle did in Luke 17:5. When we have faith we need nothing more, for it brings with it the Holy Spirit, who then teaches us not only all things, but also establishes us firmly in it, and leads us through death and hell to heaven.

14 Now observe, we have given these answers, that the Scriptures have

15

such passages concerning works, on account of such dreamers and self-invented faith; not that man should become good by works, but that man should thereby prove and see the difference between false and true faith. For wherever faith is right it does good. If it does no good, it is then certainly a dream and a false idea of faith. So, just as the fruit on the tree does not make the tree good, but nevertheless outwardly proves and testifies that the tree is good, as Christ says, "By their fruits ye shall know them"—thus we should also learn to know faith by its fruits.

[15] From this you see, there is a great difference between being good, and to be known as good; or to become good and to prove and show that you are good. Faith makes good, but works prove the faith and goodness to be right. Thus the Scriptures speak in the plain way, which prevails among the common people, as when a father says unto his son: "Go and be merciful, good and friendly to this or to that poor person." By which he does not command him to be merciful, good and friendly, but because he is already good and merciful, he requires that he should also show and prove it outwardly toward the poor by his act, in order that the goodness which he has in himself may also be known to others and be helpful to them.

[16] So you should explain all passages of Scripture referring to works, that God thereby desires to let the goodness received in faith express and prove itself, and become a benefit to others, so that false faith may become known and rooted out of the heart. For God gives no one His grace that it may remain inactive and accomplish nothing good, but in order that it may bear interest, and by being publicly known and proved externally draw every one to God; as Christ says: "Even so let your light shine before men, that they may see your good works, and glorify your Father who is in heaven." Otherwise it would be but a buried treasure and a hidden light. But what profit is there in either? Yea, goodness does not only thereby become known to others, but we ourselves also become certain that we are honest, as St. Peter says: "Wherefore, brethren, give the more diligence to make your calling and election sure." For where works do not follow, a man cannot know whether his faith is right; yea, he may be certain that his faith is a dream, and not right as it should be. Thus Abraham became certain of his faith, and that he feared God, when he offered up his son. As God by the angel said to Abraham: "Now I know, that is, it is manifest, that thou fearest God, seeing thou hast not withheld thy son, thine only son, from me."

[17] Then abide by the truth, that man is internally, in spirit before God, justified by faith alone without works, but externally and publicly before men and himself, he is justified by works, that he is at heart an honest believer and pious. The one you may call a public or outward justification, the other an inner justification, yet in the sense that the public or external justification is only the fruit, the result and proof of the justification in the heart, that a man does not become just thereby before God, but must previously be just before Him. So you may call the fruit of the tree the public or outward good of the tree, which is only the result and proof of its inner and natural goodness.

¹⁸ This is what St. James means when he says in his Epistle: "Faith without works is dead." That is, as the works do not follow, it is a sure sign that there is no faith there; but only an empty thought and dream, which they falsely call faith. Now we understand the word of Christ: "Make to yourselves friends by means of the mammon of unrighteousness." That is, prove your faith publicly by your outward gifts, by which you win friends, that the poor may be witnesses of your public work, that your faith is genuine. For mere external giving in itself can never make friends, unless it proceed from faith, as Christ rejects the alms of the Pharisees that they thereby make no friends because their heart is false. Thus no heart can ever be right without faith, so that even nature forces the confession that no work makes one good, but that the heart must first be good and upright.

II. *All works must be done freely and gratuitously, without seeking gain by them.*

¹⁹ Christ means this when He says: "Freely ye receive, freely give." For just as Christ with all His works did not merit heaven for Himself, because it was His before; but He served us thereby, not regarding or seeking His own, but these two things, namely, our benefit and the glory of God His Father; so also should we never seek our own in our good works, either temporal or eternal, but glorify God by freely and gratuitously doing good to our neighbor. This St. Paul teaches the Philippians, "Have this mind in you which was also in Christ Jesus: who, existing in the form of God, counted not the being on an equality with God a thing to be grasped, but emptied himself, taking the form of a servant, being made in the likeness of men; and being found in fashion as a man, he humbled himself, becoming obedient unto death, yea, the death of the cross." That is, for Himself he had enough, since in Him dwelt all the fulness of the Godhead bodily; and yet He served us and became our servant.

²⁰ And this is the cause; for since faith justifies and destroys sin before God, so it gives life and salvation. And now it would be a lasting shame and disgrace, and injurious to faith, if any one by his life and works would desire to obtain what faith already possesses and brings with it. Just as Christ would have only disgraced Himself had He done good in order to become the Son of God and Lord over all things, which He already was before. So faith makes us God's children, as John says: "But as many as received him, to them gave he the right to become the children of God, even to them that believe on his name." But if they are children, then they are heirs, as St. Paul says, "How then can we do anything to obtain the inheritance, which we already have by faith?"

²¹ But what shall we say of passages that insist on a good life for the sake of an external reward as this one does: "Make to yourselves friends by means of the mammon of unrighteousness"? And in Matthew: "But if thou wouldst enter into life, keep the commandments." "Lay up for yourselves treasures in heaven." We will say this: that those who do not know faith, only speak and think of the reward, as of works. For they think that the same rule obtains here as in human affairs, that they must earn the Kingdom of heaven

17

by their works. These, too, are dreams and false views, of which Malachi speaks: "Oh, that there were one among you that would shut the doors, that ye might not kindle fire on mine altar in vain!" They are slaves and greedy self-enjoying hirelings and day laborers, who receive their reward here on earth, like the Pharisees with their praying and fasting, as Christ says.

22 However, in regard to the eternal reward it is thus: inasmuch as works naturally follow faith, as I said, it is not necessary to command them, for it is impossible for faith not to do them without being commanded, in order that we may learn to distinguish the false from the true faith. Hence the eternal reward also follows true faith, naturally, without any seeking, so that it is impossible that it should not, although it may never be desired or sought, yet it is appropriated and promised in order that true and false believers may be known, and that every one may understand that a good life follows naturally of itself.

23 As an illustration of this take a rude comparison: behold, hell and death are also threatened to the sinner, and naturally follow sin without any seeking; for no one does wickedly because he wants to be damned, but would much rather escape it. Yet, the result is there, and it is not necessary to declare it, for it will come of itself. Yet, it is declared that man might know what follows a wicked life. So here, a wicked life has its own reward without seeking it. Hence a good life will find its reward without any seeking it. When you drink good or poor wine, although you do not drink it for the taste, yet the taste naturally follows of itself.

24 Now when Christ says: "make to yourselves friends," "lay up for yourselves treasures," and the like, you see that He means: do good, and it will follow of itself without your seeking, that you will have friends, find treasures in heaven, and receive a reward. But your eyes must simply be directed to a good life, and care nothing about the reward, but be satisfied to know and be assured that it will follow, and let God see to that. For those who look for a reward become lazy and unwilling laborers, and love the reward more than the work, yea, they become enemies of work. In this way God's will also becomes hateful, who has commanded us to work, and hence God's command and will must finally become burdensome to such a heart.

III. *It is not the saints, but God only who receives us into the eternal tabernacles, and bestows the reward.*

25 This is so clear that it needs no proof. For how can the saints receive us into heaven, as every one himself must depend on God alone to receive him into heaven, and every saint scarcely has enough for himself? This the wise virgins prove, who did not wish to give of their oil to the foolish virgins, and St. Peter says: "The righteous is scarcely saved." And Christ declares: "No one hath ascended into heaven, but he that descended out of heaven, even the Son of Man, who is in heaven."

26 What then shall we reply to: "Make to yourselves friends out of the mammon of unrighteousness; that, when it shall fail, they may receive you into the eternal tabernacles"? We say this: that this passage says nothing about the saints in heaven, but of the poor and needy on earth, who live

among us. As though He would say: "Why do you build churches, make saints and serve my mother, St. Peter, St. Paul and other departed saints? They do not need this or any other service of yours, they are not your friends, but friends of those who lived in their days and to whom they did good; but do service to your friends, that is, the poor who live in your time and among you, your nearest neighbors who need your help, make them your friends with your mammon."

27 Again, we must not understand this reception into the eternal tabernacles as being done by man; however, man will be an instrument and witness to our faith, exercised and shown in their behalf, on account of which God receives us into the eternal tabernacles. For thus the Scriptures are accustomed to speak when they say: sin condemns, faith saves; that means, sin is the cause why God condemns, and faith is the cause why He saves. As man also is at all times accustomed to say: your wickedness will bring you misfortune, which means, your wickedness is the cause and source of your misfortune. Thus our friends receive us into heaven, when they are the cause, through our faith shown to them, of entering heaven. This is enough on these three points.

28 In this connection we will explain three questions, that we may better understand this Gospel. What is mammon? Why is it unrighteous? And why Christ commands us to imitate the unjust steward, who worked for his own gain at his master's expense, which without doubt is unjust and a sin?

29 First, mammon is a Hebrew word meaning riches or temporal goods, namely, whatever any one owns over and above what his needs require, and with which he can benefit others without injuring himself. For Hamon in Hebrew means multitude, or a great crowd or many, from which Mahamon or Mammon, that is, multitude of riches or goods, is derived.

30 Second, it is called unrighteous, not because obtained by injustice and usury, for with unrighteous possessions no good can be done, for it must be returned, as Isaiah says: "I, Jehovah, love justice, I hate robbery with iniquity." And Solomon says: "Withhold not good from them to whom it is due, when it is in the power of thy hand to do it." But it is called unrighteous because it stands in the service of unrighteousness, as St. Paul says to the Ephesians, that the days are evil, although God made them and they are good, but they are evil because wicked men misuse them, in which they do many sins, offend and endanger souls.

31 Therefore, riches are unrighteous, because the people misuse and abuse them. For we know that wherever riches are, the saying holds good: money rules the world, men creep for it, they lie for it, they act the hypocrite for it, and do all manner of wickedness against their neighbor to obtain it, to keep it, and increase it to possess the friendship of the rich.

32 But it is especially before God an unrighteous mammon because man does not serve his neighbor with it; for where my neighbor is in need and I do not help him when I have the means to do so, I unjustly keep what is his, as I am indebted to give to him according to the law of nature: "Whatsoever you would that men should do to you, do you even so to them." And

19

again Christ says: "Give to him that asketh thee." And John in his first Epistle says: "But whoso hath the world's goods, and beholdeth his brother in need, and shutteth up his compassion from him, how doth the love of God abide in him?" And few see this unrighteousness in mammon because it is spiritual, and is found also in those possessions which are obtained by the fairest means, which deceive them that they think they do no one any harm, because they do no coarse outward injustice, by robbing, stealing and usury.

[33] In the third place it has been a matter of very great concern to many to know who the unjust steward is whom Christ so highly recommends? This, in short, is the simple answer: Christ does not commend unto us the steward on account of his unrighteousness, but on account of his wisdom and his shrewdness, that with all his unrighteousness, he so wisely helps himself. As though I would urge some one to watch, pray and study, and would say: "Look here, murderers and thieves wake at night to rob and steal, why then do you not wake to pray and study?" By this I do not praise murderers and thieves for their crimes, but for their wisdom and foresight, that they so wisely obtain the goods of unrighteousness. Again, as though I would say: An unchaste woman adorns herself with gold and silk to tempt young boys; why will you not also adorn yourself with faith to please Christ? By this I do not praise fornication, but the diligence employed.

[34] In this way Paul compares Adam and Christ, saying: "Adam was a figure of him that was to come." Although from Adam we have nothing but sin, and from Christ nothing but grace, yet these are greatly opposed to each other. But the comparison and type consisted only in the consequences of birth, not in virtue or vice. As to birth, Adam is the father of all sinners, so Christ is the father of all the righteous. And as all sinners come from one Adam, so all the righteous come from one Christ. Thus the unjust steward is here typified to us only in his cunning and wisdom, who knows so well how to help himself, that we should also consider in the right way the welfare of our souls as he did in the wrong way that of his body and life. With this we will let it suffice, and pray God for grace.

From *The Pilgrim's Progress*

As I walked through the wilderness of this world I lighted on a certain place where was a den, and laid me down in that place to sleep; and as I slept I dreamed a dream. I dreamed, and behold, I saw a man clothed with rags standing in a certain place, with his face from his own house, a book in his hand, and a great burden upon his back. I looked and saw him open the book, and read therein; and as he read he wept and trembled; and not being able longer to contain, he brake out with a lamentable cry, saying, "What shall I do?"

2 In this plight, therefore, he went home, and restrained himself as long as he could, that his wife and children should not perceive his distress; but he could not be silent long, because that his trouble increased. Wherefore at length he brake his mind to his wife and children, and thus he began to talk to them: "O my dear wife," said he, "and you, the children of my bowels, I, your dear friend, am in myself undone by reason of a burden that lieth hard upon me; moreover, I am certainly informed that this our city will be burned with fire from heaven, in which fearful overthrow, both myself, with thee my wife, and you my sweet babes, shall miserably come to ruin, except (the which I see not) some way of escape can be found whereby we may be delivered." At this his relations were sore amazed; not for that they believed that what he had said to them was true, but because they thought that some frenzy distemper had got into his head, therefore, it drawing towards night, and they hoping that sleep might settle his brains, with all haste they got him to bed. But the night was as troublesome to him as the day; wherefore, instead of sleeping, he spent it in sighs and tears. So when the morning was come, they would know how he did. He told them, "Worse and worse;" he also set to talking with them again; but they began to be hardened. They also thought to drive away his distemper by harsh and surly carriage to him; sometimes they would deride, sometimes they would chide, and sometimes they would quite neglect him. Wherefore he began to retire himself to his chamber to pray for and pity them, and also to condole his own misery; he would also walk solitarily in the fields, sometimes reading, and sometimes praying: and thus for some days he spent his time.

3 Now I saw, upon a time, when he was walking in the fields, that he was (as he was wont) reading in his book, and greatly distressed in his mind;

The beginning and ending passages (Chicago and New York: Belford, Clarke & Co., 1884).

and as he read, he burst out, as he had done before, crying, "What shall I do to be saved?"

⁴ I saw also that he looked this way, and that way, as if he would run; yet he stood still because (as I perceived) he could not tell which way to go. I looked then, and saw a man named Evangelist coming to him, and he asked, "Wherefore dost thou cry?"

⁵ He answered, "Sir, I perceive, by the book in my hand, that I am condemned to die, and after that to come to judgment; and I find that I am not willing to do the first, nor able to do the second."

⁶ Then said Evangelist, "Why not willing to die, since this life is attended with so many evils?" The man answered, "Because I fear that this burden that is upon my back will sink me lower than the grave, and I shall fall into Tophet. And, sir, if I be not fit to go to prison, I am not fit to go to judgment, and from thence to execution; and the thoughts of these things make me cry."

⁷ Then said Evangelist, "If this be thy condition, why standest thou still?" He answered, "Because I know not whither to go." Then he gave him a parchment roll, and there was written within, "Fly from the wrath to come."

⁸ The man therefore read it, and, looking upon Evangelist very carefully, said, "Whither must I fly?" Then said Evangelist pointing with his finger over a very wide field, "Do you see yonder wicket gate?" The man said, "No." Then said the other, "Do you see yonder shining light?" He said, "I think I do." Then said Evangelist, "Keep that light in your eye, and go up directly thereto; so shalt thou see the gate; at which, when thou knockest, it shall be told thee what thou shalt do."

. . . .

⁹ After this it was noised abroad that Mr. Valiant-for-truth was taken with a summons by the same post as the other, and had this for a token that the summons was true, "that his pitcher was broken at the fountain." When he understood it, he called for his friends, and told them of it. Then said he, I am going to my Father's; and though with great difficulty I have got hither, yet now I do not repent me of all the trouble I have been at to arrive where I am. My sword I give to him that shall succeed me in my pilgrimage, and my courage and skill to him that can get it. My marks and scars I carry with me to be a witness for me that I have fought His battles who will now be my rewarder.

¹⁰ When the day that he must go hence was come, many accompanied him to the riverside, into which, as he went, he said, "Death, where is thy sting?" And as he went down deeper he said, "Grave, where is thy victory?" So he passed over, and all the trumpets sounded for him on the other side.

The Scripture Way of Salvation

Ye are saved through faith.—Eph. 2:8

NOTHING can be more intricate, complex, and hard to be understood, than religion, as it has been often described. And this is not only true concerning the religion of the Heathens, even many of the wisest of them, but concerning the religion of those also who were in some sense, Christians; yea, and men of great name in the Christian world; men who seemed to be pillars thereof. Yet how easy to be understood, how plain and simple a thing, is the genuine religion of Jesus Christ; provided only that we take it in its native form, just as it is described in the oracles of God! It is exactly suited, by the wise Creator and Governor of the world, to the weak understanding and narrow capacity of man in his present state. How observable is this, both with regard to the end it proposes, and the means to attain that end! The end is, in one word, salvation; the means to attain it, faith.

² 2. It is easily discerned, that these two words, I mean faith and salvation, include the substance of all the Bible, the marrow, as it were, of the whole Scripture. So much the more should we take all possible care to avoid all mistake concerning them, and to form a true and accurate judgment concerning both the one and the other.

³ 3. Let us then seriously inquire.—

   I. WHAT IS SALVATION?

   II. WHAT IS THAT FAITH WHEREBY WE ARE SAVED? AND,

   III. HOW ARE WE SAVED BY IT?

⁴ I. 1. And, first, let us inquire, What is salvation? The salvation which is here spoken of is not what is frequently understood by that word, the going to heaven, eternal happiness. It is not the soul's going to paradise, termed by our Lord, "Abraham's bosom." It is not a blessing which lies on the other side death; or, as we usually speak, in the other world. The very words of the text itself put this beyond all question: *"Ye are saved."* It is not something at a distance: it is a present thing; a blessing which, through the free mercy of God, ye are now in possession of. Nay, the words may be rendered, and that with equal propriety, "Ye *have been* saved": so that the salvation which is here spoken of might be extended to the entire work of God, from the first dawning of grace in the soul, till it is consummated in glory.

From *Wesley's Standard Sermons,* ed. Edward H. Sugden (Nashville: Publishing House M. E. Church, South).

[5] 2. If we take this in its utmost extent, it will include all that is wrought in the soul by what is frequently termed "natural conscience," but more properly, "preventing grace"; all the drawings of the Father—the desires after God, which, if we yield to them, increase more and more; all that light wherewith the Son of God "enlighteneth every one that cometh into the world"—showing every man "to do justly, to love mercy, and to walk humbly with his God"; all the convictions which His spirit, from time to time, works in every child of man—although it is true, the generality of men stifle them as soon as possible, and after a while forget, or at least deny, that they ever had them at all.

[6] 3. But we are at present concerned only with that salvation which the Apostle is directly speaking of. And this consists of two general parts, justification and sanctification.

[7] Justification is another word for pardon. It is the forgiveness of all our sins; and, what is necessarily implied therein, our acceptance with God. The price whereby this hath been procured for us (commonly termed "the meritorious cause of our justification"), is the blood and righteousness of Christ; or, to express it a little more clearly, all that Christ hath done and suffered for us, till He "pours out His soul for the transgressors." The immediate effects of justification are, the peace of God, a "peace that passeth all understanding," and a "rejoicing in hope of the glory of God" "with joy unspeakable and full of glory."

[8] 4. And at the same time that we are justified, yea, in that very moment, sanctification begins. In that instant we are born again, born from above, born of the Spirit: there is a *real* as well as a *relative* change. We are inwardly renewed by the power of God. We feel "the love of God shed abroad in our heart by the Holy Ghost which is given unto us"; producing love to all mankind, and more especially to the children of God; expelling the love of the world, the love of pleasure, of ease, of honour, of money, together with pride, anger, self-will, and every other evil temper; in a word, changing the earthly, sensual, devilish mind, into "the mind which was in Christ Jesus."

[9] 5. How naturally do those who experience such a change imagine that all sin is gone; that it is utterly rooted out of their heart, and has no more any place therein! How easily do they draw that inference, "I *feel* no sin; therefore, I *have* none: it does not *stir;* therefore, it does not *exist:* it has no *motion;* therefore, it has no *being!*"

[10] 6. But it is seldom long before they are undeceived, finding sin was only suspended, not destroyed. Temptations return, and sin revives; showing it was but stunned before, not dead. They now feel two principles in themselves, plainly contrary to each other; "the flesh lusting against the Spirit"; nature opposing the grace of God. They cannot deny, that although they still feel power to believe in Christ, and to love God; and although His "Spirit" still "witnesses with their spirits, that they are children of God;" yet they feel in themselves sometimes pride or self-will, sometimes anger or unbelief. They find one or more of these frequently *stirring* in their heart,

though not *conquering;* yea, perhaps, "thrusting sore at them that they may fall"; but the Lord is their help.

¹¹ 7. How exactly did Macarius, fourteen hundred years ago, describe the present experience of the children of God: "The unskilful," or unexperienced, "when grace operates, presently imagine they have no more sin. Whereas they that have discretion cannot deny, that even we who have the grace of God may be molested again. For we have often had instances of some among the brethren, who have experienced such grace as to affirm that they had no sin in them; and yet, after all, when they thought themselves entirely freed from it, the corruption that lurked within was stirred up anew, and they were well-nigh burned up."

¹² 8. From the time of our being born again, the gradual work of sanctification takes place. We are enabled "by the Spirit" to "mortify the deeds of the body," of our evil nature; and as we are more and more dead to sin, we are more and more alive to God. We go on from grace to grace, while we are careful to "abstain from all appearances of evil," and are "zealous of good works," as we have opportunity, doing good to all men; while we walk in all his ordinances blameless, therein worshipping Him in spirit and in truth; while we take up our cross, and deny ourselves every pleasure that does not lead us to God.

¹³ 9. It is thus that we wait for entire sanctification; for a full salvation from all our sins—from pride, self-will, anger, unbelief; or, as the Apostle expresses it, "go on unto perfection." But what is perfection? The word has various senses: here it means perfect love. It is love excluding sin; love filling the heart, taking up the whole capacity of the soul. It is love "rejoicing evermore, praying without ceasing, in everything giving thanks."

¹⁴ II. But what is that faith through which we are saved? This is the second point to be considered.

¹⁵ Faith, in general, is defined by the Apostle, πραγμάτων ἔλεγχος οὐ βλεπομένων—*an evidence*, a divine *evidence and conviction* (the word means both) *of things not seen;* not visible, not perceivable either by sight, or by any other of the external senses. It implies both a supernatural *evidence* of God, and of the things of God; a kind of spiritual *light* exhibited to the soul, and a supernatural *sight* or perception thereof. Accordingly, the Scripture speaks of God's giving sometimes light, sometimes a power of discerning it. So St. Paul: "God, who commanded light to shine out of darkness, hath shined in our hearts, to give us the light of the knowledge of the glory of God in the face of Jesus Christ." And elsewhere the same Apostle speaks of "the eyes of" our "understanding being opened." By this two-fold operation of the Holy Spirit, having the eyes of our soul both *opened* and *enlightened,* we see the things which the natural "eye hath not seen, neither the ear hears." We have a prospect of the invisible things of God; we see the *spiritual world,* which is all round about us, and yet no more discerned by our natural faculties than if it had no being. And we see the *eternal world,* which is all round about us, and yet no more discerned by our natural faculties than if it had

no being. And we see the *eternal world;* piercing through the veil which hangs between time and eternity. Clouds and darkness then rest upon it no more, but we already see the glory which shall be revealed.

¹⁶ 2. Taking the word in a more particular sense, faith is a divine evidence and conviction not only that "God was in Christ, reconciling the world unto Himself," but also that Christ loved *me,* and gave Himself for *me.* It is by this faith (whether we term it the *essence,* or rather a *property* thereof) that we *receive Christ;* that we receive Him in all His offices, as our Prophet, Priest, and King. It is by this that He is "made of God unto us wisdom, and righteousness, and sanctification, and redemption."

¹⁷ 3. "But is this the *faith of assurance,* or *faith of adherence?*" The Scripture mentions no such distinction. The Apostle says, "There is one faith, and one hope of our calling"; one Christian, saving faith; "as there is one Lord," in whom we believe, and "one God and Father of us all." And it is certain, this faith necessarily implies an *assurance* (which is here only another word for *evidence,* it being hard to tell the difference between them), that Christ loved me, and gave Himself for me. For "he that believeth" with the true living faith "hath the witness in himself": "the Spirit witnesseth with his spirit that he is a child of God." "Because he is a son, God hath sent forth the Spirit of His Son into his heart, crying, Abba, Father"; giving him an assurance that he is so, and a childlike confidence in Him. But let it be observed, that, in the very nature of the thing, the assurance goes before the confidence. For a man cannot have a childlike confidence in God until he knows he is a child of God. Therefore, confidence, trust, reliance, adherence, or whatever else it be called, is not the first, as some have supposed, but the second, branch or act of faith.

¹⁸ 4. It is by this faith we are saved, justified, and sanctified; taking that word in its highest sense. But how are we justified and sanctified by faith? This is our third head of inquiry. And this being the main point in question, and a point of no ordinary importance, it will not be improper to give it a more distinct and particular consideration.

¹⁹ III. 1. And, first, how are we justified by faith? In what sense is this to be understood? I answer, Faith is the condition, and the only condition, of justification. It is the *condition:* none is justified but he that believes: without faith no man is justified. And it is the *only condition:* this alone is sufficient for justification. Everyone that believes is justified, whatever else he has or has not. In other words: no man is justified till he believes; every man when he believes is justified.

²⁰ 2. "But does not God command us to repent also? Yea, and to bring forth fruits meet for repentance—to cease, for instance, from doing evil, and learn to do well? And is not both the one and the other of the utmost necessity, insomuch that if we willingly neglect either, we cannot reasonably expect to be justified at all? But if this be so, how can it be said that faith is the only condition of justification?"

²¹ God does undoubtedly command us both to repent, and to bring forth fruits meet for repentance; which if we willingly neglect, we cannot reason-

ably expect to be justified at all: therefore both repentance, and fruits meet for repentance, are, in some sense, necessary to justification. But they are not necessary in the *same sense* with faith, nor in the *same degree*. Not in the *same degree;* for those fruits are only necessary *conditionally;* if there be time and opportunity for them. Otherwise a man may be justified without them, as was the *thief* upon the cross (if we may call him so; for a late writer has discovered that he was no thief, but a very honest and respectable person!); but he cannot be justified without faith; this is impossible. Likewise, let a man have ever so much repentance, or ever so many of the fruits meet for repentance, yet all this does not at all avail; he is not justified till he believes. But the moment he believes, with or without these fruits, yea, with more or less repentance, he is justified.—Not in the *same sense;* for repentance and its fruits are only *remotely* necessary; necessary in order to faith; whereas faith is *immediately* and *directly* necessary to justification. It remains, that faith is the only condition which is *immediately* and *proximately* necessary to justification.

22 3. "But do you believe we are sanctified by faith? We know you believe that we are justified by faith; but do not you believe, and accordingly teach, that we are sanctified by our works?" So it has been roundly and vehemently affirmed for these five-and-twenty years: but I have constantly declared just the contrary; and that in all manner of ways. I have continually testified in private and in public, that we are sanctified as well as justified by faith. And indeed the one of those great truths does exceedingly illustrate the other. Exactly as we are justified by faith, so are we sanctified by faith. Faith is the condition, and the only condition, of sanctification, exactly as it is of justification. It is the *condition:* none is sanctified but he that believes; without faith no man is sanctified. And it is the *only condition:* this alone is sufficient for sanctification. Every one that believes is sanctified, whatever else he has or has not. In other words, no man is sanctified till he believes: every man when he believes is sanctified.

23 4. "But is there not a repentance consequent upon, as well as a repentance previous to, justification? And is it not incumbent on all that are justified to be zealous of good works? Yea, are not these so necessary, that if a man willingly neglect them he cannot reasonably expect that he shall ever be sanctified in the full sense; that is, perfected in love? Nay, can he grow at all in grace, in the loving knowledge of our Lord Jesus Christ? Yea, can he retain the grace which God has already given him? Can he continue in the faith which he has received, or in the favour of God? Do not you yourself allow all this, and continually assert it? But, if this be so, how can it be said that faith is the only condition of sanctification?"

24 5. I do allow all this, and continually maintain it as the truth of God. I allow there is a repentance consequent upon, as well as a repentance previous to, justification. It is incumbent on all that are justified to be zealous of good works. And these are so necessary, that if a man willingly neglect them, he cannot reasonably expect that he shall ever be sanctified; he cannot grow in grace, in the image of God, the mind which was in Christ Jesus; nay, he can-

not retain the grace he has received; he cannot continue in faith, or in the favour of God.

25 What is the inference we must draw herefrom? Why, that both repentance, rightly understood, and the practice of all good works—works of piety, as well as works of mercy (now properly so called, since they spring from faith), are, in some sense, necessary to sanctification.

26 6. I say, "repentance rightly understood"; for this must not be confounded with the former repentance. The repentance consequent upon justification is widely different from that which is antecedent to it. This implies no guilt, no sense of condemnation, no consciousness of the wrath of God. It does not suppose any doubt of the favour of God, or any "fear that hath torment." It is properly a conviction, wrought by the Holy Ghost, of the *sin* which still *remains* in our hearts; of the φρόνημα σαρκός, *the carnal mind*, which "does still *remain*" (as our Church speaks), "even in them that are regenerate"; although it does no longer *reign;* it has not now dominion over them. It is a conviction of our proneness to evil, of an heart bent to backsliding, of the still continuing tendency of the flesh to lust against the spirit. Sometimes, unless we continually watch and pray, it lusteth to pride, sometimes to anger, sometimes to love of the world, love of ease, love of honour, or love of pleasure more than of God. It is a conviction of the tendency of our heart to self-will, to Atheism, or idolatry; and above all, to unbelief; whereby, in a thousand ways, and under a thousand pretences, we are ever departing, more or less, from the living God.

27 7. With this conviction of the sin remaining in our hearts, there is joined a clear conviction of the sin remaining in our lives; still *cleaving* to all our words and actions. In the best of these we now discern a mixture of evil, either in the spirit, the matter, or the manner of them; something that could not endure the righteous judgment of God, were He extreme to mark what is done amiss. Where we least suspected it, we find a taint of pride or self-will, or unbelief or idolatry; so that we are now more ashamed of our best duties than formerly of our worst sins: and hence we cannot but feel that these are so far from having anything meritorious in them, yea, so far from being able to stand in sight of the divine justice, that for those also we should be guilty before God, were it not for the blood of the covenant.

28 8. Experience shows that, together with this conviction of sin *remaining* in our hearts, and *cleaving* to all our words and actions; as well as the guilt which on account thereof we should incur, were we not continually sprinkled with the atoning blood; one thing more is implied in this repentance; namely a conviction of our helplessness, of our utter inability to think one good thought or to form one good desire; and much more to speak one word aright, or to perform one good action, but through His free, almighty grace, first preventing us, and then accompanying us every moment.

29 9. "But what good works are those, the practice of which you affirm to be necessary to sanctification?" First, all works of piety; such as public prayer, family prayer, and praying in our closet; receiving the supper of the Lord; searching the Scriptures, by hearing, reading, meditating; and using such a measure of fasting or abstinence as our bodily health allows.

³⁰ 10. Secondly, all works of mercy; whether they relate to the bodies or souls of men; such as the feeding of the hungry, clothing the naked, entertaining the stranger, visiting those that are in prison, or sick, or variously afflicted; such as the endeavoring to instruct the ignorant, to awaken the stupid sinner, to quicken the lukewarm, to confirm the wavering, to comfort the feeble-minded, to succour the tempted, or contribute in any manner to the saving of souls from death. This is the repentance, and these the "fruits meet for repentance," which are necessary to full sanctification. This is the way wherein God hath appointed His children to wait for complete salvation.

³¹ 11. Hence may appear the extreme mischievousness of that seemingly innocent opinion, that there is no sin in a believer; that all sin is destroyed, root and branch, the moment a man is justified. By totally preventing that repentance, it quite blocks up the way to sanctification. There is no place for repentance in him who believes there is no sin either in his life or heart: consequently, there is no place for his being perfected in love, to which that repentance is indispensably necessary.

³² 12. Hence it may likewise appear, that there is no possible danger in *thus* expecting full salvation. For suppose we were mistaken, suppose no such blessing ever was or can be attained, yet we lose nothing: nay, that very expectation quickens us in using all the talents which God has given us; yea, in improving them all; so that when our Lord cometh, He will receive His own with increase.

³³ 13. But to return. Though it be allowed, that both this repentance and its fruits are necessary to full salvation; yet they are not necessary either in the same sense with faith, or in the same degree.—Not in the *same degree;* for these fruits are only necessary *conditionally*, if there be time and opportunity for them; otherwise a man may be sanctified without them. But he cannot be sanctified without faith. Likewise, let a man have ever so much of this repentance, or ever so many good works, yet all this does not at all avail: he is not sanctified till he believes. But the moment he believes, with or without those fruits, yea, with more or less of this repentance, he is sanctified.—Not in the *same sense;* for this repentance and these fruits are only *remotely* necessary—necessary in order to the continuance of his faith, as well as the increase of it; whereas faith is *immediately* and *directly* necessary to sanctification. It remains, that faith is the only condition which is *immediately* and *proximately* necessary to sanctification.

³⁴ 14. "But what is that faith whereby we are sanctified,—saved from sin, and perfected in love?" It is a divine evidence and conviction, first that God hath promised it in the holy Scripture. Till we are thoroughly satisfied of this, there is no moving one step further. And one would imagine there needed not one word more to satisfy a reasonable man of this, than the ancient promise, "Then will I circumcise thy heart, and the heart of thy seed, to love the Lord thy God with all thy heart, and with all thy soul, and with all thy mind." How clearly does this express the being perfected

in love!—how strongly imply the being saved from all sin! For as long as love takes up the whole heart, what room is there for sin therein?

³⁵ 15. It is a divine evidence and conviction, secondly, that what God hath promised He is able to perform. Admitting, therefore, that "with men it is impossible" to "bring a clean thing out of an unclean," to purify the heart from all sin, and to fill it with all holiness; yet this creates no difficulty in the case, seeing "with God all things are possible." And surely no one ever imagined it was possible to any power less than that of the Almighty! But if God speaks, it shall be done. God saith, "Let there be light;" and there is "light"!

³⁶ 16. It is, thirdly, a divine evidence and conviction that He is able and willing to do it now. And why not? Is not a moment to Him the same as thousand years? He cannot want more time to accomplish whatever is His will. And He cannot wait or stay for any more *worthiness* or *fitness* in the persons He is pleased to honour. We may therefore boldly say, at any point of time, "Now is the day of salvation!" "To-day, if ye will hear His voice, harden not your hearts!" "Behold, all things are now ready; come unto the marriage!"

³⁷ 17. To this confidence, that God is both able and willing to sanctify us now, there needs to be added one thing more,—a divine evidence and conviction that He doeth it. In that hour it is done: God says to the inmost soul, "According to thy faith be it unto thee!" Then the soul is pure from every spot of sin; it is clean "from all unrighteousness." The believer then experiences the deep meaning of those solemn words, "If we walk in the light as He is in the light, we have fellowship one with another, and the blood of Jesus Christ His Son cleanseth us from all sin."

³⁸ 18. "But does God work this great work in the soul gradually or instantaneously?" Perhaps it may be gradually wrought in some; I mean in this sense,—they do not advert to the particular moment wherein sin ceases to be. But it is infinitely desirable, were it the will of God, that it should be done instantaneously; that the Lord should destroy sin "by the breath of His mouth," in a moment, in the twinkling of an eye. And so He generally does; a plain fact, of which there is evidence enough to satisfy any unprejudiced person. *Thou* therefore look for it every moment! Look for it in the way above described; in all those *good works* whereunto thou art "created anew in Christ Jesus." There is then no danger: you can be no worse, if you are no better, for that expectation. For were you to be disappointed of your hope, still you lose nothing. But you shall not be disappointed of your hope: it will come, and will not tarry. Look for it then every day, every hour, every moment! Why not this hour, this moment? Certainly you may look for it *now*, if you believe it is by faith. And by this token you may surely know whether you seek it by faith or by works. If by works, you want something to be done *first*, *before* you are sanctified. You think, I must first *be* or *do* thus or thus. Then you are seeking it by works unto this day. If you seek it by faith, you may expect it *as you are;* and if as you are, then expect it *now*. It is of importance to observe, that there is an

inseparable connection between these three points,—expect it *as you are;* and expect it *now.* To deny one of them, is to deny them all; to allow one, is to allow them all. Do *you* believe we are sanctified by faith? Be true then to your principle; and look for this blessing just as you are, neither better nor worse; as a poor sinner that has still nothing to pay, nothing to plead, but *"Christ died."* And if you look for it as you are, then expect it *now.* Stay for nothing: why should you? Christ is ready; and He is all you want. He is waiting for you. He is at the door! Let your inmost soul cry out,

> Come in, come in, Thou heavenly Guest!
>   Nor hence again remove;
> But sup with me, and let the feast
>   Be everlasting love.

The Burning Bush

And he looked, and behold the bush burned with fire,
and the bush was not consumed; and Moses said, I will
now turn aside, and see this great sight, why the bush is
not burnt.   —Exod. 3:2-3

IT IS a common saying, and common sayings are generally founded on matter of fact, that it is always darkest just before break of day; and I am persuaded, that if we do justice to our own experience, as well as consider God's dealings with his people in preceding ages, we shall find that man's extremity has been usually made God's opportunity, and that *when the enemy has broke in like a flood, the spirit and providence of God has lifted up a standard against him:* and I believe at the same time, that however we may dream of a continued scene of prosperity in church or state, either in respect to our bodies, souls, or temporal affairs, we shall find this life to be chequered, that the clouds return after the rain, and the most prosperous state attended with such cloudy days, as may make even the people of God sometimes cry, *all men are liars, and God has forgotten to be gracious.*

2 The chapter in which is our text, is an instance of this. What a glorious day of the Son of man was that when Joseph sent for his father to Egypt; and the good old patriarch, after he had thought his son had been dead many years, agreeably surprised by a message from him to come to him, with all his family, and are by him comfortably settled in Goshen; where the good old patriarch, after many a stormy day, died in peace, and was highly honored at his funeral by Pharaoh and his servants, and attended to the sepulcher of his fathers in Canaan by all his sons. After which, Joseph continued to live in splendor, lord of all the land of Egypt; and his brethren, doubtless, in the height of prosperity; but how sadly did the scene change at Pharaoh's death, soon after which, *another king arose that knew not Joseph,* verifying the observation, "new lords, new laws," by whom the descendants of Jacob, instead of reigning in Goshen, were made bond slaves; many, many long years, employed in making bricks, and in all probability, had what we call their Bibles taken from them, by being forced to conform to the idolatry of Egypt, and so were in a worse state than the unhappy negroes in America

---

From John Gillis, *The Memoirs of Rev. George Whitefield* (Hartford: Edwin Hunt, 1848).

are at this day. No doubt, numbers of them either wondered that ever they had been prospered at all, or that God had forgotten them now; but what a mercy it is that *a thousand years in God's sight are but as one day*, and therefore when God's time is come, the set time he has appointed, he will defeat all the opposition of men and devils—he will come down and deliver his people, and in such a manner, that the enemy shall know, as well as friends, it is the Lord's doings. A deliverer is born and bred in Pharaoh's court, a Moses is brought up in all the learning of the Egyptians, for Pharaoh intended him for a high and exalted post: but when offers of the highest preferment are made to him, he did not catch at them as some folks now do, who are very good and humble till something occurs to take them from God. Young as he was, he refused the highest dignity, and spurned at it with a holy contempt; and chose rather to suffer affliction with the people of God, than enjoy all the grandeur and pleasures of, perhaps, one of the greatest courts on earth.

³ Forty years continued he in a state of obscurity, in which time he acquired such a competent degree, and variety of knowledge, as qualified him for everything God intended him for: the occasion of this was his kind attempt to compose a difference between two of his brethren, one of whom accused him of murder, on which he that was to be king in Jeshurun, is forced to fly into a strange land; there he submits to the humble office of servant, marries, and lives in a state of subjection for forty years, as was said before. At length when he was eighty years old, dreaming of no such thing, behold God calls, and commands him to go and deliver his people: as he himself informs us, who is the author of this book, verse 1. "Now Moses kept the flock of Jethro his father-in-law, priest of Midian." He might have said, What, such a scholar as I keep a parcel of sheep! such a learned man as I am, employed in such menial service! Some proud hearts would break first, but you never knew a truly great man but would stoop; some that are called great men, swell till they burst; like sturdy oaks, they think they can stand every wind, till some dreadful storm comes and blows them up by the roots, while the humble reed bends and rises again. Moses was one of the latter, he keeps the flocks of Jethro his father-in-law, and leads them to the mountain of God, even to Horeb. This shows how persons ought to methodize their time: but however the name of a Methodist is despised, they will never be bad servants and masters; you would be only weathercocks, unless you took care to order things in proper seasons: the devotion and business of a Methodist go hand in hand; I will assure you Moses was a Methodist, a very fine one, a very strong one too; he kept his flock, but that did not hinder his going to Horeb, he took them to the desert, and being thus employed in his lawful business, God met him. Some say, we encourage people in idleness; I deny it; we say, people ought to be industrious; and I defy any one to say, a person is called by God that is negligent in his calling. "The angel of the Lord appeared to him in a flame of fire out of the bush:" some think this angel was Gabriel, but most agree, and I believe with the great probability, that it was Jesus Christ, *the angel of the ever-*

lasting covenant; and an expositor tells you, that the eternal *Logos,* longing to become man, often visited this earth in that form, as an evidence of his coming by and by, and dying a cursed death for man. The manner of this angel's appearing is taken particular notice of; it was to Moses when nobody was with him. I do not hear he had so much as a boy, or one companion; and I mention this, because I believe we have often found that we are never less alone than when with God; we often want this and that companion, but happy they that can say, Lord, thy company is enough. Moses was startled at the sight and I do not know that he is to be discouraged for it, it was not to gratify a bare curiosity, but seeing a bush burning, it engaged his attention, and made him think that there was something uncommon; *the bush burned with fire and yet was not consumed;* this startled him, as it was intended to do: for where God designs to speak, he will first gain attention from the person spoken to; Moses therefore says, *I will now turn aside and see this great sight, why the bush is not burned;* he did not know but the bush might take fire by some accident; he saw no fire come from above, he saw no fire around the bush, yet that did not so much startle him, as to see, though it did burn, it was not consumed, or in the least diminished; it was a strange sight, but it was, my brethren, a glorious one; a sight which, I pray God, you and I may behold with faith and comfort this evening; for, my dear hearers, this bush, and the account of it, was given for our instruction; and I will venture to say, could Moses arise from the dead, he would not be angry with me for telling you this is of no private interpretation, but is intended as a standing lesson, as a significant emblem of the church, and every individual child of God, till time itself shall be no more. I would therefore observe to you, that this bush,

4 In the first place, is typical of the church of God in all ages; the bush was burning; why might it not be a tall cedar; why might it not be some large or some glorious tree; why should the great God choose a bush, a little bush of briers and thorns, above any other thing? But because the church of Christ generally consists of poor, mean, despicable creatures; though it is all glorious within, yet it is all despicable without. It is observable, that when the church came to prosper when Constantine smiled on it, it was soon hugged to death; and that great poet Milton observes, that when that emperor gave ministers rich vestments, high honors, great livings, and golden pulpits, there was a voice heard from heaven, saying this day there is a poison come into the church; and I have sometimes said in discourse, I do not doubt but if any one made an experiment, and left £100,000 or 200,000 only among the Methodists, there would be hundreds and thousands that would not be reckoned Methodists now, that would turn Methodists presently, that would buy a hymn book because a part of the legacy would pay for the hymn book, and would wish to have a living into the bargain; but though "not many mighty men, not many noble are called," yet some are; if any of you are rich here and are Christians, thank God for it, you ought to be doubly thankful for it; God's people are but like a little bramble bush. I remember an eminent minister said once, when I heard him preach upon Christmas day, *Christ per-*

34

sonal is very rich, but Christ mystical is very poor; and Jesus Christ does this on purpose to confound the world. When he comes to judgment, millions that have their thousands now, will be damned and burnt to all eternity, and Christ's church will be rich to all eternity, that is now a bramble all on fire.

⁵ *The bush burned,* what is that for? It showed that Christ's church while in this world, will be a bush burning with fiery trials and afflictions of various kinds; this was a lively emblem of the state of religion, and liberty of Israel at that time: they were busy in making brick, and there were consequently burnings continually; as though the Lord had said, this bush is burning with fire, so my people are burning with slavery. Ah, but say you, that was only the case of the Israelites when they were under Pharaoh; pray is not that the case of the church in all ages? Yes, it has been; read your Bibles, and you may instantly see that it is little else than an historical account of a burning bush; and though there might be some periods wherein the church had rest, yet these periods have been of a short date; and if God's people have *walked in the comforts of the Holy Ghost,* it is only like a calm that precedes an earthquake. If you remember, before the last earthquake, it was a fine morning, and who when they arose in the morning, would have thought the earth should shake under them before night; and so with the church when they are in a calm, and all seems safe there, then comes a storm. God prepare us for it.

⁶ But this is not only the case with the church of Christ collected, but also it is so with individual believers, especially those that God intends to make great use of as prophets in his church. I know very well that it is said, that now the case is altered; modern commentators, therefore, and our great Dr. Young, calls them downy doctors: they tell us, now we have a Christian king and governor, and are under the toleration act, we shall have no persecution; and blessed be God, we have had none since this family has been on the throne: may God continue it till time shall be no more. Yet my dear hearers, we shall find, if God's word is true, whether we are born under a despotic power, or free government, that they that will live godly in Christ Jesus must suffer persecution.

⁷ You have heard of that saying, *Wonder not at the fiery trial wherewith you are to be tried;* And God said, *I have chosen thee,* which is applicable to every believer, *in the furnace of affliction.* Now the furnace is a hot place, and they that are tried in the furnace must be burned surely. Now what must the Christian burn with? With tribulation and persecution. I heard a person not long ago say, I have no enemies. Bishop Latimer came to a house one day, and the man of the house said, he had not met with a cross in all his life; give me my horse, says the good bishop, I am sure God is not here where no cross is. But suppose we are not persecuted by the world, is there one Christian but is persecuted by his friends? if there is an Isaac in the family, I warrant there is an Ishmael to mock at him. *Wo is me,* says David, *that I must dwell with Mesheck, and in Kedar:* and in one's own family, one's own brothers and sisters, one's own dependents, though they wait for our death, and perhaps, long to have us gone, that they may run away with our sub-

stance, to have these persons mock at us, and if they dare not speak out, yet let us see they hate the God we worship; if this be thy case, why, God knows, poor soul thou art a burning bush: but if we have no such things as mocking, yet if we are surrounded with afflictions, domestic trials, the loss of dear and near friends, the bad conduct of our children, the dreadful misconduct of those that are dependent upon us; O there is many a parent here that is a burning bush; burning with what? With family afflictions: some do not care what becomes of their children; O, thank God, I have left my boy so much, and my daughter a coach, perhaps; ah! well your son and daughter may ride in that coach post to the devil: but the godly man says, I want an eternal inheritance for my son: I want God's blessing for him; this is the poor man's prayer, while the poor deluded youth mocks him: or, supposing this is not the case, a person may burn with an inward temptation; you have heard of the fiery darts of the devil, and were you to feel them, I believe you would find them fiery darts indeed! and you have great reason to suspect your experience, your having any interest in the love of the Son of God at all, if you never found the fiery darts of the devil. O, says one, I never felt the devil; I am sure thou mayest feel him now; thou art father's own child; thou art speaking the very language of the devil, and he is teaching thee to deny thy own father; therefore graceless child of the devil, if you never felt the devil's fiery darts, it is because the devil is sure of thee; he has lulled thee into a damnable slumber; may the God of love wake thee before real damnation comes! The fiery darts of Satan are poisoned, and wherever they stick they fill the persons with tormenting pains like fire; this I mention, because there are some poor souls perhaps here to-night, whom the devil tells, thou hast committed the unpardonable sin; you are afraid to come to sacrament, you are afraid to go to prayer, because at these seasons the devil disturbs thee most, and tempts you to leave these seasons; and some go on thus burning a great while. My brethren, the time would fail, and I should draw this discourse to too great a length, and hinder you from your families, if I were to mention but a few more of those thousands that the believer burns with, the trials without, and what is still worse, his trials within. Why, says one, it is very strange you talk thus to-night. I am sorry it is strange to any of you; sure you are not much acquainted with your Bibles, and less with your hearts, if you know not this. Why, sure, say some, you make God a tyrant; no, but having made ourselves devils incarnate, we are now in a state of preparation, and these various trials are intended, by the great God, to train us up for heaven; and therefore, that you may not think I am drawing a picture without any life, give me leave to observe, that it is particularly remarkable, that though *the bush burned, it was not consumed:* it was this that struck Moses, he looked to see why the bush was not consumed. But the burning I have been here painting forth to you is not a consuming, but a purifying fire. Is not that enough to answer the shade that has been already drawn? It is true the bush burns, the Christian is persecuted, the Christian is oppressed, the Christian is burned with inward trials, he is perplexed at times, he is *cast down, but* blessed be God, *he is not destroyed,* he is not in despair.

Who is he, that says he is in such an estate that nothing disturbs him? Vain man! he discovers an ignorance of Christ; are you greater than the apostle Paul? Some people think that the apostles had no trials; so they think perhaps of some ministers, that they are always on the mount, while, perhaps, they have been in the burning to get that sermon for them. We that are to speak for others, must expect to be tempted in all things like to our brethren, or we should be only poor preachers, and never reach men's hearts. But whether ministers or people burn, the great God, the angel of the everlasting covenant, spoke to Moses out of the bush; he did not stand at a distance from the bush, he did not speak to him so much as one yard or foot from the bush, but he spoke to him out of the bush; he said, Moses, Moses, my people shall burn in this bush to the end of time, but be not afraid, I will succor them; when they burn, I will burn too. There is a scripture vastly strong to this purpose, in which it is not said, *the good will of him that* was *in the bush,* but *the good will of him that* dwelt *in the bush.* Amazing! I thought God dwelt in heaven; but as a poor woman who was once in darkness fourteen years, before she was brought out of it, said, God has two homes, one in heaven, the other in the lowest heart. He dwells in the bush, and I am sure if he did not, the devil and their own cursed hearts would burn the bush to ashes. How is it that it is not consumed? Why, it is because God has declared it shall not be consumed; he has made an everlasting covenant, and I pity those that are not acquainted with an interest in God's covenant; and it would be better that people would pity them, than dispute with them. I really believe that a disputing devil is one of the worst devils that can be brought into God's church, for he comes with his own gown and book in his hand, and I should always suspect the devil when he comes in his gown and band and this is the cause they agree and disagree. Some, who it is to be hoped are God's children, if you tell them that God has loved them with an everlasting love, they are afraid to receive it, and especially if you mention the word election, or that hard word predestination, they will be quite frightened; but talk to them in another way, their dear hearts will rejoice. God has said, "As the waters of Noah shall cease for ever, so he will not forget the covenant of his peace: nothing shall pluck them out of his hand." Ah! say some, the apostle has said, "that neither things present, nor things to come shall separate us from the love of Christ;" but he has not said an evil heart shall not: I fancy that is one of the *present things.* The bush is not consumed, because if the devil is in the bush, God is in the bush too; if the devil acts one way, the Lord, the Spirit, acts another to balance it, and the Spirit of God is engaged to train up the souls of his people; and God has determined the bush shall not be consumed; his Spirit stands near believers to support and guide and make them more than conquerors: all that are given to Jesus Christ shall come, he will not lose one of them; this is food for the children of God; a bad mind will turn every thing to poison; and if it were not for this, that God had promised to keep them, my soul within these thirty years would have sunk a thousand times over. Come then, O suffering saints, to you the word of this salvation is sent. I do not know who of you are the followers of the Lamb; may the Spirit of the living God point them out; may every one be enabled to say, I am the man. O, says one, I have been watching and very attentive to-night, but you have not mentioned my burnings; what do you think of my burning lusts? What do you think of my burning corruptions? What do you think of my burning pride? O, perhaps some of you will say, thank God, I have no pride at all; like the bishop of Cambray, as mentioned by Dr. Watts, who said, he had received many sins from his father Adam, but, thank God, he had no pride! Alas! alas! we are all as proud as the devil. Pray what do you think of passion, that burns not only themselves, but all around them? What do you think of enmity? What do you think of jealousy; is not this something that burns the bush? And there are some people that pride themselves, they have not so much of the beast about them, they never get drunk, scorn to commit murder, and at the same time are full of enmity, of envy, malice, and pride, as the devil. The Lord God help such to see their condition.

⁸ Happy is it, Christ can dwell in the bush when we cannot dwell ourselves there; there are few Christians can live together, very few relations can live together under one roof; we can take that from other people that we cannot bear from our own flesh and blood: and if God did not bear with us more than we bear with one another, we should all have been destroyed every day. Does the devil make you say, that you will give up all; I will go to the Tabernacle no more; I will lay on my couch and take my ease. Oh! if this is the case of any to-night, thus tempted by Satan, may God rescue their souls. O poor, dear soul, you never will have such sweet words from God as when you are in the bush; our suffering times will be our best times. I know I had more comfort in Moorfields, on Kennington Common, and especially when the rotten eggs, the cats and dogs were thrown upon me, and my gown was filled with clods of dirt that I could scarce move it; I have had more comfort in this burning bush than when I have been at ease. I remember when I was preaching at Exeter, a stone came and made my forehead bleed; I found at that very time the word came with double power to a laborer that was gazing at me, who was wounded at the same time by another stone; I felt for the lad more than for myself, went to a friend, and the lad came to me, "Sir," says he, "the man gave me a wound, but Jesus healed me; I never had my bonds broke till I had my head broke." I appeal to you whether you were not better when it was colder than now, because your nerves were braced up; you have a day like a dog day, now you are weak, and are obliged to fan yourselves: thus it is prosperity lulls the soul, and I fear Christians are spoiled by it.

⁹ Whatever your trials are, let this be your prayer, Lord, though the bush is burning, let it not be consumed. I think that is too low, let it be thus: Lord, when the bush is burning, let it not burn lower as the fire does, but let me burn higher and higher: I thank thee, my God, for trouble; I thank thee, my God, for putting me into these afflictions one after another; I thought I could sing a requiem to myself, that I should have a little rest, but trouble came from that very quarter where I might reasonably expect the greatest comfort:

I thank thee for knocking my hands off from the creature; Lord, I believe, help my unbelief. Thus you will go on blessing God to all eternity: by and by the bush shall be translated to the paradise of God; no burning bush in heaven, except the fire of love, wonder, and gratitude; no trials there: troubles are limited to this earth; above, our enemies cannot reach us.

[10] Perhaps some of you here are saying, *burning bush, a bush burnt and not consumed!* I do not know what to make of this nonsense. Come, come, go on, I am used to it, and I guess what are the thoughts of your heart. I pray God, that every one of you here may be afraid of comfort, lest they should be tossed about by the devil. What is it I have said? How have I talked in such an unintelligible manner? Why, say you, what do you mean by a burning bush? Why, thou art the very man. How so? Why, you are burning with the devil in your hearts; you are burning with foppery, with nonsense, with *the lust of the flesh,* with *the lust of the eye, and the pride of life;* and if you do not get out of this state, as Lot said to his sons-in-law, ere long you shall be burning in hell, and not consumed: the same angel of the covenant who spake to Moses out of the bush, he shall ere long descend, surrounded with millions of the heavenly host, and sentence you to everlasting burnings. O you frighten me! Did you think I did not intend to frighten you? Would to God I might frighten you enough! I believe it will be no harm for you to be frightened out of hell, to be frightened out of an unconverted state. O go and tell your companions that the madman said, that wicked men are as firebrands of hell. God pluck you as brands out of that burning. Blessed be God, that there is yet a day of grace. Oh! that this might prove the accepted time. Oh! that this might prove *the day of salvation.* Oh! the angel of the everlasting covenant, come down; thou blessed, dear comforter, have mercy, mercy, mercy upon the unconverted, upon our unconverted friends, upon the unconverted part of this auditory; *speak, and it shall be done; command, O Lord, and it shall come to pass:* turn the burning bushes of the devil into burning bushes of the Son of God. Who knows but God may hear our prayer—who knows but God may hear this cry, *I have seen, I have seen the afflictions of my people: the cry of the children of Israel is come up to me, and I am come down to deliver them.* God grant this may be his word to you under all your trouble; God grant he may be your comforter. The Lord awaken you that are dead in sin, and though on the precipice of hell, God keep you from tumbling in: and you that are God's burning bushes, God help you to stand to keep this coat of arms, to say when you go home, blessed be God, *the bush is burning but not consumed.* Amen! Even so, Lord Jesus. Amen.

The Christian Pilgrim

or

The True Christian's Life a Journey Towards Heaven

*And confessed that they were strangers and pilgrims
on the earth. For they that say such things, declare plainly
that they seek a country.*   —Heb. 11:13-14

T HE APOSTLE is here setting forth the excellencies of the grace of faith, by the glorious effects and happy issue of it in the saints of the Old Testament. He had spoken in the preceding part of the chapter particularly, of Abel, Enoch, Noah, Abraham and Sarah, Isaac and Jacob. Having enumerated those instances, he takes notice that "these all died in faith, not having received the promises, but having seen them afar off, were persuaded of them, and embraced them, and confessed that they were strangers, &c."—In these words the apostle seems to have a more particular respect to Abraham and Sarah, and their kindred, who came with them from Haran, and from Ur of the Chaldees, as appears by the 15th verse, where the apostle says, "and truly if they had been mindful of that country from whence they came out, they might have had opportunity to have returned."

Two things may be observed here:

2 1. What these saints confessed of themselves, viz. *that they were strangers and pilgrims on the earth.*—Thus we have a particular account concerning Abraham, "I am a stranger and a sojourner with you." And it seems to have been the general sense of the patriarchs, by what Jacob says to Pharaoh. "And Jacob said to Pharaoh, the days of the years of my pilgrimage are an hundred and thirty years: few and evil have the days of the years of my life been, and have not attained to the days of the years of the life of my fathers in the days of their pilgrimage." "I am a stranger and a sojourner with thee, as all my fathers were."

3 2. The inference that the apostle draws from hence, viz. *that they sought another country as their home.* "For they that say such things, declare plainly that they seek a country." In confessing that they were strangers, they plainly declared that this is not their country; that this is not the place where they are at home. And in confessing themselves to be pilgrims, they declared

From *The Works of President Edwards* (8 vol. ed., Leeds, England: Edward Baines, 1807), Vol. V.

plainly that this is not their settled abode; but that they have respect to some other country, which they seek, and to which they are travelling.

SECT. I. *That this life ought to be so spent by us, as to be only a journey or pilgrimage towards heaven.*

Here I would observe,

⁴ 1. That we ought not to rest in the world and its enjoyments, but should desire heaven. We should *seek first the kingdom of God.* We ought above all things to desire a heavenly happiness; to be with God; and dwell with Jesus Christ. Though surrounded with outward enjoyments, and settled in families with desirable friends and relations; though we have companions whose society is delightful, and children in whom we see many promising qualifications; though we live by good neighbours, and are generally beloved where known; yet we ought not to take our rest in these things as our portion. We should be so far from resting in them, that we should desire to leave them all, in God's due time. We ought to possess, enjoy, and use them, with no other view but readily to quit them, whenever we are called to it, and to change them willingly and cheerfully for heaven.

⁵ A traveller is not wont to rest in what he meets with, however comfortable and pleasing on the road. If he passes through pleasant places, flowery meadows, or shady groves; he does not take up his content in these things, but only takes a transient view of them as he goes along. He is not enticed by fine appearances to put off the thought of proceeding. No, but his journey's end is in his mind. If he meets with comfortable accommodations at an inn: he entertains no thoughts of settling there. He considers that these things are not his own, that he is but a stranger, and when he has refreshed himself, or tarried for a night, he is for going forward. And it is pleasant to him to think that so much of the way is gone.

⁶ So should we desire heaven more than the comforts and enjoyments of this life. The apostle mentions it as an encouraging, comfortable consideration to Christians, that they draw nearer their happiness. "Now is our salvation nearer than when we believed."—Our hearts ought to be loose to these things, as that of a man on a journey; that we may as cheerfully part with them, whenever God calls. "But this I say, brethren, the time is short, it remaineth, that both they that have wives, be as though they had none; and they that weep, as though they wept not; and they that rejoice, as though they rejoiced not; and they that buy, as though they possessed not; and they that use this world, as not abusing it; for the fashion of this world passeth away."— These things, as only lent to us for a little while, to serve a present turn; but we should set our *hearts* on heaven, as our inheritance forever.

2. We ought to seek heaven, by travelling in the way that leads thither. This is a way of holiness. We should chuse and desire to travel thither in this way and in no other; and part with all those carnal appetites which, as weights, will tend to hinder us. "Let us lay aside every weight, and the sin which doth so easily beset us, and let us run with patience the race set before

41

us." However pleasant the gratification of any appetite may be, we must lay it aside, if it be any hindrance, or a stumbling-block in the way to heaven.

⁷ We should travel on in the way of obedience to all God's commands, even the difficult as well as the easy; denying all our sinful inclinations and interests. The way to heaven is ascending; we must be content to travel up hill, though it be hard and tiresome, and contrary to the natural bias of our flesh. We should follow Christ; the path he travelled, was the right way to heaven. We should take up our cross and follow him, in meekness and lowliness of heart, obedience and charity, diligence to do good, and patience under afflictions. The way to heaven is a heavenly life; an imitation of those that are in heaven, in their holy enjoyments, loving, adoring, serving, and praising God and the Lamb. Even if we *could* go to heaven with the gratification of our lusts, we should prefer a way of holiness and conformity to the spiritual self-denying rules of the gospel.

⁸ We should travel on in this way in a laborious manner.—Long journeys are attended by toil and fatigue; especially if through a wilderness. Persons in such a case expect no other than to suffer hardships and weariness.—So we should travel in this way of holiness, improving our time and strength, to surmount the difficulties and obstacles that are in the way. The land we have to travel through, is a wilderness; there are many mountains, rocks, and rough places that we must go over, and therefore there is a necessity that we should lay out our strength.

⁹ 4. Our whole lives ought to be spent in travelling this road.—We ought to begin *early*. This should be the *first* concern, when persons become capable of acting. When they first set out in the *world,* they should set out on *this* journey.—And we ought to travel on with *assiduity*. It ought to be the work of every day. We should often think of our journey's end; and make it our daily work to travel on in the way that leads to it.—He who is on a journey, is often thinking of the destined place; and it is his daily care and business to get along; and to improve his time to get towards his journey's end. Thus should heaven be continually in our thought; and the immediate entrance or passage to it, viz. death should be present with us.—We ought to *persevere* in this way as long as we live.

¹⁰ "Let us run with patience the race that is set before us." Though the road be difficult, and toilsome, we must hold out with patience, and be content to endure hardships. Though the journey be long, yet we must not stop short; but hold on till we arrive at the place we seek. Nor should we be discouraged with the length and difficulties of the way, as the children of Israel were, and be for turning back again. All our thought and design should be to press forward till we arrive.

¹¹ 5. We ought to be continually growing in holiness; and in that respect coming nearer and nearer to heaven.—We should be endeavouring to come nearer to heaven, in being more heavenly; becoming more and more like the inhabitants of heaven, in respect of holiness and conformity to God; the knowledge of God and Christ; in clear views of the glory of God, the beauty of Christ, and the excellency of divine things, as we come nearer

42

to the beatific vision.—We should labour to be continually growing in divine love—that this may be an increasing flame in our hearts, till they ascend wholly in this flame—in obedience and an heavenly conversation; that we may do the will of God on earth as the angels do in heaven: in comfort and spiritual joy; in sensible communion with God and Jesus Christ. Our path should be as "the shining light, that shines more and more to the perfect day." We ought to be hungering and thirsting after righteousness; after an increase in righteousness. "As new born babes desire the sincere milk of the word, that ye may grow thereby." The perfection of heaven should be our mark. "This one thing I do, forgetting those things which are behind, and reaching forth unto those things that are before, I press toward the mark, for the prize of the high calling of God in Christ Jesus."

[12] 6. All other concerns of life ought to be entirely subordinate to this.— When a man is on a journey, all the steps he takes are subordinated to the aim of getting to his journey's end. And if he carries money or provisions with him, it is to supply him in his journey. So we ought wholly to subordinate all our other business, and all our temporal enjoyments, to this affair of travelling to heaven. When any thing we have, becomes a clog and hindrance to us, we should quit it immediately. The use of our worldly enjoyments and possessions, should be with such a view, and in such a manner, as to further us in our way heaven-ward. Thus we should eat, and drink, and clothe ourselves, and improve the conversation and enjoyment of friends. And whatever business we are setting about, whatever design we are engaging in, we should enquire with ourselves, whether this business or undertaking will forward us in our way to heaven? And if not, we should quit our design.

Sect. II. *Why the Christian's life is a journey, or pilgrimage?*

[13] 1. This world is not our abiding place. Our continuance here is but very short. Man's days on the earth, are as a shadow. It was never designed by God that this world should be our home. Neither did God give us these temporal accommodations for that end. If God has given us ample estates, and children or other pleasant friends, it is with no such design, that we should be furnished here, as for a settled abode; but with a design that we should use them for the present, and leave them in a very little time. When we are called to any secular business, or charged with the care of a family, it is if we improve our lives to any other purpose, than as a journey toward heaven, all our labour will be lost. If we spend our lives in the pursuit of a temporal happiness; as riches or sensual pleasures; credit and esteem from men; delight in our children, and the prospect of seeing them well brought up, and well settled, &c.—All these things will be of little significancy to us. Death will blow up all our hopes, and will put an end to these enjoyments. "The places that have known us, will know us no more:" and "the eye that has seen us, shall see us no more." We must be taken away for ever from all these things: and it is uncertain when: it may be soon after we are put into the

possession of them. And then, where will be all our worldly employments and enjoyments, when we are laid in the silent grave! "So man lieth down and riseth not again, till the heavens be no more."

14 2. The future world was designed to be our settled and everlasting abode. There it was intended that we should be fixed; and there alone is a lasting habitation, and a lasting inheritance. The present state is short and transitory; but our state in the other world, is everlasting. And as we are there at first, so we must be without change. Our state in the future world, therefore, being eternal, is of so much greater importance than our state here, that all our concerns in this world should be wholly subordinate to it.

15 3. Heaven is that place where our highest end, and highest good is to be obtained. God hath made us for himself. "Of him, and through him, and to him are all things." Therefore, then do we attain to our highest end, when we are brought to God: but that is by being brought to heaven; for that is God's throne, the place of his special presence. There is but a very imperfect union with God to be had in this world, a very imperfect knowledge of him in the midst of much darkness; a very imperfect conformity to God, mingled with abundance of estrangement. Here we can serve and glorify God, but in a very imperfect manner; our service being mingled with sin which dishonours God.—But when we get to heaven, (if ever that be) we shall be brought to a perfect union with God, and have more clear views of him. There we shall be fully conformed to God, without any remaining sin; for "we shall see him as he is." There we shall serve God perfectly; and glorify him in an exalted manner, even to the utmost of the powers and capacity of our nature. Then we shall perfectly give up ourselves to God; our hearts will be pure and holy offerings, presented in a flame of divine love.

16 God is the highest good of the reasonable creature; and the enjoyment of him is the only happiness with which our souls can be satisfied.—To go to heaven, fully to enjoy God, is *infinitely* better than the most pleasant accommodations here. Fathers and mothers, husbands, wives or children, or the company of earthly friends, are but shadows; but the enjoyment of God is the substance. These are but scattered beams; but God is the sun. These are but streams; but God is the fountain. These are but drops; but God is the ocean.—Therefore it becomes us to spend this life only as a journey towards heaven, as it becomes us to make the seeking of our highest end and proper good, the whole work of our lives; to which we should subordinate all other concerns of life. Why should we labour for, or set our hearts on any thing else, but that which is our proper end, and true happiness?

17 4. Our present state, and all that belongs to it, is designed by him that made all things, to be wholly in order to another world.—This world was made for a place of preparation for another. Man's mortal life was given him, that he might be prepared for his fixed state. And all that God has here given us, is given to this purpose. The sun shines, and the rain falls upon us; and the earth yields her increase to us for this end. Civil, ecclesiastical, and family affairs, and all our personal concerns, are designed and ordered in subordina-

tion to a future world, by the maker and disposer of all things. To this therefore they ought to be subordinated by us.

SECT. III. *Instruction afforded by the consideration, that life is a journey, or pilgrimage, towards heaven.*

[18] 1. This doctrine may teach us moderation in our mourning for the loss of such dear friends, who, while they lived, improved their lives to right purposes.—If they lived a holy life, then their lives were a journey towards heaven. And why should we be immoderate in mourning, when they are got to their journey's end? Death, though it appears to us with a frightful aspect, is to them a great blessing. Their end is happy, and better than their beginning. *"The day of their death, is better to them than the day of their birth."* While they lived, they desired heaven, and chose it above this world, or any of its enjoyments. For this they earnestly longed, and why should we grieve that they have obtained it?—Now they have got to their Father's house. They find more comfort a thousand times, now they are got home, than they did in their journey. In this world they underwent much labour and toil; it was a wilderness they passed through. There were many difficulties in the way; mountains and rough places. It was laborious and fatiguing to travel the road; and they had many wearisome days and nights; but now they have got to their everlasting rest. "And I heard a voice from heaven, saying unto me, Write, blessed are the dead which die in the Lord, from henceforth: yea, saith the spirit, that they may rest from their labours; and their works do follow them." They look back upon the difficulties, and sorrows, and dangers of life, rejoicing that they have surmounted them all.

[19] We are ready to look upon death as their calamity, and to mourn, that those who were so dear to us, should be in the dark grave; that they are there transformed to corruption and worms; taken away from their dear children and enjoyments, &c. as though they were in awful circumstances. But this is owning to our infirmity; They are in a happy condition, inconceivably blessed. They do not mourn, but rejoice with exceeding joy: their mouths are filled with joyful songs, and they drink at rivers of pleasure. They find no mixture of grief, that they have changed their earthly enjoyments, and the company of mortals, for heaven. Their life here, though in the best circumstances, was attended with much that was adverse and afflictive: but now there is an end to all adversity. "They shall hunger no more, nor thirst any more; neither shall the sun light on them, nor any heat. For the Lamb which is in the midst of the throne, shall feed them, and shall lead them unto living fountains of water: and God shall wipe away all tears from their eyes."

[20] It is true, we shall see them no more in this world, yet we ought to consider that we are travelling towards the same place; and why should we break our hearts that they have got there before us? We are following after them, and hope, as soon as we get to our journey's end, to be with them again, in better circumstances. A degree of mourning for near relations when departed is not inconsistent with Christianity, but very agreeable to it; for

as long as we are flesh and blood, we have animal propensities and affections. But we have just reason that our mourning should be mingled with joy. "But I would not have you to be ignorant, brethren, concerning them that are asleep, that ye sorrow not, even as others that have no hope:" (*i. e.*) that they should not sorrow as the heathen, who had no knowledge of a future happiness. This appears by the following verse; "*for if we believe that Jesus died and rose again, even so them also which sleep in Jesus, will God bring with him.*"

[21] 2. If our lives ought to be only a journey towards heaven; how ill do they improve their lives, that spend them in travelling towards hell?—Some men spend their whole lives, from their infancy to their dying day, in going down the broad way to destruction. They not only draw nearer to hell as to time, but they every day grow more ripe for destruction; they are more assimilated to the inhabitants of the infernal world. While others press forward in the strait and narrow way to life, and laboriously travel up the hill toward Zion, against the inclinations and tendency of the flesh; these run with a swift career down to eternal death. This is the employment of every day, with all wicked men; and the whole day is spent in it. As soon as ever they awake in the morning, they set out anew in the way to hell, and spend every waking moment in it. They begin in early days. "The wicked are estranged from the womb, they go astray as soon as they are born, speaking lies." They hold on in it with perseverance. Many of them who live to be old, are never weary in it; though they live to be an hundred years old, they will not cease travelling in the way to hell, till they arrive there. And all the concerns of life are subordinated to this employment. A wicked man is a servant of sin; his powers and faculties are employed in the service of sin, and in fitness for hell. And all his possessions are so used by him as to be subservient to the same purpose. Men spend their time in treasuring up wrath against the day of wrath. Thus do all unclean persons, who live in lascivious practices in secret; all malicious persons; all prophane persons, that neglect the duties of religion. Thus do all unjust persons; and those who are fraudulent and oppressive in their dealings. Thus do all backbiters and revilers; all covetous persons, that set their hearts chiefly on the riches of this world. Thus do tavern-haunters, and frequenters of evil company; and many other kinds that might be mentioned. Thus the bulk of mankind are hasting onward in the broad way to destruction; which is, as it were, filled up with the multitude that are going in it with one accord. And they are every day going into hell out of this broad way by thousands. Multitudes are continually flowing down into the great lake of fire and brimstone, as some mighty river constantly disembogues its water into the ocean.

[22] 3. Hence when persons are converted, they do but begin their work, and set out in the way they have to go.—They never till then do any thing at that work in which their whole lives ought to be spent. Persons before conversion never take a step that way. Then does a man first set out on his journey, when he is brought home to Christ; and so far is he from having

46

done his work, that his care and labour in his Christian work and business, is then but begun, in which he must spend the remaining part of his life.

²³ Those persons do ill, who when they are converted, and have obtained a hope of their being in a good condition, do not strive as earnestly as they did before, while they were under awakenings. They ought, henceforward, as long as they live, to be as earnest and laborious, as watchful and careful as ever; yea, they should increase more and more. It is no just excuse, that now they have obtained conversion. Should not we be as diligent that we may serve and glorify God, as that we ourselves may be happy? And if we have obtained grace, yet we ought to strive as much that we may obtain the other degrees that are before, as we did to obtain that small degree that is behind. The Apostle tells us, that he forgot what was behind, and reached forth towards what was before.

²⁴ Yea those who are converted, have now a further reason to strive for grace; for they have seen something of its excellency. A man who has once tasted the blessings of Canaan, has more reason to press towards it, than he had before. And they who are converted, should strive to "make their calling and election sure." All those who are converted are not sure of it; and those who are sure, do not know that they shall be always so; and still seeking and serving God with the utmost diligence, is the way to have assurance, and to have it maintained.

SECT. IV. *An exhortation, so to spend the present life, that it may only be a journey towards heaven.*

²⁵ Labour to obtain such a disposition of mind that you may chuse heaven for your inheritance and home; and may earnestly long for it and be willing to change this world, and all its enjoyments for heaven. Labour to have your heart taken up so much about heaven, and heavenly enjoyments, as that you may rejoice when God calls you to leave your best earthly friends, and comforts for heaven, there to enjoy God and Christ.

²⁶ Be persuaded to travel in the way that leads to heaven; *viz.* in holiness, self-denial, mortification, obedience to all the commands of God, following Christ's example; in a way of a heavenly life, or imitation of the saints and angels in heaven. Let it be your daily work, from morning to night, and hold out in it to the end; let nothing stop or discourage you, or turn aside from this road. And let all other concerns be subordinated to this. Consider the reasons that have been mentioned why you should thus spend your life; that this world is not your abiding place, that the future world is to be your everlasting abode; and that the enjoyments and concerns of this world, are given entirely in order to another. And consider further for motive,

²⁷ 1. How worthy is heaven that your life should be wholly spent as a journey towards it.—To what better purpose can you spend your life, whether you respect your duty or your interest? What better end can you propose to your journey, than to obtain heaven? You are placed in this world, with a choice given you, that you may travel which way you please;

and one way leads to heaven. Now can you direct your course better than this way? All men have some aim or other in living. Some mainly seek worldly things; they spend their days in such pursuits. But is not heaven, where is fulness of joy for ever, much more worthy to be sought by you? How can you better employ your strength, use your means, and spend your days, than in travelling the road that leads to the everlasting enjoyment of God; to his glorious presence; to the new Jerusalem: to the heavenly mount Zion; where all your desires will be filled, and no danger of ever losing your happiness?—No man is at home in this world, whether he chuse heaven or not; here he is but a transient person. Where can you chuse your home better than in heaven?

²⁸ 2. This is the way to have death comfortable to us.—To spend our lives so as to be only a journeying towards heaven, is the way to be free from bondage, and to have the prospect and forethought of death comfortable. Does the traveller think of his journey's end with fear and terror? Is it terrible to him to think that he has almost got to his journey's end? Were the children of Israel sorry, after forty years of travel in the wilderness, when they had almost got to Canaan? This is the way to be able to part with the world without grief. Does it grieve the traveller when he has got home, quit his staff and load of provisions that he had to sustain him by the way?

²⁹ 3. No more of your life will be pleasant to think of when you come to die, than has been spent after this manner.—If you have spent none of your life this way, your whole life will be terrible to you to think of, unless you die under some great delusion. You will see then, that all of your life that has been spent otherwise, is lost. You will then see the vanity of all other aims that you may have proposed to yourself. The thought of what you here possessed and enjoyed, will not be pleasant to you unless you can think also that you have subordinated them to this purpose.

³⁰ 4. Consider that those who are willing thus to spend their lives as a journey towards heaven may have heaven.—Heaven, however high and glorious is attainable for such poor worthless creatures as we are. We may attain that glorious region which is the habitation of angels; yea, the dwelling-place of the Son of God; and where is the glorious presence of the great Jehovah. And we may have it freely; without money and without price; if we are but willing to travel the road that leads to it, and bend our course that way as long as we live; we may and shall have heaven for our eternal resting place.

³¹ 5. Let it be considered that if our lives be not a journey towards heaven, they will be a journey to hell. All mankind, after they have been here a short while, go to either of the two great receptacles of all that depart out of this world; the one is *heaven;* whither a small number, in comparison travel; and the other is *hell,* whither the bulk of mankind throng. And one or the other of these must be the issue of our course in this world.

I shall conclude by giving a few *directions:*

³² 1. Labour to get a sense of the vanity of this world; on account of the little satisfaction that is to be enjoyed here: its short continuance, and un-

serviceableness when we most stand in need of help, *viz.* on a death bed.—All men, that live any considerable time in the world, might see enough to convince them of its vanity, if they would but consider.—Be persuaded therefore to exercise consideration, when you see and hear, from time to time of the death of others. Labour to turn your thoughts this way. See the vanity of the world in such a glass.

³³ 2. Labour to be much acquainted with heaven.—If you are not acquainted with it, you will not be likely to spend your life as a journey thither. You will not be sensible of its worth, nor will you long for it. Unless you are much conversant in your mind with a better good, it will be exceeding difficult to you to have your hearts loose from these things, and to use them only in subordination to something else, and be ready to part with them for the sake of that better good.—Labour therefore to obtain a realizing sense of a heavenly world, to get a firm belief of its reality, and to be very much conversant with it in your thoughts.

³⁴ 3. Seek heaven only by Jesus Christ.—Christ tells us that he is the way, and the truth and the life. He tells us that he is the door of the sheep. "I am the door, by me if any man enter in he shall be saved; and go in and out and find pasture." If we therefore would improve our lives as a journey towards heaven, we must seek it by him, and not by our own righteousness; as expecting to obtain it only for his sake, looking to him, having our dependence on him, who has procured it for us by his merit. And expect strength to walk in holiness, the way that leads to heaven, only from him.

³⁵ 4. Let christians help one another in going this journey.—There are many ways whereby christians might greatly forward one another in their way to heaven, as by religious conference, &c. Therefore let them be exhorted to go this journey as it were in company, conversing together, and assisting one another. Company is very desirable in a journey, but in none so much as this.—Let them go united, and not fall out by the way, which would be to hinder one another; but use all means they can to help each other up the hill.—This would ensure a more successful travelling, and a more joyful meeting at their Father's house in glory.

The Expulsive Power of a New Affection

Love not the world, neither the things that are in the
world. If any man love the world, the love of the Father
is not in him.   —I John 2:15

THERE are two ways in which a practical moralist may attempt to dis-
place from the human heart its love of the world—either by a demonstration of the world's vanity, so that the heart shall be prevailed upon
simply to withdraw its regards from an object that is not worthy of it;
or, by setting forth another object, even God, as more worthy of its
attachment, so that the heart shall be prevailed upon not to resign an old
affection, which shall have nothing to succeed it, but to exchange an old
affection for a new one. My purpose is to show that from the constitution
of our nature, the former method is altogether incompetent and ineffectual,
and that the latter method will alone suffice for the rescue and recovery of
the heart from the wrong affection that domineers over it. After having
accomplished this purpose, I shall attempt a few practical observations.

2 Love may be regarded in two different conditions. The first is, when
its object is at a distance, and then it becomes love in a state of desire. The
second is, when its object is in possession, and then it becomes love in a
state of indulgence. Under the impulse of desire, man feels himself urged
onward in some path or pursuit of activity for its gratification. The faculties
of his mind are put into busy exercise. In the steady direction of one great
and engrossing interest, his attention is recalled from the many reveries into
which it might otherwise have wandered; and the powers of his body are
forced away from an indolence into which it also might have languished;
and that time is crowded with occupation, which but for some object of
keen and devoted ambition might have driveled along in successive hours
of weariness and distaste; and though hope does not always enliven, and
success does not always crown this career of exertion, yet in the midst of
this very variety, and with the alternations of occasional disappointment,
is the machinery of the whole man kept in a sort of congenial play, and
upholden in that tone and temper which are most agreeable to it. Insomuch,
that if through the extirpation of that desire which forms the originating

---

From *The Works of Thomas Chalmers* (New York: Robert Carter & Bros., 1830),
Vol. II.

principle of all this movement the machinery were to stop, and to receive no impulse from another desire substituted in its place, the man would be left with all his propensities to action in a state of most painful and unnatural abandonment. A sensitive being suffers and is in violence if, after having thoroughly rested from his fatigue, or been relieved from his pain, he continue in possession of powers without any excitement to those powers, if he possess a capacity of desire without having an object of desire, or if he have a spare energy upon his person, without a counterpart, and without a stimulus to call it into operation. The misery of such a condition is often realized by him who is retired from business, or who is retired from law, or even the occupations of the chase, and of the gaming table. Such is the demand of our nature for an object in pursuit, that no accumulation of previous success can extinguish it—and thus it is that the most prosperous merchant, and the most victorious general, and the most fortunate gamester, when the labour of their respective vocations has come to a close, are often found to languish in the midst of all their acquisitions, as if out of their kindred and rejoicing element. It is quite in vain to attempt cutting away from him the spring or the principle of one employment without providing him with another. The whole heart and habit will rise in resistance against such an undertaking. The else unoccupied female, who spends the hours of every evening at some play of hazard, knows as well as you that pecuniary gain or the honorable triumph of a successful contest is altogether paltry. It is not such a demonstration of vanity that will force her away from her dear and delightful occupation. The habit cannot be displaced so as to leave nothing but a negative and cheerless vacancy behind it—though it may be so supplanted as to be followed up by another habit of employment, to which the power of some new affection has constrained her. It is willingly suspended, for example, on any single evening, should the time that is wont to be allotted to gambling require to be spent on the preparation for an approaching assembly.

[3] The ascendant power of a second affection will do what no exposition, however forcible, of the folly and worthlessness of the first, ever could effectuate. And it is the same in the great world. You will never be able to arrest any of its leading pursuits, by a naked demonstration of their vanity. It is quite in vain to think of stopping one of those pursuits in any way else but by stimulating to another. In attempting to bring a worldly man, intent and busied with the prosecution of his objects, to a dead stand, you have not merely to encounter the charm which he annexes to those objects—but you have to encounter the pleasure which he feels in the very prosecution of them. It is not enough, then, that you dissipate the charm by your moral, and eloquent, and effective exposure of its illusiveness. You must address to the eye of his mind another object with a charm powerful enough to dispossess the first of its influence, and to engage him in some other prosecution as full of interest, and hope, and congenial activity, as the former. It is this which stamps an impotency upon all moral and pathetic declamation about the insignificance of the world. A man will no more

51

consent to the misery of being without an object, because that object is a trifle, or of being without a pursuit, because that pursuit terminates in some frivolous or fugitive acquirement, than he would voluntarily submit himself to the torture because that torture is to be of short duration. If to be without desire and without exertion altogether is a state of violence and discomfort, then the present desire, with its correspondent train of exertion is not to be got rid of simply by destroying it. It must be by substituting another desire, and another line or habit of exertion in its place; and the most effectual way of withdrawing the mind from one object is not by turning it away upon desolate and unpeopled vacancy, but by presenting to its regard another object still more alluring.

4 These remarks apply not merely to love considered in its state of desire for an object not yet attained. They apply also to love considered in its state of indulgence, or placid gratification, with an object already in possession. It is seldom that any of our tastes are made to disappear by a mere process of natural extinction. At least, it is very seldom that this is done through the instrumentality of reasoning. It may be done by excessive pampering—but it is almost never done by the mere force of mental determination. But what cannot be thus destroyed may be dispossessed—and one taste may be made to give way to another, and to lose its power entirely as the reigning affection of the mind. It is thus that the boy ceases at length to be the slave of his appetite, but it is because a manlier taste has now brought it into subordination—and that the youth ceases to idolize pleasure, but it is because the idol of wealth has become the stronger and gotten the ascendancy. Even the love of money ceases to have the mastery over the heart of many a citizen, but it is because drawn into the whirl of city politics, another affection has been wrought into his moral system, and he is now lorded over by love of power. There is not one of these transformations in which the heart is left without an object. Its desire for one particular object may be conquered; but as to its desire for having some one object or other, this is unconquerable. Its adhesion to that on which it has fastened the preference of its regards, cannot willingly be overcome by the rending away of a simple separation. It can be done only by the application of something else, to which it may feel the adhesion of a still stronger and more powerful preference. Such is the grasping tendency of the human heart that it must have a something to lay hold of, and which, if wrested away without the substitution of another something in its place, would leave a void and a vacancy as painful to the mind, as hunger is to the natural system. It may be dispossessed of one object, or of any, but it cannot be desolated of all. Let there be a breathing and a sensitive heart, but without a liking and without affinity to any of the things that are around it, and in a state of cheerless abandonment it would be alive to nothing but the burden of its own consciousness, and feel it to be intolerable. It would make no difference to its owner, whether he dwelt in the midst of a gay and goodly world, or placed afar beyond the outskirts of creation, he dwelt a solitary unit in dark and unpeopled nothingness. The heart must have something to cling

to, and never by its own voluntary consent will it so denude itself of all its attachments that there shall not be one remaining object that can draw or solicit it.

⁵ The misery of a heart thus bereft of all relish for that which wont to minister enjoyment, is strikingly exemplified in those, who, satiated with indulgence, have been so belaboured, as it were, with the variety and the poignancy of the pleasurable sensations that they have experienced, that they are at length fatigued out of all capacity for sensation whatever. The disease of ennui is more frequent in the French metropolis, where amusement is more exclusively the occupation of higher classes, than it is in the British metropolis, where the longings of the heart are more diversified by the resources of business and politics. There are the votaries of fashion, who, in this way, have at length become the victims of fashionable excess—in whom the very multitude of their enjoyments, has at last extinguished their power of enjoyment—who, with the gratifications of art and nature at command, now look upon all that is around them with an eye of tastelessness—who, plied with the delights of sense and of splendour even to weariness, and incapable of higher delights, have come to the end of all their perfection, and like Solomon of old, found it to be vanity and vexation. The man whose heart has thus been turned into a desert, can vouch for the insupportable languor which must ensue, when one affection is thus plucked away from the bosom, without another to replace it. It is not necessary that a man receive pain from any thing, in order to become miserable. It is barely enough that he looks with distaste to every thing—and in that asylum which is the repository of minds out of joint, and where the organ of feeling as well as the organ of intellect, has been impaired, it is not in the cell of loud and frantic outcries where you will meet with the acme of mental suffering. But that is the individual who outpeers in wretchedness all his fellows, who throughout the whole expanse of nature and society, meets not an object that has at all the power to detain or to interest him; who neither in earth beneath, nor in heaven above, knows of a single charm to which his heart can send forth one desirous or responding movement; to whom the world, in his eye a vast and empty desolation, has left him nothing but his own consciousness to feed upon—dead to all that is without him, and alive to nothing but to the load of his own torpid and useless existence.

⁶ It will now be seen, perhaps, why it is that the heart keeps by its present affections with so much tenacity, when the attempt is to do them away by a mere process of extirpation. It will not consent to be so desolated. The strong man whose dwelling-place is there may be compelled to give way to another occupier, but unless another stronger than he has power to dispossess and succeed him, he will keep his present lodgment inviolable. The heart would revolt against its own emptiness. It could not bear to be so left in a state of waste and cheerless insipidity. The moralist who tries such a process of dispossession as this upon the heart is thwarted at every step by the recoil of its own mechanism. You have all heard that Nature abhors a vacuum. Such at least is the nature of the heart that though the room

which is in it may change one inmate for another, it cannot be left void without the pain of most intolerable suffering. It is not enough then to argue the folly of an existing affection. It is not enough, in the terms of a forcible or an affecting demonstration, to make good the evanescence of its object. It may not even be enough to associate the threats and terrors of some coming vengeance, with the indulgence of it. The heart may still resist the every application, by obedience to which it would finally be conducted to a state so much at war with all its appetites as that of downright inanition. So to tear away an affection from the heart as to leave it bare of all its regards, and of all its preferences were a hard and a hopeless undertaking; and it would appear as if the alone powerful engine of dispossession were to bring the mastery of another affection to bear upon it.

7 We know a more sweeping interdict upon the affections of Nature, than that which is delivered by the Apostle in the verse before us. To bid a man into whom there is not entered the great and ascendant influence of the principle of regeneration, to bid him withdraw his love from all the things that are in the world, is to bid him give up all the affections that are in his heart. The world is the all of a natural man. He has not a taste, nor a desire, that points not to a something placed within the confines of its visible horizon. He loves nothing above it, and he cares for nothing beyond it; and to bid him love not the world, is to pass a sentence of expulsion on all the inmates of his bosom. To estimate the magnitude and the difficulty of such a surrender, let us only think that it were just as arduous to prevail on him to set wilful fire to his own property. This he might do with sore and painful reluctance, if he saw that a new property of tenfold value was instantly to emerge upon the wreck of the old one. In this case there is something more than the mere displacement of an affection. There is the overbearing of one affection by another. But to desolate his heart of all love for the things of the world, without the substitution of any love in its place, were to him a process of as unnatural violence, as to destroy all the things he has in the world, and give him nothing in their room. So that, if to love not the world be indispensable to one's Christianity, then the crucifixion of the old man is not too strong a term to mark that transition in his history, when all old things are done away, and all things are become new.

8 We hope that by this time, you understand the impotency of a mere demonstration of this world's insignificance. Its sole practical effect, if it had any, would be to leave the heart in a state which to every heart is insupportable, and that is a mere state of nakedness and negation. You may remember the fond and unbroken tenacity with which your heart has often recurred to pursuits over the utter frivolity of which it sighed and wept but yesterday. The arithmetic of your short-lived days may on Sabbath make the clearest impression upon your understanding—and from his fancied bed of death, may the preacher cause a voice to descend in rebuke and mockery on all the pursuits of earthliness—and as he pictures before you the fleeting generations of men, with the absorbing grave, whither all the joys and interests of the world hasten to their sure and speedy oblivion,

may you, touched and solemnized by his argument, feel for a moment as if on the eve of a practical and permanent emancipation from a scene of so much vanity. But the morrow comes, and the business of the world, and the objects of the world, and the moving forces of the world come along with it—and the machinery of the heart, in virtue of which it must have something to grasp, or something to adhere to, brings it under a kind of moral necessity to be actuated just as before—and in utter repulsion towards a state so unkindly as that of being frozen out both of delight and of desire, does it feel all the warmth and the urgency of its wonted solicitations—not in the habit and history of the whole man, can we detect so much as one symptom of the new creature—so that the church, instead of being to him a school of obedience, has been a mere sauntering place for the luxury of a passing and theatrical emotion; and the preaching which is mighty to compel the attendance of multitudes, which is mighty to still and to solemnize the hearers into a kind of tragic sensibility, which is mighty in the play of variety and vigour that it can keep up around the imagination, is not mighty to the pulling down of strong-holds.

⁹ The love of the world cannot be expunged by a mere demonstration of the world's worthlessness. But may it not be supplanted by the love of that which is more worthy than itself? The heart cannot be prevailed upon to part with the world by a simple act of resignation. But may not the heart be prevailed upon to admit into its preference another who shall subordinate the world, and bring it down from its wonted ascendancy? If the throne which is placed there, must have an occupier, and the tyrant that now reigns has occupied it wrongfully, he may not leave a bosom which would rather detain him, than be left in desolation. But may he not give way to the lawful sovereign, appearing with every charm that can secure his willing admittance, and taking unto himself his great power to subdue the moral nature of man, and to reign over it? In a word, if the way to disengage the heart from the positive love of one great and ascendant object is to fasten it in positive love to another, then it is not by exposing the worthlessness of the former, but by addressing to the mental eye the worth and excellence of the latter, that all old things are to be done away, and all things are to become new.

¹⁰ To obliterate all our present affections, by simply expunging them, and so as to leave the seat of them unoccupied, would be to destroy the old character, and to substitute no new character in its place. But when they take their departure upon the ingress of other visitors; when they resign their sway to the power and the predominance of new affections, when, abandoning the heart to solitude, they merely give place to a successor who turns it into as busy a residence of desire and interest and expectation as before, there is nothing in all this to thwart or to overbear any of the laws of our sentient nature; and we see how, in fullest accord with the mechanism of the heart, a great moral revolution may be made to take place upon it.

¹¹ This, we trust, will explain the operation of that charm which accompanies the effectual preaching of the Gospel. The love of God and the

love of the world are two affections, not merely in a state of rivalship but in a state of enmity, and that so irreconcilable, that they cannot dwell together in the same bosom. We have already affirmed how impossible it were for the heart, by any innate elasticity of its own, to cast the world away from it, and thus reduce itself to a wilderness. The heart is not so constituted, and the only way to dispossess it of an old affection is by the expulsive power of a new one. Nothing can exceed the magnitude of the required change in a man's character—when bidden as he is in the New Testament to not love the world; no, nor any of the things that are in the world, for this so comprehends all that is dear to him in existence, as to strike him dumb. But the same revelation which dictates so mighty an obedience places within our reach as mighty an instrument of obedience. It brings for admittance to the very door of our hearts an affection which, once seated upon its throne, will either subordinate every previous inmate, or bid it away. Beside the world, it places before the eye of the mind Him who made the world, and with this peculiarity, which is all its own—that in the Gospel do we so behold God that we may love God. It is there, and there only, where God stands revealed as an object of confidence to sinners, and where our desire after Him is not chilled into apathy, by that barrier of human guilt which intercepts every approach that is not made to Him through the appointed Mediator. It is the bringing in of this better hope whereby we draw nigh unto God; and to live without hope is to live without God; and if the heart be without God, then the world will have the ascendancy. It is God apprehended by the believer as God in Christ, who alone can dispost it from this ascendancy. It is when He stands dismantled of the terrors which belong to Him as an offended Lawgiver, and when we are enabled by faith to see His glory in the face of Jesus Christ, and to hear His beseeching voice, as it protests good will to men, and entreats the return of all who will to a full pardon and a gracious acceptance—it is then that a love paramount to the love of the world, and at length expulsive of it, first arises in the regenerating bosom. It is when released from the spirit of bondage, with which love cannot dwell, and when admitted into the number of God's children, through the faith that is in Jesus Christ, the spirit of adoption is poured upon us—it is then that the heart, brought under the mastery of one great and predominant affection, is delivered from the tyranny of its former desires, and in the only way in which deliverance is possible. And that faith which is revealed to us from heaven as indispensable to a sinner's justification in the sight of God, is also the instrument of the greatest of all moral and spiritual achievements on a nature dead to the influence and beyond the reach of every other application.

12 Thus may we come to perceive what it is that makes the most effective kind of preaching. It is not enough to hold out to the world's eye the mirror of its own imperfections. It is not enough to come forth with a demonstration, however pathetic, of the evanescent character of all its enjoyments. It is not enough to travel the walk of experience along with you, and speak to your own conscience, and your own recollection of the deceitfulness of the heart,

and the deceitfulness of all that the heart is set upon. There is many a bearer of the Gospel message, who has not shrewdness of natural discernment enough, and who has not power of characteristic description enough, and who has not the talent of moral delineation enough, to present you with a vivid and faithful sketch of the existing follies of society. But that very corruption which he has not the faculty of representing in its visible details, he may practically be the instrument of eradicating in its principle. Let him be but a faithful expounder of the Gospel testimony—unable as he may be to apply a descriptive hand to the character of the present world,—unskilled as he is in the work of so anatomizing the heart, as with the power of a novelist to create a graphical or impressive exhibition of the worthlessness of its many affections—let him only deal in those mysteries of peculiar doctrine, on which the best of novelists have thrown the wantonness of their derision. He may not be able, with the eye of shrewd and satirical observation, to expose to the ready recognition of his hearers the desires of worldliness—but with the tidings of the Gospel in commission, he may wield the only engine that can extirpate them. He cannot do what some have done, when, as if by the hand of a magician, they have brought out to view, from the hidden recesses of our nature, the foibles and lurking appetites which belong to it. But he has a truth in his possession, which into whatever heart it enters, will, like the rod of Aaron, swallow up them all—and unqualified as he may be to describe the old man in all the nicer shadings of his natural and constitutional varieties, with him is deposited that ascendant influence under which the leading tastes and tendencies of the old man are destroyed, and he becomes a new creature in Jesus Christ our Lord.

[13] Let us not cease then to ply the only instrument of powerful and positive operation, to do away from you the love of the world. Let us try every legitimate method of finding access to your hearts for the love of Him who is greater than the world. For this purpose, let us, if possible, clear away that shroud of unbelief which so hides and darkens the face of the Deity. Let us insist on His claims to your affection, and whether in the way of gratitude, or in the shape of esteem, let us never cease to affirm that in the whole of that wondrous economy, the purpose of which is to reclaim a sinful world unto himself—He, the God of love, so sets himself forth in character of endearment that nought but faith and nought but understanding are wanting on your part to call forth the love of your hearts back again.

[14] And here let me advert to the incredulity of a worldly man; when he brings his own sound and secular experience to bear upon the high doctrines of Christianity—when he looks on regeneration as a thing impossible —when feeling as he does, the obstinacies of his own heart on the side of things present, and casting an intelligent eye, much exercised perhaps in the observation of human life, on the equal obstinacies of all who are around him, he pronounces this whole matter about the crucifixion of the old man, and the resurrection of a new man in his place, to be in downright opposition to all that is known and witnessed of the real nature of humanity. We think that we have seen such men, who, firmly trenched in their own vigorous and

homebred sagacity, and shrewdly regardful of all that passes before them through the week, and upon the scenes of ordinary business, look on that transition of the heart by which it gradually dies unto time, and awakens in all the life of a new-felt and ever-growing desire towards God, as a mere Sabbath speculation; and who thus, with all their attention engrossed upon the concerns of earthiness, continue unmoved, to the end of their days, amongst the feelings, and the appetites, and the pursuits of earthliness. If the thought of death, and another state of being after it, comes across them at all, it is not with a change so radical as that of being born again, that they ever connect the idea of preparation. They have some vague conception of its being quite enough that they acquit themselves in some decent and tolerable way of their relative obligations; and that, upon the strength of some such social and domestic moralities as are often realized by him in whose heart the love of God has never entered, they will be transplanted in safety from this world, where God is the Being with whom it may almost be said they have had nothing to do, to that world where God is the Being with whom they will have mainly and immediately to do throughout all eternity. They admit all that is said of the utter vanity of time, when taken up with as a resting place. But they resist every application made upon the heart of man with the view of so shifting its tendencies, that it shall not henceforth find in the interests of time, all its rest and all its refreshment. They, in fact, regard such an attempt as an enterprise that is altogether aerial—and with a tone of secular wisdom, caught from the familiarities of every-day experience, do they see a visionary character in all that is said of setting our affections on the things that are above; and of walking by faith; and of keeping our hearts in such a love of God as shall shut out from them the love of the world; and of having no confidence in the flesh; and of so renouncing earthly things as to have our conversation in heaven.

[15] Now, it is altogether worthy of being remarked of those men who thus disrelish spiritual Christianity, and, in fact, deem it an impracticable acquirement, how much of a piece of their incredulity about the demands of Christianity, and their incredulity about the doctrines of Christianity, are with one another. No wonder that they feel the work of the New Testament to be beyond their strength, so long as they hold the words of the New Testament to be beneath their attention. Neither they nor any one else can dispossess the heart of an old affection, but by the impulsive power of a new one—and, if that new affection be the love of God, neither they nor any one else can be made to entertain it, but on such representation of the Deity, as shall draw the heart of the sinner towards him. Now it is just their unbelief which screens from the discernment of their minds this representation. They do not see the love of God in sending his Son into the world. They do not see the expression of his tenderness to men, in sparing him not, but giving him up unto the death for us all. They do not see the sufficiency of the atonement or of the sufferings that were endured by him who bore the burden that sinners should have borne. They do not see the blended holiness and compassion of the Godhead, in that he passed by the transgressions

58

of his creatures, yet could not pass them by without an expiation. It is a mystery to them, how a man should pass to the state of godliness from a state of nature—but had they only a believing view of God manifest in the flesh, this would resolve for them the whole mystery of godliness. As it is, they cannot get quit of their old affections, because they are out of sight from all those truths which have influence to raise a new one. They are like the children of Israel in the land of Egypt, when required to make bricks without straw—they cannot love God, while they want the only food which can aliment this affection in a sinner's bosom—and however great their errors may be both in resisting the demands of the Gospel as impracticable, and in rejecting the doctrines of the Gospel as inadmissible, yet there is not a spiritual man (and it is the prerogative of him who is spiritual to judge all men) who will not perceive that there is a consistency in these errors.

16 But if there be a consistency in the errors, in like manner is there a consistency in the truths which are opposite to them. The man who believes in the peculiar doctrines, will readily bow to the peculiar demands of Christianity. When he is told to love God supremely, this may startle another, but it will not startle him to whom God has been revealed in peace, and in pardon, and in all the freeness of an offered reconciliation. When told to shut out the world from his heart, this may be impossible with him who has nothing to replace it—but not impossible with him, who has found in God a sure and a satisfying portion. When told to withdraw his affections from the things that are beneath, this were laying an order of self-extinction upon the man, who knows not another quarter in the whole sphere of his contemplation, to which he could transfer them—but it were not grievous to him whose view has been opened up to the loveliness and glory of the things that are above, and can there find, for every feeling of his soul, a most ample and delighted occupation. When told to look not to the things that are seen and temporal, this were blotting out the light of all that is visible from the prospect of him in whose eye there is a wall of partition between guilty nature and the joys of eternity—but he who believes that Christ hath broken down this wall, finds a gathering radiance upon his soul, as he looks onwards in faith to the things that are unseen and eternal. Tell a man to be holy—and how can he compass such a performance, when his alone fellowship with holiness is a fellowship of despair? It is the atonement of the cross reconciling the holiness of the lawgiver with the safety of the offender, that hath opened the way for a sanctifying influence into the sinner's heart, and he can take a kindred impression from the character of God now brought nigh, and now at peace with him. Separate the demand from the doctrine, and you have either a system of righteousness that is impracticable, or a barren orthodoxy. Bring the demand and the doctrine together—and the true disciple of Christ is able to do the one, through the other strengthening him. The motive is adequate to the movement; and the bidden obedience of the Gospel is not beyond the measure of his acceptance. The shield of faith, and the hope of salvation, and the Word of God, and the girdle of truth—these are the armour

59

that he has put on; and with these the battle is won, and the eminence is reached, and the man stands on the vantage ground of a new field and a new prospect. The effect is great, but the cause is equal to it—and stupendous as this moral resurrection to the precepts of Christianity undoubtedly is, there is an element of strength enough to give it being and continuance in the principles of Christianity.

[17] The object of the Gospel is both to pacify the sinner's conscience and to purify his heart, and it is of importance to observe that what mars the one of these objects mars the other also. The best way of casting out an impure affection is to admit a pure one; and by the love of God to expel the love of what is evil. Thus it is that the freer the Gospel, the more sanctifying is the Gospel, and the more it is received as a doctrine of grace, the more will it be felt as a doctrine according to godliness. This is one of the secrets of the Christian life, that the more a man holds to God as a pensioner, the greater is the payment of service that he renders back again. On the tenure of "Do this and live," a spirit of fearfulness is sure to enter; and the jealousies of a legal bargain chase away all confidence from the intercourse between God and man; and the creature striving to be square and even with his Creator, is, in fact, pursuing all the while his own selfishness instead of God's glory; and with all the conformities which he labours to accomplish, the soul of obedience is not there, the mind is not subject to the law of God, nor indeed under such an economy ever can be. It is only when, as in the Gospel, acceptance is bestowed as a present, without money and without price, that the security which man feels in God is placed beyond the reach of disturbance, or that he can repose in Him as one friend reposes in another, or that any liberal and generous understanding can be established betwixt them, the one party rejoicing over the other to do him good, the other finding that the truest gladness of his heart lies in the impulse of a gratitude, by which it is awakened to the charms of a new moral existence. Salvation by grace, salvation by free grace, salvation not of works but according to the mercy of God, salvation on such a footing is not more indispensable to the deliverance of our persons from the hand of justice than it is to the deliverance of our hearts from the chill and the weight of ungodliness. Retain a single shred or fragment of legality with the Gospel, and you raise a topic of distrust between man and God. You take away from the power of the Gospel to melt and to conciliate. For this purpose, the freer it is, the better it is. That very peculiarity which so many dread as the germ of Antinomianism, is, in fact, the germ of a new spirit, and a new inclination against it. Along with the light of a free Gospel, does there enter the love of the Gospel, which in proportion as you impair the freeness, you are sure to chase away. And never does the sinner find within himself so mighty a moral transformation, as when under the belief that he is saved by grace, he feels constrained thereby to offer his heart a devoted thing, and to deny ungodliness.

[18] To do any work in the best manner, you must make use of the fittest

tools. And we trust that what has been said may serve in some degree for the practical guidance of those who would like to reach the great moral achievement of our text—but feel that the tendencies and desires of Nature are too strong for them. We know of no other way by which to keep the love of the world out of our hearts than to keep in our hearts the love of God, and no other way to keep our hearts in the love of God than by building ourselves up in our most holy faith. That denial of the world which is not possible to him that dissents from the Gospel testimony is possible even as all things are possible to him that believeth. To try this without faith, is to work without the right tool or the right instrument. But faith worketh by love; and the way of expelling from the heart the love that transgresseth the law is to admit into its receptacles the love that fulfilleth the law.

[19] Conceive a man to be standing on the margin of this green world; and that, when he looked towards it, he saw abundance smiling upon every field, and all the blessings which earth can afford, scattered in profusion throughout every family, and the light of the sun sweetly resting upon all the pleasant habitations, and the joys of human companionship brightening many a happy circle of society—conceive this to be the general character of the scene upon one side of his contemplation; and that on the other, beyond the verge of the goodly planet on which he was situated, he could descry nothing but a dark and fathomless unknown. Think you that he would bid a voluntary adieu to all the brightness and all the beauty that were before him upon earth, and commit himself to the frightful solitude away from it? Would he leave its peopled dwelling places, and become a solitary wanderer through the fields of nonentity? If space offered him nothing but a wilderness, would he for it abandon the homebred scenes of life and cheerfulness that lay so near, and exerted such a power of urgency to detain him? Would not he cling to the regions of sense, and of life, and of society?—And shrinking away from the desolation that was beyond it, would not he be glad to keep his firm footing on the territory of this world, and to take shelter under the canopy that was stretched over it?

[20] But if during the time of his contemplation some happy island of the blest had floated by; and there had burst upon his senses the light of its surpassing glories, and its sounds of sweeter melody; and he clearly saw, that there, a purer beauty rested upon every field, and a more heartfelt joy spread itself among all the families; and he could discern there a peace, and a piety, and a benevolence, which put a moral gladness into every bosom, and united the whole society in one rejoicing sympathy with each other, and with the beneficent Father of them all;—Could he further see that pain and mortality were there unknown; and above all, that signals of welcome were hung out, and an avenue of communication was made for him;—perceive you not, that what was before the wilderness would become the land of invitation; and that now the world would be the wilderness? What unpeopled space could not do can be done by space teeming with beatific

scenes and beatific society. And let the existing tendencies of the heart be what they may to the scene that is near and visible around us, still if another stood revealed to the prospect of man, either through the channel of faith or through the channel of his senses—then, without violence done to the constitution of his moral nature, may he die unto this present world, and live to the lovelier world that stands in the distance away from it.

The Character of Christ

This is my beloved Son, in whom I am well pleased.
—Matt. 17:5

THE character of Christ may be studied for various purposes. It is singularly fitted to call forth the heart, to awaken love, admiration, and moral delight. As an example, it has no rival. As an evidence of his religion, perhaps it yields to no other proof; perhaps no other has so often conquered unbelief. It is chiefly to this last view of it, that I now ask your attention. The character of Christ is a strong confirmation of the truth of his religion. As such, I would now place it before you. I shall not, however, think only of confirming your faith; the very illustrations, which I shall adduce for this purpose will show the claims of Jesus to our reverence, obedience, imitation, and fervent love.

2 The more we contemplate Christ's character, as exhibited in the Gospel, the more we shall be impressed with its genuineness and reality. It was plainly drawn from the life. The narratives of the Evangelists bear the marks of truth, perhaps beyond all other histories. They set before us the most extraordinary being who ever appeared on earth, and yet they are as artless as the stories of childhood. The authors do not think of themselves. They have plainly but one aim, to show us their Master; and they manifest the deep veneration which he inspired, by leaving him to reveal himself, by giving us his actions and sayings without comment, explanation, or eulogy. You see in these narratives no varnishing, no high coloring, no attempts to make his actions striking, or to bring out the beauties of his character. We are never pointed to any circumstance as illustrative of his greatness. The Evangelists write with a calm trust in his character, with a feeling that it needed no aid from their hands, and with a deep veneration, as if comment or praise of their own were not worthy to mingle with the recital of such a life.

3 It is the effect of our familiarity with the history of Jesus, that we are not struck by it as we ought to be. We read it before we are capable of understanding its excellence. His stupendous works become as familiar to us as the events of ordinary life, and his high offices seem as much matters of

From *The Works of William E. Channing* (complete ed.; Boston: American Unitarian Association, 1875).

course, as the common relations which men bear to each other. On this account, it is fit for the ministers of religion to do what the Evangelists did not attempt, to offer comments on Christ's character, to bring out its features, to point men to its higher beauties, to awaken their awe by unfolding its wonderful majesty. Indeed, one of our most important functions, as teachers, is to give freshness and vividness to truths which have become worn, I had almost said tarnished, by long and familiar handling. We have to fight with the power of habit. Through habit, men look on this glorious creation with insensibility, and are less moved by the all-enlightening sun than by a show of fire-works. It is the duty of a moral and religious teacher, almost to create a new sense in men, that they may learn in what a world of beauty and magnificence they live. And so in regard to Christ's character; men become used to it, until they imagine, that there is something more admirable in a great man of their own day, a statesman or a conqueror, than in Him, the latchet of whose shoes statesmen and conquerors are not worthy to unloose.

⁴ In this discourse, I wish to show that the character of Christ, taken as a whole, is one which could not have entered the thoughts of man, could not have been imagined or feigned; that it bears every mark of genuineness and truth; that it ought therefore to be acknowledged as real and of divine original.

⁵ It is all-important, my friends, if we would feel the force of this argument, to transport ourselves to the times when Jesus lived. We are very apt to think, that he was moving about in such a city as this, or among a people agreeing with ourselves in modes of thinking and habits of life. But the truth is, he lived in a state of society singularly remote from our own. Of all nations, the Jewish was the most strongly marked. The Jew hardly felt himself to belong to the human family. He was accustomed to speak of himself as chosen by God, holy, clean; whilst the Gentiles were sinners, dogs, polluted, unclean. His common dress, the phylactery on his brow or arm, the hem of his garment, his food, the ordinary circumstances of his life, as well as his temple, his sacrifices, his ablutions, all held him up to himself, as a peculiar favorite of God, and all separated him from the rest of the world. With other nations he could not eat or marry. They were unworthy of his communion. Still, with all these notions of superiority, he saw himself conquered by those whom he despised. He was obliged to wear the shackles of Rome, to see Roman legions in his territory, a Roman guard near his temple, and a Roman tax-gatherer extorting, for the support of an idolatrous government and an idolatrous worship, what he regarded as due only to God. The hatred which burned in the breast of the Jew towards his foreign oppressor, perhaps never glowed with equal intensiveness in any other conquered state. He had, however, his secret consolation. The time was near, the prophetic age was at hand, when Judea was to break her chains and rise from the dust. Her long-promised king and deliverer was near, and was coming to wear the crown of universal empire. From Jerusalem was to go forth his law, and all nations were to serve the chosen people of

God. To this conqueror the Jews indeed ascribed the office of promoting religion; but the religion of Moses, corrupted into an outward service, was to them the perfection of human nature. They clung to its forms with the whole energy of their souls. To the Mosaic institution, they ascribed their distinction from all other nations. It lay at the foundation of their hopes of dominion. I believe no strength of prejudice ever equalled the intense attachment of the Jew to his peculiar national religion. You may judge of its power by the fact of its having been transmitted through so many ages, amidst persecution and sufferings which would have subdued any spirit but that of a Jew. You must bring these things to your mind. You must place yourselves in the midst of this singular people.

⁶ Among this singular people, burning with impatient expectation, appeared Jesus of Nazareth. His first words were, "Repent, for the kingdom of heaven is at hand." These words we hear with little emotion; but to the Jews, who had been watching for this kingdom for ages, and who were looking for its immediate manifestation, they must have been awakening as an earthquake. Accordingly we find Jesus thronged by multitudes which no building could contain. He repairs to a mountain, as affording him advantages for addressing the crowd. I see them surrounding him with eager looks, and ready to drink in every word from his lips. And what do I hear? Not one word of Judea, of Rome, of freedom, of conquest, of the glories of God's chosen people, and of the thronging of all nations to the temple on Mount Zion. Almost every word was a death-blow to the hopes and feelings, which had glowed through the whole people, and were consecrated under the name of religion. He speaks of the long-expected Kingdom of Heaven; but speaks of it as a felicity promised to, and only to be partaken by, the humble and pure in heart. The righteousness of the Pharisees, that which was deemed the perfection of religion, and which the new deliverer was expected to spread far and wide, he pronounces worthless, and declares the kingdom of Heaven, or of the Messiah, to be shut against all who do not cultivate a new, spiritual, and disinterested virtue. Instead of war and victory, he commands his impatient hearers to love, to forgive, to bless their enemies; and holds forth this spirit of benignity, mercy, peace, as the special badge of the people of the true Messiah. Instead of national interests and glories, he commands them to seek first a spirit of impartial charity and love, unconfined by the bounds of tribe or nation, and proclaims this to be the happiness and honor of the reign for which they hoped. Instead of this world's riches, which they expected to flow from all lands into their own, he commands them to lay up treasures in heaven, and directs them to an incorruptible, immortal life, as the true end of their being. Nor is this all. He does not merely offer himself as a spiritual deliverer, as the founder of a new empire of inward piety and universal charity; he closes with language announcing a more mysterious office. "Many will say unto me in that day, Lord, Lord, have we not prophesied in thy name? and in thy name done many wonderful works? And then will I profess unto them, I never knew you; depart from me, ye that work iniquity." Here I meet the annunciation of a character as

65

august as it must have been startling. I hear him foretelling a dominion to be exercised in the future world. He begins to announce, what entered largely into his future teaching, that his power was not bounded to this earth. These words I better understand, when I hear him subsequently declaring, that, after a painful death, he was to rise again, and ascend to heaven, and there, in a state of preeminent power and glory, was to be the advocate and judge of the human race.

7 Such are some of the views given by Jesus, of his character and reign, in the Sermon on the Mount. Immediately afterwards, I hear another lesson from him, bringing out some of these truths still more strongly. A Roman centurion makes application to him for the cure of a servant, whom he particularly valued; and on expressing, in a strong manner, his conviction of the power of Jesus to heal at a distance, Jesus, according to the historian, "marvelled, and said to those that followed, Verily I say unto you, I have not found so great faith in Israel; and I say unto you, that many shall come from the east and west, and shall sit down with Abraham, and Isaac, and Jacob in the kingdom of heaven; but the children of the kingdom" (that is, the Jews) "shall be cast out." Here all the hopes which the Jews had cherished of an exclusive or peculiar possession of the Messiah's kingdom, were crushed; and the reception of the despised Gentile world to all his blessings, or, in other words, the extension of his pure religion to the ends of the earth, began to be proclaimed.

8 Here I pause for the present, and I ask you, whether the character of Jesus be not the most extraordinary in history, and wholly inexplicable on human principles. Review the ground over which we have gone. Recollect that he was born and grew up a Jew, in the midst of Jews, a people burning with one passion, and throwing their whole souls into the expectation of a national and earthly deliverer. He grew up among them in poverty, seclusion, and labors fitted to contract his thoughts, purposes, and hopes; and yet we find him escaping every influence of education and society. We find him as untouched by the feelings which prevailed universally around him, which religion and patriotism concurred to consecrate, which the mother breathed into the ear of the child, and which the teacher of the synagogue strengthened in the adult, as if he had been brought up in another world. We find him conceiving a sublime purpose, such as had never dawned on sage or hero, and see him possessed with a consciousness of sustaining a relation to God and mankind, and of being invested with powers in this world and the world to come, such as had never entered the human mind. Whence now, I ask, came the conception of this character?

9 Will any say it had its origin in imposture; that it was a fabrication of a deceiver? I answer, the character claimed by Christ excludes this supposition, by its very nature. It was so remote from all the ideas and anticipations of the times, so unfit to awaken sympathy, so unattractive to the heathen, so exasperating to the Jew, that it was the last to enter the mind of an impostor. A deceiver of the dullest vision might have foreseen, that it would expose him to bitter scorn, abhorrence, and persecution, and that he would be left

to carry on his work alone, just as Jesus always stood alone, and could find not an individual to enter into his spirit and design. What allurements an unprincipled, self-seeking man could find to such an enterprise, no common ingenuity can discover.

10 I affirm next, that the sublimity of the character claimed by Christ forbids us to trace it to imposture. That a selfish, designing, depraved mind could have formed the idea and purpose of a work unparalleled in beneficence, in vastness, and in moral grandeur, would certainly be a strange departure from the laws of the human mind. I would add, that if an impostor could have lighted on the conception of so sublime and wonderful a work as that claimed by Jesus, he could not, I say, he *could* not have thrown into his personation of it the truth and reality. The part would have been too high for him. He would have overacted it or fallen short of it perpetually. His true character would have rebelled against his assumed one. We should have seen something strained, forced, artificial, awkward, showing that he was not in his true sphere. To act up to a character so singular and grand, and one for which no precedent could be found, seems to me utterly impossible for a man who had not the true spirit of it, or who was only wearing it as a mask.

11 Now, how stands the case with Jesus? Bred a Jewish peasant or carpenter, he issues from obscurity, and claims for himself a divine office, a superhuman dignity, such as had not been imagined; and in no instance does he fall below the character. The peasant, and still more the Jew, wholly disappears. We feel that a new being, of a new order of mind, is taking a part in human affairs. There is a native tone of grandeur and authority in his teaching. He speaks as a being related to the whole human race. His mind never shrinks within the ordinary limits of human agency. A narrower sphere than the world never enters his thoughts. He speaks in a natural, spontaneous style, of accomplishing the most arduous and important change in human affairs. This unlabored manner of expressing great thoughts is particularly worthy of attention. You never hear from Jesus that swelling, pompous, ostentatious language, which almost necessarily springs from an attempt to sustain a character above our powers. He talks of his glories as one to whom they were familiar, and of his intimacy and oneness with God, as simply as a child speaks of his connexion with his parents. He speaks of saving and judging the world, of drawing all men to himself, and of giving everlasting life, as we speak of the ordinary powers which we exert. He makes no set harangues about the grandeur of his office and character. His consciousness of it gives a hue to his whole language, breaks out in indirect, undesigned expressions, showing that it was the deepest and most familiar of his convictions. This argument is only to be understood by reading the Gospels with a wakeful mind and heart. It does not lie on their surface, and it is the stronger for lying beneath it. When I read these books with care, when I trace the unaffected majesty which runs through the life of Jesus, and see him never falling below his sublime claims amidst poverty, and scorn, and in his last agony; I have a feeling of the

reality of his character which I cannot express. I feel that the Jewish carpenter could no more have conceived and sustained this character under motives of imposture, than an infant's arm could repeat the deeds of Hercules, or his unawakened intellect comprehend and rival the matchless works of genius.

¹² Am I told that the claims of Jesus had their origin, not in imposture but in enthusiasm; that the imagination, kindled by strong feeling, overpowered the judgment so far as to give him the notion of being destined to some strange and unparalleled work? I know that enthusiasm, or a kindled imagination, has great power; and we are never to lose sight of it, in judging of the claims of religious teachers. But I say first, that, except in cases where it amounts to insanity, enthusiasm works, in a greater or less degree, according to a man's previous conceptions and modes of thought. In Judea, where the minds of men were burning with feverish expectation of a Messiah, I can easily conceive of a Jew imagining that in himself this ardent conception, this ideal of glory, was to be realized. I can conceive of his seating himself in fancy on the throne of David, and secretly pondering the means of his appointed triumphs. But that a Jew should fancy himself the Messiah, and at the same time should strip that character of all the attributes which had fired his youthful imagination and heart,—that he should start aside from all the feelings and hopes of his age, and should acquire a consciousness of being destined to a wholly new career, and one as unbounded as it was new, this is exceedingly improbable; and one thing is certain, that an imagination so erratic, so ungoverned, and able to generate the conviction of being destined to a work so immeasurably disproportioned to the power of the individual, must have partaken of insanity. Now, is it conceivable, that an individual, mastered by so wild and fervid an imagination, should have sustained the dignity claimed by Christ, should have acted worthily the highest part ever assumed on earth? Would not his enthusiasm have broken out amidst the peculiar excitements of the life of Jesus, and have left a touch of madness on his teaching and conduct? Is it to such a man that we should look for the inculcation of a new and perfect form of virtue, and for the exemplification of humanity in its fairest form?

¹³ The charge of an extravagant, self-deluding enthusiasm is the last to be fastened on Jesus. Where can we find the traces of it in his history? Do we detect them in the calm authority of his precepts; in the mild, practical, and beneficent spirit of his religion; in the unlabored simplicity of the language with which he unfolds his high powers, and the sublime truths of religion; or in the good sense, the knowledge of human nature, which he always discovers in his estimate and treatment of the different classes of men with whom he acted? Do we discover this enthusiasm in the singular fact, that whilst he claimed power in the future world, and always turned men's minds to Heaven, he never indulged his own imagination, or stimulated that of his disciples, by giving vivid pictures, or any minute description, of that unseen state? The truth is, that, remarkable as was the

character of Jesus, it was distinguished by nothing more than by calmness and self-possession. This trait pervades his other excellences. How calm was his piety! Point me, if you can, to one vehement, passionate expression of his religious feelings. Does the Lord's Prayer breathe a feverish enthusiasm? The habitual style of Jesus on the subject of religion, if introduced into many churches by his followers at the present day, would be charged with coldness. The calm and the rational character of his piety is particularly seen in the doctrine which he so earnestly inculcates, that disinterested love and self-denying service to our fellow-creatures are the most acceptable worship we can offer to our Creator. His benevolence, too, though singularly earnest and deep, was composed and serene. He never lost the possession of himself in his sympathy with others; was never hurried into the impatient and rash enterprises of an enthusiastic philanthropy; but did good with the tranquility and constancy which mark the providence of God. The depth of his calmness may best be understood by considering the opposition made to his claims. His labors were everywhere insidiously watched and industriously thwarted by vindictive foes, who had even conspired to compass, through his death, the ruin of his cause. Now, a feverish enthusiasm, which fancies itself to be intrusted with a great work of God, is singularly liable to impatient indignation under furious and malignant opposition. Obstacles increase its vehemence; it becomes more eager and hurried in the accomplishment of its purposes, in proportion as they are withstood. Be it therefore remembered, that the malignity of Christ's foes, though never surpassed, and for the time triumphant, never robbed him of self-possession, roused no passion, and threw no vehemence or precipitation into his exertions. He did not disguise from himself or his followers the impression made on the multitude by his adversaries. He distinctly foresaw the violent death towards which he was fast approaching. Yet, confiding in God, and in the silent progress of his truth, he possessed his soul in peace. Not only was he calm, but his calmness rises into sublimity when we consider the storms which raged around him, and the vastness of the prospects in which his spirit found repose. I say, then, that serenity and self-possession were peculiarly the attributes of Jesus. I affirm, that the singular and sublime character claimed by Jesus, can be traced neither to imposture, nor to an ungoverned, insane imagination. It can only be accounted for by its truth, its reality.

14 I began with observing how our long familiarity with Jesus blunts our minds to his singular excellence. We probably have often heard of the character which he claimed, without a thought of its extraordinary nature. But I know nothing so sublime. The plans and labors of statesmen sink into the sports of children, when compared with the work which Jesus announced, and to which he devoted himself in life and death, with a thorough consciousness of its reality. The idea of changing the moral aspect of the whole earth, of recovering all nations to the pure and inward worship of one God, and to a spirit of divine and fraternal love, was one of which we meet not a trace in philosopher or legislator before him. The human mind had

given no promise of this extent of view. The conception of this enterprise, and the calm, unshaken expectation of success, in one who had no station and no wealth, who cast from him the sword with abhorrence, and who forbade his disciples to use any weapons but those of love, discover a wonderful trust in the power of God and the power of love; and when to this we add that Jesus looked not only to the triumph of his pure faith in the present world, but to a mighty and beneficent power in Heaven, we witness a vastness of purpose, a grandeur of thought and feeling, so original, so superior to the workings of all other minds, that nothing but our familiarity can prevent our contemplation of it with wonder and profound awe. I confess, when I can escape the deadening power of habit, and can receive the full import of such passages as the following,—"Come unto me, all ye that labor and are heavy laden, and I will give you rest,"—"I am come to seek and to save that which was lost,"—"He that confesseth me before men, him will I confess before my Father in Heaven,"—"Whosoever shall be ashamed of me before men, of him shall the Son of Man be ashamed when he cometh in the glory of the Father with the holy angels,"—"In my Father's house are many mansions; I go to prepare a place for you:"—I say, when I can succeed in realizing the import of such passages, I feel myself listening to a being, such as never before and never since spoke in human language. I am awed by the consciousness of greatness which these simple words express; and when I connect this greatness with the proofs of Christ's miracles which I gave you in a former discourse, I am compelled to exclaim with the centurion, "Truly, this was the Son of God."

15 I have thus, my friends, set before you one view of Jesus Christ, which shows him to have been the most extraordinary being who ever lived. I invite your attention to another; and I am not sure, but that it is still more striking. You have seen the consciousness of greatness which Jesus possessed; I now ask you to consider how, with this consciousne, he lived among men. To convey my meaning more distinctly, let me avail myself of an imaginary case. Suppose you had never heard the particulars of Christ's history, but were told in general that, ages ago, an extraordinary man appeared in the world, whose mind was wholly possessed with the idea of having come from God, who regarded himself as clothed with divine power and charged with the sublimest work in the universe, who had the consciousness of sustaining a relation of unexampled authority and beneficence, not to one nation or age, but to all nations and all times,—and who anticipated a spiritual kingdom and everlasting power beyond the grave. Suppose you should be told, that, on entering the world, he found not one mind able to comprehend his views, and felt himself immeasurably exalted in thought and purpose above all around him, and suppose you should then be asked what appearance, what mode of life, what tone, what air, what deportment, what intercourse with the multitude seemed to you to suit such a character, and were probably adopted by him; how would you represent him to your minds? Would you not suppose, that, with this peculiar character, he adopted some peculiar mode of life, expressive of his superiority to and separation from all other

70

men? Would you not expect something distinctive in his appearance? Would you not expect him to assume some badge, and to exact some homage? Would you not expect, that, with a mind revolving such vast thoughts, and raised above the earth he would look coldly on the ordinary gratifications of men? that, with a mind spreading itself over the world, and meditating its subjection to his truth, he would take little interest in ordinary individuals? and that, possessing, in his own doctrine and character, a standard of sublime virtue, he would attach little importance to the low attainments of the ignorant and superstitious around him? Would you not make him a public character, and expect to see him laboring to establish his ascendency among public men? Would you not expect to see his natural affections absorbed in his universal philanthropy; and would not private attachments seem to you quite inconsistent with his vast superiority, and the immensity of his purposes? Would you not expect him to avail himself of the best accommodations the world could afford? Would you not expect the great Teacher to select the most sacred spots for his teaching, and the Lord of all to erect some conspicuous seat, from which should go forth the laws which were to reach the ends of the earth? Would you not, in a word, expect this extraordinary personage to surround himself with extraordinary circumstances, and to maintain a separation from the degraded multitude around him?

[16] Such, I believe, would be the expectation of us all; and what was the case with Jesus? Read his history. He comes with the consciousness of more than human greatness, to accomplish an infinite work; and where do you find him? What is his look? what his manner? How does he converse, how live with men? His appearance, mode of life, and intercourse are directly the reverse of what we should have supposed. He comes in the ordinary dress of the class of society in which he had grown up. He retreats to no solitude, like John, to strike awe, nor seeks any spot which had been consecrated in Jewish history? Would you find him? Go to the house of Peter, the fisherman. Go to the well of Samaria, where he rests after the fatigues of his journey. Would you hear him teach? You may find him, indeed, sometimes in the temple, for that was a place of general resort; but commonly you may find him instructing in the open air, now from a boat on the Galilean lake, now on a mount, and now in the streets of the crowded city. He has no place wherein to lay his head, nor will he have one. A rich ruler comes and falls at his feet. He says, "Go, sell what thou hast, and give to the poor, and then come and follow me." Nor was this all. Something more striking remains to be told. He did not merely live in the streets, and in the houses of fishermen. In these places, had he pleased, he might have cleared a space around him, and raised a barrier between himself and others. But in these places, and everywhere, he lived with men as a man, a brother, a friend, sometimes as a servant; and entered, with a deep, unexampled sympathy, into the feelings, interests, wants, sorrows of individuals, of ordinary men, and even of the most depressed, despised, and forsaken of the race. Here is the most striking view of Jesus. This combination

71

of the spirit of humanity, in its lowliest, tenderest form, with the consciousness of unrivalled and divine glories, is the most wonderful distinction of this wonderful character. Here we learn the chief reason, why he chose poverty, and refused every peculiarity of manner and appearance. He did this because he desired to come near to the multitude of men, to make himself accessible to all, to pour out the fullness of his sympathy upon all, to know and weep over their sorrows and sins, and to manifest his interest in their affections and joys.

[17] I can offer but a few instances of this sympathy of Christ with human nature in all its varieties of character and condition. But how beautiful are they! At the very opening of his ministry, we find him present at a marriage, to which he and his disciples had been called. Among the Jews this was an occasion of peculiar exhilaration and festivity; but Jesus did not therefore decline it. He knew what affections, joys, sorrows, and moral influences are bound up in this institution, and he went to the celebration, not as an ascetic, to frown on its bright hopes and warm congratulations, but to sanction it by his presence, and to heighten its enjoyments. How little does this comport with the solitary dignity which we should have pronounced most accordant with his character, and what a spirit of humanity does it breathe! But this event stands almost alone in his history. His chief sympathy was not with them that rejoice, but with the ignorant, sinful, sorrowful; and with these we find him cultivating an habitual intimacy. Though so exalted in thought and purpose, he chose uneducated men to be his chief disciples; and he lived with them, not as a superior, giving occasional and formal instruction, but became their companion, travelled with them on foot, slept in their dwellnigs, sat at their tables, partook their plain fare, communicated to them his truth in the simplest form; and though they constantly misunderstood him, and never received his full meaning, he was never wearied with teaching them. So familiar was his intercourse, that we find Peter reproving him with an affectionate zeal, for announcing his approaching death, and we find John leaning on his bosom. Of his last discourse to these disciples I need not speak. It stands alone among all writings for the union of tenderness and majesty. His own sorrows are forgotten in his solicitude to speak peace and comfort to his humble followers.

[18] The depth of his human sympathies was beautifully manifested when children were brought to him. His disciples, judging as all men would judge, thought that he who was sent to wear the crown of universal empire, had too great a work before him to give his time and attention to children, and reproved the parents who brought them; but Jesus, rebuking his disciples, called to him the children. Never, I believe, did childhood awaken such deep love as at that moment. He took them in his arms and blessed them, and not only said that "of such was the kingdom of heaven," but added, "He that receiveth a little child in my name, receiveth me;" so entirely did he identify himself with this primitive, innocent, beautiful form of human nature.

[19] There was no class of human beings so low as to be beneath his sym-

pathy. He not merely taught the publican and sinner, but, with all his consciousness of purity, sat down and dined with them, and, when reproved by the malignant Pharisee for such companionship, answered by the touching parables of the Lost Sheep and the Prodigal Son, and said, "I am come to seek and to save that which was lost."

20 No personal suffering dried up this fountain of love in his breast. On his way to the cross, he heard some women of Jerusalem bewailing him, and at the sound, forgetting his own grief, he turned to them and said, "Women of Jerusalem, weep not for me, but weep for yourselves and your children." On the cross, whilst his mind was divided between intense suffering, and the contemplation of the infinite blessings in which his sufferings were to issue, his eye lighted on his mother and John, and the sensibilities of a son and a friend mingled with the sublime consciousness of the universal Lord and Saviour. Never before did natural affection find so tender and beautiful an utterance. To his mother he said, directing her to John, "*Behold thy son;* I leave my beloved disciple to take my place, to perform my filial offices, and to enjoy a share of that affection with which you have followed me through life;" and to John he said, "*Behold thy mother;* I bequeath to you the happiness of ministering to my dearest earthly friend." Nor is this all. The spirit of humanity had one higher triumph. Whilst his enemies surrounded him with a malignity unsoftened by his last agonies, and, to give the keenest edge to insult, reminded him scoffingly of the high character and office which he had claimed, his only notice of them was the prayer, "Father, forgive them, they know not what they do."

21 Thus Jesus lived with men; with the consciousness of unutterable majesty, he joined a lowliness, gentleness, humanity, and sympathy, which have no example in human history. I ask you to contemplate this wonderful union. In proportion to the superiority of Jesus to all around him, was the intimacy, the brotherly love, with which he bound himself to them. I maintain, that this is a character wholly remote from human conception. To imagine it to be the production of imposture or enthusiasm, shows a strange unsoundness of mind. I contemplate it with a veneration second only to the profound awe with which I look up to God. It bears no mark of human invention. It was real. It belonged to and it manifested the beloved Son of God.

22 But I have not done. May I ask your attention a few moments more? We have not yet reached the depth of Christ's character. We have not touched the great principle on which his wonderful sympathy was founded, and which endeared to him his office of universal Saviour. Do you ask what this deep principle was? I answer, it was his conviction of the greatness of the human soul. He saw in man the impress and image of the divinity, and therefore thirsted for his redemption, and took the tenderest interest in him, whatever might be the rank, character, or condition in which he was found. This spiritual view of man pervades and distinguishes the teaching of Christ. Jesus looked on men with an eye which pierced beneath the

73

material frame. The body vanished before him. The trappings of the rich, the rags of the poor, were nothing to him. He looked through them, as though they did not exist, to the soul; and there, amidst clouds of ignorance and plague spots of sin, he recognized a spiritual and immortal nature, and the germs of power and perfection which might be unfolded forever. In the most fallen and depraved man he saw a being who might become an angel of light. Still more, he felt that there was nothing in himself to which men might not ascend. His own lofty consciousness did not sever him from the multitude; for he saw in his own greatness the model of what men might become. So deeply was he thus impressed, that again and again, in speaking of his future glories, he announced that in these his true followers were to share. They were to sit on His throne, and partake of His beneficent power.

[23] Here I pause, and indeed I know not what can be added to heighten the wonder, reverence, and love, which are due to Jesus. When I consider him, not only as possessed of the consciousness of an unexampled and unbounded majestiy, but as recognizing a kindred nature in human beings, and living and dying to raise them to a participation of his divine glories; and when I see him under these views allying himself to men by the tenderest ties, embracing them with a spirit of humanity, which no insult, injury, or pain could for a moment repel or overpower, I am filled with wonder as well as reverence and love. I feel that this character is not of human invention, that it was not assumed through fraud, or struck out by enthusiasm; for it is .infinitely above their reach. When I add this character of Jesus to the other evidences of his religion, it gives to what before seemed so strong, a new and a vast accession of strength; I feel as if I could not be deceived. The Gospels must be true; they were drawn from a living original; they were founded on reality. The character of Jesus is not a fiction; he was what he claimed to be, and what his followers attested. Nor is this all. Jesus not only *was*, he is still, the Son of God, the Saviour of the world. He exists now; he has entered that Heaven to which he always looked forward on earth. There he lives and reigns. With a clear, calm faith, I see him in that state of glory; and I confidently expect, at no distant period, to see him face to face. We have indeed no absent friend whom we shall so surely meet. Let us then, my hearers, by imitation of his virtues and obedience to his word, prepare ourselves to join him in those pure mansions, where he is surrounding himself with the good and pure of our race, and will communicate to them forever his own spirit, power, and joy.

Every Man's Life a Plan of God

I girded thee, though thou hast not known me.—Isa. 45:5

S o BEAUTIFUL is the character and history of Cyrus, the person here addressed, that many have doubted whether the sketch given by Xenophon
was not intended as an idealizing, or merely romantic picture. And yet, there
have been examples of as great beauty unfolded, here and there, in all the
darkest recesses of the heathen world, and it accords entirely with the
hypothesis of historic verity in the account given us of this remarkable man,
that he is designated and named by our prophet, even before he is born,
as a chosen foster-son of God. "I have surnamed thee," he declares, "I
have girded thee, though thou hast not known me." And what should he
be but a model of all princely beauty, of bravery, of justice, of impartial
honor to the lowly, of greatness and true magnanimity in every form, when
God has girded him, unseen, to be the minister of his own great and sovereign
purposes to the nations of his time.

² Something of the same kind will also be detected in the history and
personal consciousness of almost every great and remarkable character.
Christ himself testifies to the girding of the Almighty, when he says,—
"To this end was I born, and for this purpose came I into the world."
Abraham was girded for a particular work and mission, in what is otherwise
denominated his call. Joseph, in Egypt, distinguishes the girding of God's
hand, when he comforts his guilty brothers in the assurance,—"So, it was
not you that sent me hither, but God." Moses and Samuel were even
called by name, and set to their great life-work, in the same manner. And
what is Paul endeavoring, in all the stress and pressure of his mighty apostle-
ship, but to perform the work for which God's Spirit girded him at his
call, and to apprehend that for which he was apprehended of Christ Jesus?
And yet these great master-spirits of the world are not so much distinguished,
after all, by the acts they do, as by the sense itself of some mysterious
girding of the Almighty upon them, whose behests they are set to fulfill.
And all men may have this; for the humblest and commonest have a place
and a work assigned them, in the same manner, and have it for their privilege
to be always ennobled in the same lofty consciousness. God is girding every
man for a place and a calling, in which, taking it from him, even though

From *Sermons for the New Life* (New York: Charles Scribner, 1858).

75

it be internally humble, he may be as consciously exalted as if he held the rule of a kingdom. The truth I propose then for your consideration is this,—

That God has a definite life-plan for every human person, girding him, visibly or invisibly, for some exact thing, which it will be the true significance and glory of his life to have accomplished.

³ Many persons, I am well aware, never even think of any such thing. They suppose that, for most men, life is a necessarily stale and common affair. What it means for them they do not know, and they scarcely conceive that it means any thing. They even complain, venting heavy sighs, that, while some few are set forward by God to do great works and fill important places, they are not allowed to believe that there is any particular object in their existence. It is remarkable, considering how generally this kind of impression prevails, that the Holy Scriptures never give way to it, but seem, as it were, in all possible ways, to be holding up the dignity of common life, and giving a meaning to its appointments, which the natural dullness and lowness of mere human opinion can not apprehend.

⁴ They not only show us explicitly, as we have seen, that God has a definite purpose in the lives of men already great, but they show us how frequently, in the conditions of obscurity and depression, preparations of counsel going on, by which the commonest offices are to become the necessary first chapter of a great and powerful history. David among the sheep; Elisha following after the plough; Nehemiah bearing the cup; Hannah, who can say nothing less common than that she is the wife of Elkanah and a woman of a sorrowful spirit,—who, that looks on these humble people, at their humble post of service, and discovers at last, how dear a purpose God was cherishing in them, can be justified in thinking that God has no particular plan for him, because he is not signalized by any kind of distinction?

⁵ Besides, what do the scriptures show us, but that God has a particular care for every man, a personal interest in him and a sympathy with him and his trials, watching for the uses of his one talent as attentively and kindly and approving him as heartily, in the right employment of it, as if he had given him ten; and, what is the giving out of the talents itself, but an exhibition of the fact that God has a definite purpose, charge and work, be it this or that, for every man?

⁶ They also make it the privilege of every man to live in the secret guidance of God; which is plainly nugatory, unless there is some chosen work, or sphere, into which he may be guided; for how shall God guide him, having nothing appointed or marked out for him to be guided into? No field opened for him, no course set down which is to be his wisdom?

⁷ God also professes in his Word to have purposes pre-arranged for all events; to govern by a plan which is from eternity even, and which, in some proper sense, comprehends every thing. And what is this but another way of conceiving that God has a definite place and plan adjusted for every human being? And, without such a plan, he could not even govern the world intelligently, or make a proper universe of the created system; for it

76

becomes a universe only in the grand unity of reason, which includes it. Otherwise, it were only a jumble of fortuities, without counsel, end or law.

8 Turning, now, from the scriptures to the works of God, how constantly are we met here by the fact, everywhere visible, that ends and uses are the regulative reasons of all existing things. This we discover often, when we are least able to understand the speculative mystery of objects; for it is precisely the *uses* of things that are most palpable. These uses are to God, no doubt, as to us, the significance of his works. And they compose, taken together, a grand reciprocal system, in which part answers actively to part, constructing thus an all-comprehensive and glorious whole. And the system is, in fact, so perfect, that the loss or displacement of any member would fatally derange the general order. If there were any smallest star in heaven that had no place to fill, that oversight would beget a disturbance which no Leverrier could compute; because it would be a real and eternal, not merely casual or apparent disorder. One grain, more or less, of sand would disturb, or even fatally disorder the whole scheme of the heavenly motions. So nicely balanced, and so carefully hung, are the worlds, that even the grains of their dust are counted, and their places adjusted to a correspondent nicety. There is nothing included in the gross, or total sum, that could be dispensed with. The same is true in regard to forces that are apparently irregular. Every particle of air is moved by laws of as great precision as the laws of the heavenly bodies, or, indeed, by the same laws; keeping its appointed place, and serving its appointed use. Every odor exhales in the nicest conformity with its appointed place and law. Even the viewless and mysterious heat, stealing through the dark centers and impenetrable depths of the worlds, obeys its uses with unfaltering exactness, dissolving never so much as an atom that was not to be dissolved. What now shall we say of man, appearing, as it were, in the center of this great circle uses? They are all adjusted for him: has he, then, no ends appointed for himself? Noblest of all creatures, and closest to God, as he certainly is, are we to say that his Creator has no definite thoughts concerning him, no place prepared for him to fill, no use for him to serve, which is the reason of his existence?

9 There is, then, I conclude, a definite and proper end, or issue, for every man's existence; an end, which, to the heart of God, is the good intended for him, or for which he was intended; that which he is privileged to become, called to become, ought to become; that which God will assist him to become and which he can not miss, save by his own fault. Every human soul has a complete and perfect plan, cherished for it in the heart of God— a divine biography marked out, which it enters into life to live. This life, rightly unfolded, will be a complete and beautiful whole, an experience led on by God and unfolded by his secret nurture, as the trees and the flowers, by the secret nurture of the world; a drama cast in the mould of a perfect art, with no part wanting; a divine study for the man himself, and for others; a study that shall forever unfold, in wondrous beauty, the love and faithfulness of God; great in its conception, great in the Divine skill

by which it is shaped; above all, great in the momentous and glorious issues it prepares. What a thought is this for every human soul to cherish! What dignity does it add to life! What support does it bring to the trials of life! What instigations does it add to send us onward in every thing that constitutes our excellence! We live in the Divine thought. We fill a place in the great everlasting plan of God's intelligence. We never sink below his care, never drop out of his counsel.

10 But there is, I must add, a single but very important and even fearful qualification. Things serve their uses, and never break out of their place. They have no power to do it. Not so with us. We are able, as free beings, to refuse the place and the duties God appoints; which, if we do, then we sink into something lower and less worthy of us. That highest and best condition for which God designed us is no more possible. We are fallen out of it, and it can not be wholly recovered. And yet, as that was the best thing possible for us in the reach of God's original counsel, so there is a place designed for us now, which is the next best possible. God calls us now to the best thing left, and will do so till all good possibility is narrowed down and spent. And then, when he can not use us any more for our own good, he will use us for the good of others,—an example of the misery and horrible desperation to which any soul must come, when all the good ends, and all the holy callings of God's friendly and fatherly purpose are exhausted. Or it may be now that, remitting all other plans and purposes in our behalf, he will henceforth use us, wholly against our will, to be the demonstration of his justice and avenging power before the eyes of mankind; saying over us, as he did over Pharaoh in the day of his judgments, "Even for this same purpose have I raised thee up, that I might show my power in thee, and that my name might be declared throughout all the earth." Doubtless, He had other and more genial plans to serve in this bad man, if only he could have accepted such; but knowing his certain rejection of these, God turned his mighty counsel in him wholly on the use to be made of him as a reprobate. How many Pharaohs in common life refuse every other use God will make of them, choosing only to figure, in their small way, as reprobates; and descending, in that manner, to fate that painfully mimics his.

11 God has, then, I conclude, a definite life-plan set for every man; one that, being accepted and followed, will conduct him to the best and noblest end possible. No qualification of this doctrine is needed, save the fearful one just named; that we, by our perversity, so often refuse to take the place and do the work he gives us.

12 It follows, in the same way, that, as God, in fixing on our end or use, will choose the best end or use possible, so he will appoint for us the best manner possible of attaining it; for, as it is a part of God's perfection to choose the best things, and not things partially good, so it will be in all the methods he prescribes for their attainment. And so, as you pass on, stage by stage, in your courses of experience, it is made clear to you that, whatever you have laid upon you to do or to suffer, whatever to want, what-

ever to surrender or to conquer, is exactly best for you. Your life is a school, exactly adapted to your lesson, and that to the best, last end of your existence.

[13] No room for a discouraged or depressed feeling, therefore, is left you. Enough that you exist for a purpose high enough to give meaning to life, and to support a genuine inspiration. If your sphere is outwardly humble, if it even appears to be quite insignificant, God understands it better than you do, and it is a part of his wisdom to bring out great sentiments in humble conditions, great principles in works that are outwardly trivial, great characters under great adversities and heavy loads of encumbrance. The tallest saints of God will often be those who walk in the deepest obscurity, and are even despised or overlooked by man. Let it be enough that God is in your history and that the plan of the biography is His, the issue that He has set for it the highest and the best. Away then, O man, with thy feeble complaints and feverish despondencies. There is no place left for this kind of nonsense. Let it fill thee with cheerfulness and exalted feeling, however deep in obscurity your lot may be, that God is leading you on, girding you for a work, preparing you to a good that is worthy of his Divine magnificence. If God is really preparing us at all to become that which is the very highest and best thing possible, there ought never to be a discouraged or uncheerful being in the world.

[14] Nor is it any detraction from such a kind of life that the helm of its guidance is, by the supposition, to be in God, and not in our own will and wisdom. This, in fact, is its dignity: it is a kind of divine order, a creation moulded by the loving thoughts of God; in that view, to the man himself a continual discovery, as it is unfolded both of himself and God. A discovery of some kind it must be to all; for, however resolutely or defiantly we undertake to accomplish our own objects, and cut our own way through to a definite self-appointed future, it will never be true, for one moment, that we are certain of this future, and will almost always be true that we are met by changes and conditions unexpected. This, in fact, is one of the common mitigations even of a selfish and self-directed life, that its events come up out of the unknown and overtake the subject, as discoveries he could not shun, or anticipate. Evil itself is far less evil, even to the worldly man, that it comes by surprises. Were the scenes of necessary bitterness, wrong, trial, disappointment, self-accusation, every such man has to pass through in his life, distinctly set before him at the beginning, how forbidding generally, and how dismal the prospect. We say, therefore, how frequently, "I could not have endured these distasteful, painful years, these emptinesses, these trials and torments that have rent me, one after another, if I had definitely known beforehand what kind of lot was before me." And yet, how poor a comfort is it to such pains and disasters that they overtook the sufferer as surprises and sorrows not set down beforehand in the self-appointed programme of life. How different, how inspiring and magnificent, instead, to live, by holy consent, a life all discovery; to see it unfolding, moment by moment, a plan of God, our own life-plan conceived in his paternal love; each event, incident, experience, whether bright or dark, having its mission from him,

and revealing, either now or in its future issues, the magnificence of his favoring counsel; to be sure, in the dark day, of a light that will follow, that loss will terminate in gain, that trial will issue in rest, doubt in satisfaction, suffering in patience, patience in purity, and all in a consummation of greatness and dignity that even God will look on with a smile. How magnificent, how strong in its repose, how full of rest is such a kind of life! Call it human still, decry it, let it down by whatever diminutives can be invented, still it is great; a charge which ought even to inspire a dull-minded man with energy and holy enthusiasm.

15 But, the inquiry will be made, supposing all this to be true in the manner stated, how can we ever get hold of this life plan God has made for us, or find our way into it? Here, to many, if not all, will be the main stress of doubt and practical suspense.

16 Observe, then, first of all, some negatives that are important and must be avoided. They are these:

17 You will never come into God's plan if you study singularity; for, if God has a design or plan for every man's life, then it is exactly appropriate to his nature; and, as every man's nature is singular and peculiar to himself,— as peculiar as his face or look,—then it follows that God will lead every man into a singular, original and peculiar life, without any study of singularity on his part. Let him seek to be just what God will have him, and the talents, the duties and circumstances of his life will require him to be, and then he will be just peculiar enough. He will have a life of his own; a life that is naturally and, therefore, healthily peculiar; a simple, unaffected, unambitious life, whose plan is not in himself, but in God.

18 As little will he seek to copy the life of another. No man is ever called to be another. God has as many plans for men as he has men; and, therefore, he never requires them to measure their life exactly by any other life. We are not to require it of ourselves to have the precise feelings, or exercises, or do the works, or pass through the trials of other men; for God will handle us according to what we are, and not according to what other men are. And whoever undertakes to be exercised by any given fashion, or to be any given character, such as he knows or has read of, will find it impossible, even as it is to make himself another nature. God's plan must hold and we must seek no other. To strain after something new and peculiar is fantastic and weak, and is also as nearly wicked as that kind of weakness can be. To be a copyist, working at the reproduction of a human model, is to have no faith in one's significance, to judge that God means nothing in his particular life, but only in the life of some other man. Submitting himself, in this manner, to the fixed opinion that his life means nothing, and that nothing is left for him but to borrow or beg a life-plan from some other man, what can the copyist become but an affectation or a dull imposture.

19 In this view also, you are never to complain of your birth, your training, your employments, your hardships; never to fancy that you could be something if only you had a different lot and sphere assigned you. God understands his own plan, and he knows what you want a great deal better than you do.

The very things that you most deprecate, as fatal limitations or obstructions, are probably what you most want. What you call hindrances, obstacles, discouragements, are probably God's opportunities; and it is nothing new that the patient should dislike his medicines, or any certain proof that they are poisons. No! A truce to all such impatience! Choke that devilish envy which gnaws at your heart, because you are not in the same lot with others; bring down your soul, or, rather, bring it up to receive God's will and do his work, in your lot, in your sphere, under your cloud of obscurity, against your temptations; and then you shall find that your condition is never opposed to your good, but really consistent with it. Hence it was that an apostle required his converts to abide each one in that calling wherein he was called; to fill his place till he opens a way, by filling it, to some other; the bondman to fill his house of bondage with love and duty, the laborer to labor, the woman to be a woman, the men to show themselves men,—all to acknowledge God's hand in their lot, and seek to cooperate with that good design which he most assuredly cherishes for them.

[20] Another frequent mistake to be carefully avoided is that, while you surrender and renounce all thought of making up a plan, or choosing out a plan, for yourself, as one that you set by your own will, you also give up the hope or expectation that God will set you in any scheme of life, where the whole course of it will be known, or set down beforehand. If you go to him to be guided, he will guide you; but he will not comfort your distrust, or half trust of him, by showing you the chart of all his purposes concerning you. He will only show you into a way where, if you go cheerfully and trustfully forward, he will show you on still further. No contract will be made with you save that he engages, if you trust him, to lead you into the best things, all the way through. And, if they are better than you can either ask or think beforehand, they will be none the worse for that.

[21] But we must not stop in negatives. How, then, or by what more positive directions can a man, who really desires to do it, come into the plan God lays for him, so as to live it and rationally believe that he does? You are on the point of choosing, it may be, this or that calling, wanting to know where duty lies and what the course God himself would have you take. Beginning at a point most remote, and where the generality of truth is widest,

[22] Consider (1) the character of God, and you will draw a large deduction from that; for, all that God designs for you will be in harmony with his character. He is a being infinitely good, just, true. Therefore, you are to know that he cannot really seek any thing contrary to this in you. You may make yourselves contrary, in every attribute of character, to God; but he never made you to become any thing different from, or unworthy of, himself. A good being could not make another to be a bad being, as the proper issue and desired end of his existence; least of all could one infinitely good. A great many employments or callings are, by these first principles, forever cut off. No thought is permitted you, even for a moment, of any work or calling

that does not represent the industry, justice, truth, beneficence, mercy of God.

²³ (2)Consider relation to him as a creature. All created wills have their natural center and rest in God's will. In him they all come into a play of harmony, and the proper harmony of being is possible only in this way. Thus, you know that you are called to have a will perfectly harmonized with God's and rested in his, and that gives you a large insight into what you are to be, or what is the real end of your being. In fact, nine-tenths of your particular duties may be settled, at once, by a simple reference in this manner to what God wills.

²⁴ (3) You have a conscience, which is given to be an interpreter of his will and thus of your duty, and, in both, of what you are to become.

²⁵ (4) God's law and his written Word are guides to present duty, which, if faithfully accepted, will help to set you in accordance with the mind of God and the plan he has laid for you. "I am a stranger in the earth," said one, "hide not thy commandments from me;" knowing that God's commandments would give him a clue to the true meaning and business of his life.

²⁶ (5) Be an observer of Providence; for God is showing you ever, by the way in which he leads you, whither he means to lead. Study your trials, your talents, the world's wants, and stand ready to serve God now, in whatever he brings to your hand.

²⁷ Again (6), consult your friends, and especially those who are most in the teaching of God. They know your talents and personal qualifications better, in some respects, than you do yourself. Ask their judgment of you and of the spheres and works to which you are best adapted.

²⁸ Once more (7) go to God himself, and ask for the calling of God; for, as certainly as he has a plan or calling for you, he will somehow guide you into it. And this is the proper office and work of his Spirit. By this private teaching he can show us, and will, into the very plan that is set for us. And this is the significance of what is prescribed as our duty, viz., living and walking in the Spirit; for the Spirit of God is a kind of universal presence, or inspiration, in the world's bosom; an unfailing inner light, which if we accept and live in, we are guided thereby into a consenting choice, so that what God wills for us we also will for ourselves,—settling into it as the needle to the pole. By this hidden union with God, or intercourse with him, we get a wisdom or insight deeper than we know ourselves; a sympathy, a oneness with the Divine will and love. We go into the very plan of God for us, and are led along in it by him, consenting, cooperating, answering to him, we know not how, and working out, with nicest exactness, that good end for which his unseen counsel girded us and sent us into the world. In this manner, not neglecting the other methods just named, but gathering in all their separate lights, to be interpreted in the higher light of the Spirit, we can never be greatly at a loss to find our way into God's counsel and plan. The duties of the present moment we shall meet as they rise and these will open a gate into the next, and we shall thus pass on, trustfully and securely, almost never in doubt as to what God calls us to do.

82

²⁹ It is not to be supposed that you have followed me, in such a subject as this, without encountering questions from within that are piercing. It has put you on reflection; it has set you to the inquiry, what you have been doing and becoming thus far in your course, and what you are hereafter to be? Ten, twenty, fifty, seventy years ago, you came into this living world, and began to breathe this mortal air. The guardian angel that came to take charge of you said, "To this end is he born, for this cause is he come into the world." Or, if this be a Jewish fancy, God said the same himself. He had a definite plan for you, a good end settled and cherished for you in his heart. This it was that gave a meaning and glory to your life. Apart from this, it was not, in his view, life for you to live; it was accident, frustration, death. What now, O soul, hast thou done? what progress hast thou made? how much of the blessed life-plan of thy Father hast thou executed? How far on thy way art thou to the good, best end thy God has designed for thee?

³⁰ Do I hear thy soul confessing, with a suppressed sob within thee, that, up to this time, thou hast never sought God's chosen plan at all? Hast thou, even to this hour, and during so many years, been following a way and a plan of thine own, regardless, hitherto, of all God's purposes in thee? Well, if it be so, what hast thou gotten? How does thy plan work? Does it bring thee peace, content, dignity of aim and feeling, purity, rest; or, does it plunge thee into mires of disturbance, scorch thee in flames of passion, worry thee with cares, burden thee with bitter reflections, cross thee, disappoint, sadden, sour thee? And what are thy prospects? what is the issue to come? After thou hast worked out this hard plan of thine own, will it come to a good end? Hast thou courage now to go on and work it through?

³¹ Perhaps you may be entertaining yourself, for the time, with a notion of your prosperity, counting yourself happy in past successes, and counting on greater successes to come. Do you call it, then, success, that you are getting on in a plan of your own? There can not be a greater delusion. You set up a plan that is not God's, and rejoice that it seems to prosper; not observing that you are just as much farther off from God's plan for you and from all true wisdom, as you seem to prosper more. And the day is coming when just this truth will be revealed to you, as the bitterest pang of your defeat and shame.

³² No matter which it be, prosperity or acknowledged defeat, the case is much the same in one as in the other, if you stand apart from God and his counsel. There is nothing good preparing for any man who will not live in God's plan. If he goes a prospecting for himself, and will not apprehend that for which he is apprehended, it can not be to any good purpose.

³³ And really, I know not any thing, my hearers, more sad and painful to think of, to a soul properly enlightened by reason and God's truth, than so many years of Divine good squandered and lost; whole years, possibly many years, of that great and blessed biography which God designed for you, occupied by a frivolous and foolish invention of your own, substituted for the good counsel of God's infinite wisdom and love. O, let the past suffice!

³⁴ Young man, or woman, this is the day of hope to you. All your best

opportunities are still before you. Now, too, you are laying your plans for the future. Why not lay them in God? Who has planned for you as wisely and faithfully as he? Let your life begin with him. Believe that you are girded by your God for a holy and great calling. Go to him and consecrate your life to him, knowing assuredly that he will lead you into just that life which is your highest honor and blessing.

[35] And what shall I say to the older man, who is further on his course and is still without God in the world? The beginning of wisdom, my friend, you have yet to learn. You have really done nothing, as yet, that you were sent into the world to do. All your best opportunities, too, are gone or going by. The best end, the next best, and the next are gone, and nothing but the dregs of opportunity is left. And still Christ calls even you. There is a place still left for you; not the best and brightest, but an humble and good one. To this you are called, for this you are apprehended of Christ Jesus still. O, come, repent of your dusty and dull and weary way, and take the call that is offered.

[36] All men, living without God, are adventurers out upon God's world, in neglect of him, to choose their own course. Hence the sorrowful, sad looking host they make. O, that I could show them whence their bitterness, their dryness, their unutterable sorrows, come. O, that I could silence, for one hour, the noisy tumult of their works, and get them to look in upon that better, higher life of fruitfulness and blessing to which their God has appointed them. Will they ever see it? Alas! I fear!

[37] Friends of God, disciples of the Son of God, how inspiring and magnificent the promise, or privilege, that is offered here to you! Does it still encounter only unbelief in your heart? does it seem to you impossible that you can ever find your way into a path prepared for you by God, and be led along in it by his mighty counsel? Let me tell you a secret. It requires a very close, well-kept life to do this; a life in which the soul can have confidence always toward God; a life which allows the Spirit always to abide and reign, driven away by no affront of selfishness. There must be a complete renunciation of self-will. God and religion must be practically first; and the testimony that we please God must be the element of our peace. And such a disciple I have never known who did not have it for his joy that God was leading him on, shaping his life for him, bringing him along out of one moment into the next, year by year. To such a disciple, there is nothing strained or difficult in saying that God's plan can be found, or that this is the true mode and privilege of life. Nothing to him is easier or more natural. He knows God ever present, feels that God determines all things for him, rejoices in the confidence that the everlasting counsel of his Friend is shaping every turn of his experience. He does not go hunting after this confidence; it comes to him, abides in him, fortifies his breast, and makes his existence itself an element of peace. And this, my brethren, is your privilege, if only you can live close enough to have the secret of the Lord with you.

[38] How sacred, how strong in its repose, how majestic, how nearly divine is a life thus ordered! The simple thought of a life which is to be the

84

unfolding, in this manner, of a Divine plan, is too beautiful, too captivating, to suffer one indifferent or heedless moment. Living in this manner, every turn of your experience will be a discovery to you of God, every change a token of his Fatherly counsel. Whatever obscurity, darkness, trial, suffering falls upon you; your defeats, losses, injuries; your outward state, employment, relations; what seems hard, unaccountable, severe, or, as nature might say, vexatious,—all these you will see are parts or constitutive elements in God's beautiful and good plan for you, and, as such, are to be accepted with a smile. Trust God! have an implicit trust in God! and these very things will impart the highest zest to life. If you were in your own will, you could not bear them; and if you fall, at any time, into your own will, they will break you down. But, the glory of your condition, as a Christian, is that you are in the mighty and good will of God. Hence it was that Bunyan called his hero Great Heart; for, no heart can be weak that is in the confidence of God. See how it was with Paul: counting all things but loss for the excellency of the knowledge; enduring with godlike patience, unspeakable sufferings; casting every thing behind him, and following on to apprehend that for which he was apprehended. He had a great and mighty will, but no self-will: therefore, he was strong, a true lion of the faith. Away, then, with all feeble complaints, all meagre and mean anxieties. Take your duty, and be strong in it, as God will make you strong. The harder it is, the stronger, in fact, you will be. Understand, also, that the great question here is, not what you will get, but what you will become. The greatest wealth you can ever get will be in yourself. Take your burdens, and troubles, and losses, and wrongs, if come they must and will, as your opportunities, knowing that God has girded you for greater things than these. O, to live out such a life as God appoints, how great a thing it is!—to do the duties, make the sacrifices, bear the adversities, finish the plan, and then to say, with Christ, (who of us will be able?)—"It is finished!"

The God of Comfort

*Blessed be God, even the Father of our Lord Jesus
Christ, the Father of mercies, and the God of all comfort;
who comforteth us in all our tribulation, that we may be
able to comfort them which are in any trouble by the
comfort wherewith we ourselves are comforted of God.*
—II Cor. 1:3-4

I CALL the New Testament the Book of Joy. There is not in the world
a book which is pervaded with such a spirit of exhilaration. Nowhere does
it pour forth a melancholy strain. Often pathetic, it is never gloomy. Full
of sorrows, it is full of victory over sorrow. In all the round of literature,
there is not another book that can cast such cheer and inspire such hope.
Yet it eschews humor, and foregoes wit. It is intensely earnest, and yet full
of quiet. It is profoundly solemn, and yet there is not a strain of morbid
feeling in it.

² Some books have recognized the wretchedness of man's condition on
earth, and in some sense have produced exhilaration; but it has been rather
by amusing their readers. They have turned life into a comedy. They have
held up men's weakness to mirth. They have turned men's passions to
ridicule, sharply puncturing their folly by wit. Thus they have under-
valued human nature. They have relieved men's sorrowful thoughts of human
life by teaching them substantially to despise life and its duties. They have
kept down the nobler sentiments, and worked up the jollity of men's lower
nature, and sought to redeem them from suffering by taking out all earnestness, all faith, all urgent convictions.

³ Not so the Christian Scriptures. They never jest; they never ridicule;
they never deal in any wise in comic scenes. They disdain, in short, all those
methods by which other writings have inspired cheer; and yet, by a method
of their own, they produce in all who accept them a reasonable sympathy,
elevation of mind, high hope, and cheerful resignation.

⁴ Other writers gild the nature of man with the light of an indiscriminating
benevolence. They tell us, in substance, that wickedness is not so wicked
as we think; that we put too much emphasis on conduct, and attach too much
importance to events; that we must look upon men more as if they were

From *The Sermons of Henry Ward Beecher in Plymouth Church*, first series (New
York: J. B. Ford & Co., 1869).

clouds coming and going in the sky, or like leaves which flutter, without self-help, as the wind determines; and that good and evil should not afflict and agitate us, since they are accidents, like the bark of trees, smooth or rough, by some occult law, rather than by any intelligent purpose of their own; and that we should be charitable. Thus men are taught to be charitable at the expense of moral convictions, and of sensibility to that which is right or wrong.

⁵ And so these writers relieve our spirits of melancholy by flattening all of life to a tame level—lowering the dignity of human nature by belittling man's destiny. If life *is* nothing, and *means* nothing; if it comes from nothing, and returns to nothing, why should men take events too burdensomely? why not say, "Let us eat and drink, for to-morrow we die"?

⁶ But the New Testament unfolds the nature of man in the darkest colors. It lifts over his head a cloud full of bolts, liable at any moment to fall destructively. It creates him a responsible agent; and, rolling back the horizon-curtains, reveals the everlasting future, on which, as upon a daguerrean plate, this life is picturing itself. It recites the evils of the human heart, drawing in lurid colors the revel of appetites; in sharp lines sketching the features of the human passions. It recites the wicked deeds which pride and vanity and selfishness have evermore produced in mankind. It paints no paradise of innocent sufferers. It sweeps a circle around a guilty race, lost in trespasses and sins, and so given over to them that all strength for recovery is gone; and Death, universal and final, towers and glooms over the race, like a black storm that will soon burst forth, unless some kind wind arises to bear it back, and sweep it out of the hemisphere.

⁷ Strange as it is in statement, it is while dealing with such a scene that the New Testament writers suffuse their compositions with a transcendent joy; and not once, nor twice, but always, and all the way through, they flash with radiant hope and cheer. This is without a parallel. It puts it, as a marvel in literature, that the most profound conceptions of the sin and guilt of mankind, arraignments and condemnations of conduct and character the most relentless, and denunciations and prophecies of the future fate of evil-doers the most fearful, are yet the subject-matters of a sacred literature more natural and wholesome, more cheerful and hopeful, more invigorating and comforting, than any that has ever existed. There is not a morbid line in the New Testament.

⁸ If one would contrast the writers who have most severely dealt with human weaknesses, let him read Rabelais, if he can, holding his nose, the while, as he walks through his nastiness; let him read the lurid lines and heartless sneers of that demoniac genius, Byron, or go back to the biting ugliness of Dean Swift; and then let him listen to the wide and various representations of human wickedness in the New Testament, simple, earnest, truthful, beginning with Christ's lament over Jerusalem, which is the one key-note of the whole lore and symphony of the wickedness of man, as represented in the New Testament literature.

⁹ What is the source of this strange cheer overhanging so strange a subject?

87

What is the source of that joy which glances from every argument, from every line almost, while treating of such tremendous realities of sadness? How comes it that the sacred writers are so inspiriting? As birds fly easier against the wind, if it be not too strong, than in a calm, does joy, too, rise more easily against the breath of this world's great sorrows? How is it?

10 The fountain and unfailing source of this sober exhilaration was found in the divine nature, as it had been revealed to the apostles. Our text is an admirable expression of this representation of the divine nature. And I will attempt so to open this passage as to give some insight into those experiences, both of sorrow and of consolation, which have made the apostles the leaders of men for so many ages.

11 God is here styled *the Father of mercies, and the God of all comfort.* We are not to take our conceptions of God from human systems; for these systems have been built up out of selections from the Word of God. But God's word is a vast forest; and as a man can build, out of the timber that is growing in the forest, a hut, or a common mansion, or a palatial residence, so out of the Word of God man can build a poor theology, or a rich theology, or a glorious one, according as he is skillful in his selections.

12 Men had heard of God who *created* all things, who *governed* all things, who weighed and measured all human thoughts and feelings, and stamped with ineffaceable lines the moral character of the race. This magisterial and juridical Deity, revealed to men through the types of civil government, was powerful to incite fear and to restrain from evil. This vision of God must always remain, having certain purposes, and having in it the office of representing certain truths respecting the divine nature. But this view does not express God. To represent a being as perfectly holy, and as sitting in the circle of holiness, holding the race to absolute purity, almost without sympathy, except that which is doled out on certain conditions—that is not to represent God, though it is to represent something about God.

13 Men, too, had heard of a God perfect in holiness. Their thoughts had ranged until weary through that vast circle inhabited by the ideal of perfect justice and truth.

14 It was the latest disclosure of the divine nature that, within that august power which had been revealed, and beating like a heart within that perfect holiness, there was a nature of exquisite sympathy and tenderness; that the energies of that Almighty Being were exerted in the service of mercy and kindness; that the direction of God's nature was toward love; and that, although alternatively there were justice and judgment, yet they were but alternative; while the length and breadth, the height and depth of God was in the sphere of love—potential, fruitful.

15 Consider what that nature must be which is here styled *the Father of mercies.* When a man begets children, they are in his own likeness. God groups all the mercies of the universe into a great family of children, of which he is the head. Mercies tell us what God is. They are his children. He is the father of them, in all their forms, combinations, multiplications, derivations, offices. Mercies in their length and breadth, in their multitudes

88

infinite, uncountable—these are God's offspring, and they represent their Father. Judgments are *effects* of God's power. Pains and penalties go forth from his hand. Mercies are God himself. They are the issues of his heart. If he rears up a scheme of discipline and education which requires and justifies the application of pains and penalties for special purposes, the God that stands behind all special systems and all special administrations, in his own interior nature pronounces himself *the Father of mercies, and the God of all comfort.* Of mercies it is said that they are *children.* They are part of God's *nature.* They are not what he *does* so much as what he *is.*

16 But even more strongly is it said that he is *the God of all comfort.* By *comfort,* we mean those influences which succor distress; which soothe suffering; which alleviate grief, and convert the whole experience of sorrow to gladness.

17 Consider that God is declared, *not* at times and upon fit occasions, to *produce* comfort, but that he is the very God of it. If we might imagine a kingdom wide and rich in all the elements of consolation, where every ill found its remedy, and every sorrow its cure—a celestial sanitarium, out of which issued winds bearing health everywhither—then there, in its own centre, and exalted to the highest place, is God, sovereign and active *in comforting.* For this he thinks; for this he plans; for this he executes; for this he waits; for this he lives.

18 Oh! what a realm of sorrow lies under this kingdom. Oh! what a need there has been in this world that there should be somebody to comfort. "The whole creation has groaned and travailed in pain until now." Men have been born, it would seem, that they might be sufferers. Nations have been wrapped in darkness. Tribulation has come like the sheeted doom of storms, and swept whole continents. Ages have been stained with blood. Tears have been so abundant that they have been too cheap to count. Weeping has had more work in this world than laughing. Trouble has ruled more than joy. Even yet, large-built, and high advanced in the causes of a better living, and in the very midst of civilization, men, if you read their title, by which we see what sign experience has hung out upon their face, are scarcely creatures of joy, but more of care and trouble and sorrow. Every household, every heart, in its turn, is pierced. Men go lonely, yearning, longing, unsatisfied. They are bereaved. They are filled with shocks of calamities. They are overturned. All their life is at times darkened. They are subverted. In midday, there walk ten thousand men in these cities, that say, "Our life is done. We have sown to the wind, and reaped the whirlwind." There are thousands of dying children, and thousands of mothers that would die. There are armies of men beguiling their leisure by destroying armies of men. There are nations organized so as to suppress manhood. The very laws of nature are employed as forces to curtail men's conveniences by impoverishing them. Commerce and manufacturing, and work itself, man's best friend—these are putting on bands and gyves. The city makes suffering, and the town makes suffering; and man himself heaps up in himself, by his own work, ten thousand sources of misery. And it is true that "the whole creation groans

and travails in pain." We march like so many soldiers, but march to a requiem, not to a pean; and the sounds that fill the world are sounds of mourning and of sorrow.

[19] Oh! what need there is that up out of this darkness and trouble and sadness, out of these calamities, there should be exalted, somewhere, an image that writes upon itself, "I am the God of comfort." That brings God right home to man's need. The world would die if it had not some hope of finding such a God.

[20] He penetrates and pervades the universe with his nature and with his disposition. My flagging faith has need of some such assurance. I have walked very much in thought with those old philosophers that believed that there was a God, too, of evil, as well as of good; and I am more willingly a disciple, therefore, of that inspired teaching which declares that evil is not a personage. It is not even an empire. Like the emery and sand with which we scour off rude surfaces, evil and trouble in this world are but instruments. And they are in the hands of God. If they bite with sharp attrition, it is because we need more scouring. It is because men's troubles need ruder handling and chiseling, that evils float in the air, swim in the sea, and spring up from out of the ground. But all is under the control of *the God of consolation*, as it is said elsewhere; *the God of comfort, and the Father of mercies*, as it is said here. More are the tender thoughts, the inspired potential actions, in God, than the stars in the heavens. Innumerable are the sweet influences which he sends down from his realm above. More and purer are his blessings than the drops of dew which night shakes down on the flowers and grass. He penetrates and pervades the world with more saving mercies than does the sun with particles of light and heat. He declares that this nature in himself is boundless; that this heart of mercy is inexhaustible; that this work of comfort is endless.

[21] Listen to this symphony and chant of the apostle, wherewith he prays that "we might be able to comprehend with all saints"—Stand back as he builds the statue, glowing at every touch with supernal brightness! "That we might be able to comprehend" what? That wire-drawn, fine, finical character that too often theology has skeletonized; that filmy and silky substance abstracted almost beyond the grasp of the understanding, reduced, for the sake of a certain notion of perfection, to an abstraction that is absolutely unusable in practical life—is this God? No. As he builds, listen: "That Christ may dwell in your hearts by faith; that ye, being rooted and grounded in *love*, may be able to comprehend"—Ah! old hoary student, do you think because you can read Hebrew, and Syriac, and Arabic, and Greek, and Latin, that you can teach me about God? Ah! old grammarian, that comes fighting me on doctrines, that marshals sentences, with exegesis, sharp both at the point and at the edge, cutting both ways, do you think that because you are so wise in construction, you can teach me of God? He is not found by either. "That ye, being rooted and grounded in *love*"—which is the only interpreter of the divine nature—"may be able to comprehend, with all saints, what is the breadth"—look from where the sun

90

comes to where he sets; and look again from where he sets to where he comes, if you would gain any measure—"that ye may be able to comprehend, with all saints, what is the breadth, and length, and depth, and height; and to know the love of Christ which passeth knowledge, that ye might be filled with all the fullness of God."

22 This is the true conception of God. This is that majestic and mighty Heart, rich, glowing, glorious, yearning and desiring good, and scattering it as through the spheres he scatters light and atmosphere. This is that vast, voluminous God that, when Paul looked up out from the cloudy world, from amidst its rain-drops, he saw riding triumphantly, and spreading His bow over the storms which beat and afflicted him in this lower mortal state. This is the God that declares himself to be, in this wicked, sin-smitten, ruined world, *the God of all comfort*—the great-breasted God, the mother-God, into whose arms come those that weep, where he comforts them, even as a mother comforts her child. And the earth itself is rocked, as it were, by that same tending, nursing, loving God, if only its inhabitants knew what is the consolation that is addressed to them.

23 This view of Christ was the peculiar manifestation. Would that we could have it again, as they had it in their time. For, when the apostles lived, most of them had seen him. Even Paul—in some respects better—had seen him by celestial vision; and he lived in all the fresh remembrances of the whole lore of Christ's love, his words, and his actions; and it is very plain that Christians, during the first hundred years, lived in the presence of Christ, as a person near and dear to them, as if he had been born in their own household, and had gone out from them as a child or a parent goes. The apostles saw Christ; but they did not see or think of him as we do in modern times. It is difficult for me to make you understand when I say that it is right to philosophize in respect to the nature of God, that indeed it must be done, and that yet this philosophy can never take hold of the soul and satisfy it. You shall read all the writings of the apostles, and you shall not find that once the nature of God in Christ Jesus arose to them as a question of mental philosophy. Yet, handed from school to school, from theory to theory, almost our whole conception of God is one that has been philosophized. We are ranking him; we are counting his attributes; we are telling how much makes God less than that which can not be God; we are declaring his functions; we are philosophizing, analyzing, synthetizing; and our Divinity is one that is largely made up from the stand-point of mental philosophy. For theology is nothing but mental philosophy applied to the divine mind and the divine government. But the apostles looked upon God from a different point of view. They saw him in respect to his practical relations to the wants of the individual heart, and the wants of the world. They thought of him in his adaptation of the needs of the human soul, and to the world's need, and seemed to say in themselves, "Here are all the troubles of life; here is this beneficent Being, that carries with him cure." And to their view he was God, because he supplied the universal need; because he had that without which the world's life would die out of it. It was this practical adaptation of the

divine nature to the wants of the suffering world that made Christ so un-questionably divine. The questions that are still discussed in the church re-specting the divinity of Christ would long since have ceased as useless, evaporated as worthless, if men had more habitually contemplated Christ as a life-power, as a Redeemer and a Saviour.

²⁴ The apostles held for certain that, in spite of nature, organization, the drift of things, kingdoms, powers, and influences, this meridian mercy, this divine consolation, would yet regulate the world. The world was not, there-fore, a pit of hopeless incurables. The matchless power of God would finally overcome all evil, and sweep it out of the universe. And they lived in the anticipation of victory. So, then, they neither were so disgusted as many are with the wrong-doing of men, nor were they so hopeless as others are who believe that a world so wicked, banded and hereditated in wickedness, can never be changed nor repaired. They looked up at the power which is above, and then they said, "There is hope for the world. Men can be regener-ated. Men can be transformed. A new heaven there shall yet be, and a new earth in which dwells righteousness." Therefore their conception of the char-acter of God, and of its relations to this world, filled them with a surprise of perpetual joy, and with the inspiration of hope. This vision of God, the Comforter, and the One most merciful, lifted them up. And as the star after the storm guides the weary mariner; as the sun, after being long hidden by the thick cloud that half-shrouded the heaven, gives him knowledge as to where he is, and cheers his hope again; as he derives his inspiration, not from the ocean, nor from the wind, nor from the cloud, nor from the sail, nor from the hull, but borrows every thing from the heaven above him; so did the apostles, and so have the noble and worthy followers of the apostles in every day since, borrowed every thing of joy and comfort from God. For they are the descendants, the lineal successors, of the apostles, who are like them in heart—not those who have some sort of touch on the shell.

²⁵ They were inspired, too, by the example of Christ, to make their sorrows so many medicines for others. In other words, they learned that the business of sorrow was not simply to be comforted; that the comfort which they re-ceived was to make itself the comforter of others.

Blessed be God, even the Father of our Lord Jesus Christ, the Father of mercies, and the God of all comfort; who comforteth us in all our tribula-tion, that we may be able to comfort them which are in any trouble by the comfort wherewith we ourselves are comforted of God.

²⁶ Not longer to expand this matter, let me in application make a few points.

²⁷ 1. This world is not an orb broke loose and snarled with immedicable evils. If we would know what this world is coming to, we must not look too low. Have you never noticed, in summer days, when the sun stands at the very meridian height, how white and clear the light is; how the trees stand revealed; how all things are transparently clear? But let the sun sink and droop till it shoots level beams along the surface of the earth, and those beams are caught and choked up with a thousand vapors, with dust, with all the day's breedings from swamp, morass, and river, and fen, and the sunlight

grows thick and murky. We call it *roseate*, and *orange*, and what not; but it is the poisoned light of the sun, which, in its own nature, is white and pure. And so when men's eyes glance along the surface of the world, looking at moral questions, they look through the vapors which the world itself has generated, and can not see clearly. Therefore it is that many men think this world is bound to wickedness, and that all philanthropic attempts are mere efforts of weakness and inexperience. There be many men that arrogate to themselves great superiority, and that are proud of their cynical wisdom, who sit with a kind of impudent, pitying leer, looking upon men that instruct the ignorant, that clothe and feed the poor and the needy, that spend— *waste* as they say—their time in going out into the highways to do good. "What matters it," say they, "whether this great beast of a world dies with its hair licked one way or another? What matters it, if all the wombs of time are generating wickedness, and if man is born to wickedness, whether any thing is done for him or not? You might as well attempt to cure volcanoes with pills, as to attempt to cure the human heart by any of your poor medicaments." They say that they despise such attempts. And yet, no man who does not take his inspirations from the ordinary conceptions of the nature of God, can have right views of human life. No man can be a charitable man who does not believe that his fellow-men are depraved. I will not say *totally;* for I do not believe in the doctrine of total depravity. They are depraved, and that is enough. There is very little difference between *enough* and *totally*— not enough to dispute about. You are wicked in every faculty, and you will keep being wicked in every faculty. The salient play of the understanding is itself full of imperfections, and at times is stained with sin and wrong. The lecherous imagination goes to and fro, a robber of purity, throughout the universe. The moral sentiments—how are they perpetually suborned to do the work of wickedness! How are the best affections wreathed around, oftentimes, with idols! How are the passions flagrant, despotic, oppressive! Men are wicked; and no man can be charitable with men who does not start with the belief that they are wicked in all parts of their nature. And then, no man can be charitable with men who does not believe that it is the essential nature of God to cure, and not to condemn; that his first and latest thought is, "O Israel, thou hast destroyed thyself; but in me is thy remedy." God is himself a vast medicine. God's soul and nature are the blood of the universe. Ask the physician what it is that he trusts to throw out morbific influences from the human system. If there be diseased organs, what cures them? Do you think pills do the work? They do but little except to say to the lazy organ, "Wake up and go to work, and throw out the enemy that is preying upon you." What is medicine? It is merely a coaxer. Its business is to say to the part affected, "Lazy dog! wake up and get well." If a man gets well, he cures himself—often, thanks to the doctor; oftener, thanks to the nurse; always, thanks to nature. That does the work, if it is done at all. What is the stream that carries reparation to the wasted parts, that carries stimulation to the dormant parts, that carries nutrition to the exhausted parts? What is it that fights? It is the blood.

93

[28] And throughout the vast heaven, throughout time and the universe, the blood of the world comes from the heart of God. The mercies of the loving God throb everywhere—above and below, within and without, endless in circuits, vast in distribution, infinitely potential. It is the heart of God that carries restoration, inspiration, aspiration, and final victory. And as long as God lives, and is what he is, "the Father of mercies, and the God of all comfort"—so long this world is not going to rack and ruin. And let men despond as much as they please, let the work seem to be delayed as long as it pleases, let men watch as in the night for the slow coming of the sun of a winter morning; nevertheless, he that has taken his observation, and has based his faith on the character and nature of God, knows that though a thousand years, or cycles of thousands of years may intervene, in the end there shall be a new heaven and a new earth in which shall dwell righteousness. The earth is to stand up. The earth is not forever to groan. Methinks there is to come a day when God shall sound the note from the throne where he is, and when from afar off, catching that key-note and theme, this old earth, so long dismal, and rolling, and wailing, as it rolls, the sad requiem of sin and death, shall surprise the spheres, and fill all the universe with that chanting song of victory, "Christ hath redeemed us, and he reigns in every heart, and over all the earth." The time shall come.

[29] Work on then, brother! Work on, sister! Not a tear that you drop to wash away any person's trouble, not a blow that you strike in imitation of the strokes of the Almighty arm, shall be forgotten. And when you stand in the presence of the Lord Jesus Christ, and he says to you, "Inasmuch as ye have done it unto one of the least of these my disciples, ye have done it unto me," it shall be more to you than if you wore the crowns of the Caesars and carried all the honors of the earth. The world shall be redeemed; for our God's name is Mercy and Comfort. The Redeemer of Israel is his name.

[30] 2. There are no troubles which befall our suffering hearts individually for which there is not in God a remedy, if only we rise to receive it. God's nature is medicinal to ours. You have troubles; I have troubles. We have needless troubles; but then, we have troubles necessary, troubles that will abide, troubles that harass, that weigh, that fever, that fret.

[31] Now, there is victory for each true Christian heart over its troubles. Not by disowning them; not by sloughing them. Every man runs that way. The first impact of pain and trouble leads every man to say, "Cast it out!" Every man's prayer to God is, "Lord, remove this thorn in the flesh." He has not a thought of any thing but that. "Thrice," says the apostle, the most heroic of mortal men, "I besought the Lord." And his answer was what? "My grace shall be sufficient for thee." He whose crown of thorns is now more illustrious and radiant than previous stones could make a crown, says to every one of his disciples that have thorns piercing them, "My grace shall be sufficient for you." Then bear, *bear*, BEAR!

[32] Bear how? resignedly? Oh! If you can not do any better, be resigned. That is better than murmuring—only just, though. I hear persons in great trouble and affliction saying, "I strive to be resigned." Well, strive for that;

94

strive for any thing; strive for the lowest degree of Christian attainment rather than not strive at all. If you are resigned, say so; but do not say it as a whipped child says it is sorry because it is whipped, and would not say it if it were not afraid of being whipped again. Saying that, is good as far as it goes. It is much better to do the least right thing than to do nothing, or the wrong thing. Say *resignation;* but resignation is not the word. Resignation is a negative thing. It is the consent of the soul to receive without replication, without revulsion, without murmuring, without resistance, without rebellion. It is giving up a contest or conflict.

[33] But oh! is the disciple better than the Master? Would you, if you could, reach forth your hand and take back one single sorrow, gloomy then, but gorgeous now, that made Christ to you what he is? Is it not the power of Jesus in heaven, and to all eternity will it not be his glory, that he was the Sufferer, and that he bore suffering in such a way that he vanquished suffering? And is he not the Lord over all by reason of that? Now you are his followers; and will you follow Christ, and will you desire to be worthy of his leadership, by slinking away from suffering? Do not seek it; but if it comes, remember that no sorrow comes but with his knowledge. If he does not draw the golden bow that sends the silver arrow to your heart, he knows it is sent, and sees it fall. You are never in trouble that he does not know it. And what is trouble but that very influence that brings you nearer to the heart of God than prayers or hymns? I think sorrows bring us closer to God than joys, usually; but sorrows, to be of use, must be borne, as Christ's were, victoriously, carrying with them intimations and sacred prophecies to the heart of Hope, not only that we shall not be overborne by them, but that by them we shall be strengthened and ennobled and enlarged.

[34] How is it, brother? I do not ask you whether you like the cup which you are now drinking; but look back twenty years. Almost every one of you can think of some trouble which you experienced twenty, or ten, or five years ago, and which at the time seemed to you like midnight. It bowed you down; and you felt as though your heart was bursting in twain. Now it is all over, and it has wrought out its effect on you; and I ask you, Would you give out of your education those twists and twirls which you suffered under? Would you have removed the experience of that burden which you thought would crush you, but which you fought in such a way that you came out a strong man? What has made you so versatile? What has made you so patient? What has made you so broad, so deep, and so rich? God put pickaxes into you, though you did not like it. He dug wells of salvation in you. He took you in his strong hand, and shook you by his north wind, and rolled you in his snows, and fed you with the coarsest food, and clothed you in the coarsest raiment, and beat you as a flail beats grain till the straw is gone and the wheat is left. And you are what you are by the grace of God's providence, many of you. By fire, by anvil-strokes, by the hammer that breaks the flinty rock, you are made what you are. You were gold in the rock; and God played miner, and blasted you out of the rock; and then he played stamper, and crushed you; and then he played smelter, and melted you; and now you

95

are gold free from the rock by the grace of God's severity to you. And as you look back upon those experiences of five, or ten, or twenty years ago, and see what they have done for you, and what you are now, you say, "I would not exchange what I learned from these things for all the world."

³⁵ What is the reason you have never learned to apply the same philosophy to the trouble of to-day? Why is that, when trouble comes on you to-day, your heart can not rise up and say, "O God of darkness, I know thee. Clouds are around about thee; but justice and judgment are the habitations of thy throne"? Why can not you do by God as your children do by you? If you play with your children—and every body ought to—if you dress yourself and come at your children with shapes of terror, how half-scared, and yet not scared, they run at you, with strokes, and pull away the covering from your face, and rejoice when they begin to see the features of their father, who is playing with them. That which terrified them is the life of their sport when they find you out. And when God comes to you wrapped and wreathed in clouds, and in storms, why should we not recognize him, and say, "I know thee, God; and I will not fear thee. Though thou slay me, I will trust thee"? If a man could see God in his troubles, and take sorrow to be the lore of inspiration, the light of interpretation, the sweet discipline of a bitter medicament that brings health, though the taste is not agreeable—if one could so look upon his God, how would sorrows make him strong!

³⁶ 3. Once more. No person is ordained until his sorrows put into his hands the power of comforting others. Did any body but Paul ever think as Paul did? See what a genuine nobleness and benevolence there was in every thing he did. Sorrow is apt to be very selfish, it is apt to be self-indulgent; but see how sorrow worked in the apostle. "Blessed be God," said he, "even the Father of our Lord Jesus Christ, the Father of mercies, and the God of all comfort; who comforteth us in all our tribulation, that we may be able to comfort them which are in any trouble by the comfort wherewith we ourselves are comforted of God."

³⁷ There is a universal instance and illustration of it. When the daughter is married, and goes from home, much as she loves her chosen companion, how often her heart goes back to her father's house! Father and mother are never so dear as about two or three years after the child has been separated from them—just long enough to get over the novelty of being independent. At no other time—and this is a comfort to you, mothers, who cry when your daughters get married, and you think they love somebody else besides you— do they so much come back to their parents for counsel. And that is as it should be; for father and mother are the true counselors of the child. As time goes on, the daughter suffers from sickness, children are multiplied in the family, she does not know which way to turn; and the mother comes to her, journeying from afar. And oh, what a light there is in the dwelling! The mother's face is more than stars in the night, more than the sun in the daytime, to the home-sick child. The mother tarries in the family. The children are sick; there is trouble in the household; but the daughter says, "Mother is here." And when from her lips fall sweet words of consolation,

and she says, "My dear child, nothing surprising has befallen you; I have gone through it all," and she narrates some of the inward history of her own life, of the troubles that she has experienced, while yet she is telling her story, strangely, as if exhaled, all these drops of trouble that have been sprinkled on the child's heart have gone, and she is comforted. Why? Because the consolations by which the mother's heart was comforted, have gone over and rested on the child's mind.

[38] Now, the apostle says, "When Christ comforts your grief, he makes you mother to somebody else."

[39] I know some people who, when they have griefs, become paupers and mendicants. I do not like to talk so contemptuously, though I feel it at first; but I despise, until I stop and think, those people who want to parade their griefs and sorrows. There are persons who, having had losses, go around with a hat in their hand begging a penny of comfort from this one and that one, on account of their bereavements. Wherever they go, they want to have somebody talk about their griefs, and ask about them; and if people do not ask about them, they tell about them without being asked. They carry a tail to their griefs as long as a comet's tail. All the time their omnivorous mouth is open to give forth something concerning their griefs. They want every body to be interested in their griefs, and sympathize with them on account of them. They make their griefs an occasion of mendicancy.

[40] And what does the apostle say? That when God comforts your griefs, he ordains you to be a minister of comfort to others who are in trouble. You are not to seek comfort for yourselves, but are, out of your experience of heart, to pour comfort into other people's wounded hearts. That is the ministration of sorrow.

[41] Christian brethren, does God so comfort you that you are able to bear the yoke, and to endure the piercing thorn? And when God enables you to bear it, is your first thought this, "I am now marked with the cross, as one that bears for others; I am lifted up among my fellow-men, not to be praised, but that I may go about as my Master did, and minister to them the consolations by which I myself have been comforted"? Do not any of you say, "The cup is too large and too bitter." Never. The Hand that was pierced for you takes the cup, and gives it to you; and Christ loves you too much to give you a cup that you can not drink. Do not say, "The burden is too great; I can not bear it." He that loves you, as you do not even yourself love yourself, the Redeemer, "the God of all comfort," "the Father of mercies," lays every burden on you; and he that lays the burden on, will give you strength to bear it. Take up your cross. God gives every body, I think, a cross, when he enters upon a Christian life. When it comes into his hands, what is it? It is the rude oak, four-square, full of splinters and slivers, and rudely tacked together. And after forty years I see some men carrying their cross just as rude as it was at first. Others, I perceive, begin to wind around about it faith, and hope, and patience; and after a time, like Aaron's rod, it blossoms all over. And at last their cross has been so covered with holy affections that it does not seem any more to be a cross. They carry it so easily, and are so much

more strengthened than burdened by it, that men almost forget that it is a cross, by the triumph with which they carry it. Carry *your* cross in such a way that there shall be victory in it; and let every tear, as it drops from your eye, glance also, as the light strikes through it, with the consolations of the Holy Ghost.

⁴² There be many of you that are standing in dark hours now, and that need just these consolations. My dear child, my daughter, my son, be not surprised—certainly not out of your faith. God is not angry with you. It is not necessarily for your sins that you are afflicted—though we are all sinful. For your *good* God afflicts you; and he says to you, "What father is he that chastiseth not his son? If ye endure chastisement, ye are my sons. Whom the Lord loveth he chasteneth." O glorious fact! O blessed truth! These are God's love-letters, written in dark ink. "Whom the Lord loveth he chasteneth, and scourgeth every son whom he receiveth. If ye endure chastening," ye are *the sons* of God; if not, *bastards.*

⁴³ Grant, O God! that we may be sons. Now speak, and see if thou canst scare us. Now thunder, and see if we tremble. Now write, and see if we do not press thy messages to our heart. Afflict us, only do not forget us. Comfort us, and we will bear to others *the comfort wherewith we are comforted.*

The Loneliness of Christ

Jesus answered them, Do ye now believe? Behold the
hour cometh, yea, is now come, that ye shall be scat-
tered, every man to his own, and shall leave me alone; and
yet I am not alone, because the Father is with me.
                                        —John 16:31-32

THERE are two kinds of solitude: the first consisting of insulation in space, the other of isolation in spirit. The first is simply separation by distance. When we are seen, touched, heard by none, we are said to be alone. And all hearts respond to the truth of that saying, This is not solitude; for sympathy can people our solitude with a crowd. The fisherman on the ocean alone at night is not alone when he remembers the earnest longings which are arising up to heaven at home for his safety; the traveller is not alone when the faces which will greet him on his arrival seem to beam upon him as he trudges on; the solitary student is not alone when he feels that human hearts will respond to the truths which he is preparing to address to them.

² The other is loneliness of soul. There are times when hands touch ours, but only send an icy chill of unsympathetic indifference to the heart: when eyes gaze into ours, but with a glazed look which cannot read into the bottom of our souls: when words pass from our lips, but only come back as an echo reverberated without reply through a dreary solitude: when the multitude throng and press us, and we cannot say, as Christ said, "Somebody hath *touched* me:" for the contact has been not between soul and soul, but only between form and form.

³ And there are two kinds of men who feel this last solitude in different ways. The first are men of self-reliance: self-dependent: who ask no counsel, and crave no sympathy: who act and resolve alone—who can go sternly through duty, and scarcely shrink let what will be crushed in them. Such men command respect: for whoever respects himself, constrains the reverence of others. They are invaluable in all those professions of life in which sensitive feelings would be a superfluity; they make iron commanders: surgeons who do not shrink; and statesmen who do not flinch from their purpose for the dread of unpopularity. But mere self-dependence is weakness: and the conflict is terrible when a human sense of weakness is felt by such men.

From *Sermons Preached at Brighton* (1-vol. ed.; New York: Harper & Bros., 1898).

⁴ Jacob was alone when he slept in his way to Padan-aram, the first night that he was away from his father's roof, with the world before him, and all the old associations broken up: and Elijah was alone in the wilderness when the court had deserted him, and he said, "They have digged down Thine altars, and slain Thy prophets with the sword: and I, even I, only am left, and they seek my life to take it away." But the loneliness of the tender Jacob was very different from that of the stern Elijah. To Jacob the sympathy he yearned for was realized in the form of a simple dream. A ladder raised from earth to heaven figured the possibility of communion between the spirit of man and the Spirit of God. In Elijah's case, the storm, and the earthquake, and the fire, did their convulsing work in the soul, before a still, small voice told him that he was not alone. In such a spirit the sense of weakness comes with a burst of agony, and the dreadful conviction of being alone manifests itself with a rending of the heart of rock. It is only so that such souls can be taught that the Father is with them, and that they are not alone.

⁵ There is another class of men who live in sympathy. These are affectionate minds which tremble at the thought of being alone: not from want of courage, nor from weakness of intellect comes their dependence upon others, but from the intensity of their affections. It is the trembling spirit of Humanity in them. They want not aid, nor even countenance: but only sympathy. And the trial comes to them not in the shape of fierce struggle, but of chill and utter loneliness, when they are called upon to perform a duty on which the world looks coldly, or to embrace a truth which has not found lodgment yet in the breasts of others.

⁶ It is to this latter and not to the former class that we must look if we would understand the spirit in which the words of the text were pronounced. The deep Humanity of the Soul of Christ was gifted with those finer sensibilities of affectionate nature which stand in need of sympathy. He not only gave sympathy, but wanted it too, from others. He who selected the gentle John to be his friend—who found solace in female sympathy, attended by the women who ministered to him out of their substance—who in the trial-hour could not bear even to pray without the human presence, which is the pledge and reminder of God's presence, had nothing in Him of the hard, merely self-dependent character. Even this verse testifies to the same fact. A stern spirit never could have said, "I am not alone: the Father is with me"—never would have felt the loneliness which needed the balancing truth. These words tell of a struggle: an inward reasoning: a difficulty and a reply: a sense of solitude—"I shall be alone;" and an immediate correction of that, "not alone—the Father is with Me."

⁷ There is no thought connected with the Life of Christ more touching, none that seems so peculiarly to characterize His spirit than the solitariness in which He lived. Those who understood Him best only half understood Him. Those who knew Him best scarcely could be said to *know* Him. On this occasion the disciples thought—Now we do understand—now we believe. The lonely spirit answered, "Do ye now believe? Behold the hour cometh that ye shall be scattered, every man to his own, and shall leave Me alone."

[8] Very impressive was that trait in His history. He was in the world alone.

I. First then we meditate on the loneliness of Christ.

II. On the temper of His solitude.

[9] 1. The Loneliness of Christ was caused by the Divine elevation of His character. His infinite superiority severed Him from sympathy—His exquisite affectionateness made that want of sympathy a keen trial.

[10] There is a second-rate greatness which the world can comprehend. If we take two who are brought into direct contrast by Christ Himself, the one the type of human, the other that of Divine excellence, the Son of Man and John the Baptist, this becomes clearly manifest. John's life had a certain rude, rugged goodness, on which was written, in characters that needed no magnifying-glass to read, spiritual excellence. The world on the whole accepted him. Pharisees and Sadducees went to his baptism. The people idolized him as a prophet. And if he had not chanced to cross the path of a weak prince and a revengeful woman, we can see no reason why John might not have finished his course with joy, recognised as irreproachable. If we inquire why it was that the world accepted John and rejected Christ, one reply appears to be that the life of the one was finitely simple and one-sided, that of the Other divinely complex.

[11] In physical nature, the naturalist finds no difficulty in comprehending the simple structure of the lowest organization of animal life, where one uniform texture, and one organ performing the office of brain and heart and lungs, at once, leave little to perplex. But when he comes to study the complex anatomy of man, he has the labour of a lifetime before him. It is not difficult to master the constitution of a single country; but when you try to understand the entire universe, you find infinite appearances of contradiction: law opposed to law: motion balanced by motion: happiness blended with misery: and the power to elicit a divine order and unity out of this complex variety is given to only a few of the gifted of the race. That which the structure of man is to the structure of the limpet: that which the universe is to a single country, the complex and boundless soul of Christ was to the souls of other men.

[12] Therefore, to the superficial observer, His life was a mass of inconsistencies and contradictions. All thought themselves qualified to point out the discrepancies. The Pharisees could not comprehend how a holy Teacher could eat with publicans and sinners. His own brethren could not reconcile His assumption of a public office with the privacy which He aimed at keeping. "If thou doest these things, show thyself to the world." Some thought He was "a good man,"—others said, "Nay—but He deceiveth the people." And hence it was that He lived to see all that acceptance which had marked the earlier stage of His career, as, for instance, at Capernaum, melt away. First the Pharisees took the alarm: then the Sadducees: then the political party of the Herodians: then the people. That was the most terrible of all: for the enmity of the upper classes is impotent; but when the cry of brute force is stirred from the deeps of society, as deaf to the voice of reason as the ocean in its strength churned into raving foam by the winds, the heart of

101

mere earthly oak quails before that. The apostles, at all events, did quail. One denied: another betrayed: all deserted. They "were scattered, each to his own:" and the Truth Himself was left alone in Pilate's judgment-hall.

13 Now we learn from this a very important distinction. To feel solitary is no uncommon thing. To complain of being alone, without sympathy and misunderstood, is general enough. In every place, in many a family, these victims of diseased sensibility are to be found, and they might find a weakening satisfaction in observing a parallel between their feelings and those of Jesus. But before that parallel is assumed, be very sure that it is, as in His case, the elevation of your character which severs you from your species. The world has small sympathy for Divine goodness: but it also has little for a great many other qualities which are disagreeable to it. You meet with no response—you are passed by—find yourself unpopular—meet with little communion—Well? Is that because you are *above* the world, nobler, devising and executing grand plans which they cannot comprehend: vindicating the wronged, proclaiming and living on great principles: offending it by the saintliness of your purity, and the unworldliness of your aspirations? Then yours is the loneliness of Christ. Or is it that you are wrapped up in self—cold, disobliging, sentimental, indifferent about the welfare of others, and very much astonished that they are not deeply interested in you? *You* must not use these words of Christ. They have nothing to do with you.

14 Let us look at one or two of the occasions on which this loneliness was felt.

The first time was when He was but twelve years old, when His parents found Him in the temple, hearing the doctors and asking them questions. High thoughts were in the Child's soul: expanding views of life: larger views of duty and His own destiny.

15 There is a moment in every true life—to some it comes very early—when the old routine of duty is not large enough—when the parental roof seems too low, because the Infinite above is arching over the soul—when the old formulas, in creeds, catechisms, and articles, seem to be narrow, and they must either be thrown aside, or else transformed into living and breathing realities—when the earthly father's authority is being superseded by the claims of a Father in heaven.

16 That is a lonely, lonely moment, when the young soul first feels God—when this earth is recognised as an "awful place, yea, the very gate of heaven." When the dream ladder is seen planted against the skies, and we wake, the dream haunts us as a sublime reality.

17 You may detect the approach of that moment in the young man or the young woman by the awakened spirit of inquiry: by a certain restlessness of look, and an eager earnestness of tone: by the devouring study of all kinds of books: by the waning of your own influence, while the inquirer is asking the truth of the doctors and teachers in the vast temple of the world: by a certain opinionativeness, which is austere and disagreeable enough: but the austerest moment of the fruit's taste is that in which it is passing from greenness into ripeness. If you wait in patience, the sour will become sweet. Rightly

looked at, that opinionativeness is more truly anguish: the fearful solitude of feeling the insecurity of all that is human; the discovery that life is real, and many forms of social and religious existence hollow. The old moorings are torn away, and the soul is drifting, drifting, drifting, very often without compass, except the guidance of an unseen hand, into the vast infinite of God. Then come the lonely words, and no wonder, "How is it that ye sought me? Wist ye not that I must be about my Father's business?"

18 2. That solitude was felt by Christ in trial. In the desert, in Pilate's judgment-hall, in the garden, He was alone—and alone must every son of man meet his trial-hour. The individuality of the soul necessitates that. Each man is a new soul in this world: untried, with a boundless possible before him. No one can predict what he may become, prescribe his duties, or mark out his obligations. Each man's own nature has its own peculiar rules: and he must take up his life-plan alone, and persevere in it in a perfect privacy with which no stranger intermeddleth. Each man's temptations are made up of a host of peculiarities, internal and external, which no other mind can measure. You are tried alone—alone you pass into the desert—alone you must bear and conquer in the agony—alone you must be sifted by the world. There are moments known only to a man's own self, when he must sit by the poisoned springs of existence, "yearning for a morrow which shall free him from the strife." And there are trials more terrible than that. Not when vicious inclinations are opposed to holy, but when virtue conflicts with virtue, is the real rending of the soul in twain. A temptation, in which the lower nature struggles for mastery, can be met by the whole united force of the spirit. But it is when obedience to a heavenly Father can be only paid by disobedience to an earthly one: or fidelity to duty can be only kept by infidelity to some entangling engagement: or the straight path must be taken over the misery of others: or the counsel of the affectionate friend must be met with a "Get thee behind me, Satan,"—Oh! it is then, when human advice is unavailable, that the soul feels what it is to be alone.

19 Once more—the Redeemer's soul was alone in dying. The hour had come—they were all gone, and He was, as He predicted, left alone. All that is human drops from us in that hour. Human faces flit and fade, and the sounds of the world become confused. "I shall die alone"—yes, and alone you live. The philosopher tells us that no atom in creation touches another atom—they only approach within a certain distance; then the attraction ceases, and an invisible something repels—they only *seem* to touch. No soul touches another soul except at one or two points; and those chiefly external,— a fearful and a lonely thought; but one of the truest of life. Death only realizes that which has been the fact all along. In the central deeps of our being we are all alone.

20 II. The spirit or temper of that solitude.

1. Observe its grandeur. I am alone, yet not alone. There is a feeble and sentimental way in which we speak of the Man of Sorrows. We turn to the Cross, and the agony, and the loneliness, to touch the softer feelings, to arouse compassion. You degrade *that* loneliness by your compassion. Compassion!

103

compassion for Him? Adore if you will—respect and reverence that sublime solitariness with which none but the Father was—but no pity: let it draw out the firmer and manlier graces of the soul. Even tender sympathy seems out of place.

²¹ For even in human things, the strength that is in a man can be only learnt when he is thrown upon his own resources and left alone. What a man can do in conjunction with others does not test the man. Tell us what he can do alone. It is one thing to defend the truth when you know that your audience are already prepossessed, and that every argument will meet a willing response: and it is another thing to hold the truth when truth must be supported, if at all, alone—met by cold looks and unsympathizing suspicion. It is one thing to rush on to danger with the shouts and the sympathy of numbers: it is another thing when the lonely chieftain of the sinking ship sees the last boatful disengage itself, and folds his arms to go down into the majesty of darkness, crushed, but not subdued.

²² Such and greater far was the strength and majesty of the Saviour's solitariness. It was not the trial of the lonely hermit. There is a certain gentle and pleasing melancholy in the life which is lived alone. But there are the forms of nature to speak to him, and he has not the positive opposition of mankind if he has the absence of actual sympathy. It is a solemn thing doubtless, to be apart from men, and to feel eternity rushing by like an arrowy river. But the solitude of Christ was the solitude of a crowd. In that single human bosom dwelt the thought which was to be the germ of the world's life: a thought unshared, misunderstood, or rejected. Can you not feel the grandeur of those words, when the Man reposing on His solitary strength, felt the last shadow of perfect isolation pass across His soul: "My God, my God, why hast *Thou* forsaken me?"

²³ Next, learn from these words self-reliance. "Ye shall leave me alone." Alone then the Son of man was content to be. He threw Himself on His own solitary thought: did not go down to meet the world; but waited, though it might be for ages, till the world should come round to Him. He appealed to the future, did not aim at seeming consistent: left His contradictions unexplained. "I came from the Father, I leave the world, and go to the Father." "Now," said they, "thou speakest no proverb:" that is, enigma. But many a hard and enigmatical saying before He had spoken, and He left them all. A thread runs through all true acts, stringing them together into one harmonious chain: but it is not for the Son of God to be anxious to prove their consistency with each other.

²⁴ This is self-reliance—to repose calmly on the thought which is deepest in our bosoms, and be unmoved if the world will not accept it yet. To live on your own convictions against the world, is to overcome the world—to believe that what is truest in you is true for all: to abide by that, and not be over-anxious to be heard or understood, or sympathized with, certain that at last all must acknowledge the same, and that while you stand firm, the world will come round to you: that is independence. It is not difficult to get away into retirement, and there live upon your own convictions: nor is

it difficult to mix with men, and follow their convictions: but to enter into the world, and there live out firmly and fearlessly according to your own conscience, that is Christian greatness.

²⁵ There is a cowardice in this age which is not Christian. We shrink from the consequences of truth. We look round and cling dependently. We ask what men will think—what others will say—whether they will not stare in astonishment. Perhaps they will; but he who is calculating that, will accomplish nothing in this life. The Father—the Father who is with us and in us—what does He think? God's work cannot be done without a spirit of independence. A man is got some way in the Christian life when he has learned to say humbly and yet majestically, "I dare to be alone."

²⁶ Lastly,—I remark the humility of this loneliness. Had the Son of Man simply said, I can be alone, He would have said no more than any proud, self-relying man can say. But when He added "because the Father is with me," that independence assumed another character, and self-reliance became only another form of reliance upon God. Distinguish between genuine and spurious humility. There is a false humility which says, "It is my own poor thought, and I must not trust it. I must distrust my own reason and judgment, because they are my own. I must not accept the dictates of my own conscience, for it is not my own, and is not trust in self the great fault of our fallen nature?"

²⁷ Very well. Now remember something else. There is a Spirit which beareth witness with our spirits—there is a God who "is not far from any one of us"—there is a "Light which lighteth every man which cometh into the world." Do not be unnaturally humble. The thought of your mind perchance is the thought of God. To refuse to follow *that* may be to disown God. To take the judgment and conscience of other men to live by,—where is the humility of that? From whence did their conscience and judgment come? Was the fountain from which they drew exhausted for you? If they refuse like you to rely on their own conscience, and you rely upon it, how are you sure that it is more the mind of God, than your own which you have refused to hear?

²⁸ Look at it another way. The charm of the words of great men, those grand sayings which are recognised as true as soon as heard, is this, that you recognise them as wisdom which has passed across your own mind. You feel that they are your own thoughts come back to you, else you would not at once admit them: "All that floated across me before, only I could not say it, and did not feel confident enough to assert it: or had not conviction enough to put it into words." Yes, God spoke to you what He did to them: only they believed it, said it, trusted the Word within them, and you did not. Be sure that often when you say, "It is only my own poor thought, and I am alone,"—the real correcting thought is this, "alone, but the Father is with me,"—therefore I can live that lonely conviction.

²⁹ There is no danger in this, whatever tender minds may think—no danger of mistake, if the character be a true one. For we are not left in uncertainty in this matter. It is given us to know our base from our noble hours: to

105

distinguish between the voice which is from above, and that which speaks from below, out of the abyss of our animal and selfish nature. Samuel could distinguish between the impulse, quite a human one, which would have made him select Eliab out of Jesse's sons, and the deeper judgment by which "the Lord said, Look not on his countenance, nor on the height of his stature, for I have refused him." Doubtless deep truth of character is required for this: for the whispering voices get mixed together, and we dare not abide by our own thoughts, because we think them our own, and not God's: and this because we only now and then endeavour to know in earnest. It is only given to the habitually true to know the difference. He knew it, because all His blessed life long He could say, "My judgment is just, *because* I seek not my own will, but the will of Him which sent me."

³⁰ The practical result and inference of all this is a very simple, but a very deep one: the deepest of existence. Let life be a life of faith. Do not go timorously about, inquiring what others think, what others believe, and what others say. It seems the easiest, it is the most difficult thing in life to do this—believe in God. God is near you. Throw yourself fearlessly upon Him. Trembling mortal, there is an unknown might within your soul which will wake when you command it. The day may come when all that is human, man and woman, will fall off from you, as they did from Him. Let His strength be yours. Be independent of them all now. The Father is with you. Look to Him, and He will save you.

Love and Forgiveness

Her sins, which are many, are forgiven, for she loved
much.   —Luke 7:47

THIS story contains three figures, three persons, who may stand for us as types or representatives of the Divine love and of all its operation in the world, of the way in which it is received or rejected, and of the causes and consequences of its reception or rejection. There is the unloving, cleanly, respectable, self-complacent Pharisee, with all his contempt for "this woman." There is the woman, with gross sin and mighty penitence, the great burst of love that is flowing out of her heart sweeping away before it, as it were, all the guilt of her transgressions. And, high over all, brooding over all, loving each, knowing each, pitying each, willing to save and be the Friend and Brother of each, is the embodied and manifested Divine Love, the knowledge of whom is love in our hearts, and is "life eternal." So that now I have simply to ask you to look with me, for a little while, at these three persons, as representing for us the Divine love that comes forth among sinners, and the twofold form in which that love is received. There is first, Christ The Love of God *appearing amongst men—the foundation of all our love to Him.* Then there is The Woman, *the penitent sinner, lovingly recognizing the Divine love.* And then, last, there is the Pharisee, *the self-righteous man, ignorant of himself, and empty of all love to God.*

² These are the three figures to which I ask your attention now. In the first place, we have Christ *here standing as a manifestation of the divine love coming forth amongst sinners.* His person and His words, the part He plays in this narrative, and the parable that He speaks in the course of it, have to be noticed under this head.

³ First, then, you have this idea,—that He, as bringing to us the love of God, shows it to us, as *not at all dependent upon our merits or deserts:* "He *frankly* forgave them both," are the deep words in which He would point us to the source and the ground of all the love of God. Brethren, have you ever thought what a wonderful and blessed truth there lies in the old words of one of the Jewish prophets, "I do not this for your sakes, O house of Israel, but for mine holy Name's sake"? The foundation of all God's love to

---

From *Sermons Preached in Manchester,* first series (London: Macmillan & Co., 1887).

us sinful men, that passage tells us, lies not in us, nor in anything about us, not in anything external to God Himself. He, and He alone, is the cause and reason, the motive and the end, of His own love to our world. And unless we have grasped that magnificent thought as the foundation of all our acceptance in Him, I think we have not yet learnt half of the fullness which, even in this world, may belong to our conceptions of the love of God—a love that has no motive but Himself; a love that is not evoked even (if I may so say) by regard to His creatures' wants; a love, therefore, which is eternal, being in that Divine heart before there were creatures upon whom it could rest; a love that is its own guarantee, its own cause—safe and firm, therefore, with all the firmness and serenity of the Divine nature—incapable of being affected by our transgression, deeper than all our sins, more ancient than our very existence, the very essence and being of God Himself. "He frankly forgave them both." If you seek the source of Divine love, you must go high up into the mountains of God, and learn that it, as all other of His (shall I say) emotions, and feelings, and resolutions, and purposes, owns no reason but Himself, no motive but Himself; lies wrapped in the secret of his nature, who is all-sufficient for His own blessedness, and all whose work and being is caused by, and satisfied, and terminates in His own fullness. "God is love:" therefore beneath all considerations of what we may want,—deeper and more blessed than all thoughts of a compassion that springs from the feeling of human distress and the sight of man's misery,—lies the thought of an affection which does not need the presence of sorrow to evoke it, which does not want the touch of our finger to flow out, but by its very nature is everlasting, by its very nature is infinite, by its very nature *must be* pouring out the flood of its own joyous fullness for ever and ever!

4 Then again, Christ standing here for us as the representative and revelation of this Divine Love which He manifests to us, tells us that *whilst it is not caused by us*, but comes from the nature of God, *it is not turned away by our sins*. "This man, if he were a prophet, would have known who and what manner of woman this is that toucheth Him," says the unloving self-righteous heart, "for she is a sinner." Ah! there is nothing more beautiful than the difference between the thought about sinful creatures which is natural to a *holy* being, and the thought about sinful creatures which is natural to a *self-righteous* being. The one is all contempt; the other, all pity. He knew what she was, and therefore He let her come close to Him with the touch of her polluted hand, and pour out the gains of her lawless life upon His blessed and holy head. His knowledge of her as a sinner, what did it do to His love for her? It made that love gentle and tender, as knowing that she could not bear the revelation of the blaze of His purity. It smoothed His face and softened His tones, and breathed through all His knowledge and notice of her timid and yet confident approach. "Daughter, I know all about it—all thy wanderings and thy vile transgressions: I know them all, and My love is mightier than all these. *They* may be as the great sea, but My love is like the everlasting mountains, whose roots go down beneath the ocean; and My love is like the everlasting heaven, whose brightness covers it all over."

God's love is Christ's love; Christ's love is God's love. And this is the lesson that we gather—infinite and Divine loving-kindness does not turn away from thee, my brother and my friend, because thou art a sinner, but remains hovering about thee, with wooing invitations and with gentle touches, if it may draw thee to repentance, and open a fountain of answering affection in thy seared and dry heart. The love of God is deeper than all our sins. "For His great love wherewith He loved us, when we were dead in sins, He quickened us."

⁵ Sin is but the cloud behind which the everlasting sun lies in all its power and warmth, unaffected by the cloud; and the light will yet strike, the light of His love will yet pierce through, with its merciful shafts bringing healing in their beams, and dispersing all the murkiness of man's transgressions. And as the mists gather themselves up and roll away, dissipated by the heat of that sun in the upper sky, and reveal the fair earth below,—so the love of Christ shines in, melting the mist and dissipating the fog, thinning it off in its thickest places, and at last piercing its way right through it, down to the heart of the man that has been lying beneath the oppression of this thick darkness, and who thought that the fog was the sky, and that there was no sun there above. God be thanked! the everlasting love of God that comes from the heart of His own being, and is there because of Himself, will never be quenched because of man's sin.

⁶ And so, in the next place, Christ teaches us here that this *Divine love, when it comes forth among sinners, necessarily manifests itself first in the form of forgiveness.* There was nothing to be done with the debtors until the debt was wiped out; there was no possibility of other gifts of the highest sort being granted to them, until the great score was cancelled and done away with. When the love of God comes down into a sinful world, it must come down first and foremost as pardoning mercy. There are no other terms on which there can be a union betwixt the loving-kindness of God and the emptiness and sinfulness of my heart, except only this—first of all there shall be the clearing away from my soul of the sins which I have gathered there, and then there is space for all other Divine things to work and to manifest themselves. Only do not fancy that when we speak about forgiveness, we simply mean that a man's position in regard to the penalties of sin is altered. That is not all the depth of the scriptural notion of forgiveness. It includes far more than the removal of outward penalties. The heart of it all is, that the love of God rests upon the sinner, unturned away even by his sins, passing over his sins, and removing his sins for the sake of Christ. My friend, if you are talking in general terms about a great Divine loving-kindness that wraps you round, if you have a great deal to say, apart from the Gospel, about the love of God as being your hope and confidence, I want you to reflect on this, that the first word which the love of God speaks to sinful men is *pardon;* and unless that is your notion of God's love, unless you look to that as the first thing of all, let me tell you, you may have before you a very fair picture of a beautiful, tender, good-natured benevolence, but you have not nearly reached the height of the vigor and yet the tenderness of

the Scripture notion of the love of God. It is not a love which says, "Well, put sin on one side, and give the man the blessings all the same," not a love which has nothing to say about that great fact of transgression, not a love which gives it the go-by, and leaves it standing: but a love which passes into the heart through the portal of pardon, a love which grapples with the fact of sin first, and has nothing to say to a man until it has said that message to him.

⁷ And but one word more on this part of my subject—here we see the love of God thus coming from Himself; not turned away by man's sins; being the cause of forgiveness; expressing itself in pardon; and last of all, *demanding service.* "Simon, thou gavest me no water, thou gavest me no kiss, my head thou didst not anoint. I expected all these things from thee—I desired them all from thee: my love came that they might spring up in thy heart;—thou hast not given them; my love is wounded, as it were disappointed, and it turns away from thee." Yes, after all that we have said about the freeness and fulness, the unmerited, and uncaused, and unmotivated nature of that divine affection, after all that we have said about its being the source of every blessing to man, asking nothing from him, but giving everything to him; it still remains true that God's love, when it comes to men, comes that it may evoke an answering echo in the human heart, and "though it might be much bold to enjoin, yet for love's sake rather beseeches" us to give unto Him who has given all unto us. There, then, stands forth in the narrative Christ as a revelation of the Divine love among sinners.

⁸ II. Now, in the second place, let us look for a moment, at "THIS WOMAN," as the representative of a class of character—THE PENITENT LOVINGLY RECOGNIZING THE DIVINE LOVE. The words which I have read as a text contain a statement as to the woman's character: "Her sins, which are many, are forgiven; for she loved much." Allow me just one word of explanation, in the shape of exposition, on these words. Great blunders have been built upon them. I daresay you have seen epitaphs—(I have)—written often on gravestones with this misplaced idea on them,—"Very sinful; but there was a great deal of love in the person; and for the sake of the love, God passed by the sin!" Now, when Christ says "she loved much," He does not mean to say that her love was the cause of her forgiveness—not at all. He means to say that her love was the proof of her forgiveness, and that it was so because her love was a consequence of her forgiveness. As, for instance, we might say, "the woman is in great distress, for she weeps;" but we do not mean thereby that the weeping is the reason of the distress, but the means of our knowing the sorrow. It is the proof because it is the consequence. Or (to put it into the simplest shape) the love does not go before the forgiveness, but the forgiveness goes before the love; and because the love comes after the forgiveness, it is the sign of the forgiveness. That this is the true interpretation, you will see, if you look back for a moment at the narrative which precedes, where He says, "He frankly forgave them both: tell me, therefore, which of them will love him most?" Pardon is the pre-requisite of love, and love is a consequence of the sense of forgiveness.

⁹ This, then, is the first thing to observe: all true love to God is preceded

110

in the heart by these two things—a sense of sin, and an assurance of pardon. Brethren, there is no love possible—real, deep, genuine, worthy of being called love of God—which does not start with the belief of my own transgression, and with the thankful reception of forgiveness in Christ. You do nothing to get pardon for yourselves; but unless you *have* the pardon you have no love to God. I know that sounds a very hard thing—I know that many will say it is very narrow and bigoted, and will ask, "Do you mean to tell me that the man whose bosom glows with gratitude because of earthly blessings, has no love—that all natural religion which is in people, apart from this sense of forgiveness in Christ, do you mean to tell me that this is not all genuine?" Yes, most assuredly; and I believe the Bible and man's conscience say the same thing. I do not for one moment deny that there may be in the hearts of those who are in the grossest ignorance of themselves as transgressors, certain emotions of instinctive gratitude and natural religiousness, directed to some higher power dimly thought of as the author of their blessings and the source of much gladness: but has *that* kind of thing got any living power in it? I demur to its right to be called love to God at all, for this reason—because it seems to me that the object that is loved is not God, but a fragment of God. He who but says, "I owe to Him breath and all things; in Him I live and move, and have my being," has left out one-half at least of the Scriptural conception of God. Your God, my friend, is not the God of the Bible, unless He stands before you clothed in infinite loving-kindness indeed; but clothed also in strict and rigid justice. Is your God perfect and entire? If you say that you love Him, and if you do so, is it as the God and Father of our Lord Jesus Christ? Have you meditated on the depths of the requirements of His law? Have you stood silent and stricken at the thought of the blaze of His righteousness? Have you passed through all the thick darkness and the clouds with which He surrounds His throne, and forced your way at last into the inner light where He dwells? Or is it a vague divinity that you worship and love? Which? Ah, if a man study his Bible, and try to find out for himself, from its veracious records, who and what manner of God the living God is, there will be no love in his heart to that Being except only when he has flung himself at His feet, and said, "Father of eternal purity, and God of all holiness and righteousness, forgive Thy child, a sinful broken man—forgive Thy child, for the sake of Thy Son!" That, and that alone, is the road by which we come to possess the love of God, as a practical power, filling and sanctifying our souls; and such is the God to whom alone our love ought to be rendered;—and I tell you (or rather the Bible tells you, and the Gospel and the cross of Christ tell you), *no love without pardon*, no fellowship and sonship without the sense of sin and the acknowledgment of foul transgression!

¹⁰ So much, then, for what precedes the love of Christ in the heart; now a word as to what follows. "Her sins, which are many, are forgiven: for she loved much." The sense of sin precedes forgiveness: forgiveness precedes love; love precedes all acceptable and faithful service. If you want *to do, love*. If you want *to know, love!* This poor woman, she knew Christ a vast deal

better than that Pharisee there. He said, "This man is not a prophet; He does not understand the woman." Ay, but the woman knew herself better than the Pharisee knew himself, knew herself better than the Pharisee knew her, knew Christ, above all, a vast deal better than he did. Love is the *gate of all knowledge*.

[11] This poor woman brings her box of ointment, a relic perhaps of past evil life, and once meant for her own adornment, and pours it on His head, lavishes offices of service which to the unloving heart seem bold in the giver and cumbersome to the receiver. It is little she can do, but she does it. Her full heart demands expression, and is relieved by utterance in deeds. The deeds are spontaneous, welling out at the bidding of an inward impulse, not drawn out by the force of an external command. It matters not what practical purpose they serve. The motive of them makes their glory. Love prompts them, love justifies them, and His love interprets them, and His love accepts them. The love which flows from the sense of forgiveness is *the source of all obedience* as well as the means of all knowledge.

[12] Brethren, we differ from each other in all respects but one, "We have all sinned and come short of the glory of God;" we all need the love of Christ; it is offered to us all; but believe me, the sole handle by which you can lay hold of it, is the feeling of your own sinfulness and need of pardon. I preach to you a love that you do not want to buy, a mercy that you do not need to bribe, a grace that is all independent of your character, and condition, and merits, which issues from God for ever, and is lying at your doors if you will take it. You are a sinful man; Christ died for you. He comes to give you His forgiving mercy. Take it, be at rest. So shalt thou love and know and do, and so shall He love and guide *thee!*

[13] III. Now one word, and then I have done. A third character stands here— THE UNLOVING AND SELF-RIGHTEOUS MAN, ALL IGNORANT OF THE LOVE OF CHRIST. He is the antithesis of the woman and her character. You remember the traditional peculiarities and characteristics of the class to which he belonged. He is a fair specimen of the whole of them. Respectable in life, rigid in morality, unquestionable in orthodoxy; no sound of suspicion having ever come near his belief in all the traditions of the elders; intelligent and learned, high up among the ranks of Israel! What was it that made this man's morality a piece of dead nothingness? What was it that made his orthodoxy just so many dry words, from out of which all the life had gone? What was it? This one thing: there was no love in it. As I said, Love is the foundation of all obedience. Without it, religion degenerates into mere casuistry. Love is the foundation of all knowledge. Without it, religion degenerates into a chattering about Moses, and doctrines, and theories; a thing that will neither kill nor make alive, that never gave life to a single soul or blessing to a single heart, and never put strength into any hand in the conflict and strife of daily life. There is no more contemptible and impotent thing on the face of the earth than morality divorced from love, and religious thoughts divorced from a heart full of the love of God. Quick corruption or long decay, and in either case death and putrefaction, are the end of these! You and I need that lesson,

my friends. It is of no use for us to condemn Pharisees that have been dead and in their graves for eighteen hundred years. The same thing besets us all; we all of us try to get away from the centre, and dwell contented on the surface. We are satisfied to take the flowers, and stick them into our little gardens, without roots to them; when of course they will die. People may try to cultivate virtue without religion, and to acquire correct notions of moral and spiritual truth, and partially and temporarily they may succeed; but the one will be a yoke of bondage, and the other a barren theory. I repeat, *love* is the basis of all knowledge and of all right-doing. If you have got that firm foundation laid in the soul, then the knowledge and the practice will be builded in God's own good time; and if not, the higher you build the temple, and the more aspiring are its cloud-pointing pinnacles, the more certain will be its toppling some day, and the more awful will be the ruin when it comes. The Pharisee was contented with himself; and so there was no sense of sin in him, there was no penitent recognition of Christ as forgiving and loving him, therefore there was no love to Christ. Because there was no love, there was neither light nor heat in his soul, his knowledge was barren notions, and his painful doings were soul-destructive self-righteousness.

14 And so it all comes round to the one blessed message: My friend, God hath loved us with an everlasting love. He has provided an eternal redemption and pardon for us. If you would know Christ at all, you must go to Him as a sinful man, or you are shut out from Him altogether. If you *will* go to Him as a sinful being, fling yourself down there, not try to make yourself better, but say, "I am all full of unrighteousness and transgression: let Thy love fall upon me and heal me;" you will get the answer, and in your heart there shall begin to live and grow a root of love to Him, which shall at last effloresce into all knowledge and into all purity of obedience; for he that hath had much forgiven, loveth much; and "he that loveth knoweth God," and "dwelleth in God, and God in him."

Songs in the Night

But none saith, Where is God my Maker, who giveth
songs in the night?   —Job 35:10

Elihu was a wise man, exceeding wise, though not so wise as the all-wise Jehovah, who sees light in the clouds, and finds order in confusion; hence Elihu, being much puzzled at beholding Job thus afflicted, cast about him to find the cause, and he very wisely hit upon one of the most likely reasons, although it did not happen to be the right one in Job's case. He said within himself, "Surely if men be troubled exceedingly, it is because, while they think about their troubles and distress themselves about their fears, they do not say, 'Where is God my Maker, who giveth songs in the night?' " Elihu's reason was right in the majority of cases. The great cause of the Christian's distress, the reason of the depths of sorrow into which many believers are plunged, is simply this—that while they are looking about, on the right hand and on the left, to see how they may escape their troubles, they forget to look to the hills whence all real help cometh; they do not say, "Where is God my Maker, who giveth songs in the night?" We shall, however, leave that inquiry, and dwell upon those sweet words, "God, my Maker, who giveth songs in the night."

2 The world hath its night. It seemeth necessary that it should have one. The sun shineth by day, and men go forth to their labors; but they grow weary, and nightfall cometh on, like a sweet boon from heaven. The darkness draweth the curtains, and shutteth out the light, which might prevent our eyes from slumber; while the sweet, calm stillness of the night permits us to rest upon the lap of ease, and there forget awhile our cares, until the morning sun appeareth, and an angel puts his hand upon the curtain, and undraws it once again, touches our eyelids, and bids us rise, and proceed to the labors of the day. Night is one of the greatest blessings men enjoy; we have many reasons to thank God for it. Yet night is to many a gloomy season. There is "the pestilence that walketh in darkness;" there is the terror by night; there is the dread of robbers and of fell disease, with all those fears that the timorous know, when they have no light wherewith they can

---

From *Sermons*, second series (New York: Sheldon, Blakeman & Co., 1857).

SONGS IN THE NIGHT

discern objects. It is then they fancy that spiritual creatures walk the earth; though, if they knew rightly, they would find it to be true, that

> Millions of spiritual creatures walk this earth
> Unseen, both when we sleep and when we wake,

and that at all times they are round about us—not more by night than by day. Night is the season of terror and alarm to most men. Yet even night has its songs. Have you never stood by the seaside at night, and heard the pebbles sing, and the waves chant God's glories? Or have you never risen from your couch, and thrown up the window of your chamber, and listened there? Listened to what? Silence—save now and then a murmuring sound, which seems sweet music then. And have you not fancied that you heard the harp of God playing in heaven? Did you not conceive, that yon stars, that those eyes of God, looking down on you, were also mouths of song—that every star was singing God's glory, singing, as it shone, its mighty Maker, and his lawful, well-deserved praise? Night hath its songs. We need not much poetry in our spirit, to catch the song of night, and hear the spheres as they chant praises which are loud to the heart, though they be silent to the ear—the praises of the mighty God, who bears up the unpillared arch of heaven, and moves the stars in their courses.

³ Man, too, like the great world in which he lives, must have his night. For it is true that man is like the world around him; he is a little world; he resembles the world in almost every thing; and if the world hath its night, so hath man. And many a night do we have—nights of sorrow, nights of persecution, nights of doubt, nights of bewilderment, nights of anxiety, nights of oppression, nights of ignorance—nights of all kinds, which press upon our spirits and terrify our souls. But, blessed be God, the Christian man can say, "My God giveth me songs in the night."

⁴ It is not necessary, I take it, to prove to you that Christian men have nights; for if you are Christians, you will find that *you* have them, and you will not want any proof, for nights will come quite often enough. I will, therefore, proceed at once to the subject; and I will speak this evening upon songs in the night, *their source*—God giveth them; songs in the night, *their matter*—what do we sing about in the night? songs in the night, *their excellence*—they are hearty songs, and they are sweet ones; songs in the night, *their uses*—their benefits to ourselves and others.

⁵ I. First, songs in the night—WHO IS THE AUTHOR OF THEM? "God," says the text, our "Maker:" he "giveth songs in the night."

⁶ Any fool can sing in the day. When the cup is full, man draws inspiration from it; when wealth rolls in abundance round about him, any man can sing to the praise of a God who gives a plenteous harvest, or sends home a loaded argosy. It is easy enough for an Æolian harp to whisper music when the winds blow; the difficulty is for music to come when no wind bloweth. It is easy to sing when we can read the notes by daylight; but the skillful singer is he who can sing when there is not a ray of light to read by—who sings from his

115

heart, and not from a book that he can see, because he has no means of reading, save from that inward book in his own living spirit, whence notes of gratitude pour out in songs of praise. No man can make a song in the night by himself; he may attempt it, but he will feel how difficult it is. Let all things go as I please—I will weave songs, weave them wherever I go, with the flowers that grow upon my path; but put me in a desert, where no flowers are, and wherewith shall I weave a chorus of praise to God? How shall I make a crown for him? Let this voice be free, and this body be full of health, and I can sing God's praise; but stop this tongue, lay me upon the bed of languishing; and it is not easy to sing from the bed, and chant high praises in the fires. Give me the bliss of spiritual liberty, and let me mount up to my God, get near the throne, and I will sing, ay, sing as sweet as seraphs; but confine me, fetter my spirit, clip my wings, make me exceeding sad, so that I become old like the eagle—ah! then it is hard to sing. It is not in man's power to sing, when all is adverse. It is not natural to sing in trouble—"Bless the Lord, O my soul, and all that is within me bless his holy name:" for that is a daylight song. But it was a divine song which Habakkuk sang, when in the night he said— "Though the fig-tree shall not blossom," and so on, "yet will I trust in the Lord, and stay myself in the God of Jacob." Methinks in the Red Sea any man could have made a song like that of Moses—"The horse and his rider hath he thrown into the sea;" the difficulty would have been to compose a song before the Red Sea had been divided and to sing it before Pharaoh's hosts had been drowned, while yet the darkness of doubt and fear was resting on Israel's hosts. Songs in the night come only from God; they are not in the power of men.

7 But what does the text mean, when it asserts that God giveth songs in the night? We think we can find two answers to the question. The first is, that usually in the night of a Christian's experience *God is his only song.* If it be daylight in my heart, I can sing songs touching my graces—songs touching my sweet experience—songs touching my duties—songs touching my labors; but let the night come—my graces appear to have withered; my evidences, though they are there, are hidden; I can not

> read my title clear
> To mansions in the skies;

and now I have nothing left to sing of but my God. It is strange, that when God gives his children mercies, they generally set their hearts more on the mercies than on the Giver of them; but when the night comes, and he sweeps all the mercies away, then at once they say, "Now, my God, I have nothing to sing of but thee; I must come to thee; and to thee only. I had cisterns once; they were full of water; I drank from them then; but now the created streams are dry; sweet Lord, I quaff no stream but thine own self, I drink from no fount but from thee." Ay, child of God, thou knowest what I say; or if thou dost not understand it yet, thou wilt do so by-and-by. It is in the night we sing of God, and of God alone. Every string is tuned, and every power hath its attribute to sing, while we praise God, and nothing else. We can sacrifice to ourselves in daylight—we only sacrifice to God by night; we can sing high praises to our dear selves when all is joyful, but we can not sing praise to any save our God, when circumstances are untoward, and providences appear adverse. God alone can furnish us with songs in the night.

8 And yet again: not only does God give the song in the night, because he is the only subject upon which we can sing then, but because *he is the only one who inspires songs in the night*. Bring me a poor, melancholy, distressed child of God: I come into the pulpit, I seek to tell him sweet promises, and whisper to him sweet words of comfort; he listeneth not to me; he is like the deaf adder, he listens not to the voice of the charmer, charm he never so wisely. Send him round to all the comforting divines, and all the holy Barnabases that ever preached, and they will do very little—they will not be able to squeeze a song out of him, do what they may. He is drinking the gall of wormwood; he says, "O Lord, thou hast me drunk with weeping, I have eaten ashes like bread;" and comfort him as you may, it will be only a woeful note or two of mournful resignation that you will get from him; you will get no psalms of praise, no hallelujahs, no sonnets. But let God come to his child in the night, let him whisper in his ear as he lies on his bed, and how you see his eyes flash fire in the night! Do you not hear him say,

> 'Tis paradise, if thou art here:
> If thou depart, 'tis hell.

I could not have cheered him: it is God that has done it; and God "giveth songs in the night." It is marvelous, brethren, how one sweet word of God will make whole songs for Christians. One word of God is like a piece of gold, and the Christian is the gold-beater, and he can hammer that promise out for whole weeks. I can say myself, I have lived on one promise for weeks, and want no other. I want just simply to hammer that promise out into gold-leaf, and plate my whole existence with joy from it. The Christian gets his songs from God: God gives him inspiration, and teaches him how to sing: "God my Maker, who giveth songs in the night."

9 So, then, poor Christian, thou needest not go pumping up thy poor heart to make it glad. Go to thy Maker, and ask him to give thee a song in the night. Thou art a poor dry well: thou hast heard it said, that when a pump is dry, you must pour water down it first of all, and then you will get some up; and so, Christian, when thou art dry, go to God, ask him to pour some joy down thee, and then thou wilt get some joy up from thine own heart. Do not go to this comforter or that, for you will find them Job's comforters, after all; but go thou first and foremost to thy Maker, for he is the great composer of songs and teacher of music; he it is who can teach thee how to sing: "God, my Maker, who giveth me songs in the night."

10 II. Thus we have dwelt upon the first point. Now the second. *What is generally the matter contained in a song in the night?* What do we sing about?

11 Why, I think, when we sing at night, there are three things we sing about.

Either we sing about the yesterday that is over, or else about the night itself, or else about the morrow that is to come. Each of these are sweet themes, when God our Maker gives us songs in the night. In the midst of the night the most usual method for Christians is to sing about *the day that is over*. "Well," they say, "the night is now, but I can remember when it was daylight. Neither moon nor stars appear at present; but I remember when I saw the sun. I have no evidence just now; but there was a time when I could say, 'I know that my Redeemer liveth.' I have my doubts and fears at this present moment; but it is not long since I could say with full assurance, 'I know that he shed his blood for me; I know that my Redeemer liveth, and when he shall stand a second time upon the earth, though the worms devour this body, yet in my flesh I shall see God.' It may be darkness now; but I know the promises *were* sweet; I know I had blessed seasons in his house. I am quite sure of this; I used to enjoy myself in the ways of the Lord; and though now my paths are strewn with thorns, I know it is the King's highway. It was a way of pleasantness once; it will be a way of pleasantness again. 'I will remember the days of old; I will meditate upon the years of the right hand of the Most High.' " Christian, perhaps the best song thou canst sing, to cheer thee in the night, is the song of yester-morn. Remember, it was not always night with thee: night is a new thing to thee. Once thou hadst a glad heart, a buoyant spirit; once thine eye was full of fire; once thy foot was light; once thou couldst sing for very joy and ecstasy of heart. Well, then, remember that God, who made thee sing yesterday, has not left thee in the night. He is not a daylight God, who can not know his children in darkness; but he loves thee now as much as ever: though he has left thee a little, it is to prove thee, to make thee trust him better, and serve him more. Let me tell you some of the sweet things of which a Christian may make a song when he is in the night.

[12] If we are going to sing of the things of yesterday, let us begin with what God did for us in past times. My beloved brethren, you will find it a sweet subject for a song at times, to begin to sing of electing love and covenanted mercies. When thou thyself art low, it is well to sing of the fountain-head of mercy; of that blessed decree wherein thou wast ordained to eternal life, and of that glorious Man who undertook thy redemption; of that solemn covenant signed, and sealed, and ratified, in all things ordered well; of that everlasting love which, ere the hoary mountains were begotten, or ere the aged hills were children, chose thee, loved thee firmly, loved thee fast, loved thee well, loved thee eternally. I tell thee, believer, if thou canst go back to the years of eternity; if thou canst in thy mind run back to that period, or ere the everlasting hills were fashioned, or the fountains of the great deep were scooped out, and if thou canst see thy God inscribing thy name in his eternal book; if thou canst see in his heart eternal thoughts of love to thee, thou wilt find this a charming means of giving thee songs in the night. No songs like those which come from electing love; no sonnets like those that are dictated by meditations on discriminating mercy. Some, indeed, can not sing of election: the Lord open their mouths a little wider! Some there are that

are afraid of the very term; but we only despise men who are afraid of what they believe, afraid of what God has taught them in his Bible. No, in our darker hours it is our joy to sing:

> Sons we are through God's election,
>   Who in Jesus Christ believe;
> By eternal destination,
>   Sovereign grace we now receive.
> Lord, thy favor,
>   Shall both grace and glory give.

Think, Christian, of the yesterday, I say, and thou wilt get a song in the night. But if thou hast not a voice tuned to so high a key as that, let me suggest some other mercies thou mayest sing of; and they are the mercies thou hast experienced. What! man, canst thou not sing a little of that blessed hour when Jesus met thee; when, a blind slave, thou wast sporting with death, and he saw thee, and said: "Come, poor slave, come with me?" Canst thou not sing of that rapturous moment when he snapped thy fetters, dashed thy chains to the earth, and said: "I am the Breaker; I came to break thy chains, and set thee free?" What though thou art ever so gloomy now, canst thou forget that happy morning, when in the house of God thy voice was loud, almost a seraph's voice, in praise? for thou couldst sing: "I am forgiven; I am forgiven":

> A monument of grace,
> A sinner saved by blood.

Go back, man; sing of that moment, and then thou wilt have a song in the night. Or if thou hast almost forgotten that, then sure thou hast some precious milestone along the road of life that is not quite grown over with moss, on which thou canst read some happy inscription of his mercy toward thee! What! didst thou never have a sickness like that which thou art suffering now, and did he not raise thee up from that? Wast thou never poor before, and did he not supply thy wants? Wast thou never in straits before, and did he not deliver thee? Come, man! I beseech thee, go to the river of thine experience, and pull up a few bulrushes, and weave them into an ark, wherein thine infant faith may float safely on the stream. I bid thee not forget what God hath done. What! hast thou buried thine own diary? I beseech thee, man, turn over the book of thy remembrance. Canst thou not see some sweet hill Mizar? Canst thou not think of some blessed hour when the Lord met with thee at Hermon? Hast thou never been on the Delectable Mountains? Hast thou never escaped the jaw of the lion and the paw of the bear? Nay, O man, I know thou hast; go back, then, a little way, and take the mercies of yesterday, and they shall glitter through the darkness, and thou shalt find that God hath given thee a song in the night.

[13] "Ay," says one, "but you know, that when we are in the dark, we can not see the mercies God has given us. It is all very well for you to tell

119

us this; but we can not get hold of them." I remember an old experimental Christian speaking about the great pillars of our faith; he was a sailor; we were then on board ship, and there were sundry huge posts on the shore, to which the ships were usually fastened, by throwing a cable over them. After I had told him a great many promises, he said, "I know they are good strong promises, but I can not get near enough to shore to throw my cable around them; that is the difficulty."

14 Now, it often happens that God's past mercies and loving kindnesses would be good sure posts to hold on to, but we have not got faith enough to throw our cable round them, and so we go slipping down the stream of unbelief, because we can not stay ourselves by our former mercies. I will, however, give you something that I think you can throw your cable over. If God has never been kind to you, one thing you surely know, and that is, he has been kind to others. Come, now; if thou art in ever so great straits, sure there were others in greater straits. What! art thou lower down than poor Jonah was, when he went down to the bottoms of the mountains? Art thou more poorly off than thy Master, when he had not a place where to lay his head? What! conceivest thou thyself to be the worst of the worst? Look at Job there, scraping himself with a potsherd, and sitting on a dunghill. Art thou as bad as he? And yet Job rose up, and was richer than before; and out of the depths Jonah came, and preached the Word; and our Saviour Jesus hath mounted to his throne. O Christian! only think of what he has done for others! If thou canst not recollect that he has done any thing for thee, yet remember, I beseech thee, what his usual rule is, and do not judge hardly by my God. You remember Benhadad, when he was overcome and conquered, and Ahab was after him. Some said to him, "We know that the kings of Israel are merciful kings; let us send therefore unto Ahab, and it may be he will spare our lives." Benhadad sent to the king; he had received no kindness from Ahab before, he had only heard that he was a merciful king; so to the king he went; and what said the king? "Is my brother, Benhadad, yet alive?" Truly, poor soul, if thou hast never had a merciful God, yet others have had; the King is a merciful King; go and try him. If thou art ever so low in thy troubles, look to "the hills, from whence cometh thy help." Others have had help therefrom, and so mayest thou. Up might start hundreds of God's children, and show us their hands full of comforts and mercies; and they could say, "the Lord gave us these without money and without price; and why should he not give to thee also, seeing that thou also art a king's son?" Thus, Christian, thou wilt get a song in the night out of other people, if thou canst not get a song from thyself. Never be ashamed of taking a leaf out of another man's experience book. If thou canst find no gold leaf in thine own, tear one out of someone's else; and if thou hast no cause to be grateful to God in darkness, or canst not find cause in thine own experience, go to some one else, and, if thou canst, harp his praise in the dark, and like the nightingale sing his praise sweetly when all the world has gone to rest. We can sing in the night of the mercies of yesterday.

15 But I think, beloved, there is never so dark a night, but there is some-

thing to sing about, even *concerning that night;* for there is one thing I am sure we can sing about, let the night be ever so dark, and that is, "It is of the Lord's mercies that we are not consumed, and because his compassions fail not." If we can not sing very loud, yet we can sing a little low tune, something like this—"He hath not dealt with us after our sins, nor rewarded us according to our iniquities." "O!" says one, "I do not know where to get my dinner from tomorrow. I am a poor wretch." So you may be, my dear friend; but you are not so poor as you deserve to be. Do not be mightily offended about that; if you are, you are no child of God; for the child of God acknowledges that he has no right to the least of God's mercies, but that they come through the channel of grace alone. As long as I am out of hell, I have no right to grumble; and if I were in hell I should have no right to complain, for I feel, when convinced of sin, that never creature deserved to go there more than I do. We have no cause to murmur; we can lift up our hands, and say, "Night! thou art dark, but thou mightest have been darker. I am poor, but if I could not have been poorer, I might have been sick. I am poor and sick—well, I have some friend left; my lot can not be so bad, but it might have been worse." And therefore, Christian, you will always have one thing to sing about—"Lord, I thank thee, it is not all darkness!" Besides, Christian, however dark the night is, there is always a star or moon. There is scarce ever a night that we have, but there are just one or two little lamps burning up there. However dark it may be, I think you may find some little comfort, some little joy, some little mercy left, and some little promise to cheer thy spirit. The stars are not put out, are they? Nay, if thou canst not see them, they are there; but methinks one or two must be shining on thee; therefore give God a song in the night. If thou hast only one star, bless God for that one, perhaps he will make it two; and if thou hast only two stars, bless God twice for the two stars, and perhaps he will make them four. Try, then, if thou canst not find a song in the night.

16 But, beloved, there is another thing of which we can sing yet more sweetly; and that is, we can sing of *the day that is to come*. I am preaching tonight for the poor weavers of Spitalfields. Perhaps there are not to be found a class of men in London who are suffering a darker night than they are; for while many classes have been befriended and defended, there are few who speak up for them, and (if I am rightly informed) they are generally ground down within an inch of their lives. I suppose their masters intend that their bread shall be very sweet, on the principle, that the nearer the ground, the sweeter the grass; for I should think no people have their grass so near the ground as the weavers of Spitalfields. In an inquiry by the House of Commons last week, it was given in evidence that their average wages amount to seven or eight shillings a week; and then they have to furnish themselves with a room and work at expensive articles, which my friends the ladies are wearing now, and which they buy as cheaply as possible; but perhaps they do not know that they are made with the blood and bones and marrow of the Spitalfields weavers who, many of them, work for less than man ought to have to subsist upon. Some of them waited upon me

121

the other day; I was exceedingly pleased with one of them. He said, "Well, sir, it is very hard, but I hope there is better times coming for us." "Well, my friend," I said, "I am afraid you can not hope for much better times, unless the Lord Jesus Christ comes a second time." "That is just what we hope for," said he. "We do not see there is any chance of deliverance, unless the Lord Jesus Christ comes to establish his kingdom upon earth; and then he will judge the oppressed, and break the oppressors in pieces with an iron rod, and dash them in pieces like a potter's vessel." I was glad my friend had got a song in the night, and was singing about the morning that was coming. Often do I cheer myself with the thought of the coming of the Lord. We preach now, perhaps, with little success; "the kingdoms of this world" are not "become the kingdoms of our Lord and of his Christ;" we send out missionaries; they are for the most part unsuccessful. We are laboring, but we do not see the fruit of our labors. Well, what then? Try a little while; we shall not always labor in vain, or spend our strength for naught. A day is coming, and now is, when every minister of Christ shall speak with unction, when all the servants of God shall preach with power, and when colossal systems of heathenism shall tumble from their pedestals, and mighty, gigantic delusions shall be scattered to the winds. The shout shall be heard, "Alleluia! Alleluia! the Lord God Omnipotent reigneth." For that day do I look; it is to the bright horizon of that second coming that I turn my eyes. My anxious expectation is that the sweet Sun of righteousness will arise with healing beneath his wings, that the oppressed shall be righted, that despotisms shall be cut down, that liberty shall be established, that peace shall be made lasting, and that the glorious liberty of the gospel of God shall be extended throughout the known world. Christian! if thou art in a night, think of the morrow; cheer up thy heart with the thought of the coming of thy Lord. Be patient, for "Lo! he comes, with clouds descending." Be patient! The husbandman waits until he reaps his harvest. Be patient; for you know who has said, "Behold, I come quickly, and my reward is with me, to give to every man according as his works shall be."

¹⁷ One thought more upon that point. There is another sweet tomorrow of which we hope to sing in the night. Soon, beloved, you and I shall lie on our dying-bed, and we shall want a song in the night then; and I do not know where we shall get it, if we do not get it from the tomorrow. Kneeling by the bed of an apparently dying saint last night, I said, "Well, sister, he has been precious to you; you can rejoice in his covenant mercies, and his past loving-kindnesses." She put out her hand and said, "Ah! sir, do not talk about them now; I want the sinner's Saviour as much now as ever; it is not a saint's Saviour I want; it is still a sinner's Saviour that I am in need of, for I am a sinner still." I found that I could not comfort her with the past; so I reminded her of the golden streets, of the gates of pearl, of the walls of jasper, of the harps of gold, of the songs of bliss; and then her eye glistened; she said, "Yes, I shall be there soon; I shall meet them by-and-by;"

and then she seemed so glad! Ah! believer, you may always cheer yourself
with that thought; for if you are ever so low now, remember that

> A few more rolling suns at most,
> Will land thee on fair Canaan's coast.

18 Thy head may be crowned with thorny troubles now, but it shall wear
a starry crown directly; thy hand may be filled with cares—it shall grasp
a harp soon, a harp full of music. Thy garments may be soiled with dust
now; they shall be white by-and-by. Wait a little longer. Ah! beloved,
how depicable our troubles and trials will seem when we look back upon
them! Looking at them here in the prospect, they seem immense; but when
we get to heaven, we shall then,

> With transporting joys, recount
> The labors of our feet.

Our trials will seem to us nothing at all. We shall talk to one another about
them in heaven, and find all the more to converse about, according as we
have suffered more here below. Let us go on, therefore; and if the night be
ever so dark, remember there is not a night that shall not have a morning;
and that morning is to come by-and-by. When sinners are lost in darkness,
we shall lift up our eyes in everlasting light. Surely I need not dwell longer
on this thought. There is matter enough for songs in the night in the past,
the present, and the future.

19 III. And now I want to tell you, very briefly, *What are the excellencies
of songs in the night above all other songs.*

20 In the first place, when you hear a man singing a song in the night—
I mean in the night of trouble—you may be quite sure it is *a hearty one.* Many
of you sang very prettily just now, didn't you? I wonder whether you would
sing very prettily, if there were a stake or two in Smithfield for all of you
who dared to do it? If you sang under pain and penalty, that would show
your heart to be in your song. We can all sing very nicely indeed when
every body else sings. It is the easiest thing in the world to open your
mouth, and let the words come out; but when the devil puts his hand over
your mouth, can you sing then? Can you say, "Though he slay me, yet will
I trust in him?" That is hearty singing; that is real song that springs up in
the night. The nightingale singeth most sweetly because she singeth in the
night. We know a poet has said, that if she sang by day, she might be thought
to sing no more sweetly than the wren. It is the stillness of the night that
makes her song sweet. And so doth a Christian's song become sweet and
hearty, because it is in the night.

21 Again: the songs we warble in the night are those that show we have
real faith in God. Many men have just enough faith to trust God as far as
they can see him, and they always sing as far as they can see providence
go right; but true faith can sing when its possessors can not see. It can take
hold of God when they can not discern him.

123

²² Songs in the night, too, prove that we have *true courage*. Many sing by day who are silent by night; they are afraid of thieves and robbers; but the Christain who sings in the night proves himself to be a courageous character. It is the bold Christian who can sing God's sonnets in the darkness.

²³ He who can sing songs in the night, too, proves that he has *true love* to Christ. It is not love to Christ to praise him while every body else praises him; to walk arm in arm with him when he has the crown on his head is no great need, I wot; to walk with Christ in rags is something. To believe in Christ when he is shrouded in darkness, to stick hard and fast by the Saviour when all men speak ill of him and forsake him—that is true faith. He who singeth a song to Christ in the night, singeth the best song in all the world; for he singeth from the heart.

²⁴ IV. I am afraid of wearying you; therefore I will not dwell on the excellencies of night songs, but just, in the last place, *show you their uses*.

²⁵ Well, beloved, it is very useful to sing in the night of our troubles, first, *because it will cheer ourselves*. When you were boys living in the country, and had some distance to go alone at night, don't you remember how you whistled and sang to keep your courage up? Well, what we do in the natural world we ought to do in the spiritual. There is nothing like singing to keep your spirits alive. When we have been in trouble, we have often thought ourselves to be well-nigh overwhelmed with difficulty; and we have said, "Let us have a song." We have begun to sing; and Martin Luther says, "The devil can not bear singing." That is about the truth; he does not like music. It was so in Saul's days: an evil spirit rested on Saul; but when David played on his harp, the evil spirit went away from him. This is usually the case: if we can begin to sing we shall remove our fears. I like to hear servants sometimes humming a tune at their work; I love to hear a plowman in the country singing as he goes along with his horses. Why not? You say he has no time to praise God; but he can sing a song—surely he can sing a Psalm; it will take no more time. Singing is the best thing to purge ourselves of evil thoughts. Keep your mouth full of songs, and you will often keep your heart full of praises; keep on singing as long as you can; you will find it is a good method of driving away your fears.

²⁶ Sing in the night, again, because *God loves to hear his people sing in the night*. At no time does God love his children's singing so well as when they give a serenade of praise under his window, when he has hidden his face from them, and will not appear to them at all. They are all in darkness; but they come under his window, and they begin to sing there. "Ah!" says God, "that is true faith, that can make them sing praises when I will not look at them; I know there is some faith in them, that makes them lift up their hearts, even when I seem to take away all my tender mercies and all my compassions." Sing, Christian, for singing pleases God. In heaven we read, the angels are employed in singing: do you be employed in the same way; for by no better means can you gratify the Almighty One of Israel, who stoops from his high throne to observe the poor creature of a day.

²⁷ Sing, again, for another reason: *because it will cheer your companions*.

124

If any of them are in the valley and in the darkness with you, it will be a great help to comfort them. John Bunyan tells us that as Christian was going through the valley he found it a dreadful dark place, and terrible demons and goblins were all about him, and poor Christian thought he must perish for certain; but just when his doubts were the strongest, he heard a sweet voice; he listened to it, and he heard a man in front of him saying, "Yea, when I pass through the valley of the shadow of death, I will fear no evil." Now, that man did not know who was near him, but he was unwittingly singing to cheer a man behind. Christian, when you are in trouble, sing; you do not know who is near you. Sing! perhaps you will get a good companion by it. Sing! perhaps there will be many a heart cheered by your song. There is some broken spirit, it may be, that will be bound up by your sonnets. Sing! There is some poor distressed brother, perhaps, shut up in the Castle of Despair, who, like King Richard, will hear your song inside the walls, and sing to you again, and you may be the means of getting him a ransom. Sing, Christian, wherever you go; try, if you can, to wash your face every morning in a bath of praise. When you go down from your chamber, never go to look on men till you have first looked on your God; and when you have looked on him, seek to come down with a face beaming with joy; carry a smile, for you will cheer up many a poor way-worn pilgrim by it. And when thou fastest, Christian—when thou hast an aching heart, do not appear to men to fast; appear cheerful and happy; anoint thy head, and wash thy face; be happy for thy brother's sake; it will tend to cheer him up, and help him through the valley.

[28] One more reason; and I know it will be a good one for you. Try and sing in the night, Christian, *for that is one of the best arguments* in all the world in favor of your religion. Our divines, now-a-days, spend a great deal of time in trying to prove Christianity against those who disbelieve it. I should like to have seen Paul trying that! Elymas the sorcerer withstood him: how did our friend Paul treat him? He said "O, full of all subtlety and all mischief, thou child of the devil, thou enemy of all righteousness, wilt thou not cease to pervert the right ways of the Lord?" That is about the politeness such men ought to have who deny God's truth. We start with this assumption: we will prove that the Bible is God's word, but we are not going to prove God's word. If you do not like to believe it, we will shake hands, and bid you good-by; we will not argue with you. The gospel has gained little by discussion. The greatest piece of folly on earth has been to send a man round the country, to follow another up who has been lecturing on infidelity just to make himself notorious.

[29] Why, let them lecture on; this is a free country; why should we follow them about? The truth will win the day. Christianity need not wish for controversy; it is strong enough for it, if it wishes it; but that is not God's way. God's direction is, "Preach, teach, dogmatize." Do not stand disputing; claim a divine mission; tell men that God says it, and there leave it. Say to them, "He that believeth shall be saved, and he that believeth not shall be damned;" and when you have done that, you have done enough. For what

reason should our missionaries stand disputing with Brahmins? Why should they be wasting their time by attempting to refute first this dogma, and then another, of heathenism? Why not just go and say, "The God whom ye ignorantly worship, I declare unto you; believe me, and you will be saved; believe me not, and the Bible says you are lost." And then, having thus asserted God's word, say, "I leave it; I declare it unto you; it is a thing for you to believe, not a thing for you to reason about." Religion is not a thing merely for your intellect; a thing to prove your own talent upon, by making a syllogism on it; it is a thing that demands your faith. As a messenger of heaven, I demand that faith; if you do not choose to give it, on your own head be the doom, if there be such; if there be not, you are prepared to risk it. But I have done my duty; I have told you the truth; that is enough, and there I leave it. O, Christian, instead of disputing, let me tell thee how to prove your religion. Live it out! live it out! Give the external as well as the internal evidence; give the external evidence of your own life. You are sick; there is your neighbor, who laughs at religion; let him come into your house. When he was sick, he said, "O, send for the doctor;" and there he was fretting, and fuming, and whining, and making all manner of noises. When you are sick, send for him; tell him that you are resigned to the Lord's will; that you will kiss the chastening rod; that you will take the cup, and drink it, because your Father gives it. You need not make a boast of this, or it will lose all its power; but do it because you can not help doing it. Your neighbor will say, "There is something in that." And when you come to the borders of the grave—he was there once, and you heard how he shrieked, and how frightened he was—give him your hand, and say to him, "Ah! I have a Christ that will do to die by; I have a religion that will make me sing in the night." Let him hear how you can sing, "Victory, victory, victory!" through him that loved you. I tell you, we may preach fifty thousand sermons to prove the gospel, but we shall not prove it half so well as you will through singing in the night. Keep a cheerful frame; keep a happy heart; keep a contented spirit; keep your eye up; and your heart aloft, and you will prove Christianity better than all the Butlers, and all the wise men that ever lived. Give them the analogy of a holy life, and then you will prove religion to them; give them the evidence of internal piety, developed externally, and you will give the best possible proof of Christianity. Try and sing songs in the night; for they are so rare, that if thou canst sing them, thou wilt honor thy God.

[30] I have been preaching all this while to the children of God, and now there is a sad turn that this subject must take, just one moment or so, and then we have done. There is a night coming, in which there will be no songs of joy—a night in which no one will even attempt to lead a chorus. There is a night coming when a song shall be sung, of which misery shall be the subject, set to the music of wailing and gnashing of teeth; there is a night coming when woe, unutterable woe, shall be the matter of an awful terrible *miserere*—when the orchestra shall be composed of damned men,

and howling fiends, and yelling demons; and mark you, I speak what I do know, and testify the Scriptures. There is a night coming for a poor soul within this house tonight; and unless he repent, it will be a night wherein he will have to growl, and howl, and sigh, and cry, and moan and groan forever. "Who is that?" sayest thou. Thyself, my friend, if thou art godless and Christless. "What!" sayest thou, "am I in danger of hell-fire?" In danger, my friend! Ay, more: thou art damned already. So saith the Bible. Sayest thou, "And can you leave me without telling me what I must do to be saved? Can you believe that I am in danger of perishing, and not speak to me?" I trust not; I hope I shall never preach a sermon without speaking to the ungodly, for O! how I love them. Swearer, your mouth is black with oaths now; and if you die, you must go on blaspheming throughout eternity. But list to me, blasphemer! Dost thou repent tonight? Dost thou feel thyself to have sinned against God? Dost thou feel a desire to be saved? List thee! thou mayest be saved; thou mayest be saved as much as any one that is now here. There is another: she has sinned against God enormously, and she blushes even now, while I mention her case. Dost thou repent of thy sin? There is hope for thee. Remember him who said, "Go, and sin no more." Drunkard! but a little while ago thou wast reeling down the street, and now thou repentest. Drunkard! there is hope for thee." "Well," sayest thou, "what shall I do to be saved?" Then again let me tell thee the old way of salvation. It is, "Believe in the Lord Jesus Christ, and thou art saved." We can get no further than that, do what we will; this is the sum and substance of the gospel. Believe in the Lord Jesus Christ, and be baptized, and thou shalt be saved. So saith the Scripture. Dost thou ask, "What is it to believe?" Am I to tell thee again? I can not tell thee, except that it is to look at Christ. Dost thou see that Saviour there? He is hanging on the cross; there are his dear hands, pierced with nails, nailed to a tree, as if they were waiting for the tardy footsteps, because thou wouldst not come. Dost thou see his dear head there? It is hanging on his breast, as if he would lean over, and kiss thy poor soul. Dost thou see his blood, gushing from his head, his hands, his feet, his side? It is running after thee; because he well knew that thou wouldst never run after it. Sinner! to be saved, all that thou hast to do is to look at that Man. Canst thou do it now? "No," sayest thou, "I do not believe it will save me." Ah! my poor friend, try it; and if thou dost not succeed, when thou hast tried it, I am bondsman for my Lord—here, take me, bind me, and I will suffer thy doom for thee. This I will venture to say: if thou castest thyself on Christ, and he deserteth thee, I will be willing to go halves with thee in all thy misery and woe. For he will never do it: never, never, never!

> No sinner was ever
> Empty sent back,
> Who came seeking mercy
> For Jesus' sake.

I beseech thee, therefore, try him, and thou shalt not try him in vain, but shalt find him "able to save to the uttermost them that come unto God by him." Thou shalt be saved now, and saved forever.

May God give you his blessing! I can not preach as earnestly as I could wish; but, nevertheless, may God accept these words, and send them home to some hearts this night! and may you, my dear brethren and sisters, have songs in the night!

PHILLIPS BROOKS   SERMON **13**

The Fire and the Calf

*So they gave it me: then I cast it into the fire, and there
came out this calf.*   —Exod. 32:24

I N THE story from which these words are taken we see Moses go up into
the mountain to hold communion with God. While he is gone the Israelites begin to murmur and complain. They want other gods, gods of their own.
Aaron, the brother of Moses, was their priest. He yielded to the people, and
when they brought him their golden earrings he made out of them a golden
calf for them to worship. When Moses came down from the mountain he
found the people deep in their idolatry. He was indignant. First he destroyed
the idol, "He burnt it in the fire, and ground it to powder, and strawed it
upon the water, and made the children of Israel drink of it." Then he turned
to Aaron: "What did this people unto thee that thou hast brought so great
sin upon them?" And Aaron meanly answered: "Let not the anger of my
Lord wax hot: thou knowest the people, that they are set on mischief. For
they said unto me, Make us gods which shall go before us . . . And I said
unto them, Whosoever hath any gold, let them break it off. So they gave
it me: then I cast it into the fire, and there came out this calf." That was
his mean reply. The real story of what happened had been written earlier
in the chapter. When the people brought Aaron their golden earrings "he
received them at their hand, and fashioned it with a graving tool, after he
had made it a molten calf: and they said, These be thy gods, O Israel, which
brought thee up out of the land of Egypt." That was what really happened,
and this is the description which Aaron gave of it to Moses: "So they gave
it me: then I cast it into the fire, and there came out this calf."

2 Aaron was frightened at what he had done. He was afraid of the act itself, and of what Moses would say. Like all timid men, he trembled before
the storm which he had raised. And so he tried to persuade Moses, and perhaps in some degree even to persuade himself, that it was not he that had done
this thing. He lays the blame upon the furnace. "The fire did it," he declares.
He will not blankly face his sin, and yet he will not tell a lie in words. He
tells what is literally true. He had cast the earrings into the fire, and this
calf had come out. But he leaves out the one important point, his own personal agency in it all; the fact that he had moulded the earrings into the calf's

---

From *Sermons Preached in English Churches* (New York: E. P. Dutton & Co., 1883).

shape, and that he had taken it out and set it on its pedestal for the people to adore. He tells it so that it shall all look automatic. It is a curious, ingenious, but transparent lie.

[3] Let us look at Aaron's speech a little while this morning and see what it represents, for it does represent something. There never was a speech more true to our human nature. We are all ready to lay the blame upon the furnaces. "The fire did it," we are all of us ready to say. Here is a man all gross and sensual, a man still young, who has lost the freshness and the glory and the purity of youth. He is profane; he is cruel; he is licentious; all his brightness has grown lurid; all his wit is ribaldry. You know the man. As far as a man can be, he is a brute. Suppose you question him about his life. You expect him to be ashamed, repentant. There is not a sign of anything like that! He says, "I am the victim of circumstances. What a corrupt, licentious, profane age is this in which we live! When I was in college I got into a bad set. When I went into business I was surrounded by bad influences. When I grew rich, men flattered me. When I grew poor, men bullied me. The world has made me what I am, this fiery, passionate, wicked world. I had in my hands the gold of my boyhood which God gave me. Then I cast it into the fire, and there came out this calf." So the poor wronged miserable creature looks into your face with his bleared eyes and asks your pity. Another man is not a profligate, but a miser, or a mere business machine. "What can you ask of me?" he says. "This is a mercantile community. The business man who does not attend to his business goes to the wall. I am what this intense commercial life has made me. I put my life in there, and it came out this." And he gazes fondly at his golden calf and his knees bend under him with the old habit of worshipping it, and he loves it still, even while he abuses and disowns it. And so with the woman of society. "The fire made me this," she says of her frivolity and pride. And so of the politician and his selfishness and partisanship. "I put my principles into the furnace and this came out." And so of the bigot and his bigotry, the one-sided conservative with his stubborn resistance to all progress, the one-sided radical with his ruthless iconoclasm. So of all partial and fanatical men. "The furnace made us," they are ready to declare. "These things compel us to be this. In better times we might have been better, broader men; but, now behold, God put us into the fire, and we came out this." It is what one is perpetually hearing about disbelief. "The times have made me sceptical. How is it possible for a man to live in days like these and yet believe in God and Jesus and the Resurrection? You ask me how I, who was brought up in the faith and in the Church, became a disbeliever. "Oh, you remember that I lived five years here," or "three years there." "You know I have been very much thrown with this set or with that. You know the temper of our town. I cast myself into the fire, and I came out this." One is all ready to understand, my friends, how the true soul, struggling for truth, seems often to be worsted in the struggle. One is ready to have tolerance, respect, and hope for any man who, reaching after God, is awed by God's immensity and his own littleness, and falls back crushed and doubtful. His is a doubt which is born in the secret chambers of

his own personal conscientiousness. It is independent of his circumstances and surroundings. The soul which has truly come to a personal doubt finds it hard to conceive of any ages of the most implicit faith in which it could have lived in which that doubt would not have been in it. It faces its doubt in a solitude where there is none but it and God. All that one understands, and the more he understands it the more unintelligible does it seem to him, that any earnest soul can really lay its doubt upon the age, the set, or the society it lives in. No; our age, our society is what, with this figure taken out of the old story of Exodus, we have been calling it. It is the furnace. Its fire can set and fix and fasten what the man puts into it. But, properly speaking, it can create no character. It can make no truly faithful soul a doubter. It never did. It never can.

⁴ Remember that the subtlety and attractiveness of this excuse, this plausible attributing of power to inanimate things and exterior conditions to create what only man can make, extends not only to the results which we see coming forth in ourselves; it covers also the fortunes of those for whom we are responsible. The father says of his profligate son whom he has never done one wise or vigorous thing to make a noble and pure-minded man: "I cannot tell how it has come. It has not been my fault. I put him into the world and this came out." The father whose faith has been mean and selfish says the same of his boy who is a sceptic. Everywhere there is this cowardly casting off of responsibilities upon the dead circumstances around us. It is a very hard treatment of the poor, dumb, helpless world which cannot answer to defend itself. It takes us as we give ourselves to it. It is our minister fulfilling our commissions for us upon our own souls. If we say to it, "Make us noble," it does make us noble. If we say to it, "Make us mean," it does make us mean. And then we take the nobility and say, "Behold, how noble I have made myself." And we take the meanness and say, "See how mean the world has made me."

⁵ You see, I am sure, how perpetual a thing the temper of Aaron is, how his excuse is heard everywhere and always. I need not multiply illustrations. But now, if all the world is full of it, the next question is, What does it mean? Is it mere pure deception, or is there also delusion, self-deception in it? Take Aaron's case. Was he simply telling a lie to Moses and trying to hide the truth from his brother whom he dreaded, when he said, "I cast the earrings into the fire, and this calf came out"? Or was he in some dim degree, in some half-conscious way, deceiving himself? Was he allowing himself to attribute some power to the furnace in the making of the calf? Perhaps as we read the verse above in which it is so distinctly said that Aaron fashioned the idol with a graving tool, any such supposition seems incredible. But yet I cannot but think that some degree, however dim, of such self-deception was in Aaron's heart. The fire was mysterious. He was a priest. Who could say that some strange creative power had not been at work in the heart of the furnace which had done for him what he seemed to do for himself. There was a human heart under that ancient ephod, and it is hard to think that Aaron did not succeed in bringing himself to be somewhat imposed upon by his own

131

words, and hiding his responsibility in the heart of the hot furnace. But however it may have been with Aaron, there can be no doubt that in almost all cases this is so. Very rarely indeed does a man excuse himself to other men and yet remain absolutely unexcused in his own eyes. When Pilate stands washing the responsibility of Christ's murder from his hands before the people, was he not feeling himself as if his hands grew cleaner while he washed? When Shakespeare paints Macbeth with the guilty ambition which was to be his ruin first rising in his heart, you remember how he makes him hide his new-born purpose to be king even from himself, and pretend that he is willing to accept the kingdom only if it shall come to him out of the working of things, for which he is not responsible, without an effort of his own.

> If chance will have me king, why, chance may crown me,
> Without my stir.

That was the first stage of the growing crime which finally was murder. Often it takes this form. Often the very way to help ourselves most to a result which we have set before ourselves is just to put ourselves into a current which is sweeping on that way, and then lie still and let the current do the rest; and in all such cases it is so easy to ignore or to forget the first step, which was that we chose that current for our resting place, and so to say that it is only the drift of the current which is to blame for the dreary shore on which at last our lives are cast up by the stream. Suppose you are today a scornful man, a man case-hardened in conceit and full of disbelief in anything generous or supernatural, destitute of all enthusiasm, contemptuous, supercilious. You say the time you live in has made you so. You point to one large tendency in the community which always sets that way. You parade the specimens of enthusiastic people whom you have known who have been fanatical and silly. You tell me what your favorite journal has been saying in your ears every week for years. You bid me catch the tone of the brightest people whom you live among, and then you turn to me and say, "How could one live in such an atmosphere and not grow cynical? Behold, my times have made me what I am." What does that mean? Are you merely trying to hide from me, or are you also hiding from yourself, the certain fact that you have chosen that special current to launch your boat upon, that you have given your whole attention to certain kinds of facts and shut your eyes to certain others, that you have constantly valued the brightness which went to the depreciation of humanity and despised the urgency with which a healthier spirit has argued for the good in man and for his everlasting hope? Is it not evident that you yourself have been able to half forget all this, and so when the stream on which you launched your boat at last drives it upon the beach to which it has been flowing all the time, there is a certain lurking genuineness in the innocent surprise with which you look around upon the desolate shore on which you land, and say to yourself, "How unhappy I am that I should have fallen upon these evil days, in which it is impossible that a man should genuinely respect or love his fellowmen"?

⁶ For there are currents flowing always in all bad directions. There is a perpetual river flowing towards sensuality and vice. There is a river flowing perpetually towards hypocrisy and religious pretence. There is a river always running towards skepticism and infidelity. And when you once have given yourself up to either of these rivers, then there is quite enough in the continual pressure, in that great movement like a fate beneath your keel, to make you lose the sense and remembrance that it is by your own will that you are there, and only think of the resistless flow of the river which is always in your eyes and ears. This is the mysterious, bewildering mixture of the consciousness of guilt and the consciousness of misery in all our sin. We live in a perpetual confusion of self-pity and self-blame. We go up to the scaffolds where we are to suffer, half like culprits crawling to the gallows and half like martyrs proudly striding to their stakes. When we think of what sort of reception is to meet us in the other world as the sum and judgment of the life we have been living here, we find ourselves ready, according to the moment's mood, either for the bitterest denunciation, as of souls who have lived in deliberate sin; or for tender petting and refreshment, as of souls who have been buffeted and knocked about by all the storms of time, and for whom now there ought to be soft beds in eternity. The confusion of men's minds about the judgments of the eternal world is only the echo of their confusion about the responsibilities of the life which they are living now.

⁷ Suppose there is a man here this morning who committed a fraud in business yesterday. He did it in a hurry. He did not stop to think about it then. But now, in this quiet church, with everything calm and peaceful round him, with the words of prayer which have taken God for granted sinking into his ears, he has been thinking it over. How does it look to him? Is he not certainly sitting in the mixture of self-pity and self-reproach of which I spoke? He did the sin, and he is sorry as a sinner. The sin did itself, and he is sorry as a victim. Nay, perhaps in the next pew to him, or perhaps in the same pew, or perhaps in the same body, there is sitting a man who means to do a fraud tomorrow. In him too is there not the same confusion? One moment he looks it right in the face, and says, "Tomorrow night I shall despise myself." The next moment he is quietly thinking that the sin will do itself and give him all its advantage, and he need not interfere. "If chance will make me cheat, why chance may crown me, without my stir." Both thoughts are in his mind, and if he has listened to our service, it is likely enough that he has found something in it—even in the words of the Bible— for each thought to feed upon.

⁸ I own this freely, and yet I do believe, and I call you to bear me witness, that such self-deception almost never is absolutely complete. We feel its incompleteness the moment that anyone else attempts to excuse us with the same excuse with which we have excused ourselves. Suppose that some one of the Israelites who stood by had spoken up in Aaron's behalf and said to Moses: "Oh, he did not do it. It was not his act. He only cast the gold into the fire, and there came out this calf." Must not Aaron as he listened have felt the wretchedness of such a telling of the story, and been ashamed, and

133

even cried out and claimed his responsibility and his sin? Very often it is good for us to imagine someone saying aloud in our behalf what we are silently saying to ourselves in self-apology. We see its thinness when another hand holds it up against the sun, and we stand off and look at it. If I might turn again to Shakespeare and his wonderful treasury of human character, there is a scene in Hamlet which exactly illustrates what I mean. The king has determined that Hamlet must die, and is just sending him off upon the voyage from which he means that he is never to return. And the king has fully explained the act of his own conscience, and accepted the crime as a necessity. And then he meets the courtiers, Rosencrantz and Guildenstern, who are to have the execution of the base commission. And they, like courtiers, try to repeat to the king the arguments with which he has convinced himself. One says—

> Most holy and religious fear it is
> To keep those many many bodies safe
> That live and feed upon your majesty.

And the other takes up the strain and says—

> The single and peculiar life is bound,
> With all the strength and armour of the mind,
> To keep itself from 'noyance; but much more
> That spirit upon whose weal depend and rest
> The lives of many.

They are the king's own arguments. With them he has persuaded his own soul to tolerate the murder. But when they come to him from these other lips, he will none of them. He cuts them short. He cannot hear from others what he has said over and over to himself.

> Arm you, I pray you, to this speedy voyage.

So he cries out and interrupts them. Let the deed be done, but let not these echoes of his self-excuse parade before him the way in which he is trifling with his own soul.

So it is always. I think of the mysterious judgment-day, and sometimes it appears to me as if our souls would need no more than merely that voices outside ourselves should utter in our ears the very selfsame pleas and apologies with which we, here upon the earth, have extenuated our own wickedness. They of themselves, heard in the open air of eternity, would let us see how weak they were, and so we should be judged. Is not that partly the reason why we hate the scene of some old sin? The room in which we did it seems to ring forever with the sophistries by which we persuaded ourselves that it was right, and will not let us live in comfortable delusion. Our life there is an anticipated judgment day.

[9] I doubt not that this tendency to self-deception and apology with refer-

ence to the sins which they commit differs exceedingly with different men. Men differ, perhaps, nowhere else more than in their disposition to face the acts of their lives and to recognize their own personal part and responsibility for the things they do. Look, for instance, at this Aaron and his brother Moses. The two men are characterized by their own sins. The sin of Aaron was a denial or concealment of his own personal agency: "I cast it into the fire, and there came out this calf." The sin of Moses, you remember, was just the opposite. As he stood with his thirsty people in front of the rock of Horeb, he intruded his personal agency where it had no right. "Hear now, ye rebels; must we fetch water out of this rock?" To be sure, in the case of Moses it was a good act of mercy to which he put in his claim, while in Aaron's case it was a wicked act whose responsibility he desired to avoid. And men are always ready to claim the good deeds in which they have the slightest share, even when they try to disown the sins which are entirely their own. But still the actions seem to mark the men. Moses is the franker, manlier, braver man. In Aaron the priest there is something of that over-subtle, artificial, complicated character, that power of being morally confused even in the midst of pious feeling, that lack of simplicity, and of the disposition to look things frankly in the eye; in a word, that vague and defective sense of personality and its responsibilities which has often in the history of religion made the very name of priestcraft a reproach. Moses is the prophet. His distinct mission is the utterance of truth. He is always simple; never more simple than when he is most profound; never more sure of the fundamental principles of right and wrong, of honesty and truth, than when he is deepest in the mystery of God; never more conscious of himself and his responsibilities than when he is most conscious of God and His power.

10 And this brings me to my last point, which I must not longer delay to reach. If the world is thus full of the Aaron spirit, of the disposition to throw the blame of wrong-doing upon other things and other people, to represent to others, and to our own souls, that our sins do themselves, what is the spiritual source of such a tendency, and where are we to look to find its cure? I have just intimated what seems to me to be its source. It is a vague and defective sense of personality. Anything which makes less clear to a man the fact that he, standing here on his few inches of the earth, is a distinct separate being, in whom is lodged a unit of life, with his own soul, his own character, his own chances, his own responsibilities, distinct and separate from any other man's in all the world; anything that makes all that less clear demoralizes a man, and opens the door to endless self-excuses. And you know, surely, how many tendencies there are today which are doing just that for men. Every man's personality, in his clear sense of himself, seems to be standing where almost all the live forces of the time are making their attacks upon it. It is like a tree in the open field from which every bird carries away some fruit. The enlargement of our knowledge of the world, the growing tendency of men to work in large companies, the increased despotism of social life, the interesting studies of hereditation, the externality of a large part of our action, the rush and competition for the prizes which

135

represent the most material sort of success, the spread of knowledge by which at once all men are seen to know much, and, at the same time, no man is seen to know everything; all these causes enfeeble the sense of personality. The very prominence of the truth of a universal humanity, in which our philanthropy justly glories, obscures the clearness of the individual human life. Once it was hard to conceive of man, because the personalities of men were so distinct. Once people found it hard, as the old saying was, to see the forest for the trees. Now it is the opposite. To hundreds of people it is almost impossible to see the trees for the forest. Man is so clear that men become obscure. As the Laureate of the century sings of the time which he so well knows: "The individual withers and the race is more and more." These are the special causes, working in our time, of that which has its general causes in our human nature working everywhere and always.

11 And if this is the trouble, where, then, is the help? If this is the disease, where is the cure? I cannot look for it anywhere short of that great assertion of the human personality which is made when a man personally enters into the power of Jesus Christ. Think of it! Here is some Aaron of our modern life trying to cover up some sin which he has done. The fact of the sin is clear enough. It stands out wholly undisputed. It is not by denying that the thing was done but by beclouding the fact that he did it with his own hands, with his own will; thus it is that the man would cover up his sin. He has been nothing but an agent, nothing but a victim; so he assures his fellowmen, so he assures himself. And now suppose that while he is doing that, the great change comes to that man by which he is made a disciple and servant of Jesus Christ. It becomes known to him as a certain fact that God loves him individually, and is educating him with a separate personal education which is all his own. The clear individuality of Jesus stands distinctly out and says to him, "Follow me!" Jesus stops in front of where he is working just as evidently as He stopped in front of the booth where Matthew was sitting collecting taxes, and says, "Follow me." He is called separately, and separately he does give himself to Christ. Remember all that is essential to a Christian faith. You cannot blur it all into indistinctness and generality. In the true light of the redeeming Incarnation, every man in the multitude stands out as every blade of grass on the hillside stands distinct from every other when the sun has risen. In this sense, as in many another, this is the true light which lighteneth every man that cometh into the world.

12 The Bible calls it a new birth, and in that name too there are many meanings. And among other meanings in it must there not be this—the separateness and personality of every soul in Christ? Birth is the moment of distinctness. The meanest child in the poorest hovel of the city, who by and by is to be lost in the great whirlpool of human life, here at the outset where his being comes, a new fact, into the crowded world, is felt in his distinctness, has his own personal tending, excites his own personal emotion. When he is born and when he dies, but perhaps most of all when he is born, the commonest, the most commonplace and undistinguished of mankind asserts the fact of privilege of his separateness. And so when the possession

136

of the soul by Christ is called the "New Birth," one of the meanings of that name is this, that then there is a reassertion of personality, and the soul which had lost itself in the slavery of the multitude finds itself again in the obedience of Christ.

¹³ And now what will be the attitude of this man, with his newly-awakened selfhood, towards that sin which he has been telling himself that his hands did, but that he did not do? May he not almost say that he will need that sin for his self-identification? Who is he? A being whom Christ has forgiven, and then in virtue of that forgiveness made His servant. All his new life dates from and begins with his sin. He cannot afford to find his consciousness of himself only in the noble parts of his life, which it makes him proud and happy to remember. There is not enough of that to make for him a complete and continuous personality. It will have great gaps if he disowns the wicked demonstrations of his selfhood and says, "It was not I," wherever he has done wrong. No! Out of his sin, out of the bad, base, cowardly acts which are truly his, out of the weak and wretched passages of his life which it makes him ashamed to remember, but which he forces himself to recollect and own, out of these he gathers the consciousness of a self all astray with self-will, which he then brings to Christ and offers in submission and obedience to His perfect will.

¹⁴ You try to tell some soul rejoicing in the Lord's salvation that the sins over whose forgiveness by its Lord it is gratefully rejoicing, were not truly its; and see what strange thing comes. The soul seems to draw back from your assurance as if, if it were true, it would be robbed of all its surest confidence and brightest hope. You meant to comfort the poor penitent, and he looks into your face as if you were striking him a blow. And you can see what such a strange sight means. It is not that the poor creature loves those sins or is glad that he did them, or dreams for an instant of ever doing them again. It is only that through those sins, which are all the real experience he has had, he has found himself, and finding himself has found his Saviour and the new life.

¹⁵ So the only hope for any of us is in a perfectly honest manliness to claim our sins. "I did it! I did it," let me say of all my wickedness. Let me refuse to listen for one moment to any voice which would make my sins less mine. It is the only honest and the only hopeful way, the only way to know and be ourselves. When we have done that, then we are ready for the Gospel, ready for all that Christ wants to show us that we may become, and for all the powerful grace by which He wants to make us be it perfectly.

What Think Ye of Christ?

*Saying, What think ye of Christ? whose son is he? They
say unto him, The Son of David.*   —Matt. 22:42

I suppose there is no one here who has not thought more or less about
Christ. You have heard about Him, and read about Him, and heard
men preach about Him. For eighteen hundred years men have been talking
about Him and thinking about Him; and some have their minds made up
about who He is, and doubtless some have not. And although all these years
have rolled away, this question comes up, addressed to each of us today,
"What think ye of Christ?"

² I do not know why it should not be a proper question for one man to put
to another. If I were to ask you what you think of any of your prominent
men, you would already have your mind made up about him. If I were to ask
you what you think of our President, you would speak right out, and tell me
your opinion in a minute. If I were to ask about your governor, you would
tell me freely what you had for or against him. And why should not people
make up their minds about the Lord Jesus Christ, and take their stand for or
against Him? If you think well of Him, why not speak well of Him, and range
yourselves on His side? And if you think ill of Him, and believe Him to be an
impostor, and that He did not die to save the world, why not lift up your
voice, and say that you are against Him? It would be a happy day for
Christianity if men would just take sides—if we could know positively who
was really for Him, and who was against Him.

³ It is of very little importance what the world thinks of any one else.
All the great ones, all the noble people of this world, must soon be gone. Yes;
it matters little comparatively what we think of them. Their lives can only
interest a few; but every living soul on the face of the earth is concerned with
this Man. The question for the world is, "What think ye of Christ?" I do not
ask you what you think of the Episcopal Church, or of the Presbyterians, or
the Baptists, or the Roman Catholics; I do not ask you what you think of this
minister or that, of this doctrine or that; but I want to ask you what you
think of the living person of Christ.

⁴ I should like to ask, Was He really the Son of God—the great God-man?
Did He leave heaven and come down to this world for a purpose? Was it

From *Twelve Select Sermons* (Chicago: F. H. Revell, 1880).

really to seek and to save? I should like to begin with the manger, and follow Him up through the thirty-three years He was here upon earth. I should ask you what you think of His coming into this world, and being born in a manger when it might have been a palace; why He left the grandeur and the glory of heaven, and the royal retinue of angels; why He passed by palaces and crowns and dominion, and came down here alone?

⁵ I should like to ask you what you think of Him as a *teacher?* He spake as never man spake. I should like to take Him up as a preacher. I should like to bring you to that mountain side, that we might listen to the words as they fall from His gentle lips. Talk about the preachers of the present day! I would rather a thousand times be five minutes at the feet of Christ, than listen a lifetime to all the wise men in the world. He used just to hang truth upon anything. Yonder is a sower, a fox, a bird, and He just gathers the truth round them, so that you cannot see a fox, a sower, or a bird, without thinking what Jesus said. Yonder is a lily of the valley, you cannot see it without thinking of His words, "They toil not, neither do they spin." He makes the little sparrow chirping in the air preach to us. How fresh these wonderful sermons are, how they live to-day! How we love to tell them to our children, how the children love to hear! "Tell me a story about Jesus," how often we hear it; how the little ones love His sermons! No story-book in the world will ever interest them like the stories that He told. And yet how profound He was; how He puzzled the wise men; how the scribes and the Pharisees could never fathom Him. Oh, do you not think He was a wonderful Preacher?

⁶ I should like to ask what you think of Him as a *physician.* A man would soon have a reputation as a doctor if he could cure as Christ did. No case was ever brought to Him but what He was a match for. He had but to speak the word, and the disease fled before Him. Here comes a man covered with leprosy. "Lord, if Thou wilt Thou canst make me clean," he cries. "I will," says the Great Physician, and in an instant the leprosy is over. The world has hospitals for incurable diseases; but there were no incurable diseases with Him.

⁷ Now see Him in the little home at Bethany, binding up the wounded hearts of Martha and Mary, and tell me what you think of Him as a *Comforter.* He is a husband to the widow and a father to the fatherless. The weary find a resting place upon that breast, and the friendless may reckon Him their friend. He never varies, He never fails, He never dies. His sympathy is ever fresh. His love is ever free. O widow and orphans, O sorrowing and mourning, will you not thank God for Christ the Comforter?

⁸ But these are not the points I wish to take up. Let us go to those who knew Christ, and ask what they thought of Him. If you want to find out what a man is nowadays, you inquire about him from those who know him best. I do not wish to be partial; we will go to His enemies, and to His friends. We will ask them, What think ye of Christ? We will ask his friends and his enemies. If we went only to those who liked Him, you would say, "Oh, he is so blind; he thinks so much of the man that he can't see his faults. You

can't get any thing out of him, unless it be in his favor; it is a one-sided affair." So we shall go in the first place to His enemies, to those who hated Him, persecuted Him, cursed and slew Him. I shall put you in the jury-box, and call upon them to tell us what they think of Him.

⁹ First, among the witnesses, let us call upon the Pharisees. We know how they hated Him. Let us put a few questions to them. Come, Pharisees, tell us what you have against the Son of God. What do *you* think of Christ? Hear what they say: *This man receiveth sinners*. What an argument to bring against Him! Why, it is the very thing that makes us love Him. It is the glory of the Gospel. He receives sinners. If He had not, what would become of *us?* Have you nothing more to bring against Him than *this?* Why, it is one of the greatest compliments that was ever paid Him. Once more, when He was hanging on the tree, you had this to say of Him: "He saved others; Himself He cannot save." And so He did save others, but He could not save others and save us too. So He laid down His own life for yours and mine. Yes, Pharisees, you have told the truth for once in your lives. *He saved others*. He died for others. He was a ransom for many; so it is quite true what you think of Him: *He saved others; Himself He cannot save.*

¹⁰ Now let us call upon Caiaphas. Let him stand up here in his flowing robes; let us ask him for his evidence. "Caiaphas, you were chief priest when Christ was tried; you were president of the Sanhedrin; you were in the council-chamber when you found Him guilty; you yourself condemned Him. Tell us, what did the witnesses say? On what grounds did you judge Him? What testimony was brought against Him?"

¹¹ "He hath spoken blasphemy," says Caiaphas. "He said, 'Hereafter shall ye see the Son of Man sitting on the right hand of power, and coming in the clouds of heaven.' When I heard that, I found him guilty of blasphemy; I rent my mantle, and condemned Him to death." Yes, all that they had against Him was that He was the Son of God; and they slew Him for the promise of His coming for His bride.

¹² Now let us summon Pilate. Let him enter the witness-box. "Pilate, this man was brought before you; you examined Him; you talked with Him face to face, *what think ye of Christ?*" "I find no fault in Him," says Pilate. "He said He was the King of the Jews" (just as he wrote it over the cross); "but I find no fault in Him." Such is the testimony of the man who examined Him! And as he stands there, the centre of the Jewish mob, there comes along a man, elbowing his way, in haste. He rushes up to Pilate and, thrusting out his hand, gives him a message. He tears it open; his face turns pale as he reads: "Have nothing to do with *this just man*, for I have suffered many things this day in a dream because of Him." It is from Pilate's wife—her testimony to Christ. You want to know what His enemies thought of Him? You want to know what a heathen thought? Well, here it is: "No fault in Him"; and the wife of a heathen, "this just man."

¹³ And now, look—in comes Judas. He ought to make a good witness. Let us address him. "Come, tell us, Judas, what think ye of Christ? You knew the Master well; you sold Him for thirty pieces of silver; you betrayed Him with

140

a kiss; you saw Him perform those miracles; you were with Him in Jerusalem. In Bethany, when He summoned up Lazarus, you were there. What think ye of Him?" I can see him as he comes into the presence of the chief priests; I can hear the money ring as he dashes it upon the table—*I have betrayed innocent blood.* Here is the man who betrayed Him, and this is what he thinks of Him! Yes, my friends, God has made every man who had anything to do with the death of His Son put his testimony on record that He was an innocent Man.

¹⁴ Let us take the Centurion, who was present at the execution. He had charge of the Roman soldiers. He had told them to make Him carry His cross; he had given orders for the nails to be driven into His feet and hands, for the spear to be thrust into his side. "Centurion, you had charge of the executioners; you saw that the order for His death was carried out; you saw Him die; you heard Him speak upon the cross. Tell us, *what think ye of Christ?*" Hark! look at him; he is smiting his breast as he cries: *Truly, this man was the Son of God!*

¹⁵ I might go to the thief upon the cross, and ask what he thought of Him. At first he railed upon Him and reviled Him. But then he thought better of it. "This man hath done nothing amiss," he says. I might go further. I might summon the very devils themselves and ask them for their testimony. Have they anything to say of Him? Why, the very devils called Him the Son of God. In Mark we have the unclean spirit crying, "Jesus, Thou Son of the most High God." Men say, "I believe Christ to be the Son of God, and because I believe it intellectually, I shall be saved." I tell you, the devils did that; they did more than that, *they trembled.*

¹⁶ Let us bring in His friends. Let us call that prince of preachers, John. Let us hear the forerunner, the wilderness preacher, John. Save the Master Himself, none ever preached like this man, this man who drew all Jerusalem and Judea into the wilderness to hear him. Let John the Baptist come with his leathern girdle and his hairy coat, and let him tell what he thinks of Christ. His words, though they were echoed in the wilderness of Palestine, are written in the Book forever: "Behold the Lamb of God which taketh away the sin of the world." This is what John the Baptist thought of Him. "I bear record that He is the Son of God." No wonder he drew all Jerusalem and Judea to him, because he preached Christ. And whenever men preach Christ, they are sure to have plenty of followers.

¹⁷ Let us bring in Peter, who was with Him on the mount of transfiguration, who was with Him the night He was betrayed. "Come, Peter, tell us what you think of Christ. Stand in this witness box and testify of Him. You denied Him once. You said with a curse you did not know Him. Was it true, Peter? Don't you know him?" "Know Him!" I can imagine Peter saying: "It was a lie I told them. I *did* know Him." Afterwards I can hear him charging home their guilt upon those Jerusalem sinners. He calls Him "both Lord and Christ." Such was the testimony on the day of Pentecost. "God hath made that same Jesus both Lord and Christ." And tradition tells us that when they came to execute Peter, he felt he was not worthy to die in the way his

141

Master had died, and he requested to be crucified with his head downwards. So much did Peter think of Him!

18 Now let us hear from the beloved disciple John. He knew more about Christ than any other man. He had laid his head on his Saviour's bosom. He had heard the throbbing of that loving heart. Look into his Gospel if you wish to see what he thought of Him.

19 Matthew writes of Him as the Royal King come from His throne. Mark writes of Him as the Servant, and Luke as the Son of Man. John takes up his pen and with one stroke forever settles the question of Unitarianism. He goes right back before the time of Adam: "In the beginning was the Word, and the Word was with God, and the Word was God." Look into Revelation. He calls Him "the bright and the morning Star." So John thought well of Him—because he knew Him well.

20 We might bring in Thomas, the doubting disciple. "You doubted Him, Thomas? You would not believe He had risen from the dead, and you put your fingers into the wound in His side. What do you think of Him? "My Lord and my God!" says Thomas.

21 Then go over to Decapolis and you will find that Christ has been there casting out devils. Let us call the men of that country and ask what they think of Him. *He hath done all things well*, they say.

22 But we have other witnesses to bring in. Take the persecutor Saul, once one of the worst of His enemies. Breathing out threatenings, he meets Him. "Saul, Saul, why persecutest thou Me?" says Christ; and He might have added, "What have I done to you? Have I injured you in any way? Did I not come to bless you? Why do you treat Me thus, Saul?" Then Saul asks, "Who art Thou, Lord?" "I am Jesus of Nazareth, whom thou persecutest." You see, He was not ashamed of His name; although He had been in heaven, "I am *Jesus of Nazareth*." What a change did that one interview make to Paul! A few years after we hear him say, "I have suffered the loss of all things, and do count them but dross that I may win Christ." Such a testimony to the Saviour!

23 But I shall go still further. I shall go away from earth into the other world. I shall summon the angels and ask what they think of Christ. They saw Him in the bosom of the Father before the world was. Before the dawn of creation; before the morning stars sang together, He was there. They saw Him leave the throne and come down to the manger. What a scene for them to witness. Ask those heavenly beings what they thought of Him then. For once they are permitted to speak; for once the silence of heaven is broken. Listen to their song on the plains of Bethlehem: "Behold I bring you good tidings of great joy which shall be to all people. For unto you is born this day, in the city of David, a Saviour, which is Christ the Lord." He leaves the throne to save the world. Is it a wonder the angels thought well of Him?

24 Then there are the redeemed saints; they that see Him face to face. Here on earth He was never known, no one seemed really to be acquainted with Him; but He was known in that world where He had been from the foundation. What do they think of Him there? If we could hear from

142

heaven we should hear a shout which would glorify and magnify His name. We are told that when John was in the Spirit on the Lord's-day, and being caught up, he heard a shout around him, ten thousand times ten thousand, and thousands and thousands of voices, "Worthy is the Lamb that was slain to receive power, and riches, and wisdom, and strength, and honour, and glory, and blessing!" Yes, He is worthy of all this. Heaven cannot speak too well of Him. Oh, that earth would take up the echo, and join with heaven in singing: "WORTHY to receive power, and riches, and wisdom, and strength, and honour, and glory, and blessing!"

25 But there is yet another witness, a higher still. Some think that the God of the Old Testament is the Christ of the New. But when Jesus came out of Jordan, baptized by John, there came a voice from heaven. God the Father spoke. It was His testimony to Christ: "This is my beloved Son, in whom I am well pleased." Ah, yes! God the Father thinks well of the Son. And if God is well pleased with Him, so ought we. If the sinner and God are well pleased with Christ, then the sinner and God can meet. The moment you say, as the Father said, "I am well pleased with Him," and accept Him, you are wedded to God. Will you not believe the testimony? Will you not believe this Witness, this last of all, the Lord of Hosts, the King of Kings Himself? Once more He repeats it, that all may know it. With Peter and James and John, on the mount of transfiguration, He cries out again, "This is My beloved Son; hear Him." And that voice went echoing and re-echoing through Palestine, through all the earth from sea to sea, yes, that voice is echoing still: *Hear Him! Hear Him!*

26 My friend, will you hear Him today? Hark, what is He saying to you? "Come unto Me, all ye that labor and are heavy laden, and I will give you rest. Take My yoke upon you and learn of Me; for I am meek and lowly in heart, and ye shall find rest unto your souls. For My yoke is easy and My burden is light." Will you not think well of such a Saviour? Will you not believe Him? Will you not trust in Him with all your heart and mind? Will you not live for Him? If He laid down His life for us, is it not the least we can do to lay down ours for Him? If He bore the Cross and died on it for me, ought I not be willing to take it up for Him? Oh, have we not reason to think well of Him? Do you think it is right and noble to lift up your voice against such a Saviour? Do you think it just to cry, "Crucify Him! crucify Him?" Oh, may God help all of us to glorify the Father, by thinking well of His only-begotten Son.

Heaven

FIRST, what do I want most of all? A man in Chicago said to me one day, "If I could have all I wanted of any one thing I would take money." He would be a fool, and so would you if you would make a similar choice. There are lots of things money can't do. Money can't buy life. Money can't buy health. I want to show you the absolute and utter futility of pinning your hope to a lot of fool things that will damn your soul to hell. There is only one way to escape:

2 "As Moses lifted up the serpent in the wilderness, even so must the Son of Man be lifted up, that whosoever believeth in Him should not perish but have everlasting life. For God so loved the world that He gave His only begotten Son, that whosoever believeth in Him should not perish, but have everlasting life."

3 You can't hire a substitute in religion. You can't do some deed of kindness or act of philanthropy and substitute that for the necessity of repentance and faith in Jesus Christ. Lots of people will acknowledge their sin in the world, struggle on without Jesus Christ, and do their best to lead honorable, upright lives. Your morality will make you a better man or woman, but it will never save your soul. Morality doesn't save anybody. Your culture doesn't save you. I don't care who you are or how good you are, if you reject Jesus Christ you are doomed.

4 God hasn't one plan of salvation for the millionaire and another for the hobo. He has the same plan for everybody. God isn't going to ask you whether you like it or not. He isn't going to ask your opinion of His plan. There it is and we'll have to take it as God gives it. Simply ridding your life of the weeds of sin and not planting Jesus Christ is of no more value to you than a piece of ground is to a farmer without seed in it. And yet that is exactly what multitudes of people are doing.

5 Dismiss the idea that God owes you salvation. He gives you the opportunity, and if you don't improve it you will go to hell. Get out of your head the idea that God owes you salvation. Some people think God is like a great big Bookkeeper in heaven, and that He has a lot of angels as assistants. Every time you do a good thing He writes it down on one page, and every time you do a bad deed He writes it down on the opposite page. When you die He draws a line and adds them up. If you have done more good things than bad, you go to heaven; more bad things than good, you go to hell.

From *Billy Sunday's Sermons in Omaha* (*Omaha Daily News*, 1915). By permission of Mrs. William A. Sunday, owner of the copyright.

6 You moral man, you may be just as well off as the Christian until death knocks you down. Then you are lost, because you trust in your morality. The Christian is saved because he trusts in Jesus Christ. Some people want to wash their sins, and they whitewash them, but God wants them white. There's a lot of difference between being whitewashed and being washed white. Not only does God promise you salvation on the ground that you repent and accept Jesus Christ. He offers you eternal life as a gift.

7 I stand here and tell you that God offers you salvation through repentance and faith in Jesus Christ, and that you must accept it or be lost. You will stand up and argue the question, as though your argument could change God's plan. You can never do that. Not only has God promised you salvation on the ground of your acceptance of Jesus Christ as your Saviour. He has promised to give you a home in which to spend eternity. Listen! "In my Father's house are many mansions. If it were not so I would have told you. I go to prepare a place for you."

8 Some people say heaven is a state or condition. I don't believe it. It might possibly be better to be in a heavenly state than in a heavenly place. It might be better to be in hell in a heavenly state than to be in heaven in a hellish state. That may be true. But heaven is as much a place as the home to which you are going when I dismiss this meeting. "I go to prepare a place for you."

9 Heaven will be free from everything that curses and damns this old world here. Wouldn't this be a grand old world if it weren't for a lot of things in it? The only thing that makes Omaha a decent place to live in is the religion of Jesus Christ. There isn't a man that would live in it if you took religion out.

10 There will be no sickness in heaven, no pain, no sin, no poverty, no want, no death, no grinding toil. There are many poor men and women that never have any rest. They have to get up early and work all day. But in heaven there remaineth a rest for the people of God. Weary women that start out early to your daily toil, you will not have to get out and toil all day. No toil in heaven, no sickness there!

11 Heaven, that is a place. He has gone to prepare it for those who do His will and keep His commandments and turn away from their sin. Isn't it great? Everything will be perfect in heaven. Down here we know only in part, but there we shall know even as we are known. It is a city that hath foundations.

12 Among the last declarations of Jesus is "In my Father's house are many mansions." What a comfort to the bereaved and afflicted! Not only has God provided salvation through faith in Jesus Christ as a gift of God's outstretched hand. He has also provided a home in which you can spend eternity.

13 Surely, friends of Omaha, from the beginning of the history of man, from the time Enoch walked with God and was not, until on the Isle of Patmos John saw let down by God out of heaven the new Jerusalem, surely we have ample proof that heaven is a place. Although we cannot see it with the natural eye, it is a place, the dwelling place of God and of the angels and of the redeemed through faith in the Son of God. He says, "I go to prepare a place for you." Oh, what a time we'll have in heaven!

[14] In heaven they never mar the hillsides with spades, for they dig no graves. In heaven they never get sick. In heaven no one carries handkerchiefs, for nobody cries. In heaven they never phone for the undertaker, for nobody dies. In heaven you will never see a funeral procession going down the street, or crepe hanging on the door knob.

[15] None of the things that enter your home here will enter there. "Former things have passed away." All things have become new. In heaven the flowers never fade, the winter winds and blasts never blow. The rivers never congeal, for it never gets cold.

[16] Don't let God hang a "For Rent" sign in the mansion that He has prepared for you. Just send up word tonight, "Jesus, I've changed my mind. Put down my name for that. I'm coming, I'm coming home!"

[17] "In my Father's house are many mansions. If it were not so I would have told you. I go to prepare a place for you."

[18] Send Him word tonight to reserve one of those mansions for you!

The Magnetism of the Uplifted Lord

I, if I be lifted up from the earth, will draw all men unto
me.   —John 12:32

THE context gives us the needful illumination to see our way, *"Now there were certain Greeks among those that went up to worship at the feast: these therefore came to Philip . . . and asked him, saying, Sir, we would see Jesus."* The personality of Jesus was already becoming attractive, the magnet was beginning to draw, the sons and daughters were coming from afar! But why were these Greeks drawn unto Him? Perhaps it was only curiosity, which nevertheless is often the mother of wonder and awe, and the minister of deathless devotion. Or, perhaps it was heart-hunger, the pangs of unsatisfied craving, an unrest which philosophy was unable to soothe, a vastness of desire for which eloquence, and music, and art had no bread. "Sir, we would see Jesus!" *"Philip cometh and telleth Andrew: Andrew cometh, and Philip, and they tell Jesus."* And what will Jesus say when this first little group of enquirers from the outer world are at His door? *"And Jesus said, The hour is come, that the Son of Man should be glorified!"* Here is the beginning of the glory He seeks, the drawing of all men unto Him. Here is the little band of advance scouts which precedes a host which no man can number. But this little company is only like a small handful of precocious blades of corn upon an otherwise barren field. They are almost before their time. Before the entire field can be covered with the promising verdure there must be a winter, and in the secret virtue of that winter shall the spring and autumn glory be found. First a winter, and then, not a few straggling blades, but an uncounted number! Even now there is a little movement, some faint stirring of aspiring life, but wait until winter has added its mystic ministry, and the movement will be as the silent march of a vast army. Even now Jesus draws men. But wait until the winter is passed! First, let Jesus die! "If it die, it bringeth forth much fruit." "I, if I be lifted up, will draw all men unto Me." The tendency of this little handful of Greeks shall become the drift of the race.

² And so the magnet is to be the Lord Jesus in the wonderful energies of His transcendent sacrifice. "I, if I be lifted up." "As Moses lifted up the serpent in the wilderness, even so must the Son of Man be lifted up." No one

From *The Transfigured Church* (New York: 1910). By permission of Fleming H. Revell Co.

can really feel the pressing mystery of the cross who does not enter it possessed by the conviction of the sinlessness of Jesus, and realising something of the vast range of consciousness in which His spirit moved; His sense of the absolute oneness of Himself and God; His unwavering sense of the voluntariness of His surrender to the powers of men and the pains of earth, "No man taketh it from Me"; His expressed consciousness, that, by the raising of the eyes, He could call to His aid legions of attendant forces which would make Him invincible; His calm assurance that "all things had been given into His hands," His submission to the Cross in that assurance; all these remove His death from the ranks of common martyrdom, and place Him in an awful and glorious isolation. His martyr Stephen was forced into his death; Jesus walked into it. From the very beginning His steps were set towards it. "He set His face steadfastly to go," and with an irresistible stride He paced forward to the self-chosen consummation of sacrifice. He descended the entire slope of sacrifice, from grade to grade, until He touched death, and destroyed the power of death, until He tore out death's sting, which is sin, and in one supreme victory triumphed over both.

³ Now our Lord declares that it is in the energy of that transcendent sacrifice that His personal magnetism is to be found. The energy of His love as displayed in His life, compared with the energy in His love as displayed in His death, is as dispersed sunshine compared with focussed sunshine, sunshine concentrated in a burning heat. And it is this focussed sacrificial energy of His death, "The last pregnant syllable of God's great utterance of love," which our Lord declares is to be the ministry of attraction, by which all men are to be drawn unto Him. This teaching is not altogether strange, not altogether removed from the proof of human experience. Even upon the plane of common life, among men of narrow consciousness and sinful habit, the element of sacrifice is strangely magnetic, and allures the interest and admiration of men. We recall how the young Prince of the Netherlands, alien and unpopular, estranged from the people's hearts, drew the people to him by the energies of sacrifice. And we recall the heroic skipper, who by a midnight sacrifice drew to him the homage of kings and the affectionate acclamation of the race. Yes, and sometimes a notoriously bad man is kindled into some conspicuous act of heroic sacrifice, and in the tremendous energy of the pure flame his unworthiness seems consumed, and his infamy is forgotten. So that we are familiar with the magnetism of sacrifice even amid our own defiled and narrow lives. But what shall be the energies when the sacrificial being is the sinless Lord Himself, with strength to confront everything and never be defiled, with power to break the double tyranny of sin and death—what shall be the energy, its quantity and its quality, when He shall go "without the camp," to suffer and to die? "I, if I be lifted up, will draw all men unto Me." The energies of that self-sacrificing Redeemer constitute the mightiest magnet known among men.

⁴ There is nothing like that magnet. Test it by the individual testimony. As a matter of common experience, what draws men like the uplifted Lord? You must have noticed, as I again and again have noticed, how a silent awe

steals over an assembly, when the preacher consciously approaches the cross, and leads the contemplation to that stupendous sacrifice. If he turns to matters ecclesiastical, political, aesthetical, educational, the tension is relaxed, and we can assume an attitude of easy detachment. It is the uplifted Lord who tightens the strings, and makes us mentally and spiritually tense, and draws us to our knees. What has experience to tell us of His wonderful workings? It tells us this, that nothing so overcomes the deathly and the deadly in man as "the preaching of Jesus Christ and Him crucified." It breaks up the frozen indifference of men. It makes them graciously uneasy. It disturbs them with promising disquietude. It awakes moral pains by restoring the moral circulation, and it accomplishes resurrection through the pangs of hell and the sorrows of death. But the sacrificial Lord does more than inspire initial unrest. He converts the uneasy stirrings into definite spiritual movement. He not only breaks up inertia, He determines direction. He awakes men, and He also draws them. He draws men towards Himself, and they move to a close and personal communion. There is nothing else which works in that way, and to such swift and personal devotion. You may proclaim the Lord as a great ethical teacher, but the ethics may generate no more energy than do the Ten Commandments painted upon the cold surface of the walls of a church. You may proclaim Him as a young reformer, but the programme will no more lift me out of their deadly grooves than a party programme will lift men out of their sins. Jesus, the young prophet, may draw cheers; the uplifted Lord draws men. The young Reformer may gain men's signatures; the sacrificial Saviour wins their hearts. "I drew them with cords of a man, with bands of love."

> Just as I am, without one plea,
> But that Thy blood was shed for me,
> And that Thou bid'st me come to Thee,
> O Lamb of God, I come, I come!

[5] Test the energies of this magnet by the testimony of history as to what is the power which has most conspicuously swayed the great masses of mankind. Whenever the multitudes have been profoundly moved, whenever stagnant peoples have been stirred into newness and freshness of life, it has been by the energies of the uplifted Lord. Let us confine the range of vision to our own country, and to our own country within the limited circle of the last hundred and fifty years. I am not aware of any vast upheaval of the national sentiment which has taken place within that season which was not directly occasioned by the energies of the uplifted Lord. What we call the Evangelical Revival carries its interpretation in its name. When the England of the eighteenth century—so superficial, so cruel, so soddened in immoral indifference—began to move toward a cleaner and a sweeter and more enlightened life, the magnet that drew her was the Lamb of God. The miner in Cornwall and Northumbria, the workman in the potteries, the shepherd on the northern moors, the poor cotter in Scotland and in Ireland, all felt the pull of the magnet, and sped with eager feet toward their Lord.

Let any one turn to John Wesley's journal, and read the inner story of that wonderful revival, and he will be in no doubt as to what was the quickening ministry that created it. From shepherd and fisherman and miner alike this was the common cry, "O Lamb of God, I come!" And it has not been otherwise in a nearer day. No one has ever moved the multitudes except the men with the magnet of the uplifted Lord. Nay, it is passing strange that only the men with the uplifted Lord seem to seek the multitudes at all! Have you known of any Moody, with similar passion and similar aim, but with another magnet than this of the crucified Lord, who has moved the masses of our countrymen, and drawn them into the holy paths of higher life and service? If such there be, I should like to know of them, for as yet they have never passed across my sight. No, when the multitudes are swayed, they are swayed by the Lamb. I am not now asking you to account for it, or to accept any theory concerning it, but to accept the plain testimony of experience, that some marvellous magnetic energy attaches to the uplifted Lord, and that there is nothing to be named alongside it in its power to grip and draw the multitudes. With all my heart I believe in what Mr. Spurgeon said—and altogether apart from his supreme genius his own ministry afforded abundant proof—that there is nothing in this world which so impresses men, and nothing which at bottom they are so eager to hear, as just "the old, old story," told by men who know its power, "of Jesus and His love." That is where the Labour Church is most assuredly doomed to fail and to die, and many who are reading these words will live to see it.

6 "I, if I be lifted up, will draw *all* men unto Me." Then in the energies of this sacrificed Christ we are not only to find the dynamic of redemption, but the secret of human brotherhood. If men are drawn to Him they will be drawn nearer to one another. It will be like moving from the isolated suburbs of a great circumference down the radii to a common centre, and as we approach that centre we shall draw near to one another. The central Magnet will communicate something of its own attractive energy to every approaching soul, and by the common energy shall souls be drawn together. The secret of brotherhood is found in common nearness to the Lord. But how dare I say that when I look round upon the Churches of to-day? Is there anything less like brotherhood than the spectacle which they present to the world? So far from being possessed by some common energy of mutual attraction, we seem to be possessed by an energy which occasions mutual repulsion. If by some happy chance we find ourselves on a common platform, we either half apologise for our relationship, or we indulge in outbursts of mutual eulogy and surprise which reveal how infrequent and unreal is our communion. If it be true that by drawing near the centre we assuredly draw near to one another, what has happened to explain our position? This has happened: we have forgotten the centre, or we have made centres of our own. We have made a theory a centre, a form of ecclesiastical government a centre, and because all men will not travel toward our self-made centre, there is antagonism and repulsion, and mutual throwing of stones, and the religion which was purposed to be a minister of brotherly union becomes the em-

bittered agent of division and strife. But I tell you that wherever, in any and all denominations, men get their eyes clearly fixed upon the face of the sacrificial Lord, upon the uplifted Christ of God, they do most assuredly move and draw together, and these men, even at the present time, are living and working in co-operative service and in brotherly concord and peace. It is the man who strikes his spear and plants his standard in his own self-chosen and self-created centre, and who will not look beyond his formal creed, his rigid polity, and his fleshly succession, it is this man, wherever he may be found, who is the foe of human fellowship and Christian intimacy, and who retards the gracious oneness for which our Saviour lived and bled and died. When we get our eager eyes fixed upon the Lord, the Lord uplifted in superlative sacrifice, when we pierce through every secondary medium, and contemplate the primary glory, we shall move down the different radii of our Church relationships—Episcopalian, Methodist, Congregationalist, Presbyterian, Friend—and we shall emerge in the fair light of the oneness of a common love, and in the full, sweet harmony of a common confession, "My Lord and my God!" "I, if I be lifted up, will draw all men unto Me."

7 "I, if I be lifted up!" There is energy there to redeem us all. There is energy there to lift us out of the cold prison-house of guilt, out of the cruel tyranny of sin, out of the bitterness of death. "I will draw!" No one else can do it. "I," and this in contrast to "the prince of this world" in the previous verse. These are the combatants: "the prince of this world" versus the uplifted Lord! I place my reliance on the Lord! "Whosoever believeth on Him shall not perish, but have everlasting life."

> Drawn to the Cross which Thou hast blessed
> With healing gifts for souls distressed,
> To find in Thee my life, my rest;
>   Christ crucified, I come!
>
> To be what Thou wouldst have me be,
> Accepted, sanctified in Thee,
> Through what Thy grace shall work in me;
>   Christ crucified, I come!

WILLIAM MCCALLUM CLOW   SERMON 17

The Cross and the Memory of Sin

*Who was before a blasphemer, and a persecutor, and in-
jurious; but I obtained mercy.*   —I Tim. 1:13

G OD HAS given every faculty a part to play in the nurture and admonition of the soul. "All that is within me," in the Psalmist's
suggestive line, my desire, my imagination, my will, and every other
power, is called upon to serve in the sanctuary. On no faculty is there laid a
more vital office than on the memory. In the Old Testament the memory
was a chief minister in the religious life, the prompter to love and duty, the
source of both loyalty and devotion. "Thou shalt remember all the ways that
the Lord thy God hath led thee." "Thou shalt remember the works of the
Lord." "Thou shalt remember the right hand of him that is most high."
"Thou shalt remember that thou wast a bondman in Egypt." In the New
Testament still more solemn are the charges laid upon it. The words and
ways of Jesus are committed to its care. The anguish of an eternal doom is
made more poignant by the part memory will play in it. "Son, remember,"
said Jesus, letting us see where the rich man would feel the sting of sin. And
the most sacred and tender hour in Christian worship depends for its blessing
on the memory. "This do ye," said Jesus, "in remembrance of me."

² But there is one terrifying fact in our experience of memory. That is the
memory of sin. "I was before a blasphemer, and a persecutor, and injurious."
He is glancing back at his past. His memory has many a dark spot. The
shadow falls on his spirit and his voice is troubled. Yet the line is only one
minor note in a jubilant song. His memory has recalled more than the days
of headstrong defiance and pitiless cruelty. It has recalled his Lord, and the
gospel of forgiveness in His Cross. And as he sees again the Cross and its
salvation for the chief of sinners, he looks back with a clear and steady eye to
remember his sin, but to see it in the light of the grace of God. How does
the Cross, with its message of forgiveness and healing, affect the memory
of sin?

³ I. In the first place, *the Cross takes the sting out of the memory of sin.*
Every sin leaves a print on the memory, but the unforgiven sin leaves a
wound. That wound is quick and tender to the slightest touch. Joseph's
brethren had only to hear an Egyptian ruler speak, to find that their con-

From *The Cross in Christian Experience* (London and New York, 1908). By permission of Harper & Bros.

sciences were rousing the memory to its office. David had only to hear the words "Thou art the man" from the prophet's lips to find the pain of his unhealed though secret sore. Herod, Sadducee and worldling as he was, had only to hear of Jesus to cry out in fear, "It is John, whom I beheaded." But let a man be persuaded that he has obtained mercy through Christ and His Cross, and his wound is healed, his sting is gone. There is nothing left but a disappearing scar. Paul's recollection of his sin has little pain. "I was before a blasphemer." He saw himself, in that backward glance, standing in the Sanhedrin with his passionate invective against Christ. "A persecutor." He saw Stephen's face and the light of his holiness upon it, and he heard his prayer. He recalled the shrinking forms of the men and women he had haled to prison. "And injurious." He remembered that he had scattered the folk of the infant Church with the strong blast of his hate, and tempted weak believers to deny their Lord. But he has no wound. He can turn his eyes to Christ, and say, "I obtained mercy."

4 That is the experience which every man may repeat. You have faces which rise upon you in the hours of the backward glance, the faces of those you have tempted to evil and provoked to unbelief. You recall the names of those whom you have wronged. You know the places whose mention you hear in silence. There are streets you never pass, houses you never see, without a secret shame. You remember words and deeds from whose degradation you shrink even in thought. It is not only the sins and faults of youth, it is the more daring sins of middle-life, and the stranger and more reckless sins of old age. Take up your sin to Christ's Cross. Mark how sin scourged Him and spat upon Him, and put the crown of thorns on His head, and drove in the nails to His hands and to His feet. Be assured that He has borne your grief and carried your sorrow. Realize that He has known that pure grief of repentance which should have been yours, and that pure sorrow for sin which you have only slightly felt. Be persuaded that God for Christ's sake has forgiven you. At once you will feel that your wound is healed. Your sin has become an event of the past. Devout men sometimes thank God for the present tenses of Christian life. There is an even greater joy in the past tenses of spiritual experience. "Who *was*," said Paul, "a blasphemer, and a persecutor, and injurious; but I obtained mercy." What shall we say? Who was a man of unclean lips, of vengeful temper, of mean envy, of gross desire, of self-indulgent life, of keen worldly ambition, but I obtained mercy. The Cross has taken the sting out of the memory of sin.

5 II. In the second place, *the Cross makes the memory of sin a means of grace.* We know that through forgiveness the sting is taken out of the memory of sin, but we are often tempted to wish that the stain were also immediately purged away. Every man has much in his life that he wishes he could forget, but God leaves the stain upon the memory, not only because He will not needlessly abrogate its inviolable laws, but also to use it as a means of grace. One of these uses is that a stained memory becomes a *barrier against future sin.* When a man is trembling in the weakness of his will against a besetting sin, or when some new seductive iniquity comes with a

fresh charm and winning suggestions, the memory of the past rises up like the forbidding word of a prophet. The memory of sin is as God's angel with a drawn sword to keep the way of the gate of death. We would not repeat the old sins of which we have repented with tears; we would not be ensnared even by Satan transformed into an angel of light, if in the moment of our temptation we remembered not only the shame of iniquity, and the sting of remorse, but the pardon of the Cross of Christ. We wonder at the meekness of Moses with the murmuring Israelites. We wonder at his pleading patience with their childishness. He never forgot that godless gust of anger when he slew the Egyptian and hid him in the sand. Nothing is so beautiful in Peter's life as his lying in the prison awaiting his death in the quiet sleep of a tranquil heart. He remembered that night when he denied Christ. He remembered that he saw his sin as a hideous crime, when Jesus looked upon him, and he was able to rest in the Lord and wait patiently for Him. In the most tragical of the "Idylls of the King," Tennyson has set this truth in a convincing light. He tells the story of Queen Guinevere hiding herself in a house of holy women. She goes in with an impenitent heart. The little maid who waits upon her prattles in her artlessness, and the child's kindly words smite the unhealed wound. But she repents and is forgiven; and the sting is greatly gone. The memory of it has become a barrier against sinning. She will not even think again the thoughts that made the past so pleasant to her.

> So let me lie before your shrine,
> Do each low office of your holy house,
> Walk your dim cloister and distribute dole,
> To poor sick people, richer in His eyes,
> Who ransom'd us, and haler too than I;
> And treat their loathsome hurts and heal mine own;
> And so wear out, in almsdeeds and in prayer,
> The somber close of that voluptuous day,
> Which wrought the ruin of my lord the King.

⁶ Another use in God's grace of the stained memory is this: *It may become an equipment for service.* A stained past is not usually held to be an enrichment of a man for the service of Christ. Many men have refused Christian office, and many more are hindered in their testimony, and checked, as by a sharp pain, in their zeal, by recollection of their past. And it is much better to have no shame to remember. Nothing can compensate for the loss of purity and honour. It is enough to be tempted as Christ was, and to be without sin. Temptation gives us insight and sympathy for all we need to do. But no man can look back on a course of unblemished years. And God, by the grace of the Cross, makes the stained memory an equipment for service.

⁷ This truth shines out in the ministry of Paul. He felt, and felt justly, that no one of the apostles had sinned as he had done. Again and again, with a piteous self-abasement, he recalled his past. He was "not meet to be called an apostle." He had "beyond measure persecuted the Church and wasted it." He was "the chief of sinners." But whence came that pity for the fallen,

that gentleness with the weak, that zeal for the outcast, that tenderness over the lost, that quenchless passion for the redeeming gospel? What is the source of that power of entreaty which clothes itself in words only less persuasive than those of Jesus? Did these things lodge by nature in the heart of the young Pharisee, Saul of Tarsus? Were they ever easy graces to a man of intense dynamic like Paul? They were his equipment through the memory of sin. "A fellow feeling makes us wondrous kind." When he was dealing with some headstrong and blinded and wilful soul, he looked back and he remembered, and in that moment he became the gentlest and most beseeching teacher of men.

8 To this day it is the evangelist who remembers that he is a brand plucked from the burning, who knows how to preach the gospel to publicans and sinners. It is the man who knows how easily the strongest is swept off his feet at times, and has gone to his rest with remorseful thoughts, hardly able to pray, who will think most kindly, and will spend himself untiringly in keeping others from the slime. It is the man who recalls the coarse and un-yielding grip of an evil habit who will deal most pitifully with those who fall again and again. It is the man who has been taken out of the fearful pit and the miry clay who will despair of no man. The Pharisee in the temple had no memory of forgiven sin; had there been a stain upon it, had he recalled what the publican thought of with shame, his prayer would have been broken with penitence, he would not have stood in the holy place an offense both to God and to man. He would have been a winner of souls.

9 Another use in God's grace of the stained memory is this: it becomes *a source of love to Christ*. It is not our love to Christ that makes our calling and election sure. It is His love to us. It is not our love to Christ that saves us. It is our belief in His love to us. But we never attain the devoutness or enter into the joy of a Christian life, and we never penetrate Christ's secret until an adoring love to Him begins to beat in our hearts. We may set Christ on the throne of the universe. We may bow down in reverence before His holiness. We may thrill with awe at the wisdom and depth of His words, and the grace of His deeds. But we never love Him until we know that He has redeemed us by His Cross. It is well to remember Christ in every aspect of His ways, and to dwell upon Him by estimate and judgment; but the man who remembers with a humbling glance the sin from which he has been delivered by Christ's Cross, has the lover's desire in his thought and the lover's note in his prayers. "And, behold, a woman which was a sinner brought an alabaster box of ointment, and stood at his feet behind him weeping, and she began to wash his feet with tears, and did wipe them with the hairs of her head, and she kissed his feet, and anointed them with oint-ment." "And Jesus said, Her sins, which are many, are forgiven; for she loved much." A stained memory keeps our love to Christ in flood.

10 III. In the third place, the Cross shall finally *obliterate the memory of sin*. It is difficult for us to believe that whatever God may do, the memory of some sins shall ever be blotted out. Much may fade out of our minds, but we are inclined to think that there are one or two dark and daring sins which

can never be forgotten. Yet nothing is more simply and more notoriously true than that the words and deeds of the past, even the names and faces of those who have been very dear to us in bygone days, do fade and are utterly forgotten. The memory has been compared to a palimpsest manuscript. In old days, when fine vellum was scarce and dear, it was the custom to take an old manuscript, on which were written, perchance, the accounts of the monastery, and set a skillful and careful hand to erase the writing from the parchment by pumice stone. Then upon the cleansed surface a fresh writing could be placed, and only keen eyes could detect faint traces of the old script below. In such fashion the sins of our youth, the dark record of hours spent in wrongdoing, may be erased, and a new writing, as by the finger of God, be found on the tablets of memory.

[11] But the truth is deeper and more comforting than such a mechanical image can set forth. It is not merely the erasion of the past, not a mere cancelling of the characters leaving traces of them which may be discerned. It is an obliteration. The truth is that when a man is forgiven, and his sin ceases to haunt him, he no longer recalls its hour, it slips into oblivion. And when a man begins to contemplate Christ and His Cross, fastens his mind on His love and sacrifice, and occupies his thought with Christ's moral loveliness, the word and deed that once made a scarlet stain are wholly obliterated. They vanish as a cloud fades into the infinite azure of the blue heaven.

[12] It is a well marked phase of the action of the mind that it can completely forget what once engrossed it if new interests occupy and absorb it. In the life and letters of T. E. Brown, the poet in the Isle of Man, there occurs a notable instance of this. He is writing to a friend about the poems of his youth. One would think that a poem, the expression of a mood of passionate feeling, which had been dwelt upon with keen intellectual interest, whose words had been chosen and polished with care, would not be forgotten. Yet Brown writes: "They seem, many of them, to be strangers to me, in no way expressing a mood that is now even possible, and quite startling either in being foreign to my mind or inadequate to its conceptions." So also the man in us, sin-stained, sin-haunted, may cease to be. God restores the years that the locust has eaten. As we throw ourselves into Christ's service, and as His wisdom works into the veins of our thinking, and His life beats within our will, the past dies within us. It cannot be recalled even with an effort. It has been blotted out as completely from our minds as from the mind of God. There is a depth of forgetfulness out of which a forgiven and never recalled sin cannot emerge.

[13] So a human soul which has set up before it that everlasting mark of love and light, the Cross, and entered into the mystery of its passion and the knowledge of its power, lives in daily contemplation of its Lord and His graces, always finds the darkest, most reproachful, and most ashaming deed of time obliterated. God permits us to remember our forgiven sins only as long as they may be spurs and goads to our will, incentives to our trust, sources of our love and devotion. We sometimes wonder whether the bliss of heaven will not be marred by the stained memories we shall bear with us

from the life of earth. Sometimes we fear that we shall remember, with the rich man, the neglected beggar at our gate, the undone duty of our life, the lost opportunities of our service, the deed that ruined another's life. No, my brethren, the lash of memory will be felt, as it is felt here and now, only in hell. It is, let me repeat, the unforgiven sin whose stain is indelible. But in heaven, when men will sing that new song of the Redeemed, "Worthy is the Lamb that was slain," when the Cross shall have become a dearer and more significant symbol than on earth, when the entrancing preoccupation of a completed salvation shall seize and hold both heart and mind, the evil words and deeds of time shall pass away like a forgotten dream. No sin can live under the felt power of the Cross.

The Conquest of Fear

Fear not; I am the first and the last, and the Living One;
and I was dead, and behold, I am alive forevermore, and I
have the keys of death and of Hades.   —Rev. 1:17-18

I N THIS hour of worship, let us think together on Jesus' greatest saying concerning the conquest of fear. It is given in these words in the first chapter of the last book of the New Testament. "Fear not; I am the first and the last, and the Living One; I was dead, and behold, I am alive forevermore, and I have the keys of death and of Hades."

² It is both the mission and the message of Jesus to deliver mankind from servile, enervating, down-dragging fear. And certainly the problem of fear is a problem to be reckoned with in many lives. One of the most outstanding and surprising disclosures of our stressful, nervous, modern civilization, is the fact that many people are in the thraldom of fear. This fact obtains with all classes of people—the high and the low, the rich and the poor, the educated and ignorant, the old and the young, with all ages and classes. They have fears of all kinds—fear of themselves, of others, of the past, present and future, of sickness, of death, of poverty, and on and on.

³ A little while ago, it was my privilege to preach twice daily for a week to one of our most influential American colleges. Its student body is large, and widely influential, and more mature in years than is the student body of most of our colleges. Before my arrival there, the president of the college sent a questionnaire to every student, asking that the students indicate any subjects upon which they would have the visiting minister speak. When the answers were tabulated, the president and faculty of the college, together with the visiting minister and others, were amazed by the fact that the majority of that large and mature student body had made this request: "Let the visiting minister tell us how we may conquer fear."

⁴ The Bible is the one book which answers that very question. There are two words which stand out in the Bible, like mountain peaks—the words, *Fear not!* With those words, God comforted Abraham: "Fear not, Abram; I am thy shield and exceeding great reward." With those same words he comforted Isaac at his lonely task of digging wells in the wilderness. With the same words he comforted Jacob, when his little Joseph was lost somewhere down in Egypt. So comforted he the Israelites at the Red Sea: "And

---

From *Follow Thou Me* (Nashville, 1932). By permission of The Broadman Press.

Moses said unto the people, fear ye not, stand still, and see the salvation of the Lord, which He will show you today." These two words, *Fear not!* standing out here and there in the Bible, are a part of our great inheritance as Christians. We shall do well to note them very carefully, wherever they occur in the Bible, and to note their contextual relations.

5 The three supreme matters which concern mankind are life, death and eternity. Jesus here gives us an all-comprehensive statement concerning these three vast matters. He bids us to be unafraid of life, of death, and of eternity. It is Jesus' greatest saying concerning the conquest of fear. It was spoken to John, who was banished to Patmos, because of his fealty to Christ. Let us now earnestly summon ourselves to think on this vast message of Jesus.

6 I. And, first, Jesus bids us to be unafraid of life. He reminds us that he is "the first and the last, and the Living One." Is the fear of life real? It is poignantly so with many. The liability of fear is constant, and this fact is perhaps the explanation for many a suicide. I asked one who sought in a despondent hour to snuff out the candle of life, and was prevented from so doing: "Why did you wish to end your life?" And the pathetic answer was given: "I was afraid to go on with life." People are afraid, for one thing, because they are so dependent. They are utterly dependent upon God, and greatly dependent upon one another. Sometimes the proud expression is heard: "I am independent." Let such a one tell us of whom he is independent, and how and where and when? We are all bound together in the bundle of life. "For none of us liveth to himself, and no man dieth to himself."

7 Again, we are afraid, because we are continually in the presence of great mysteries, such as the mystery of sin, of sorrow, of God, of one's own personality, and of the strange and ofttimes trying providences that come to us in the earthly life.

8 Still again, the responsibilities of life are such that serious men and women must often tremble. Piercing questions arise to probe our hearts to the depths. Often do we ask: "Will I make good in the stern battle of life?" "Will I disappoint the expectations of my loved ones and friends?" Even Moses trembled before his mighty responsibilities, thus voicing his fear: "O my Lord, I am not eloquent, neither heretofore, nor since thou hast spoken unto thy servant: but I am slow of speech, and of a slow tongue." And even Solomon shrank before his vast responsibility, saying: "And now, O Lord my God, thou hast made thy servant king instead of David my father; and I am but a little child: I know not how to go out or come in." Often come the testing hours in life, when we cry out with Paul: "Who is sufficient for these things?" Many times are we provoked to ask that very question, as we are called upon to make important decisions and meet the critically testing experiences of life. Verily, we are many times made to tremble before the immeasurably responsible facts of life. Jesus graciously comes to us, saying: "Do not be afraid of life." "I will never leave thee nor forsake thee."

9 II. Again, he bids us be unafraid of death. He reminds us, "I was dead, and behold, I am alive forevermore." The shuddering fear of death is a very

real fact in many a life. Some are in bondage all their earthly life time, through fear of death. Maeterlinck confesses in his autobiography: "I am a frightened child in the presence of death." It is not to be wondered at that the thought of death casts its oppressive shadows about us, because death is an experience utterly strange to every one of us. "It is a bourne whence no traveler returns." "The black camel kneels at every gate." "With equal pace, impartial fate knocks at the palace and the cottage gate." It is not surprising that numbers of people have a strange fascination for prying into the secrets of death. This gruesome curiosity sometimes leads its possessor into strange quests and still stranger claims. What shall be said of these uncanny efforts to pry into the secrets of the dead? Such efforts are both profitless and presumptuous. Jesus has told us all that we need to know about death. He knows all about the grave, for he has explored its every chamber, and he has met this Waterloo of death and won. He is not now in the grave. He is alive, he is the Living One who is now bringing to bear the resources of his wisdom, mercy, power and love upon our needy world, and his will is bound to prevail. We are told that "Ideas rule the world." Very well, compare the ideas proclaimed by Jesus, with all others, and at once we see how preeminent his ideas are. The hands on his clock never turn backward. "For he must reign, till he hath put all enemies under his feet." Some day, thank God! War will be under his feet forever. And so will be all forms of intemperance, and selfishness, and sin. And so will be death itself, because it is divinely decreed that "The last enemy that shall be destroyed is death." "O death, where is thy sting? O grave, where is thy victory? . . . But thanks be to God who giveth us the victory through our Lord Jesus Christ."

10 And still further—Jesus is with his people when they come to die. The evidences of this fact are countless and glorious. Often and joyfully did John Wesley declare: "Our people die well." Many of us, even in our limited and very humble sphere, can give the same glad testimony. "Our people die well." Indeed, when we see how well they can die, how unafraid and triumphant they are, when they face the last enemy, we are fortified afresh for our work of testifying to the sufficiency of Christ's help, in every possible human experience.

11 Not long ago, I saw a timid mother die. Hers was a very humble home, the husband was a carpenter, the children were very modestly clothed, and the limitations imposed by a meager income for the home were markedly in evidence. With a calmness, fearlessness and joyfulness indescribable, that modest woman faced the final chapter of the earthly journey. She gave her sublime Christian testimony to her sorrowing husband and children; she confidently bound them to the heart of God, in a prayer that can never be forgotten by those who heard it; and then she passed into the valley of the shadows, smilingly whispering the victorious words: "Yea, though I walk through the valley of the shadow of death, I will fear no evil, for thou art with me; thy rod and thy staff they comfort me." The next day, I saw a strong husband and father pass to the great beyond. He requested that the pastor pray that the whole household might unreservedly accept God's will.

When the prayer was concluded, the strong man who was rapidly hurrying down to death sublimely said to the poignantly sorrowing wife and sons: "This is God's way; he doeth all things well; I accept his will without a question; tell me, O my dear wife and children, will you not likewise accept his will in this hour, and through all the unfolding future?" And with one voice, they said: "We will." And then, the strong man was gone, and the peace and calm of heaven filled all that house. A third day came, and I was called to witness the passing of an unusually timid girl in the Sunday school. The modest child of little more than a dozen years of age anxiously said to her mother: "Everything is getting dark, Mamma, come close to me, I'm afraid." And the gentle mother said to the little daughter: "Jesus is with us in the dark, my child, as well as in the light, and he will surely take care of all who put their trust in him." And the child's face was immediately lighted up with a joyful smile, as she said: "I am trusting him, and I'll just keep on trusting him, and he will stay close to me, for he said he would, and he always does what he says he will do." And a little later, even in life's closing moments, her voice could be heard singing: "There'll be no dark valley when Jesus comes, to gather his children home." Such illustrations of triumph in the hour of death could be indefinitely multiplied. The pastors of your churches are privileged to witness such triumphs, week by week, and they are able, therefore, to stand in their pulpits, and victoriously shout with Paul: "But thanks be to God, who giveth us the victory through our Lord Jesus Christ."

12 III. Not only does Jesus bid us be unafraid of life and of death, but he also bids us to be unafraid of eternity. The word he speaks here in his great promise is: "I have the keys of death and of Hades." That little word "keys" carries with it a large meaning. It means guidance, it means authority, it means control. Just as Jesus cares for his people in life and in death, even so will he care for them in eternity. "I go to prepare a place for you. And if I go and prepare a place for you, I will come again, and receive you unto myself; that where I am, there ye may be also."

13 Belief in God and in immortality go together. The age-old question: "If a man die, shall he live again?" is a question that will not be hushed. It is no wonder that such a question has been eagerly asked by myriads, in the recent years. The Great War laid millions of young men under sod and sea, and has sent other millions to stagger on with broken health, even down to the grave. Suffering hearts all around the encircling globe have asked and are continually asking if death is an eternal sleep, and if the grave ends all. To such questions we must give our most positive answer. The grave does not end all. The doctrine of immortality is not a dead creed, an empty speculation, an intellectual curiosity, an interesting question. The doctrine of immortality is a fact, a force, a great moral dynamic, which lifts life to high levels, and drives it to great ends. Yes, we are to live again, beyond the sunset and the night, to live on consciously, personally, and forever.

14 The nature of man demands immortality. The instinct of immortality is the prophecy of its fulfilment. Where in all nature can you find instinct falsified? The wings of the bird mean that it was made to fly. The fins of the

161

fish mean that it was made to swim. The deathless yearnings of the heart imperiously cry out for immortality. On the modest monument that marks the last resting place in France of President Roosevelt's son, who fell in the Great War, is inscribed this death-defying sentence: "He has outsoared the shadows of our night." The human heart refuses to be hushed in its cry for immortality.

15 The character of God presages immortality. When Job thought of men, he said: "If a man die, shall he live again?" When he thought of God, he said: "I know that my Redeemer liveth." Then Job went on to voice the deathless cry of the heart for immortality. God is infinitely interested in us, he cares for us, he provides for us. If he cares for the birds, as he does, surely he cares also for us. He bids us to put fear away, reminding us: "But the very hairs of your head are all numbered." "Fear ye not, therefore, ye are of more value than many sparrows." Abraham was "the friend of God." Death has not dissolved that friendship. "Enoch walked with God; and he was not, for God took him." A little girl, who heard a preacher's sermon, on this sentence, gave this report of the sermon to a little neighbor girl who did not hear the sermon: "The preacher said that Enoch took a long walk with God; and they walked, and they walked, and they walked; and at last, God told Enoch that he need not go back to live at his house any more, but he could just go on home with God, to live with him, in his house, forever." Surely, the little girl's interpretation is what our hearts demand, and it is what we steadfastly and joyfully believe to be the plan of God for his friends.

16 But the crowning argument for immortality is the experience of Jesus. He has incontestably proved it. He came to earth, and really lived, and died, and was buried, and rose again, just as he said he would do. Long years ago, the men of the Old World wondered if there was some other land, beyond the waters, to the far West. One day, a bolder spirit than others had been, set sail toward the West. And by and by, Columbus set his feet upon the shores of a new land. Even so, Jesus was the divine Columbus who has explored all the chambers of the grave, and has come back therefrom, the victorious Conqueror of death. He comforts his friends with the gracious words: "I am the resurrection and the life: he that believeth in me, though he were dead, yet shall he live. And whosoever liveth and believeth in me shall never die." In that incomparable chapter of guidance and comfort, the fourteenth chapter of John, Jesus would anchor us, once for all, with his divinely assuring words: "Because I live, ye shall live also."

> Low in the grave He lay—Jesus my Saviour!
>   Waiting the coming day, Jesus my Lord!
> Up from the grave, He arose,
>   With a mighty triumph o'er His foes;
> He arose a Victor from the dark domain,
>   And He lives forever, with His saints to reign,
> He arose! He arose!! Hallelujah! Christ arose!!

17 With our faith in that victorious Saviour, we may sing with Whittier, in his exquisite poem, "Snowbound."

> Alas for him who never sees
> The stars shine through his cypress-trees!
> Who, hopeless, lays his dead away,
> Nor looks to see the breaking day,
> Across the mournful marbles play!
> Who hath not learned, in hours of faith,
> The truth to flesh and sense unknown,
> That Life is ever lord of Death,
> And Love can never lose its own!

18 Are you trusting in Christ as your personal Saviour, and do you gladly bow to him as your rightful Master? If your hearts answer "Yes," go your many scattered ways, I pray you, without hesitation or fear. Your personal relations to Christ will determine your relations to the three vast matters: life, death and eternity, concerning which he would have us put all our fears away, now and forever more. He is our Pilot, our Righteousness, our Saviour, our Advocate, our promised and infallible Guide, even unto death, and throughout the vast beyond, forever. Well do we often sing: "He leadeth me." As we sing it now, who wishes openly to confess him and follow him?

David Livingstone's Text

I T IS THE *word of a gentleman of the most strict and sacred honour, so
there's an end of it!"* says Livingstone to himself as he places his
finger for the thousandth time on the text on which he stakes his life.
He is surrounded by hostile and infuriated savages. During the sixteen
years that he has spent in Africa, he has never before seemed in such imminent peril. Death stares him in the face. He thinks sadly of his life-work
scarcely begun. For the first time in his experience he is tempted to steal
away under cover of the darkness and to seek safety in flight. He prays!
"Leave me not, forsake me not!" he cries. But let me quote from his own
journal; it will give us the rest of the story.

² "*January* 14, 1856. *Evening.* Felt much turmoil of spirit in prospect of
having all my plans for the welfare of this great region and this teeming
population knocked on the head by savages tomorrow. But I read that Jesus
said: 'All power is given unto Me in heaven and in earth. Go ye therefore,
and teach all nations, and *lo, I am with you alway, even unto the end of the
world.*' It is the word of a gentleman of the most strict and sacred honour,
so there's an end of it. I will not cross furtively to-night as I intended. Should
such a man as I flee? Nay, verily, I shall take observations for latitude and
longitude to-night, though they may be the last. I feel quite calm now,
thank God!"

³ The words in italics are underlined in the journal, and they were underlined in his heart. Later in the same year, he pays his first visit to the Homeland. Honours are everywhere heaped upon him. The University of Glasgow
confers upon him the degree of Doctor of Laws. On such occasions the re-
cipient of the honour is usually subjected to some banter at the hands of the
students. But when Livingstone rises, bearing upon his person the marks of his
struggles and sufferings in darkest Africa, he is received in reverential silence.
He is gaunt and haggard as a result of his long exposure to the tropical sun.
On nearly thirty occasions he has been laid low by the fevers that steam
from the inland swamps, and these severe illnesses have left their mark. His
left arm, crushed by the lion, hangs helplessly at his side. A hush falls upon
the great assembly as he announces his resolve to return to the land for which
he has already endured so much. "But I return," he says, "without misgiving
and with great gladness. For would you like me to tell you what supported
me through all the years of exile among people whose language I could not

From *A Bunch of Everlastings* (New York: The Abingdon Press, 1920). By permission of The Epworth Press, London.

understand, and whose attitude towards me was always uncertain and often hostile? It was this: *'Lo, I am with you alway, even unto the end of the world!'* On those words I staked everything, and they never failed!"

"Leave me not, forsake me not!" he prays.

"Lo, I am with you alway, even unto the end of the world!" comes the response.

"It is the word of a gentleman of the most strict and sacred honour, so there's an end of it!" he tells himself.

On that pledge he hazarded his all. And it did not fail him.

4 II. When, I wonder, did David Livingstone first make that text his own? I do not know. It must have been very early. He used to say that he never had any difficulty in carrying with him his father's portrait because, in "The Cotter's Saturday Night," Robert Burns had painted it for him. Down to the last morning that he spent in his old home at Blantyre, the household joined in family worship. It was still dark when they knelt down that bleak November morning. They are up at five. The mother makes the coffee; the father prepares to walk with his boy to Glasgow; and David himself leads the household to the Throne of Grace. The thought imbedded in his text is uppermost in his mind. He is leaving those who are dearer to him than life itself; yet there is One on whose Presence he can still rely. . . . And so, in selecting the passage to be read by lamplight in the little kitchen on this memorable morning, David selects the Psalm that, more clearly than any other, promises him, on every sea and on every shore, the Presence of his Lord. . . . *The Lord shall preserve thy going out and thy coming in from this time forth, and even for evermore.* After prayers comes the anguish of farewell. But the ordeal is softened for them all by the thought that has been suggested by David's reading and by David's prayer. In the grey light of that winter morning, father and son set out on their long and cheerless tramp. I remember, years ago, standing on the Broomielaw, on the spot that witnessed their parting. I could picture the elder man turning sadly back towards his Lanarkshire home, whilst David hurried off to make his final preparations for sailing. But, deeper than their sorrow, there is in each of their hearts a song . . .—the song of the Presence—the song of the text! . . .

Lo, I am with you alway, even unto the end of the world!

And with that song singing itself in his soul, David Livingstone turns his face towards darkest Africa.

5 III. If ever a man needed a comrade, David Livingstone did. Apart from that divine companionship, his is the most lonely life in history. It is doubtless good for the world that most men are content to marry and settle down, to weave about themselves the web of domestic felicity, to face each day the task that lies nearest to them, and to work out their destiny without worrying about the remote and the unexplored. But it is equally good for the world that there are a few adventurous spirits in every age who feel themselves taunted and challenged and dared by the mystery of the great unknown. As long as there is a pole undiscovered, a sea uncharted, a forest untracked or a desert uncrossed, they are restless and ill at ease. It is the most sublime form that curiosity assumes. From the moment of his landing on African soil, Livingstone is haunted, night and day, by the visions that beckon and the voices that call from out of the undiscovered. For his poor wife's sake he tries hard, and tries repeatedly, to settle down to the life of an ordinary mission station. But it is impossible. The lure of the wilds fascinates him. He sees, away on the horizon, the smoke of a thousand native settlements in which no white man has ever been seen. It is more than he can bear. He goes to some of them and beholds, on arrival, the smoke of yet other settlements still further away. And so he wanders further and further from his starting point; and builds home after home, only to desert each home as soon as it is built! The tales that the natives tell him of vast inland seas and of wild tumultuous waters tantalize him beyond endurance. The instincts of the hydrographer tingle within him. He sees the three great rivers—the Nile, the Congo and the Zambesi—emptying themselves into three separate oceans, and he convinces himself that the man who can solve the riddle of their sources will have opened up a continent to the commerce and civilisation of the world. The treasures of history present us with few things more affecting than the hold that this ambition secures upon his heart. It lures him on and on—along the tortuous slavetracks littered everywhere with bones—through the long grass that stands up like a wall on either side of him—across the swamps, the marshes and the bogs of the watersheds—through forests dark at night and through deserts that no man has ever crossed before—on and on for more than thirty thousand miles. He makes a score of discoveries, any one of which could have established his fame; but none of these satisfy him. The unknown still calls loudly and will not be denied. Even at the last, worn to a shadow, suffering in every limb, and too feeble to put his feet to the ground, the mysterious fountains of Herodotus torture his fancy. "The fountains!" he murmurs in his delirium, "the hidden fountains!" And with death stamped upon his face, he orders his faithful blacks to bear him on a rude litter in his tireless search for the elusive streams. Yet never once does he feel really lonely. One has but to read his journal in order to see that that word of stainless honour never failed him. . . .

Lo, I am with you alway, even unto the end of the world. Thus, amidst savages and solitudes, Livingstone finds that great word grandly true.

[6] IV. *It is His word of honour!* says Livingstone; and, nothing if not practical, he straightway proceeds to act upon it. "If He be with me, I can do anything, *anything, anything.*" It is the echo of another apostolic boast: "I can do all things through Christ that strengtheneth me!" In that unwavering confidence, and with an audacity that is the best evidence of his faith, Livingstone draws up for himself a programme so colossal that it would still have seemed large had it been the project of a million men. "It is His word of honour!" he reasons; "and if He will indeed be with me, even unto the end, He and I can accomplish what a million men, unattended by the Divine Companion, would tremble to attempt." And so he draws up with a calm hand and a fearless heart that prodigious programme from which he never for a moment

swerved, and which, when all was over, was inscribed upon his tomb in Westminster Abbey. Relying on "the word of a gentleman of the most strict and sacred honour," he sets himself—

1. To evangelise the native races.
2. To explore the undiscovered secrets.
3. To abolish the desolating slave-trade.

⁷ Some men set themselves to evangelise; some make it their business to explore; others feel called to emancipate; but Livingstone, with a golden secret locked up in his heart, undertakes all three!

Evangelisation!

Exploration!

Emancipation!

Those were his watchwords. No man ever set himself a more tremendous task: no man ever confronted his lifework with a more serene and joyous confidence!

⁸ V. And how did it all work out? Was his faith justified? Was that *word of honour* strictly kept?

"Leave me not, forsake me not!" he cries.

"Lo, I am with you alway, even unto the end!"

⁹ In spite of that assurance, did he ever find himself a solitary in a strange and savage land? Was he ever left or forsaken? It sometimes looked like it.

¹⁰ It looked like it when he stood, bent with anguish beside that sad and lonely grave at Shupanga. Poor Mary Livingstone—the daughter of Robert and Mary Moffatt—was never strong enough to be the constant companion of a pioneer. For years she struggled on through dusty deserts and trackless jungles seeing no other woman but the wild women about her. But, with little children at her skirts, she could not struggle on for long. She gave it up, and stayed at home to care for the bairns and to pray for her husband as he pressed tirelessly on. But, even in Africa, people will talk. The gossips at the white settlements were incapable of comprehending any motive that could lead a man to leave his wife and plunge into the interior, save the desire to be as far from her as possible. Hearing of the scandal, and stung by it, Livingstone, in a weak moment, sent for his wife to join him. She came; she sickened; and she died. We have all been touched by that sad scene in the vast African solitude. We seem to have seen him sitting beside the rude bed, formed of boxes covered with a soft mattress, on which lies his dying wife. The man who has faced so many deaths, and braved so many dangers, is now utterly broken down. He weeps like a child. "Oh, my Mary, my Mary!" he cries, as the gentle spirit sighs itself away, "I loved you when I married you, and, the longer I lived with you, I loved you the more! How often we have longed for a quiet home since you and I were cast adrift in Africa; God pity the poor children!" He buries her under the large baobab-tree, sixty feet in circumference, and reverently marks her grave. "For the first time in my life," he says, "I feel willing to die! I am left alone in the world by one whom I felt to be a part of myself!"

"Leave me not, forsake me not!" he cried at the outset.

"I am left alone!" he cries in his anguish now.

Has the *word of honour* been violated? Has it? It certainly looks like it!

[11] VI. It looked like it, too, eleven years later, when his own time came. He is away up among the bogs and marshes near Chitambo's village in Ilala. Save only for his native helpers, he is all alone. He is all alone, and at the end of everything. He walked as long as he could walk; rode as long as he could ride; and was carried on a litter as long as he could bear it. But now, with his feet too ulcerated to bear the touch of the ground; with his frame so emaciated that it frightens him when he sees it in the glass; and with the horrible inward hemorrhage draining away his scanty remnant of vitality, he can go no further. "Knocked up quite!" he says, in the last indistinct entry in his journal. A drizzling rain is falling, and the black men hastily build a hut to shelter him. In his fever, he babbles about the fountains, the sources of the rivers, the undiscovered streams. Two of the black boys, almost as tired as their master, go to rest, appointing a third to watch the sick man's bed. But he, too, sleeps. And when he wakes, in the cold grey of the dawn, the vision that confronts him fills him with terror. The white man is not in bed, but on his knees beside it! He runs and awakens his two companions. They creep timidly to the kneeling figure. It is cold and stiff! Their great master is dead! No white man near! No woman's hand to close his eyes in that last cruel sickness! No comrade to fortify his faith with the deathless words of everlasting comfort and everlasting hope! He dies alone!

"Leave me not; forsake me not!" he cried at the beginning.

"He died alone!"—that is how it all ended!

[12] VII. But it only *looks* like it! Life is full of illusions, and so is death. Anyone who cares to read the records in the journal of that terrible experience at Shupanga will be made to feel that never for a moment did the *word of honour* really fail.

"Lo, I am with you alway, even unto the end!"

[13] The consciousness of that unfailing Presence was his one source of comfort as he sat by his wife's bedside and dug her grave. The assurance of that divine Presence was the one heartening inspiration that enabled him to take up his heavy burden and struggle on again!

"Lo, I am with you alway, even unto the end!"

[14] Yes, even to the end! Take just one more peep at the scene in the hut at Chitambo's village. He died on his knees! Then to whom was he talking when he died? He was talking even to the last moment of his life, to the constant Companion of his long, long pilgrimage! He was speaking, even in the act and article of death, to that "Gentleman of the most strict and sacred honour" whose word he had so implicitly trusted.

[15] "He will keep His word"—it is among the last entries in his journal—"He will keep His word, the Gracious One, full of grace and truth; no doubt of it. He will keep His word, and it will be all right. Doubt is here inadmissible, surely!"

"*Leave me not; forsake me not!*" he cried at the beginning.

"*Lo, I am with you alway, even unto the end!*" came the assuring response.

"*It is the word of a gentleman of the most strict and sacred honour, so there's an end of it!*"

[16] And that pathetic figure on his knees is the best testimony to the way in which that sacred pledge was kept.

Part II

Sermons by Masters
in Our Own Day

Repentance

Come unto me all ye that labor and are heavy laden.
—Matt. 11:28

JESUS calls us: "Come unto me!" Whence comes the call and whither are we called? The place where Jesus stands is nearer to us than any other place. It is perhaps for that very reason the farthest away and the least known to us. It may be that we do not see the woods for the trees. Jesus stands in the center of our lives, in the center of this world of reality, in the center indeed. What benefit to us are all the experiences of life and the knowledge of the world if we never know and enter into the center of them? It is a simple matter to find the place, easy to walk in it, if we know ourselves; that is, if we really know ourselves and not merely examine ourselves; take ourselves seriously, love or even hate ourselves. Who knows himself? And so the place where Jesus stands is everywhere and nowhere. We see Him always and yet never. Everyone knows about Him and yet no one knows Him.

2 Jesus calls us: "Come unto me!" He seeks to tell us what is true. He desires to speak truth to us. He wants to talk God to us. He, who lets himself be told, repents. Repentance is turning about to that which is nearest and which we always overlook; to the center of life which we always miss; to the simplest which is still too high and hard for us.

3 God is our Nearest. God is our Center. God is the Simple. God is—this is so natural, so plain, so self-evident, that all else seems more natural to us. God is—this is so clear, so manifest, that all else is more obvious to us. God is—this is so important that all else seems important. Just as the fact of our life is a mystery to us; just as we forget the ground on which we stand, the air in which we breathe; just as in counting we no longer think of the numeral "one" on which all counting is based. As if the first had been given, the foundation laid, the beginning made. But has it really been made? Is our life so natural, so plain, of such import, as it must be if it has its origin in God? Is our security really more than fancy or pretense? How great must the darkness in the world become to remind us that we were too quick to presume that we were like God; that we have lost and must find again the beginning; that we must turn about so that our life may become natural,

From *Come, Holy Spirit*, Sermons by Karl Barth and Eduard Thurneysen, English translation (New York: 1933). By permission.

plain, and worthful in God? That we live, move, and have our being in God is, indeed, not a platitude; it is a great and painful discovery which is to be consummated only with fear and trembling.

4 God is hidden from us. Therefore Jesus is a disturbance in our life and His call to repentance is as a stone rolled in our path. God is—this word spoken by Him, is something incomprehensibly new in the midst of all that which is natural to us; a mystery in the midst of all that which is otherwise plain to us; something hostile, alone important over against all affairs of weight. Hostile because he wishes really to give us that which ignorantly we think we already have. He wishes to open it for us—for this, first of all, must be pushed aside. He wishes to give it to us—for this, we must have first of all, empty hands. He wishes to remind us of it—for this, first of all, we must learn to forget. Jesus shatters us so that He may set us on a firm foundation. He judges us so that He may make us just. He robs us so that He may enrich us. He slays us so that He may make us alive. In no other way can that, which is, be told us. In no other way can God be spoken to us. In no other way can help be given us. Enter in through the narrow gate!

5 Jesus calls us: "Come unto me!" Other voices also call us: "Come unto me!" The voice of the church, for example. Today she calls us to the Confederation's service of thanksgiving, repentance, and prayer. The word "Confederation" reminds us of home and fatherland and of many things that are dear to us, weighty and precious. But still greater are the words "thanksgiving," "repentance," and "prayer." These words are also in the Bible. A certain similarity between them and the words of Jesus can easily be discerned. So much the more must our ears be sensitized that we may distinguish the call of Jesus from other calls of the world. More than 1900 years ago the men of the synagogue literally said almost the same thing as Jesus. Yet it was not the same, but directly the opposite. When the church says something, it is always an open question, and perhaps more than that, whether she does not say the direct opposite of what Jesus says, even when she speaks his own words. At all events it may be asked whether the word "God," spoken and heard in the church, has the least thing to do with God Himself. Perhaps the church—she and no other—has betrayed God all too often; betrayed Him to the needs and humours of man; to the spirit of the times; also quite readily to mammon; and not least, to the different fatherlands, to Switzerland, Germany, or England. Is God in the church the unheard of *new* that Jesus wished to tell us; and not rather that which is known of old, heard so often that men hear it no more? Is He the mystery: He, that dwells in light which no man can approach; and not rather something about which it is easy to chatter and which can be readily understood? Is He really the only One of consequence and not merely one among many worthful persons and things, an idol beside other idols? Does the church indeed dare to witness, in clear and unmistakable terms, how matters stand—that God is hid from us and must be sought in fear and trembling? If she dare not, then she cannot, in the way Jesus did, call men to thanksgiving, repentance, and prayer. If she dare not push aside, then she cannot open. If she dare not empty the

hands of men, then she cannot give them anything. If she dare not say *No*, then she cannot say *Yes*. If she has forgotten the cross of Jesus, the way from life to death, how can she presume to know anything of his resurrection, of the way from death to life?

⁶ Why wonder then that her call: "Come unto me!" sounds hollow and untrustworthy? "The hands are the hands of Esau but the voice is the voice of Jacob." Her call has a different meaning from that of Jesus; because, with all her speaking of God, and Christ, she does not direct man into the depth where man, through Christ in God, ends and begins. She directs him rather to heights of ecstasy and to presumably Christian ways of righteousness. Her call has another effect than the call of Jesus; for though she assures and commends, she does not know and show; though she judges and condemns, she does not speak and work the right; though she stirs up some, she moves none. Her call is something different from the call of Jesus because it is a call in this world and out of this world, and not a call out of another world; because it lacks Jesus' wisdom of death and his zeal of eternity, which alone can make it an actually redeeming attack upon this world. I must say all this just because I am a preacher, a servant of the church, and just because today is the day of prayer, the occasion most loved by the church.

⁷ The call of Jesus resounds despite the church. But the church is a great, perhaps the greatest, hindrance to repentance. If we wish to hear the call of Jesus, then we must hear it despite the church. Forget that today is the day of prayer! Forget that we are in a church! Forget that a minister stands before you! True coins can be told from counterfeit by the ring. O, that we might learn to tell the sound of the call of Jesus from its imitations.

⁸ Jesus calls us: "Come unto me!" *Who is Jesus?* We know him best by those whom he calls to himself. By the brightness into which we then enter, we know the light by which we are lighted. Come unto me, all ye! so he says at the beginning. Jesus concerns all. Jesus is here for all. He is broad and free enough to invite all to Himself, to regard all as belonging to Himself. He has confidence in His right, and above all else, in His might to draw all men unto Himself. He also is sure enough of Himself to need have no fear that He will lose what is appointed for Him when He manifests Himself and gives Himself to all. By this we know the specific purpose for which He has been sent. It can be nothing else but God. God alone concerns all men. God only is free to call all men. To this end God alone has and gives power and authority. God alone does not lose Himself when He is God for all men.

⁹ Here we see the difference between Jesus and other great men, other aims, movements, devices, even the best and most necessary. Goethe and Gottfried Keller are not for all men, not even Jeremiah Gotthelf or Dostoyevsky. Too bad, we may say, but so it is. One cannot expect that all men would be able to think seriously about God and life. Nor can one encourage all men to remain through life implicitly believing Sunday school scholars. The church, unfortunately, is not for all men; but, to be sure, neither is the mourner's bench or the Salvation Army.

¹⁰ One cannot require of all men that they become total abstainers or

socialists; neither can one ask that all men become "duty-conscious citizens." One cannot demand of all men that they be "happy, always happy, happy every day"; nor can one demand of all men that in their walk and conversation they manifest fully the seriousness of life. Unfortunately one cannot, with the hope of a favorable response, make even the simplest moral demands upon all men; for example, the demand that one's property should be assessed justly. Thousands upon thousands have never heeded it, not even with the inner ear; to say nothing that they ever obeyed it or will ever obey it according to human standards. Millions of men, in these latter years, have learned to break without a thought the commandment, "Thou shalt not kill." To them blood has no value; and by the standard of reverence for human life they are no longer to be tested. The more seriously we take the demands of moral living the more we come to realize, for example, what are the requirements of truthfulness, consideration, tact, tenderness, and love which we owe one another, of purity of heart and thought; so much the more must we recognize, to our sorrow, how the number of those who will take these requisites seriously decreases; so much the more will we be frightened at the innumerable host of men who are hopelessly shut out; if they are judged by these standards how at last scarcely one, yea, not one, Paul said, remains within. At this point we see the difference between Jesus and other masters.

¹¹ In reality He is not in a class with them. Jesus concerns all of us. Jesus attacks the entrenched positions of men not on the front, nor where they stand in armor, hardened in their great sin and guilt, the one more coarse, the other more refined; He does not lead the assault with accusations, instructions, and adjurations, not with a strategic movement, effort, or concept, not with thoughts, ideas, and demands, nor morally, and above all not with the familiar sermons of the day of prayer. He attacks men from the rear, at the point where they got into their sin and guilt and where one may still have free access to them. He attacks them from the side of God—God, whom they have lost but who has not lost them. He attacks them with forgiveness. Jesus wants nothing from men. He wants them only for God. He is for all men. All men have need of Him. Jesus at the outset excludes no one, not even in the most refined sense. He tells all men that they are included in God's love, that God counts them as His, and that they may count themselves as God's, despite their sins, despite their guilt—all men, without exception, all men without condition. The word forgiveness, when He speaks it, is the free access to all men. The word forgiveness, if they hear it from Him, is actual deliverance for all men—for the proficient and the foolish, for the cultured and the uncultured, for the converted and the unconverted, for the prisoners and the preachers in the pulpit on the day of prayer.

¹² Jesus has only one complaint against all of us: that we have gone away from God! And only one promise for all of us: that God is faithful! This all men can understand. This all men can accept without belittling themselves and without exalting themselves. Here is the key to all the prisons in which we languish. Here is the whole issue raised. Yes, Jesus is free enough

and strong enough to ask us all to come to Him. He is, also, so sure of his God that he betrays and yields nothing when he calls us all to come as we are. Precisely in these words, "Come ye all unto me!" He reveals himself as the one He is, the Son of God, the Risen One. He tells us that which, only from the standpoint of God, can be said about all of us. He alone may say it. All of us need forgiveness, and forgiveness is at hand. He who lets this be told repents. "Come unto me all ye that labor and are heavy laden!"

13 Who is Jesus? we ask ourselves once more. He who calls the laboring and the heavy laden to Himself. After all, not everyone? Yes, truly, everyone, for the words "labor and heavy laden" define the word "all." These very words show us on what side Jesus lays hold of the world to claim it for God. Jesus does not see us as we again and again would like to see ourselves; not in our fitness, not in our zeal, not in our earnestness, not in our believing, not as "warriors in the army of light," in the words of a famous novel, and not as "God's co-laborers," something which so many would like to be today. He sees us as laboring and heavy laden. He does not depreciate the good that we think, purpose, and do, surely not! but He does not praise it; He does not give it any special value; He is silent about it. He assumes that we know what is good, that we will do what we know, that we do not overvalue what we are, live and do; but that we ourselves would gladly cover it up. He is interested in our labors and in our burdens. He is interested not in our answers but in our questions, not in our security but in our restlessness, not in our finding but in our seeking. He passes the healthy and turns to the sick, goes, quietly and resolutely, past all kinds of righteous persons and turns to the publicans. He asks our young people not about their reports from school, not about their industry in the mill, not about their good repute, not even whether their parents and pastors are satisfied with them. He asks them about the remarkable dissatisfaction and longing, which disturbs every young person and which is not to be silenced by work or idleness, by obedience or license. He asks them about that doleful yearning which is so great and often so dangerous because there is no ground or name for it.

14 Jesus asks our wives not about the correctness of their housekeeping, and not about the excellence of their qualifications as wives and mothers, but about their fatigue, spiritual destitution, and helplessness because they do not know how to accommodate themselves to the lot of womanhood—which they, most of all, would like to escape. He asks us men not about our character, not about our services, not about our activity as professional people and citizens, but about our secret shame, about the wounds of egotism in our conscience, about the open or hidden tragedy of the struggle of our passions with our ideals of righteousness. He asks the socialists not about the nobility of their theory and not about results—be they ever so evident—but about the final questions of social life of which they have yet hardly thought, about the questions into which the most upright socialist cannot go farther without putting himself in the wrong. And He certainly does not ask the citizens about the points where they are right against the Bolsheviki—where it is childishly easy to be right; but about the other points, where they know that

Bolshevism uncovers only a disease, of which even they, yes, just they, suffer, and for which today a cure is sought by them in vain. And so, also, Jesus asks our pious people not about the state of their conversion and sanctification—for these are Pharisaical questions—but about their inward part from which the unredeemed soul cries out: "I believe, dear Lord, help my unbelief!"

15 For Jesus the notable thing about us is never that in which we are right, but that in which, though with much right, we are wrong. He takes account only of this—that we know that we labor and are heavy laden or that we are in some other state. He takes it for granted that we really are in this condition and that this, in all cases, is the only noteworthy thing about us. He comes into our lives when the only thing that remains to be said about us is that which can be said by God: "*forgiven!*" Because we labor and are heavy laden we belong to the "*all*" to whom his invitation is given. That, and nothing else, is for us the window open towards Jerusalem. That, and nothing else, is the side of us on which we are bound to Jesus and through him to God. Blessed are the poor in spirit! Blessed are they that mourn! Blessed are they that hunger and thirst after righteousness! Only when we labor and are heavy laden do we know Him—Him, who is not the improver, but the redeemer, of the world; Him, who restores the lost first estate. He can begin to speak and act only where in the end we must be silent and stop; where God alone can give the only answer that is left for us. His *yes* springs forth from the deepest and bitterest *no* of man in this world. His life breaks forth through death that is upon the earth. He says, *Forward!* after he has called a *Halt!* by his death on the cross, to mankind and to all that is human. He is not superior, powerful, wise, not even pious. Behold! He is the Lamb of God which bears the sins of the world. He does that *to* us, which starting with God and God alone, can be done *for* us; He puts himself beyond our good as well as beyond our evil, and confines Himself to the difficult question which remains when one takes account of both together—*He forgives us*. He confirms our only hope: the resurrection of the dead, the passing of the old man, the new creation. He, who has eyes to see, repents.

16 "Come unto me!" What does Jesus want of us? He wants nothing of us but that we come. He does not want *ours* but *us*. If we come as we are, all is well. For this is the new and all-important thing, the mystery that confronts us in Christ. Our coming consists in this, that we permit Jesus to tell us that we labor and are heavy laden. On this account it is so hard for us to come. For this we delay again and again. It is this throughout Christendom that keeps people from Jesus. To come to Him means to labor and to be heavy laden. If the issue today were to proclaim, at the direction of the church, so-called thoughts suitable for the day of prayer about our national condition, to hear them and in some measure to take them to heart, then truly we would come easily and quickly. If it were merely a matter of converting oneself for the first or second time, then, also, we would come. We would come with gladness, if Jesus were to teach us a way by which one even here on earth could climb into heaven, as, for example, among the anthroposophists in

178

Dornach—or a method by which one could set up heaven upon earth as among the "Siedler" in Germany. We would say yes, if Jesus were to demand of us that we align ourselves with the I.B.S.A.—"earnest Bible students"—and fathom the "dear God's" plan for the future; or let ourselves be taught by a jovial American how to become a happy and contented man in the easiest and simplest way. Any kind of upward move, attack, advance, upbuilding strikes us favorably.

¹⁷ But when Jesus speaks, this is not the issue; it is rather to be still, to retreat, and to tear down. On this account it is so hard for us really to come to Him, to labor and be heavy laden, and nothing but that. Mark well! here one can only *believe*. Believe, that God gives grace to the humble. Believe, that His power in the weak is mighty. Believe, that in forgiveness we have eternal life. Believe, that it is worthwhile to sell all our pearls for the sake of the pearl of great price. Believe, that Jesus is victory. It is hard for us to believe. Let us freely grant that it is harder than all that is high, great, complicated. Faith is not for every man. Much already has been gained when we recognize this. Faith begins with the insight that we have little faith. Finding begins with the pain of long futile seeking. Coming to Jesus begins with the knowledge that something difficult is asked of us. It is they who labor and are heavy laden who come to God through repentance.

GEORGE ARTHUR BUTTRICK   SERMON 21

The Sound of Silence

And after the fire a still small voice.—I Kings 19:12

THE WORDS "a still small voice" are even more surprising in the original: "a sound of thin silence." One translator has come close: "a sound of gentle stillness." Behind the words is a story that might have been written for our times, for it tells of a man to whom victory brought despair, just as V-J Day seems to have brought us to deep misgiving.

² I. The man was Elijah. On Mount Carmel he contended with the priests of Baal worship, as we contend with Nazi paganism. He challenged the false priests to call down fire on their altar, and they failed. Then he poured water on his sacrifice, filled a trench around his altar with water, and by his prayers brought fire that consumed both sacrifice and water. Then he killed the pagan priests, ended the drought that had plagued his nation, and praised God for the complete victory. You have already traced the parallel with our times.

³ Then? Then he found that paganism was not dead. The queen, who was a patron of Baal worship, sought his life; she was resolved to kill him by "tomorrow at this time." Elijah fled perforce to a cave in the desert. He was in despair: "Now let me die, for I am not better than my fathers." He may have meant that, like them, he was as good as dead; or he may have intended some bitter protest: "In every generation, theirs and mine, evil reigns. The triumph of goodness is but a mock triumph. What's the use?" A recent letter from the Pacific, commenting on the present state of our world, says, with good humor but not without seriousness, "We might as well jump into the sea." We can understand Elijah. He was suffering physical and nervous exhaustion. The taut mind had sprung back from crisis, and hung limp. That is also our case. But he was afflicted also by a real pessimism:

⁴ "Truth forever on the scaffold, wrong forever on the throne." Small people do not care what becomes of the world, but noble folk agonize. They are like Elijah at the mouth of his cave.

⁵ II. What is the answer? The diagnosis is relatively easy. What about the cure? God told this man, in a parable of actual lightning and thunder, that he should neither fear cataclysms—nor trust them. Always we are tempted to say with Omar:

By arrangement with the author.

180

> Ah Love! could you and I with Him conspire
> To grasp this sorry Scheme of Things entire,
> Would we not shatter it to bits—and then
> Remould it nearer to the Heart's desire!

But when the shattering is done, we must remold the world patiently—from the same bits. This, God said to Elijah in an acted parable. Came the tempest, but God was not in the tempest; came an earthquake, but God was not in the earthquake; came the fire, but God was not in the fire. But "after the fire," a "sound of thin silence," the beating of noiseless wings.

⁶ Catastrophe has little power to cure. That fact our generation must confront. Miami was once almost leveled by a tempest, but Miami is not a mecca of saints. San Francisco was shaken and broken by an earthquake, but San Francisco is not the "Golden Gate" to heaven. Chicago was partly demolished by fire, but not purified of dross. Besides, the tempest, earthquake, and fire that men arouse to destroy paganism may easily enthrone paganism in their own lives. The form may be different; the evil is the same recurrent evil. The convulsions of our time are not likely in themselves to bring spiritual gain; our real task has just begun.

⁷ Do not misunderstand: the sorrow and tumult need not be in vain. But their main purpose is to prepare us, if only by contrast, to hear the "still small voice." The thunderous judgments of our time are God's prelude to a gentler providence. When the storm has passed, "a sound of thin silence."

⁸ III. God told this man to trust in quiet power. Even in nature, with all its upheavals, real might moves in silence. Gravitation bases our cities which otherwise could be tossed like leaves in a gale, but gravitation comes unawares and is neither seen nor heard. The tides cleanse our shores and launch our ventures, but the tides obey the moon!

> The innocent moon, that nothing does but shine,
> Moves all the labouring surges of the world.

Spring comes with only leaves for banners: it has no fanfare or impious cannon. Nature has storms, and they bring their judgment and cleansing, but the heart of nature is a brooding beneficence in silent field and sky. So God deals with us in human nature. Tell what has deeply moved you. Not some earthquake, but seemingly trivial events. You saw in the face of an elevator man looking upward the type of all human longing. You heard Roland Hayes sing, "Were you there when they crucified my Lord?" You saw a dog run over, watched a child hug the dog in its death spasms, and thought of men being killed across a world of war. You heard great music, and one phrase haunted you for a week. You were changed, or you could have been changed, by "a sound of thin silence."

⁹ This, God said to Elijah, and cheered him by the assurance that thousands yearned secretly as he yearned: "Yet I have left me seven thousand in Israel, all the knees which have not bowed unto Baal." Paganism fulminated, but saints bided their silent time in conquering prayer. That fact holds true of

181

our generation. More and more people question our accepted ways in trade and school. They question the bombast of competing armies. They read a book like *The Robe*—read it in a wistful longing. In Norway Christian folk suddenly realize their strength, as suddenly come to political power, and then move toward Christian goals. A minister sees in this man a noble discontent of soul, and in that woman a better stoic courage as she faces death. Whence the power? It seems no stronger than a whisper in the soul. But! Three women met. One discoursed brilliantly and, as she thought, convincingly of God. Another was Madame Guyon, mystic and saint, who, tired of the argument, meditated on God in silence. The third later sought out Madame Guyon to confess her sins. "You were convinced by the argument?" Madame Guyon asked. "No," said the other, "by the silence." She was saved by a "still small voice." There are many such, God tells us.

[10] Thus God gently invited Elijah to ally himself with real power. God is in the tempest, earthquake, and fire, despite the story; but these are not His central dwelling. His home is in what sailors call "the eye of the storm"—the silence around which the tumult swirls. We covet sweeping changes, vast legislation, blinding signs. Perhaps it is because we think we are big. But God's essential nature is not in cataclysm, but in stillness. This is why men, whom God has made, can never be frightened into goodness. Even hate and anger can overcome fear, and fear fades when crisis has passed. The fear of catastrophe may prepare us to hear the sound of silence. John McNeill has told us that, when he ran away from home to serve before the mast, a terrific tempest left him as headstrong as before, but the faces of his father and mother when he returned home to Scotland—faces that searched his face to see if marks of wickedness were on him, and spoke no condemnation, but smiled only welcome—he could not forget. They turned him from his stubborn will to Christ.

[11] Christ: all roads lead home to Him. He came amid the clash of mighty empires, but not as a more dreadful thunder:

> How silently, how silently
> The wondrous gift is given!
> So God imparts to human hearts
> The blessings of His heaven.

So: not as John the Baptist had prophesied. John had said that when God the Deliverer came His ax would ring on the doomed tree, His iron flail would mercilessly drive away the chaff. But when He came, He was so gentle that He would not extinguish even a smoky lamp, or break even a broken reed. There were thunders in Him: the ground was shaken and the lightnings flashed. But these were not His heart, as any child could tell us. "So God imparts"—as Saul of Tarsus found. He was on his way to harry the Christian church in Damascus and to put its saints to the sword. A light blinded him, and some violent power flung him to the ground—a counterpart of Elijah's tempest and earthquake and fire. But these alone would never have changed Saul from a persecutor to a saint. After the flash and the buffeting came the voice. It was hardly more than "a sound of thin silence." The words could hardly have been more strange. They were a plea rather than a command: "Why persecutest thou me?" "I am Jesus, whom thou persecutest."

¹² Lincoln Steffens tells of his dismay at finding that a good mayor of his town would soon lose the election—because he had been a good mayor. People did not want a good mayor, and a tornado would not have changed them—or a world war. What would have changed them? There is always the crucial question, even though it is the question we rarely ask. The sight of the mayor dying for his faith, had he so died, might have changed them. If it would have changed them enough we do not know. Noble tragedy has cleansing power: that you know when you read a novel like *Anna Karenina*, or see a play like *Antigone*. Why tragedy befalling the noble should cleanse us, who can tell? It does, and meanwhile ennobles the noble who suffer. The cleansing is in direct proportion to the purity of the suffering. The pains of a saint cleanse far more than the pains of the selfish, for the latter may leave us with only a sense of vengeance fulfilled. Perhaps we are really saved only by—the pains of God Himself. "I am Jesus, whom thou persecutest." That is why a cross is set against the skyline of our world. That is why the best Christian preaching is not preaching at all, but a finger pointing and a voice pleading, "Behold the Man!"

¹³ "How silently, how silently"! "So God imparts . . . the blessings"! Not by the clamor of our cities, or by the threat of our wars, but by a "still small voice." The voice yet speaks: "Follow thou me." The voice is now within—"a sound of thin silence." He yet walks our streets, is still crucified, and ever rises; and Christmas comes again to remind us that in Him is our salvation. Lincoln Steffens' mayor suffering for His sake might have changed his city. At long last only so are cities changed.

¹⁴ IV. John Henry Jowett once said that if he saw a tiny church alongside a mammoth armaments factory with its forests of chimneys belching smoke and its roar of machinery like a prelude to the din of battle, he would be quite sure in which of the two real power dwelt. Would we be sure? You and I must choose between clamor and consecration, between the world's display and the soul's whisper. Shall we make the issue quite clear and close? There is the world noisy in self-assertion, saying, "Strive and gain!" Within you is—call it conscience, call it compassion—"a sound of thin silence." It does not much profit to discuss the difficulties confronting conscience in our time, or the difficulties confronting compassion. They are there, but often we have no doubt what conscience and compassion require of us. The noise of the world or the soundless word within you—which?

¹⁵ Shall we bring the issue to personal terms? Out there the raucous contending voices of the world and in us another word—some "memory" (if that description serves) of Christ. Which?

> Loud mockers in the roaring street
> Say Christ is crucified again
> Twice pierced His gospel-bearing feet,
> Twice broken His great heart in vain.

> I hear and to myself I smile,
> For Christ talks with me all the while.[1]

But which shall sway us—the roaring street or Christ? The Church has, and shall have, more power than the armaments factory if He is genuinely in the Church.

[16] After the tempest, earthquake, fire of our times, "a still small voice." That is our hope, if we will obey. The voice is as silent, yet as mighty, as a daybreak when the sun never sets.

[1] Richard le Gallienne, "The Second Crucifixion." Used by permission of Dodd, Mead & Co.

CLOVIS GILLHAM CHAPPELL   SERMON **22**

The Forks of the Road--Moses

> *By faith, Moses, when he was come to years, refused to*
> *be called the son of Pharaoh's daughter; choosing rather*
> *to suffer affliction with the people of God, than to enjoy*
> *the pleasures of sin for a season; esteeming the reproach of*
> *Christ greater riches than the treasures in Egypt; for he*
> *had respect unto the recompense of the reward.*
> —Heb. 11:24-26

MOSES is at the forks of the road. A very revealing place is this spot where the roads fork. Here every man shows himself for what he is. One man comes to the forks of the road and undertakes to stand perfectly still. He is afraid to turn either to the right hand or to the left lest he go wrong. Or he travels the road to the left for a season, then retraces his steps and for another season travels the road to the right. Such conduct indicates that he is afflicted with the fatal malady of indecision. When Moses comes to the forks of the road he refuses the one and sets himself steadfastly to travel the other. By so doing he shows himself a man of decision.

² II. There were two elements in this decision of Moses, as there are in all decisions.

³ 1. There was a negative element. "Moses when he was come to years refused." That is, there was something to which Moses said "No." And, mark you, his "No" was a full-fledged, one hundred per cent negative. It was not tinctured with a single ounce of "Yes." So often when we say "No" it is lacking in positiveness. Likewise, when we say "Yes," there is a weakness about it that indicates an admixture of the negative. Moses, when he stood at the forks of the road, looked at both roads, and to one of them he said a positive, vigorous, out and out "No."

⁴ 2. But Moses did more than say "No." He did something more than refuse to take a certain road. He also said "Yes." He refused to travel one way, not that he might stand still, but that he might travel another way. So often we content ourselves with a mere refusal. When we hear the call of Christ almost the first thought that comes into our mind is not that to which we are to say "Yes," but that to which we are to say "No." We think of the Christian life on its negative side rather than on its positive side. We

---

From *Sermons on Old Testament Characters* (New York: 1925). By permission of Harper & Brothers.

think of what we are to quit being and doing rather than what we are to become and what we are to do.

⁵ Now, it is altogether right to remember that certain things must be given up in order for us to become followers of Jesus Christ. But we must also remember this: That no amount of negatives will make us Christians. No man ever becomes a Christian by virtue of what he does not do. No amount of "don'ts" summed up will equal a saint, as no amount of ciphers summed up will equal a unit. Therefore, it is the poorest possible plea, when we respond to Christ's call to become disciples by enumerating the wicked things that we do not do. It is necessary to be able to say "No." But to simply say "No" and stop there is to end in utter moral failure.

⁶ There is a handsome wax figure in one of the stores on Main Street. When I approached him and told him where he could get a case of bootleg liquor, he refused to be interested. When I told him where he could bet on a sure thing, he was also indifferent. When I sought to amuse him with a smutty story, he had the decency not to be amused. When I complimented his competitor on the opposite side of the street, he did not turn green with envy. To every temptation he said a very positive "No." But when encouraged by his refusals to do the wrong, I invited him to prayer meeting, he was as unresponsive as the average church member. And when I passed the collection plate, he did not even see it. Therefore, I cannot call this gentlemanly wax figure a Christian. He is as far from being a saint as death is far from life.

⁷ The truth of the matter is that Christ is calling on you to say "No" not simply because he wants you to practice self-denial as an end. He is calling on you to say "No" to the lower because that is absolutely necessary in order for you to say "Yes" to the highest. He is asking you to say "No" to the darkness because in no other way can you say "Yes" to the light. He is asking you to say "No" to the mud puddle in order that you may say "Yes" to the infinite sea. He is asking you to say "No" to the ant hill in order that you may say "Yes" to the majestic mountain. He is asking you to say "No" to sin in order that you may say "Yes" to righteousness. He is asking you to say "No" to uselessness in order that you may say "Yes" to usefulness. He is asking you to say "No" to the Devil in order that you may say "Yes" to Himself.

⁸ III. This decision of Moses was costly.

1. There was much to be given up.

(1) This decision involved the giving up of the highest social position in all the land of Egypt. It was to pass in one step from this high position, not to a lower rank, but to the very lowest. It was to cease to be the son of the Egyptian princess in order to become the son of a Hebrew slave. And, mark you, social position is not a thing that we despise. There are people that are willing to pay almost any price to win and retain a high social standing. I have seen mothers willing to give their pure and tender daughters to dance with men that they knew to be libertines just in order to get into society. When, therefore, Moses said "No" to this high social position, he said "No" to something that makes a tremendous appeal to the average man and woman.

186

⁹ (2) When Moses made this decision, he said "No" to the pleasures of Egypt. The Egypt of that day was the New York of modern life. It was the playground of the world. Here every pleasure could be enjoyed, from the most fastidious and refined to the most bestial and vulgar. All these pleasures were within reach of the hand of Moses. And, therefore, when he said "No," he rejected all that could appeal to a man who was in love with worldly pleasure.

¹⁰ (3) His decision involved the giving up of the treasures of Egypt. The Egypt of that day was the granary of the world. Down from its unknown source every year came the Nile, giving to Egypt its fertility. To Egypt came the ships and caravans of many nations, carrying away her grain and leaving behind their silver and gold. Much of this treasure went into the coffers of Pharaoh. When Moses, therefore, said "No" to the treasures of Egypt, he refused to grip and hold vast wealth that might have been his for the taking.

¹¹ (4) For Moses to make this decision was to bring bitter disappointment to one who loved him, and to whom he was under very great obligations. I think we have never given sufficient credit to this Egyptian princess who was Moses' foster mother. The fact that she was a heathen did not prevent her from being a good woman. It did not rob her of a mother heart. When that strange craft afloat on the Nile was found, and when its lone occupant pelted this Egyptian princess with his weakness and cannonaded her with his tears, she had the grace and the tenderness to capitulate. She took this little waif to her heart and protected him. It was to her that he owed his life. It was to her that he owed the fact that he had been educated in the royal universities. It was by no means easy, therefore, for a big-souled man like Moses to disappoint one who had thus helped him and who tenderly loved him.

¹² 2. But the cost of this decision of Moses is not to be measured alone by what he gave up. What he chose in place of it all was also costly. When he refused all that Egypt had to offer, what did he accept in its stead? When he said "No" to the privileges that might have been his as the son of Pharaoh's daughter, to what did he say "Yes"?

¹³ (1) He chose suffering. "Moses, when he was come to years, refused to be called the son of Pharaoh's daughter, choosing rather to suffer affliction with the people of God." This is an arresting statement. Here is a man facing a road that he knows will lead him to suffering, to agony, to disappointment, to battle and conflict and tears. Yet, with his eyes wide open, he makes the choice. He does not dream for a moment that when he identifies himself with a horde of slaves he is going to have an easy time. He does not fool himself into believing that the course upon which he has decided will be all sunshine and all laughter. He knows that there will be battles to fight. He knows that there will be heavy burdens to be borne. He knows that there will be many a misunderstanding and many a disappointment and many a heartache. Yet, with his eyes wide open, and alive to all that is involved, he chooses to suffer affliction with the people of God.

¹⁴ IV. How did Moses come to make this choice?

1. He had a clear eye for distinguishing right from wrong. How easy it is

187

for us to persuade ourselves that the thing we want to do is the thing we ought to do! How easy it would have been for Moses to have accepted the career that was open to him as the son of Pharaoh's daughter! He might have reminded himself of the large service rendered by Joseph. Joseph had saved his people in the past, not by descending, but by ascending. Joseph had become a prime minister of Egypt. He himself might have promised a kindred salvation by keeping his position as the son of Pharaoh's daughter. But he refused to let his own interests blind him. He saw that to cling to his rights would be to sin. He refused to blind himself to the fact that it was not simply sinful to choose the lowest, it was also sinful to choose the second best. He realized that God was calling him to choose the highest, and to fail to so choose was to sin.

¹⁵ 2. He knew that the pleasures and gains of sin are only temporary. Sin is only charming in the present or in the immediate future. It has no charm in the past. How fascinating is sin a moment before it is committed! How absolutely necessary it seems to our happiness! But when it slips into the past its pearly teeth become ugly fangs, its shapely hands become unshapely claws, its winsome tresses become writhing serpents. The sin of the future often seems as fair as an angel from heaven, but the sin of yesterday is as ugly as a fiend from hell.

¹⁶ What a pity that we do not have this clear insight possessed by Moses. He faced the fact that there were pleasures in sin. The Bible everywhere confesses that fact. Sin had its laughter and its song and its sunshine. Sin has its pleasures, but they do not last. Its most brilliant career soon comes to an end. Its brightest day soon closes. Its sweetest draught is soon drunk. Its fairest flowers are soon faded. Choose the way of sin if you will, and though you may laugh, your laughter will be but temporary. Though you may rejoice, your joy will be as fleeting as a shadow. Then one day when the laughter has all died and your roses are all withered and your songs are all hushed, you will have a whole eternity in which to curse yourself.

¹⁷ 3. He had a keen eye for the things of real value. So clearly did he see, that he esteemed the reproach of Christ greater riches than the treasures of Egypt. It took a man deeply schooled in permanent values to reach that conclusion. The treasures of Egypt loomed large. They seemed very genuine and very weighty and very abiding. The reproach of Christ—how uninviting! How lacking in winsomeness! Yet Moses decided that the thing of real value was not the wealth of Egypt, but the reproach of Christ. What a seeing eye did this man possess!

¹⁸ 4. Then Moses looked away from everything else to the coming reward. He believed that the future belongs not to sin but to righteousness. He believed it is the heritage, not of the holders of the treasures of Egypt, but of those who share the reproach of Christ. He refused to allow temporary gain to blind him to the gain that is eternal. He looked away from everything else to the coming reward. He looked away from Egypt's splendor and power. He looked away from Egypt's molehills and ant heaps to the majestic mountains that loomed in the hazy distance. His faith gave him at once the

far view and the true view. "He had respect unto the recompense of the reward."

19 V. And what was the outcome of this decision?

1. Moses received the reward of a Christlike character. Do you see that man coming down from the mountain with face that is strangely alight? Do you find your eyes dazzled in his presence as if you were looking upon a sunrise? Whose is the face that must needs have a veil to cover it before we can look upon it? It is the face of a man who refused the treasures of Egypt and chose the reproach of Christ. The splendor of his face has not come to him from long gazing upon silver and gold. Such a gaze hardens the face and darkens all its radiance. Whence, then, came this winsome light? It has come from looking upon God. Had Moses remained in Egypt he would have missed many a conflict and struggle. He would also have missed a face lighted with the light that shines in the face of Jesus Christ.

20 2. Through this decision Moses was able to render a great service to his own nation and to the world. "Whose are those white tents in the valley?" I ask him one day. "They are the tents of God's chosen people, Israel," he answers. "Israel?" I reply in amazement. "I thought Israel was in bondage. I thought her people were slaves. I thought they were giving themselves solely to the task of brick making." "They were," he replies, "till I came. But by the grace of God I have led them from bondage to freedom."

21 But I am in doubt as to whether Moses' service in freeing his people has been greatly worth while. They are such a peevish and fretful and whining lot. They are forever lusting for the flesh pots of Egypt. They are constantly complaining to Moses because he has not left them to die in the land of bondage. I cannot convince myself that his task has been worth the doing. So I speak my mind:—"Pardon me, Moses. You have made a heroic fight. You have set your people free. But they are a cantankerous lot, and I fear your labor has been almost, if not quite, in vain."

22 But Moses does not seem to share my doubts. "Israel does not count for much now," he replies, "but remember that he is only a child. He has by no means arrived, but he is on the way. You may not believe it, but he will yet render the world a great service. One day he is going to write a Book, and that Book will do more than all other books to banish the world's wrongs and the world's night, and to bring in a reign of righteousness. One day he is going to give to the world an Isaiah with his inspired eloquence, and a Jeremiah with his broken heart and his streaming tears. One day he is going to give to the world a skylark named David and a flaming missionary named Paul. One day there is going forth from his little country the best of all good news:—"Behold, I bring you glad tidings of great joy, for there is born unto you this day a Saviour, which is Christ the Lord." Israel does not count for much yet. But he is on the way toward bringing the whole world into his debt."

23 3. Then, incidentally, this decision enabled Moses to win heaven. The New Testament makes us sure of this. Read the story of the Transfiguration. Christ has come. He is struggling under the burden of his coming Cross. He needs help such as those deeply schooled in the mystery of suffering alone can give. Therefore, two men, passed from earth long years ago, came to talk with him of his coming crucifixion. Who are they? One of them is the man who esteemed the reproach of Christ greater riches than the treasures of Egypt. Whence does he come? The One to whom he speaks, his own shining face, the whole story, answers that question. He comes from heaven. He is fresh from the house of many mansions. There he had been for long centuries. And there he is at this hour, glad with the joy of those who are forever with the Lord.

²⁴ We must conclude, therefore, that the best day's work that Moses ever did was when he made possible the writing of this sentence:—"By faith Moses, when he was come to years, refused to be called the son of Pharaoh's daughter; choosing rather to suffer affliction with the people of God than to enjoy the pleasures of sin for a season; esteeming the reproach of Christ greater riches than the treasures of Egypt; for he had respect unto the recompense of the reward." He gave up the passing and the temporal, but he won the wealth that endures. He won Christlike character. He won abiding usefulness. He won an inheritance among that elect company who "have washed their robes and made them white in the blood of the Lamb."

Forgiveness of Sins

THE ONLY persons to whom this message is addressed are those conscious of moral wrongdoing. If there is any hearer with no uneasy stirrings of conscience about his attitude toward anything or his relationship with anybody, then this sermon is not for him. For we are going to talk about forgiveness of sins.

2 Before any make up their minds, however, that they do not come within the range of this subject's interest and scope, one would like to be certain that they understand what we mean by "sin." So often when we use that word we have in the background of our minds a specific list of gross iniquities—murder, robbery, sensuality, drunkenness. Those plainly are sins. But before any person endeavors to avoid his share in the need of forgiveness, let him add at least three categories more to that carnal list.

3 Let him add sins of temperament—sullenness, vindictiveness, peevishness, jealousy, bad temper. How much more prevalent they are; how much more harm they do; how much more hidden evil they reveal than even passionate sins! In Jesus' greatest parable, the Prodigal represents sins of passion, and, ruinous as they are, he did come home again. But the Elder Brother represents sins of temper. With the Prodigal home, the house alight, music playing, dancing on, it is written of the Elder Brother that "he was angry, and would not go in." Bad temper, sullen, envious, bitter—that, as Jesus saw, keeps some people from the Father's house more hopelessly than sins of passion do.

4 If any one seeks to avoid his share in the need of forgiveness, let him add also sins of social attitude. As one of our leading sociologists has said, "The master iniquities of our time are connected with money-making." When one watches our economic system in operation, one sees how easily a man, friendly enough with individuals whom he meets, can enforce hard practices through a great organization which does more harm, works more misery, ruins more families over a wider area, than he, by his individual friendliness, ever can make up for. Cavour, the statesman, working on the unification of Italy, and using every political trick that he could think of to achieve his ends, said once to his confrères, "If we were to do for ourselves what we are doing for Italy, we should be great rogues." Just so! There are many great and small rogues today who do evil for political or economic organizations that they never would think of doing for themselves.

5 Nor should any one try to escape his share in the need of forgiveness

From *The Secret of Victorious Living* (New York: 1934). By permission of Harper & Brothers.

until he has added to the list sins of neglect. It is not alone the things we do; it is the things we leave undone that haunt us—the letters we did not write, the words we did not speak, the opportunity we did not take. How insistently Jesus stressed the importance of this type of evil! What was the matter with the man who hid his one talent in a napkin? What did he do? That was the trouble—he did nothing; he missed his chance. What was the trouble with the priest and the Levite who left the victim on the road? What did they do? That was the difficulty—they did nothing; they went by on the other side.

⁶ Sins of the flesh, sins of temper, sins of social attitude, sins of neglect— I suppose there must be others, but this ought to take in most of us and make us wonder whether, after all, we may not have a share in the need of the gospel of forgiveness.

⁷ This morning in particular I stress the difficulty of forgiving sin. So often pardon has been presented as an easy gospel, as though one light-heartedly could cry, Come, everybody, and have your sins forgiven! No, it is hard to forgive sins—hard for us; hard for Christ. "Which is easier," said Jesus in the story of the palsied man, "to say, Thy sins are forgiven thee; or to say, Arise and walk?" You see what the Master implies there. It is easier to tell a palsied man to walk—it is easier to meet any other human need— than to say, Thy sins are forgiven.

⁸ At first that sounds strange from Jesus. We should have thought it easy for him to forgive. He said so many glorious words about forgiveness; he exhibited it so marvelously in his life; he made it forever memorable on the cross. One would think forgiveness spontaneously overflowed with him. But no; it was hard for him to forgive, as it always ought to be. And a lesson is there which we modern Christians need to learn.

⁹ Why, then, was it hard for Jesus to forgive? In the first place, because he took sin seriously. It is easy to condone sin, to make light of it; but when one takes it seriously, it is hard to forgive. Suppose that some one here were a specialist in tapestries, prized them, loved them; and suppose he saw some ruffians ruining one, ignorantly, brutally ruining a lovely thing that he knew to be worth a king's ransom—would you think it easy for him to forgive that? Another man who could not tell tapestry from cheesecloth would find it easy to condone the deed, make light of it, pass it over. But for the expert to say even about that, Forgive them, for they know not what they do, would not be easy, for he takes tapestries in earnest.

¹⁰ Consider, then, the moral realm. You can go to the theater any night and hear sexual sin made light of, condoned, laughed at. But Frederick W. Robertson, the English preacher, walked down the street in Brighton once with a face terrific as the Furies and grinding his teeth in rage. He had just heard of a man plotting the ruin of a fine girl whom he knew. He took that seriously and it was hard to forgive.

¹¹ When, therefore, you hear any one talking about forgiveness light-heartedly as an easy matter, you may be sure of this: he is not forgiving sin; he is condoning it, and that is another affair altogether. There is plenty of that

192

without our adding to it. To say that sin does not matter, to make light of it, to take it easily, to be gracious and tolerant about it—there is plenty of that. But that is not forgiveness. That is moral looseness. Sin does matter—tremendously! To condone sin is easy; to forgive it is hard.

12 Here lies a familiar difference between two kinds of mothers. Some mothers have no moral depth, no moral seriousness. A superficial affectionateness distinguishes their motherhood. They have an instinctive maternity for their offspring, such as bears have for their cubs or birds for their fledglings. When the son of such a mother becomes a prodigal and wallows in vice, she will receive him again—will receive him, condoning his sin, making light of it, saying that it does not matter, making up more excuses for it than he ever could himself concoct. But some of us had mothers who never would have forgiven us that way. They would have forgiven us, but, alike for them and for us, it would have been serious. They would have borne upon their hearts the outrage of our sin as though they had committed it themselves. They would have gone with vicarious steps to the gateway of any hell we turned our feet toward, and stood grief-stricken at the door till we came out. They would have put themselves in our places, lived in our stead, felt upon their innocence the burden of our guilt. They would have forgiven us but it would have turned their hair gray. That is forgiveness. It always means self-substitution. He who gives forgiveness gives himself. And it is not easy.

13 Of course, all the seers have felt this. If Tennyson in his "Idylls of the King," portraying Arthur standing over Guinevere, fallen in penitential shame before him on the nunnery floor, had made him say some light-hearted thing as though her infidelity did not matter, we would feel the shallowness of that condoning. Moreover, Guinevere would have felt it too.

> The sombre close of that voluptuous day,
> Which wrought the ruin of my lord the King—

she knew how serious had been her sin. How then could Tennyson have made Arthur's forgiveness less solemn than this:

> Yet think not that I come to urge thy crimes;
> I did not come to curse thee, Guinevere,
> I, whose vast pity almost makes me die
> To see thee, laying there thy golden head,
> My pride in happier summers, at my feet.
> My wrath which forced my thoughts on that fierce law,
> The doom of treason and the flaming death,—
> When first I heard thee hidden here,—is past.
>
> . . . .
>
> And all is past, the sin is sinn'd, and I,
> Lo, I forgive thee, as Eternal God
> Forgives.

14 That is forgiveness, and it is not easy. "Which is easier, to say, Thy sins are forgiven thee; or to say, Arise and walk?"

[15] In the second place, Jesus found it hard to forgive because he loved people. Ah! you say, the love of people makes it easy to forgive. No, you miss the point. When you love some one deeply, and another's sin hurts that person, it is hard to forgive. And sin always does hurt other people. Nobody sins unto himself alone. When, therefore, one cares for people as Jesus did, it is hard to forgive sin.

[16] Joseph's brothers dropped him into a pit, hauled him out again, sold him as a slave to a band of Midianite merchantmen bound for Egypt, dipped his long-sleeved cloak in the blood of a goat and carried it back to the father, Jacob, trying to persuade him that Joseph was dead. Now suppose they had grown conscience-stricken, remorseful, and, unable to stand it any longer, had gone to Jacob, confessing their sin and asking his pardon. Can you not feel the first question that would have risen in the father's heart in a storm of anxious and indignant grief—Where is Joseph? What, then, has become of Joseph? You ask me to forgive you, but your sin is not simply between me and you. Where is Joseph? Somewhere in a distant land, in miserable slavery he may be today. How can I forgive you until I know that all is well with Joseph?

[17] When you love people, it is hard to forgive sin.

So in the Gospels you find it hard for Jesus. He was tremendously severe upon the scribes and Pharisees, you say, and truly he was. But what is the reason? Does it not reveal itself in verses like this, "Beware of the scribes . . . they that devour widows' houses, and for a pretence make long prayers"? Jesus was thinking of the widows and what the rapacity of the rulers did to them. His mother was a widow. We never hear of Joseph after Jesus' early boyhood. He knew what it was for a woman to be left with a family of children. More than once in Jesus' ministry a widow appeared, like the widow of Nain, and always his special gentleness overflowed. When in a parable he wanted to represent need, he pictured a widow pleading with an unjust judge. When, therefore, he was hard on the scribes, one surmises the figure of his mother in the background of his mind. "They that devour widows' houses"—that made it hard to forgive.

[18] You say he was tremendously severe on Dives. To be sure he was—picturesquely putting him in Hades with a great gulf fixed between him and paradise. But why? He thought of Lazarus, who had lain at Dives' gate, pitied by the very dogs but unsuccored by the rich man himself. Or you say the Master was hard upon the priest and Levite. So he was. But it was because he was thinking of the victim left on the road, neglected in their selfish haste.

[19] When you care for people, it is hard to forgive sin.

All the seers have felt this. Recall George Eliot's story of *Adam Bede*—Hetty Sorrel, pretty, vain, and superficial; Adam Bede, the stalwart carpenter; Arthur Donnithorne, careless, impulsive, well-meaning, rich. You remember Adam Bede's honest love for Hetty and his wish to marry her, Hetty's ruin at the hands of Donnithorne, her helpless child, her frenzied wanderings. You remember the scene where Donnithorne, having tried desperately to make amends for what never could be mended, goes to Adam Bede and

194

asks forgiveness. Well, Adam gives it, but it is not easy. "There's a sort of damage, sir," says Adam, "that can't be made up for." Aye, you whose sin hurts other folk, remember that!

20 Let no one of us evade this principle because our sins may operate in other realms. We all have bad tempers. Out of the charcoal pits of what we are, the fumes arise that blast the flowers of happiness in other lives. We may have even secret infidelities that seep through our cleverest concealments and poison the springs from which other folks must drink. Always our evil involves others.

21 My friends, forgiveness is the miracle. The first thing that we are sure of in this universe is law. Some one has said that we can no more have sin without punishment than we can have positive electricity at one end of a needle without negative electricity at the other. And it would take more than a light-hearted chatterer condoning sin to convince me that there is anything else here. Too cheap! Too easy! But when I face Christ I face one whose plummet reached to the bottom of sin. Nobody ever took it so seriously; nobody ever hated it so for what it did to people, and yet he taught forgiveness. That is the miracle: that he taught forgiveness, that he practiced it so marvelously that no poor human wreck was beyond the reach of its benedictions; and that throughout Christian history the glory of the gospel has been men and women reclaimed by pardon to a reëstablished fellowship with God. It is marvelous good news. There is a merciful side to God and he forgives, but it is a miracle. Never take it lightly. "Which is easier, to say, Thy sins are forgiven thee; or to say, Arise and walk?"

22 In the third place, Jesus found it hard to forgive because forgiveness is such a terrific experience for the man who is forgiven. Rather, I hear some one saying, it is glorious to be forgiven. My friend, if you say that light-heartedly, I am certain of one thing—you never have been forgiven. To do somebody wrong, to be alienated from him, to be ashamed of yourself, and then by free forgiveness to be restored to the old friendship and trusted again —surely that is the most humiliating experience that a proud man can go through. If there were any other way out of the remorse and guilt of sin, who wouldn't try to find it? For, you see, there is just one thing that forgiveness does—one thing only. Forgiveness does not take away the fact of sin; the Prodigal had still been in a far country. Forgiveness does not take away the memory of sin; the Prodigal will never forget it. Forgiveness does not and cannot take away all the consequences of sin. As Adam Bede, the carpenter said, "It's like a bit o' bad workmanship—you never see th' end o' th' mischief it'll do." But one thing forgiveness does; it reëstablishes the old personal relationships that have been broken by sin, and makes them deeper and sweeter, it may even be, by awakened love and responsive gratitude. That great thing forgiveness does—and to have been thus alienated and then reconciled through forgiveness is about the most searching experience that the human heart ever goes through.

23 Is not that what Christians have always meant when they associated forgiveness with the cross of Christ? I do not know what theory of the

atonement you may hold, and I might almost say I do not care whether you have any theory at all, but recognize this fact: behind all the explanations of atonement that have arisen and taken form and faded away in the history of Christian thought, this conviction has lain deep—the cross means that it was not easy even for God to forgive. It cost. And that is true to life. If you should grossly wrong your wife and then penitently ask her forgiveness and she should say, Oh, never mind; it is nothing—that would solve no problem. It would simply mean that she did not care what you did. A true-hearted woman would go deeper than that. Two things would be in her: first, a love high and deep enough to forgive; but, second, a character, an uprightness that would be wounded and crushed by your sin, an integrity that would find it hard to forgive.

24 When, therefore, the gospel has invited men to forgiveness, it never has invited them to a light-hearted place where sins are condoned. It has called them to the cross. And they have always heard the cross saying to them that it was hard even for God to forgive. It cost. It cost just what it always costs when men forgive: love putting itself in our place, bearing on its innocence the burden of our guilt. For whether a mother forgives a son or God forgives us, a cross is always at the center of it, and it is not easy.

25 Everything that we have said this morning has been leading up to this final and climactic matter: no man's sin ever is done with until it has come through this process of forgiveness. Either your sin has been forgiven or else it is yet in you as sin. I think that is about the solemnest fact in human life.

26 Do not take it from me as a Christian preacher, as though this were especially Christian, or even especially religious. It is universally human. Go back to Æschylus, hundreds of years before Christ, and read his story of Orestes, who sinned and was driven by the Furies over all the earth, finding no peace until he persuaded a jury of his fellow countrymen at Athens to vote forgiveness. Leap the centuries and come down to America. You need not go to church; go to one of the greatest novels yet written in America, *The Scarlet Letter*. See Arthur Dimmesdale, with his unconfessed, unforgiven sin. How shall he be rid of it? He is a man of intellect; he will absorb himself in thought. But that is no way out. He is a minister; he will preach sermons and save souls. But that is no way out. He is a servant and will go from door to door, humbly helping people. But that is no way out. There is only one way —penitence, confession, and forgiveness.

27 Go even to the psychiatrists, who in more ways than this are saying what Christianity has been saying for centuries. One of the leading psychiatrists in the world said to a personal friend of mine recently, "Most of the cases of mental derangement of a functional type are due to a sense of guilt."

28 And when, with all this testimony of the seers and scientists, you come to your own life, you know it is true; either your sin has been forgiven or else it is in you still as sin.

29 We know that most clearly when we are at our best. We have gross, brutal hours, when we forget our unforgiven sins, lock them in the hold, let the roar of the world fill our ears until conscience cannot be heard, but

ever and again the finer hours return, when we know that unforgiven sin still is here because unforgiven. Any minister who takes preaching in earnest cannot look out over congregations like this, Sunday after Sunday, without thinking of all the unadvertised needs that must exist beneath our respectable exteriors. Who can sum them up in their infinite variety? But deepest of all, the unforgiven sins! There must be many here this morning. Go down into that secret place. Unlock that hidden door. Take out that unforgiven sin. For your soul's sake, get rid of it! But there is only one way. Whatever theology you hold, it is the way of the cross—penitence, confession, restitution, pardon.

But When Life Tumbles In, What Then?[1]

*If thou hast run with the footmen, and they have
wearied thee, then how canst thou contend with horses?
And if in the land of peace, wherein thou trustedst, they
wearied thee, then how wilt thou do in the swelling of Jor-
dan?*   —Jer. 12:5

HERE is a man who, musing upon the bewilderments of life, has burst
into God's presence, hot, angry, stunned by His ordering of things,
with a loud babble of clamorous protest. It is unfair, he cries, unfair! And
frowningly he looks into the face of the Almighty. It is unfair! And
then suddenly he checks himself, and putting this blunt question to it,
feels his heart grow very still and very cold. For after all, he asks himself, what
is it you have to complain about so far? Nothing that everybody does not
share. Only the usual little rubs and frets and ills of life that fall to every one,
no more. And if these have broken through your guard, pushed aside your
religion, made you so sour and peevish and cross towards God—God help you,
what will happen when, sudden as a shell screaming out of the night, some one
of the great crashing dispensations bursts in your life, and leaves an emptiness
where there had been a home, a tumbled ruin of your ordered ways, a heart
so sore you wonder how it holds together? If you have caught your breath,
poor fool, when splashing through the shallow waters of some summer
brook, how will you fare when Jordan bursts its banks, and rushes, far as
the eye can see, one huge, wild swirl of angry waters, and, your feet caught
away, half choked, you are tossed nearer and nearer to the roaring of the
falls, and over it? Suppose that, to you as to Job, suddenly, out of the blue,
there leap dreadful tidings of disaster, would you have the grit to pull yourself together and to face it as he did? "The Lord gave, and the Lord hath
taken away: blessed be the name of the Lord." Suppose that to you as to
Ezekiel, that valiant soul, there comes a day when, with no second's warning,
you are given the bleak message: "Son of man, behold I take away the desire
of thine eyes at a stroke; yet neither shalt thou weep, nor let the tears run
down. So I preached unto the people in the morning: and in the evening
my wife died." Suppose that to you, as to Christ, it became evident that

---

[1] This was the first sermon preached after my wife's dramatically sudden death.

From *The Hero in Thy Soul* (New York, 1929). By permission of Charles Scribner's
Sons.

life was not to give what you expected from it, that your dreams were not to be granted, that yours was to be a steep and lonely road, that some tremendous sacrifice was to be asked of you, could you make shift to face it with a shadow of the Master's courage and the Master's calm? For there is no supposing in the matter. To a certainty to you too, in your turn, some day, these things must come.

² Yes, unbelievably they come. For years and years you and I go our sunny way and live our happy lives, and the rumors of these terrors are blown to us very faintly as from a world so distant that it seems to have nothing to do with us; and then, to us too, it happens. And when it does, nobody has the right to snivel or whimper as if something unique and inexplicable had befallen him. "Never morning wore to evening but some heart did break"—hearts just as sensitive as yours and mine. But when yours breaks, what then? It is a bit late in the day to be talking about insurance when one's house is ablaze from end to end: and somewhat tardy to be searching for something to bring one through when the test is upon one. And how are you and I, so querulous and easily fretted by the minor worries, to make shift at all in the swelling of Jordan, with the cold of it catching away our breath, and the rush of it plucking at our footing?

³ Goethe, of course, tells us that all the religions were designed to meet us and to give us help, just there; to enable us to bear the unbearable, to face the impossible, to see through with some kind of decency and honour what obviously can't be done at all.

⁴ But then so many people's religion is a fair-weather affair. A little rain, and it runs and crumbles; a touch of strain, and it snaps. How often out at the front one lay and watched an aeroplane high up in the blue and sunlight, a shimmering, glistening, beautiful thing: and then there came one shot out of a cloud, and it crashed down to earth, a broken mass of twisted metal. And many a one's religion is like that. So long as God's will runs parallel to ours, we follow blithely. But the moment that they cross, or clash, that life grows difficult, that we don't understand, how apt faith is to fail us just when we have most need of it! You remember our Lord's story of the two men who lived in the same village, and went to the same synagogue, and sat in the same pew, listening to the same services: and how one day some kind of gale blew into their lives, a fearsome storm. And in the one case, everything collapsed, and for a moment there were some poor spars tossing upon wild waters, and then, nothing at all. For that unhappy soul had built on sand, and in his day of need, everything was undermined, and vanished. But the other, though he too had to face the emptiness, the loneliness, the pain, came through it all braver and stronger and mellower and nearer God. For he had built upon the rock. Well, what of you and me? We have found it a business to march with the infantry, how will we keep up with the horsemen: if the small ills of life have frayed our faith and temper, what will we do in the roar and black swirl of Jordan?

⁵ That has always been my chief difficulty about preaching. Carlyle, you recall, used to say that the chirpy optimism of Emerson maddened him,

Emerson across whose sheltered life no cloud or shadow was allowed to blow. He seemed to me, panted the other, like a man, standing himself well back out of the least touch of the spray, who throws chatty observations on the beauty of the weather to a poor soul battling for his life in huge billows that are buffeting the breath and the life out of him, wrestling with mighty currents that keep sweeping him away. It did not help. And I, too, have had a happy life: and always when I have spoken of the Gospel, and the love of God, and Christ's brave reading of this puzzling life of ours, it has seemed to me that a very easy answer lay ready to anybody's hand who found these hard to credit. Yes, yes, they might well say irritably, if I stood in the sunshine where you are, no doubt I, too, could talk like that! But if your path ran over the cold moors, where the winds cut and whistle and pierce to the very bone, if you were set down where I am, I wonder if you would be so absolutely sure? As Shakespeare says, it is not difficult to bear other people's toothache; but when one's own jaw is throbbing, that is another matter. We will listen to Jesus Christ: for He spoke from the darkness round the Cross. We mayn't understand Him, or agree with Him, or obey him: but nobody can challenge His right to speak. But you! Wait till you stand in the rushing of Jordan, till to you there has come some fulfilment of that eerie promise, "Behold, your house is left unto you desolate," and what will you say then?

⁶ I'll tell you now. I know that we are warned in Job that the most drastic test of faith is not even these tremendous sorrows, but a long purgatory of physical and mental agony. Still, I don't think that any one will challenge my right to speak to-day. And what I have to say is this: when Claverhouse suddenly shot Brown of Priesthill, he turned to the wife and asked, the callous brute, "What think you now of your braw guidman?" And she, gathering together the scattered brain, made answer, "I aye thought muckle of him, but I think more of him now." I aye thought muckle of the Christian faith; but I think more of it now, far more. I have never claimed to understand many things in this perplexing life of ours, have always held that my dear master Browning went by much too far when he said confidently that for a Christian man there are no problems in the world or out of it. Surely the acknowledgment of God's love raises new problems. If love, then why and why and why and why? To me the essence of the faith has always seemed a certain intrepidity of loyalty that can believe undauntedly in the dark, and that still trusts God unshaken even when the evidence looks fairly damning. Do you think Christ always understood or found it easy? There was a day when He took God's will for Him into His hand, and turned it round, and looked at it. And, "Is this what You ask of Me?" He said; and for a moment His eyes looked almost incredulous. Aye, and another day when, puzzled and uncertain, He cried out, "But is this really what You mean that I should give You, this here, this now?" Yes, and another still, when the cold rushing waters roared in a raging torrent through His soul: yet He would not turn back, fought His way to the farther

200

bank, died still believing in the God who seemed to have deserted Him. And that is why He is given a name that is above every name.

7 I do not understand this life of ours. But still less can I comprehend how people in trouble and loss and bereavement can fling away peevishly from the Christian faith. In God's name, fling to what? Have we not lost enough without losing that too? If Christ is right—if, as He says, there are somehow, hidden away from our eyes as yet, still there, wisdom and planning and kindness and love in these dark dispensations—then we can see them through. But if Christ was wrong, and all that is not so; if God set His foot on my home crudely, heedlessly, blunderingly, blindly, as I unawares might tread upon some insect in my path, have I not the right to be angry and sore? If Christ was right, and immortality and the dear hopes of which He speaks do really lie a little way ahead, we can manage to make our way to them. But if it is not so, if it is all over, if there is nothing more, how dark the darkness grows! You people in the sunshine may believe the faith, but we in the shadow must believe it. We have nothing else.

8 Further, there is a grave saying in Scripture, "Receive not the grace of God in vain." That Christ should die on our behalf, that God should lavish His kindness on us, and that nothing should come of it, how terrible! And were it not pitiful if we receive the discipline of life in vain: have all the sufferng of it, pay down the price in full, yet miss what it was sent to teach! I know that at first great sorrow is just stunned, that the sore heart is too numbed to feel anything, even God's hand. When his wife died, Rossetti tells us, he passed through all that tremendous time with a mind absolutely blank, learned nothing, saw nothing, felt nothing; so that, looking back, all he could say was that, sitting in a wood with his head in his hands, somehow it was photographed permanently on his passive mind that a certain wild flower has three petals. That was all. But by and by the gale dies down, and the moon rises, and throws a lane of gold to us across the blackness and the heaving of the tumbling waters. After all it is not in the day, but in the night, that star rises after star, and constellation follows constellation, and the immensity of this bewildering universe looms up before our staggered minds. And it is in the dark that the faith becomes biggest and bravest, that its wonder grows yet more and more. "Grace," said Samuel Rutherford, "grows best in the winter." And already some things have become very clear to me.

9 This to begin, that the faith works, fulfils itself, is real; and that its most audacious promises are true. Always we must try to remember that the glorious assertions of the Scriptures are not mere suppositions and guesses. There is no perhaps about them. These splendid truths are flowers that human hands like ours plucked in the gardens of their actual experience. Why is the prophet so sure that as one whom his mother comforts so will God comfort all hurt things? How did the Psalmist know that those who are broken in their hearts and grieved in their minds God heals? Because, of course, it had happened to them, because they had themselves in their dark days felt His unfailing helpfulness and tenderness and the touch of won-

derfully gentle hands. And it is true. When we are cast into some burning fiery furnace seven times heated, we are not alone, never alone; but there is One beside us, like unto the Son of God. When our feet slip upon the slimy stones in the swelling of Jordan, a hand leaps out and catches us and steadies us. "I will not leave you comfortless," said Christ. Nor does He. There is a Presence with us, a Comforter, a Fortifier who does strengthen, does uphold, does bring us through somehow from hour to hour and day to day. Pusey once wrote that when his wife died, he felt "as if the rushing waters were up to my chin; but underneath the chin there is a hand, supporting it." And that hand is there. And as the days go by, what grows upon one more and more is the amazing tenderness of God. Like as a father pitieth his children, mused a psalmist long ago. I have been wondering these days whether he too, poor soul, had suddenly, without one second's warning, to tell his children that their mother was dead, and that remembrance of that agony made him sure all his days it is not willingly that God afflicts and grieves us children of men. Anyhow that is true.

10 There is a marvellous picture in the National Gallery. Christ hangs upon the cross in a dense darkness; and at first that is all one sees. But, as one peers into the background, gradually there stands out another form, God's form; and other hands supporting Christ, God's hands; and another face, God's face, more full of agony even than our Saviour's own. The presence, the sufficiency, the sympathy of God, these things grow very real and very sure and very wonderful.

11 Further, one becomes certain about immortality. You think that you believe in that. But wait till you have lowered your dearest into an open grave, and you will know what believing it means. I have always gazed up at Paul in staggered admiration when he burst out at the grave's mouth into his scornful challenge, his exultant ridicule of it, "O death, where is thy sting? O grave, where is thy victory?" But now it does not seem to me such a tremendous feat: for I have felt that very same. True, I can tell him where death's sting lies. Ah! it is the constant missing of what used to be always here; the bitter grudging every second of the dear body to the senseless earth, the terrible insecurity, for one is never safe—anything, nothing, and the old overwhelming pain comes rushing back. Yet when the other day I took up a magazine, it was with amazement I discovered they are still chattering about whether we people are immortal or not. I am past that. I know. "I believe in the communion of saints, the forgiveness of sins, the resurrection of the body, and the life everlasting."

12 But there is one thing I should like to say which I have never dared to say before, not feeling that I had the right. We Christian people in the mass are entirely unchristian in our thoughts of death. We have our eyes wrongly focused. We are selfish, and self-centered, and self-absorbed. We keep thinking aggrievedly of what it means to us. And that is wrong, all wrong. In the New Testament you hear very little of the families with that aching gap, huddled together in their desolate little home in some back street; but a great deal about the saints in glory, and the sunshine, and the

singing, and the splendour yonder. And, surely, that is where our thoughts should dwell. I for one want no melancholious tunes, no grey and sobbing words, but brave hymns telling of their victory. Dante had a sour mind. Yet, as he went up the hill that cleanses him that climbs, suddenly it shook and reeled beneath him. What's that? he cried out in alarm. And his guide smiled. Some happy soul, he said, has burst through into victory and every other on the mount is so praising God for that, that the whole hill rocks and staggers. And is not that the mood that best becomes us? Think out your brooding. What exactly does it mean? Would you pluck the diadem from their brows again? Would you snatch the palms of victory out of their hands? Dare you compare the clumsy nothings our poor blundering love can give them here with what they must have yonder where Christ Himself has met them, and has heaped on them who can think out what happiness and glory? I love to picture it. How, shyly, amazed, half protesting, she who never thought of self was led into the splendour of her glory. As the old poet put it centuries ago,

> Our sweet is mixed with bitter gall,
>   Our pleasure is but pain,
> Our joys scarce last the looking on,
>   Our sorrows still remain.

> But there they have such rare delights,
>   Such pleasure and such play,
> That unto them a thousand years
>   Doth seem but yesterday.

To us it will be long and lonesome: but they won't even have looked round them before we burst in. In any case, are we to let our dearest be wrenched out of our hands by force? Or, seeing that it has to be, will we not give them willingly and proudly, looking God in the eyes, and telling Him that we prefer our loneliness rather than that they should miss one tittle of their rights. When the blow fell, that was the one and only thought that kept beating like a hammer in my brain. I felt I had lost her for ever, must have lost her, that to all eternity she must shine far ahead of me; and my heart kept crying out, "I choose it, I choose it. Do not for my sake deny her anything." I know now that I have not lost her. For love is not a passing thing one leaves behind. And is it not love's way to stoop?

[13] And, after all, thank God, our gift is not an absolute one. When we are young, heaven is a vague and nebulous and shadowy place. But as our friends gather there, more and more it gains body and vividness and homeliness. And when our dearest have passed yonder, how real and evident it grows, how near it is, how often we steal yonder. For, as the Master put it: Where our treasure is, there will our heart be also. Never again will I give out that stupid lie, "There is a happy land, far, far away." It is not far. They are quite near. And the communion of the saints is a tremendous and most blessed fact.

¹⁴ Nowadays, for example, to pray is to turn home. For then they run to meet us, draw us with their dear familiar hands into the Presence, stand quite close to us the whole time we are there—quite close while we are there.

¹⁵ And for the rest, many poets have told us of Lethe, the river of forgetfulness. But Dante, in his journeyings, came on another, the Eunoe, to taste the sunny waters of which is to have recalled all the gladsome and glorious and perfect things one has ever experienced. Eunoe runs beside the track all through the valley of the shadow; and a wise soul will often kneel, and lift a handful of its waters to his thirsty lips, and, ere he rises, wonderingly thank God for the splendour he has known, that never would and could have been at all but for His marvellous grace. And so back to life again, like a healthy-minded laddie at some boarding-school, who, after the first hour of home-sickness, resolves, if he is wise, he will not mope, but throw himself into the life about him, and do his part and play the game, and enjoy every minute of it—aye, and does it too—though always, always his eyes look ahead for the term's end, and always, always his heart thrills and quickens at thought of that wonderful day when he will have not memories and letters only, but the whole of his dear ones really there, when he will be with them again and they with him. Well, that will come in time. Meanwhile, "Danton, no weakness," as that brave soul kept muttering to himself on his way to the guillotine, and he showed none.

¹⁶ I don't think you need be afraid of life. Our hearts are very frail; and there are places where the road is very steep and very lonely. But we have a wonderful God. And as Paul puts it, what can separate us from His love? Not death, he says immediately, pushing that aside at once as the most obvious of all impossibilities.

¹⁷ No, not death. For, standing in the roaring of the Jordan, cold to the heart with its dreadful chill, and very conscious of the terror of its rushing, I too, like Hopeful, can call back to you who one day in your turn will have to cross it, "Be of good cheer, my brother, for I feel the bottom, and it is sound."

Taking a City

A Sermon for the Builders of the City of God

*There was found a poor wise man, and he by his wis-
dom delivered the city.*   —Eccl. 9:15

O VER against us looms this magnificent and terrible city of Chicago.
Our problem is how to convert this city, stupendous as it is, into
the still more stupendous city of God. If only there could be found
the poor wise man of Ecclesiastes who would tell us how! What is the
wisdom whereby he might deliver us from our present, build us up to the
height of our spiritual capacity, and present us to the future the living
embodiment of the ideal society of men? How shall we make the city not
merely hog butcher, tool maker, and an emporium for commerce, but also
a reservoir of humanity at its best, a city which clothes all of its citizens
in faith, a city where the good life is lived naturally and all men know the
meaning of liberty and loyalty? How, in a word, shall we impart a soul to
Chicago?

2 I. We need a Bible.—In lieu of the poor wise man, who today seems
conspicuously absent, we shall have to turn to the historians to ask when
cities or other communities of human beings have been at their dynamic
mightiest. A first answer they might give is a strange one: people spiritually
mighty have usually—perhaps always—been people of a book. They have
been people who have accustomed themselves to look to a book for the
revelation of God's will; from it they have expected him to speak to them.
Surely it is not without significance that of the twelve historical religions
which are dead—the ancient Egyptian, the Peruvian and Mexican, Mithraism,
Manichaeism, the Babylonian, Phoenician, and Hittite, the Greek, the Roman,
the early Teutonic and Scandinavian—not one of them, according to Robert
Ernest Hume, "possessed anything which might be called a canon of sacred
Scriptures," whereas every one of the eleven living religions—Hinduism,
Jainism, Buddhism, Sikhism, Confucianism, Taoism, Shinto, Judaism,
Zoroastrianism, Mohammedanism, and Christianity—"do possess definite sets
of documents which are regarded as conveying unique divine truths which
need to be known." There is power in the Book from which God speaks.

3 And what if the Book happens to be that crown of all the others, the

From *Taking a City* (New York, 1934). By permission of Harper & Brothers.

Book in which it is set down that the God who is speaking is not the God merely of this tribe or that cult, but the Father of every human individual born into the world! That Book was rediscovered at the dawn of the Reformation after its long sleep in Latin. Wycliffe's translation into English, though only in manuscript, swept like earthquake tremors through the kingdom, and with something like the same results. A considerable sum was paid even for a few sheets of it; a load of hay became the price for permission to read in it one hour a day for a period; and some learned sections of it by heart to recite to the throngs who gathered to hear. The readers of it went to their death when captured by the authorities, who were afraid of the power of it; they were hunted down like wild beasts and burned with copies of it round their necks. But the Bible won its own way; it changed the lives of those who listened for God's word in it; eventually it revolutionized Europe.

⁴ The arresting fact about our situation here—a fact which sends one's thought of the future soaring—is that a new book of the Bible has been discovered in our day and God speaks from it as dreadfully and graciously as ever he spoke from Job or St. John. The book newly discovered is nothing else than the city of Chicago itself. Hitherto, for the most part, cities have been regarded only as cities; and to most of our fellow citizens Chicago is only a city. But we have learned that it is more. It is a scripture, an inspired scripture being written before our eyes by the awful hand of the Almighty, and communicating to us his will. What he is writing is strangely like what he has already written in his other books, now printed. "He that takes the sword—or gun—shall perish by it"—can one miss that oft-repeated text inscribed across the gangster areas? "I have made of one blood all nations of men, and belligerency between races means disaster for all"—something written in our streets in a clearer hand than writing. And as one walks through the canyon of La Salle Street, is there not posted on a score of windows, whence men in despair have flung themselves, the dark legend, "What shall it profit a man if he gain the whole world and lose his soul?" This city is a Bible from the pages of which God is speaking.

⁵ The importance of the Sacred Book has never lain in its being a book as such; the significant matter is that people have come to look there for a revelation of God's purpose. It is just this that may make the book of Chicago infinitely momentous. I am mistaken if this new and daring trait we are developing—that of holding before our eyes the flaming pages of this canonical book called Our City, and asking God what he means by it— does not have upon us the same effect of shock, contrition, amaze, and release to our higher capacities as had the open Bible of Wycliffe upon the people of his day.

⁶ We need a Bible and we have it.

⁷ II. We need a Bible with a Gospel in it.—The historians would go on to point out, I have no doubt, that the human spirit rises to its height when it has in its possession a myth, a story about God. The spirit of the greater cities of the ancient world was almost always invested in a myth. Was not

every king of Memphis the bodily son of Re, the sun god of old Egypt? Did not the fall of the statue of Diana from the skies establish the existence of the temple and city of Ephesus? Did not Athena contest with Poseidon the privilege of directing the destiny of Athens? Did not the owl-eyed goddess, offering peace and prosperity, win the privilege from the ruler of the deep, who had only war to offer? And did not the art and prowess of Athens owe more than today can be computed to the belief of the people in their myth?

8 But when a myth is true and verifiable, when it tells the story of God coming into the world to redeem it, then it becomes a Gospel that sets the world aquiver with joyous faith and gratitude. It was the true myth, the Gospel, the story of what God had actually done, which, on the lips of the Reformers, remade the then world. Always the church is in danger of slipping into the imperative mood in its teaching: do this or do that, and you shall be saved. It is a mood which puts the emphasis on the work of men—a tragic mood, therefore, since no man can save himself without God. It is not the mood of myth. What the Reformers did was to restore to the church her ancient and thrilling indicative: this has been willed and that has been done by the Almighty and you are saved. Sola gratia—by grace alone—by grace alone the world is overcome. And through grace the Reformers did indeed overcome their world.

9 Nor is this city without its myth. To some it may be, but not to us. It contains a fifth Gospel, the story of what God has actually done and how he has done it. It would not be a creditable Bible unless it held a Gospel. It is the Gospel quality that characterizes many men and women in it whom I could name. They are living announcements not primarily that God might act or should act, but that he has acted: he has reached into history and taken them for his purposes; there is an unbroken historical chain which unites God and Christ and them. Every significant person in history has had a mythical aura about him; you cannot account for them in terms of history alone; and of none may this be said more truly than of the disciples of Christ who labor in this city—in its slums and in its high places. Whence have these servants of God the motive to build upon the insight that all men are brothers? To go out on the streets and call into their hospitality drunkards and nameless wretches who never did and never would have any claim upon them? To challenge the citizens to study and think their way into nobler living? Or to heal minds broken in distraction over many things by illuminating to them the one thing needful? Did the motive for this kind of living come from materialism and animal selfishness? It came from a lovely place; it came, by a direct route, from the heart of the Eternal. Here is a story about what God has done. Here is the Gospel.

10 We need a Bible with a Gospel in it, and that, if we will look for it, is also to be found in this Chicago.

11 III. We need a Bible with a Gospel in it and the power of the Resurrection in that Gospel. An eschatology is a doctrine about the last things. It was such a doctrine that gave Buddhism its fascination for millions in its

207

heyday: follow the Buddha in his fourfold path and you come to the end of this torture misnamed existence. It is such a doctrine that gives Mohammedanism its savage beauty. It is something to know that if you die fighting for the faith your soul flies instantly to Paradise. One moment the clash of steel or the clangor of the guns; the next the quiet streams and restful gardens of eternity. It is this belief that has made the pious Moslem, throughout his history, unconquerable in battle, save when he was overwhelmed by the sheer numbers or better military equipment of the enemy.

12 There have been freakish kinds of Christianity which, though they emphasized distorted views of their own triumph at time's imminent end, did yet reveal what immense control such a belief has over a person. From the time of the Montanists who gathered at Pepuza in Asia Minor in the second century to await the end of the world, to the time of the Russellite neighbors of mine who not long ago banded together in a kind of Christian communism awaiting the same cataclysm, this doctrine that something in the nature of an end is about to happen, from which believers shall somehow enjoy redemption, has been powerful to challenge men and women to their highest spiritual daring.

13 But in true Christianity mere eschatology, the general doctrine of the nearness of heaven, potent as that is, becomes what St. Paul called the power of the resurrection. This is the power possessed by every man and woman who takes for granted the immortality of the soul, and then proceeds to live in the knowledge that this life does not exhaust his possibilities. Immediately you see what happens: such people sit loose to the circumstances of this existence, but have a firm grip on the things that are eternal. They become channels by which the heavenly graces may be transmitted to their times. They believe in the power of love, for they know it is the power of heaven. They are not thrown down and engulfed by the weltering hatreds and unhappy changefulness of this world. They know that today we are approaching the end of an age—possibly the débâcle of the race—but they are not paralyzed by fears nor made mad by despair. They salute the end. Christianity has never been afraid of the end. They recognize a crisis as the judgment of God making way for his Kingdom. Theirs is different from the eschatology of those who looked for a cataclysmic end; they know that even change is evolutionary, gradual. But they are like them in this, that they know that the redemption of God can triumph over any end.

14 Here then is a Christian sociology tremendous in its implications. It is the sociology of those who believe that the last fact of life is heaven. It is that belief that lends direction and shape and drive to their work on earth. They are realists, but realists with a deathless motive.

15 Their attitude is slightly though not greatly different from that of Emerson, who, when a millennialist rushed up to him and said, "Mr. Emerson, the world is coming to an end," responded, "Very well, madam, we'll get along without it." For they do not wish to get along without a world; it is simply that they know that their heavenly Gospel does not change with the

changes of this world. Let capitalism go, let socialism come and go, let any other doctrine rule—the Gospel of Christ is the same yesterday, today, and forever.

16 We need a Bible with a Gospel in it, and the power of the resurrection in that Gospel—and all this is to be found, if we will look in the lives of Christ's true disciples, in Chicago.

17 IV. We need a Bible with a Gospel in it and the power of the resurrection in that Gospel—and an army of saints to declare that power. The few are important and are a beginning; but they are not enough for the redemption of this vast city. Where is the army of saints to take this city for Christ? That army is here potentially; surely it can be none other than the great body of lay men and lay women of our churches.

18 One has a feeling that the day of saints has gone by, like that of the trilobites and great auks. We are inclined to think that we live in an era wholly different from that of St. Paul and the early apostles, and that the people they addressed as saints gave their days to prayer and their nights to meditation with a single-mindedness to which we do not even aspire. But if this is our idea, and we are happy in it, we had best be warned against reading the New Testament carefully.

19 It is a too illuminating exercise to name over the persons we have become accustomed to think of as saints belonging more to heaven than earth, and then to attach to each one the actual description given of him in the records. Matthew turns out to be not a Gabriel sitting on the clouds, but a man who earned his daily bread by collecting taxes. Mark was a private secretary; Luke, a physician. John, James, and Peter were engaged in the fish industry. Paul was a manufacturer; Timothy and Titus, expert organizers; Jude, a small landowner; and Philemon, the possessor of an enviable list of well-diversified securities.

20 There are your first-century saints! They were men—and women—of flesh and blood like yourselves, who had their work to do in this workaday world, but who had also a first-hand interest in the church, and the worship of God and the moral character in an immoral world, that the church stood for. It was lay men and lay women, and not lay angels who, being laid hold of by the Christian ideal, altered the course of destiny for the Roman Empire and so for our Western World.

21 We might have guessed this, to be sure, from our general knowledge of history, for it was ever so. The great eras of the Christian Church were, as Dean Hodges used to say, those of the missionaries, the monks, and the Methodists—and these were lay movements, movements of the Church as a whole, every one of them. By the missionaries he meant those quiet citizens of the first Christian century who spread the influence of Christ through the whole Roman world, to the extent that Aristides, making his defense before the Emperor Antoninus Pius, could say, "They are to your empire, Your August Highness, what a man's soul is to a man!" By the monks he meant the Franciscans: he thought of Francis himself, the young member of an importing house, who saw materialism and the commercial motive resting

like a blight on Europe, and was shocked into action at the sight; who brought to the nations a new spirit by remembering those whom the rest had forgotten, the poor, the leprous, the oppressed, and with others like himself ushered in a century which some critics call the most spacious and magnificent the human race has ever seen. By the Methodists he meant the citizens of town and country in England, rough and refined, in all walks of life, who, a hundred and twenty-five years ago, being emboldened to make their lives count for something more than cash, organized and taught the local "class meetings," as they were called, which brought to half the world a moral revolution felt to this day.

22 The priests and preachers, prophets and parsons, are very well in their way. To them is delegated supervision, necessary to any organization of people. But if lay initiative, intelligence, and consecration is lacking, they are like to become voices in Rama, producing nothing more substantial than tears. Vitality in a community is not a voice, in any case; it is a condition of rugged health suffusing the whole fabric.

23 And here all about us are men and women who, if their hearts were touched into flame, could supply that health: they could do as much for our city as ever missionary, monk, or Methodist did for theirs. We need a Bible with a Gospel in it and the power of the resurrection in that Gospel—and in the lay men and lay women of our churches we have an army of saints to declare that power and take the city for Christ.

24 Men and women of the pews, leaders of the life of our city, it is to you that in the last analysis we must turn. We have the Bible—Chicago itself —through which God is speaking; we have the Gospel, which is the story about God told in the lives of Christ's disciples; we have the power of the resurrection in those lives here among us; but without you the city cannot grow to be the city of God.

25 But with you, to what future may we not aspire? If you will take seriously your opportunities as citizens of the city of our dream, if you will put by the cheap standards of our present surroundings, if week after week you will draw down from heaven and implant in your work heaven's standards of honesty and fair dealing, sympathy and creativity, I can prophesy a flood time of spiritual power for this city such as today one cannot even conceive.

The Light on the Lord's Face

*For God, who commanded the light to shine out of
darkness, hath shined in our hearts, to give the light of the
knowledge of the glory of God in the face of Jesus Christ.*
                                                    —II Cor. 4:6

I APPROACH this text with awe. I feel about this Scripture as I imagine
a mountain climber, with several high peaks to his credit, might feel
as he views with commingled eagerness and reverence the highest peak
of all. I am sure I cannot reach the top of this mountain, perhaps not even
attain the timber line, but it will be something to tarry in the foothills of
so impressive a passage of Scripture.

2 I. *The glory of God in the face of Jesus Christ.* Now the Apostle is not
using the word "face" here merely in the sense of features. As employed
in this text, the word "face" is that figure of speech called synecdoche, where
a part is used for the whole. For example, when Enoch Arden, in Tennyson's
poem, glimpsed the infinite ocean and cried, "A sail! a sail!" meaning, of
course, a ship, he was employing synecdoche.

3 Actually, we do not know much about the features of Jesus Christ. No
portrait of Jesus was ever painted from life. No sculptor made any representation of him. The Gospel narratives do not contain a description of
the person of Jesus. There are little hints as to his eyes, his hands, his feet,
his speech; but while these are suggestive, they do not supply enough material for a picture. The artists have done fairly well in putting Jesus upon
the canvas, but their imagination has often gone astray. They have shown
us but a pale replica of the original. Let me cite a single point: the artists, in
portraying a bareheaded, out-of-doors Christ, have forgotten that no
Oriental goes without a head covering as he walks or rides beneath the
fiercely blazing sun. This is a small matter but it is significant.

4 When Paul here speaks of "the face of Jesus Christ" he means not only
his countenance but his character, personality, being. Jesus was the "good
news" incarnate, the gospel in human flesh, the way, the truth, come to life.
In a certain sense, the New Testament is Christ; the creed is Christ; the church
is Christ. The gospel is the teaching, example, religion, mind of Christ.
Christ is the Alpha and the Omega of the Christian faith. "God was in Christ,

---

From *A Man Stood Up to Preach and Fifteen Other Sermons* (St. Louis, 1943). By
permission of The Bethany Press.

reconciling the world unto himself" is a statement of tremendous implications. Be it remembered that Jesus said, "He that hath seen me hath seen the Father," also, "I and my Father are one." "The glory of God in the face of Jesus Christ" is one of the profoundest truths of our holy faith. "In him was life; and the life was the light of men."

⁵ II. *There was upon the face of Jesus the light of an incredible gladness.* There can be no doubt of this, if we take the New Testament for what it says. The artists have almost always depicted the Christ as suffering, pain drenched, a "man of sorrows." This is a partial picture, based upon but one aspect of his life and ministry. It is not the Christ of the Gospels, whom little children loved, ran to, and not away from, clambering up on his knees, seeking to be close to him.

⁶ There was something zestful and refreshing in the personality of the Master. The word "rejoice" was often on his lips. His "Be of good cheer" was like a trumpet call. Might it not be that the common people heard him gladly because of the radiance that pervaded his personality? There have been numerous sermons on "The Joy of Jesus," though there have not been as many as are warranted by the facts as set down by his biographers.

⁷ Imagine what the light on the Lord's face must have meant to those burdened, discouraged, sorrowing persons who came into Jesus' life and were never the same again. Think of what Mary Magdalene saw in that face; what the lepers discovered there; what the Canaanitish woman, the sadhearted Jairus, and that social outcast, Zacchaeus, beheld in the light of that face! This much we know; they caught a vision of a new way of life. They felt the warmth of a love that extended to the depths of their sad hearts and made them glad. Thus inspired they arose on steppingstones of their dead selves to higher things. The light on Jesus' face illumines the pages of the New Testament and shines into obscure passages, making them clear and understandable.

⁸ Jesus spoke of himself as a "bridegroom," a word that is a synonym for joy, happiness, elation, gratitude. There is an account preserved for us of that wedding feast at Cana, where Jesus was a welcome guest. Now weddings are sometimes solemn, but they are seldom sad. Normally, they are occasions for joy. A new home is about to be set up, a new family life established; and, if some ties are broken by the new relationship, other ties are taken on, and two families find a unity of hopes and dreams and aspirations for the wedded couple. We have a right, therefore, to think of Jesus as entering into festive affairs and enjoying them to the fullest.

⁹ John the Baptist was a great man. No doubt of that. But that sturdy reformer never suggests gladness or joy. Jesus paid him tribute, the highest tribute he ever paid a contemporary; but he drew a deep distinction between himself and the Baptist. John and his people were like children playing at funerals; Jesus and his circle like children playing at the happier game of marriages. The Baptist belonged to an old dispensation, wherein sternness and severity were emphasized. Jesus ushered in a new era, in which the standards were higher, and the spirit that of abounding joy, radiant faith.

212

Am I mistaken here? Read the Gospel narratives and decide for yourself.

¹⁰ That Jesus entered into the joy of a wedding occasion is not surprising, nor is it unusual that he manifested this joyous spirit when he was surrounded by little children. We should expect this. But what shall we say when the idea of joy is associated with his cross? Behold him going to Calvary with a shining face and a high heart. The author of the Epistle to the Hebrews has that incredible phrase "who for the joy that was set before him endured the cross, despising the shame." This is a joy that surpasses all understanding, though it can be studied and emulated with profit. If we cannot know it in fullness, we can at least know it in part. To do so would mean the restoration of much of that "lost radiance of Christianity." Ponder these words of Jesus, "These things have I spoken unto you, that my joy might remain in you, and that your joy might be full." These brave words can be read aright only in the light from the Lord's face.

¹¹ There are not many happy faces among us. A visitor to our shores not a great while ago observed this fact and commented upon it. He said we were not a smiling people. Look about you in a crowd and observe the faces of the people. Some are utterly sad, some sullen, features drawn and haggard. There are lines in human faces that tell a story of disappointment, grief, and envy. I have no disposition to criticize these telltale lines upon human faces and the outward signs of inward distress. Man's inhumanity to man is responsible for some of these caricatures of faces that rightly should be cheerful, radiant, and happy. "He laughs best who laughs with God." Surely one must be fortified within to be able to wear a "morning face" in the midst of darkness and despair. It was the light of an incredible gladness inspired from within which suffused the face of Jesus. He is our exemplar in this respect as in others. On the Mount of Transfiguration his face shone like the sun, a symbol of an inner light that not anything could quench.

¹² III. *There was also upon the face of Jesus the arresting light of an uncontaminated inward peace.* I remember having read somewhere a sermon in which the preacher said that the only thing that Jesus bequeathed to those about him when he died was the seamless garment for which the soldiers gambled at the foot of the cross. But surely that was the least of his legacy. A garment, even when it is of finest texture, is incidental, secondary, to character, spirit, outlook, and insight. The grandest legacy that Jesus left his disciples was his *peace*. In that Upper Room he thus spoke to his friends: "Peace I leave with you, my peace I give unto you: not as the world giveth, give I unto you. Let not your heart be troubled, neither let it be afraid."

¹³ What is the peace of Christ? Was it the peace which one finds in pastoral scenes, quiet countrysides, and flower-embroidered mountain slopes? Was it the serenity of sunset and evening star? To be sure, there were lovely pastoral surroundings and restful vistas about Nazareth. To this day it is good to dream among those hills and valleys and gaze on the shining stars and the "vitreous pour of the full moon." Yet, wherever there are human

213

beings, there is also struggle, conflict, controversy. Not necessarily cruel or debasing, to be sure, but withal vexatious, annoying, often exasperating. The clash of human wills is inevitable and universal. Whatever may have been the nature of the years at Nazareth, there can be no gainsaying that the years of Jesus' public ministry, with the possible exception of the first year, were years of tumult, conflict, and difficulty. He became a target of malicious criticism, the victim of conspiracy. He was as a storm-swept island lashed at all points by the fury of an encompassing hurricane. Yet inwardly he was at repose. He lived day by day in harmony with the Father's will; his conscience was untroubled; no memory of a misspent youth rose up to haunt him. No feeling of remorse darkened the mirror of his stainless life. Never did he say, "I was not always thus . . . remember not past years." Thus he moved amidst the fury of the storm about him, calm, courageous, knowing that "peace of God, which passeth all understanding." The peace of Jesus was an inward experience before it had an outward expression. It was spiritual before it was physical.

14 You will observe that I use the word "uncontaminated" in referring to Jesus' peace. I carefully chose this word to express just what is in my mind. Take my own peace, for instance, my inward peace. It is sufficiently strong to carry me through experiences that disappoint and disconcert, but I cannot say that this peace that I know is uncontaminated. For what is going on in this world of ours—war-scourged Europe, the suffering and the heartache —acutely affects my thinking. Even though it does not overwhelm me, it sometimes bewilders and shocks. I do not see how we can help being contaminated by the thoughts of wickedness that are within us and about us; we rise above them according to our faith, hope, love, perseverance, in thinking white. But in the case of Jesus, his peace rose on wings of a faith which carried it far above the shouting and the tumult, the darkness and the despair. Yet his feet were firmly planted on the earth, and he was touched to tears by the grief of Martha and Mary sorrowing for Lazarus. He was both idealist and realist, was Jesus of Nazareth.

15 Recall what he said to his disciples on a memorable day when they were cast down and about ready to give up. "These things I have spoken unto you, that in me ye might have peace. In the world ye shall have tribulation: but be of good cheer; I have overcome the world." This is a striking statement; the overcoming life requires much. I do not see how we can know this peace of Christ if it is contaminated by envy, hate, utter selfishness. We need to study the strategy of his life as the story is unfolded in the Gospels. He saw beyond the now; he rested his case with the Eternal Father. It might help us to remember that, however dark the day or long the night, daybreak and a new day are on their way. There'll always be a resurrection. Short views of life are troublesome; long views are clarifying and helpful.

> Great captains, with their guns and drums,
> Disturb our judgment for the hour,
> But at last silence comes.[1]

[1] James Russell Lowell, "Commemoration Ode."

Yes, silence comes at last. When the great guns fall silent and the task of building this broken world confronts us, the question will be, How shall we rebuild? What pattern shall we follow? What design for successful living? Most important is the purpose, the spirit, the ideals. We shall never have peace without until we have peace within—his peace. The arresting light on the Lord's face was that produced by an uncontaminated inward peace. He had deep wells from which to draw, springs of refreshing from the Eternal Spirit which never go dry.

16 IV. *Likewise there was the glow of a redemptive mission upon our Lord's face.* He was "sent of God," and never once did Jesus forget the mission which brought him to earth. "The Son of man is come to seek and to save that which was lost" was his battle cry of freedom. Recall his parables of seeking and finding, as recorded in the fifteenth chapetr of Luke's Gospel. How strong, persuasive, and beautiful are the stories of the Lost Sheep, the Lost Coin, the Lost Boy.

17 Human beings without a sense of worthy mission are a sorry lot, more to be pitied than condemned. They know not what they are missing yet are conscious of failure. They drift aimlessly with the tide, have no burden of lofty purpose, know no "magnificent obsession." Restless, anxious, miserable, they exist but do not really live. How far removed are they in spirit from that gallant author of "An Airman's Letter," a letter written to his mother and delivered to her after his death. He wrote: "We are sent into this world to acquire a personality and a character to take with us that can never be taken from us. Those who just eat and sleep, prosper and procreate, are no better than animals."

18 Did that glow of redemptive purpose on our Lord's face ever appear to better advantage than when he set his fact resolutely to go to Jerusalem, with all that that decision entailed—controversy bitter and prolonged, betrayal, mockery, scourging, and at last the cross and death amid a rabble cry? Little wonder that his disciples were amazed at that resolute shining face, determined to go where his enemies conspired against him and plotted his death. And no wonder at all that in the Garden those sent to take him captive fell back astounded at the calm words, "I am he." For a holy cause he came into the world.

19 When men and women are possessed of a dream and a vision of a brave new world, their faces are apt to reflect the inward fires of high resolve. There is an outward glow because of an inward grace. Thus of Stephen, on trial for his life before an unfriendly court, we read: "And all that sat in the council, looking stedfastly on him, saw his face as it had been the face of an angel." The light on Stephen's face was a beacon along the early Christian way.

20 That light on our Lord's face shone steadily with the glow of a redemptive ministry. It was as constant as the stars, as sure as the laws of seedtime and harvest. He must be about his Father's business.

> O Love Divine, that stooped to share
> Our sharpest pang, our bitterest tear,

> On Thee we cast each earth-born care,
> We smile at pain while Thou art near! [2]

Is that too strongly put? Not if read in the light that was on the Lord's face.

[21] Mediators between God and man have a hard task in the very nature of things. Moses suffered as he sought to mediate between Jehovah and the recreant Israelites. Job longed for a mediator or "umpire" between himself and God. The ministry of reconciliation requires much. Look at Abraham interceding for the city of Sodom. His is the story of the first appearance in the Scriptures of an intercessor. And how persistently that grand patriarch entreated the Almighty for the doomed city. Ponder this Scripture:

[22] "And Abraham drew near, and said, Wilt thou also destroy the righteous with the wicked? Peradventure there be fifty righteous within the city: wilt thou also destroy and not spare the place for the fifty righteous that are therein? . . . And the Lord said, If I find in Sodom fifty righteous within the city, then I will spare all the place for their sakes."

[23] Now Abraham was intensely concerned in saving the doomed city and he was not content to stop there. Would God spare the city if forty-five righteous were found in Sodom? He would. If forty, thirty, twenty, righteous were found in Sodom, would the Almighty stay his hand? Yes, God, would spare the city if twenty righteous were found there. And now Abraham makes his last stand as mediator between the Eternal and the doomed city. Humbly, yet determinedly, he states his case. If ten righteous are found, will God spare Sodom? And God said: "I will not destroy it for ten's sake." [3]

[24] Abraham stopped with ten. He stopped too soon. Suppose he had gone further, had gone all the way, and said: "O let not the Lord be angered: peradventure there be not ten righteous found in Sodom; no, not one, wilt thou spare the city for my sake?" [3] Jesus went all the way. This is the long last mile he took so bravely, so forgetful of himself, willingly losing his life for others, giving his all with superb abandon. O, the light on our Lord's face as he gave the last full measure of devotion for a despairing world!

[25] The light on the Lord's face: in thinking on this profound text, two hymns come to mind. And the first is William Cowper's comforting hymn written in 1779—

> Sometimes a light surprises
>   The Christian while he sings;
> It is the Lord who rises
>   With healing in his wings:
> When comforts are declining,
>   He grants the soul again
> A season of clear shining,
>   To cheer it after rain.

[2] Oliver Wendell Holmes.
[3] I am indebted for this impressive application of an Old Testament incident to a volume of sermons by the Reverend Hugh McLellan of Winchester, Kentucky.

And the other is the lovely hymn of George Matheson, blind Scottish poet-preacher, composed in 1882, "O Love That Wilt Not Let Me Go," and especially the second stanza—

> O Light that followest all my way,
>   I yield my flickering torch to Thee;
> My heart restores its borrowed ray,
> That in Thy sunshine's blaze its day
>   May brighter, fairer be.

And once again this Scripture of mountain-peak vastness: "For God, who commanded the light to shine out of darkness, hath shined in our hearts, to give the light of the knowledge of the glory of God in the face of Jesus Christ."

The Heart of Christianity

L ET US endeavor to recover for our thought that central conquering faith which lay at the heart of primitive Christianity, when it first became *apostolic*, which literally means "missionary." It was on its highest level a new revelation of God, and it was on the human plane an equally new revelation of man's potential nature. We have not got back to the heart of Christianity until we have recovered both of these essential aspects of Christ's life and message. They are so completely woven together that either one is apt to be missed if the other is overlooked, as has too often happened in the course of Christian history.

² Christ leaps, by a supreme spiritual insight, to a wholly new revelation of the essential character of God and consequently of life itself. God is eternally *Father*. He does not *become* Father through some mysterious change in his nature, or on account of some transaction that has occurred, nor does he ever cease to have the character traits of Father. Creation is as much an expression of Father-love as redemption is. Love is the one method of soul-making.

³ The shift of approach from the legal level to that of grace is as momentous a change of level as is the shift from the stage of matter to that of life, or from the vegetable kingdom to that of the animal. Something that would have been unthinkable on the lower level emerges on the higher level. It is as though one should pass from air-waves to radio-vibrations, or from molecular-processes to the inner process of consciousness. *The compulsion of a soul* is as much a contradiction of terms as the persuasion of a stone wall by argument would be.

⁴ Jesus was the interpreter of this way of life to a degree beyond that reached or expressed by anyone who has lived on earth. It must be said further that in the person of Christ we pass beyond what is usually meant by an *interpreter* of a way of life. His life has seemed to men in all generations to stand forth as a unique and attractive ideal of what life at its best and highest *should be*. St. Paul called him "a new Adam," a new creation, a new type of humanity. In saying that St. Paul was thinking of him primarily as the beginning of a new order of life-giving spirit—that is to say, as a typical incarnation of love and self-giving. Jesus expected to see the miracle of transformation through love work on sin-crippled men and women in every walk of life.

From *Some Problems of Life* (Nashville, 1937). By permission of Abingdon-Cokesbury Press.

⁵ This appeal of love called out the potential Cephas hidden and hardly suspected in the impulsive Simon. It raised a sinning woman, whose hope and expectation were gone, to a pure and radiant saint. It changed a self-despised tax collector into an honest and self-respecting man. It was instantly recognized by responsive little children. It had an almost miraculous effect on demoniacs who had been rendered more insane by methods of terror and compulsion.

⁶ It seemed to fail in Pilate's Hall and at Golgotha. It did not soften the hate of crafty politicians or touch the quick of Roman soldiers. The jeer of the mob drowned out the gentle voice of forgiving love. To the onlookers the "defeat" seemed obvious. But somehow that Cross has touched the heart of the world as nothing else has ever done, and it has through the ages been the most redemptive power of which history has any record.

⁷ From the very first stages of his mission Christ identified this way of grace and self-giving to which he was dedicated with the eternal character of God. His test of any quality of life was always to see whether it made the possessor of it more like God. "You are to love, even your enemies, so that you may be like God; you are to be *peacemakers* so that you may be recognized as God's children." And the inevitable doom that goes with it is that a soul *cannot be forgiven* that cannot recognize love and forgiveness when they are bestowed upon it. To lose love is by an inescapable law of life to lose God.

⁸ The parables which interpret the heart of God, with utmost naturalness and simplicity, take for granted that love is the essential aspect of his character. Lilies in the field and mother birds brooding on their nests are symbols for him of a divine care existing at the heart of things. The thoughtful gift of a cup of cold water to a little child in need stores up an increment of love in the spiritual world which is never lost or wasted.

⁹ The unforgettable parables, which we owe to St. Luke, carry this identity of love with God to its highest possible expression in words. The shepherd seeking his lost sheep, the woman hunting for her lost coin, the father meeting his returning son who had gone wrong—utterly simple stories and yet immortal frescoes of reality—carry the mind of the reader unconsciously and irresistibly from incidents of village life in Palestine to an eternal quality in the heart of God.

¹⁰ The fact that God can be revealed in a personal life carries momentous implications. It means that the divine and the human are not so far sundered as has been persistently supposed. It means that human nature *can* become an organ for the Life of God since it *has been* such an organ. It means that God is nearer to us than we supposed; more truly an Emmanuel God than we had been wont to believe. It may well be that God is all along endeavoring to break through and reveal his presence and character, the only difficulty being that he finds such poor, self-filled instruments for any true revelation to break through.

¹¹ This revealing union of the divine and the human in a life of love and service and self-giving is the clue to another central idea which belongs to

the heart of Christianity—namely, the way of life which Christ called "the Kingdom of God." This phrase has had many meanings during the period of Christian history, and, as it stands expressed in the Gospels, it is open to more than a single interpretation. The first century, in which the New Testament came to birth, was an age of apocalyptic expectations; and the despair of getting spiritual results by natural processes, which characterizes all apocalypses, is undoubtedly in evidence throughout the New Testament, as is also the fervid hope that a supernatural relief expedition was near at hand.

[12] But the remarkable fact is that there is another far deeper and more unique strand there of a wholly different type. It is easy to see how the apocalyptic hope got its place in the story; it is not so easy to account for the amazing depth and originality of the central insight which constitutes here the heart of the message, which is the expectation of a new humanity engendered by the process of the coming of the Life of God into the lives of men.

[13] The great saying, *The Kingdom of God is within you,* has been called by a modern Hindu the greatest revelation that any person has ever made. But it is not a solitary saying, apart and alone, and out of keeping with the rest of the sayings. It is rather a key which opens the whole meaning of the unique conception of the Kingdom. And it is the Kingdom which forms the deepest and most original strand of the message of "good news," which we call "Gospel."

[14] The world has suffered serious loss by the constant assumption that the Kingdom of God is a *post-mortem* state, instead of being a positive Christian ideal of life for the individual and for society here in this world where it is so desperately needed. The otherworldly emphasis in Christian teaching has accustomed us to postpone our holy cities and our rivers of the water of life to a realm beyond the grave. We have taken the Kingdom of God as a final "gift" when we should have thought of it as a present "task"—the citizenship of the new humanity according to the measure of "the new Adam," its founder.

[15] Whatever else the Kingdom of God may be in its full meaning, it is in its very nature a way of life which must begin first of all within the life of a person. Whatever more it may be, it is at least a kind of society in which the spirit of love and peace that ruled and controlled Christ's life has become the inward law and nature of those who compose it. Christ once, in a striking passage, called the method "going the second mile." He saw how much of life and religion was "legal," how many things were done because they were expected or required or compelled, and when they were performed they were counted up and cashed in for merit. To Him this first mile of compulsion, this carefully measured mile, had almost no significance for real life as it ought to be. When the second-mile spirit is born one is ready to cut off a right hand, or pluck out an eye, for the adventure, for the goal, without stopping to think of the loss.

[16] The world is so accustomed to the methods of secular calculation and

rationalization that this "other way" seems absurd and forbidding. It has never been tried on a large scale or in a bold, determined fashion. God's poor little man of Assisi went all the way through with it as his method, and the world reverently preserves the scenes of his life as among its most sacred shrines. But it is one thing to canonize a thirteenth-century saint and another to take up, adapt, and carry on his adventure in the twentieth century. John Woolman was a humble second-mile saint in the eighteenth century, and once more he demonstrated the conquering power of love and grace—"the Lamb made war against the beast and overcame it." But there is still much more territory to win. For there can be little question that this spiritual adventure with the quiet force of love and co-operative good will lies at the very heart of the Gospel of Christ, and is the main business of Christ's men in the world.

[17] We have been living in what seems to us now a long period of world-wide depression. In one way or another it has affected all our lives, and it has set its mark upon all our spirits. There are signs, or at least there are wishful hopes, that the corner of the financial depression has been turned, and that something like prosperity is on the way back.

[18] But that aspect of the situation is only a part of the troubles in which the world finds itself. We are confronted with a drift of moral and spiritual confusion. The men who have been working at the solution of the problems of depression seem like boys trying to put together a jigsaw puzzle when some of the pieces are lost. They are perhaps in the baby's crib, and the boys (in ignorance that some of the pieces are missing) cannot make the puzzle come out right. The pieces that have been missing in these years through which we have passed have been just those fundamental pieces that have to do with the unseen, the impalpable and imponderable aspects of life.

[19] W. J. Locke in one of his novels makes the hero say: "I was going about in a state of suspended animation." That has been an all too familiar state of mind. How many, like Hamlet, have been saying: "How weary, stale, flat, and unprofitable seem all the uses of this world." The first step to health and life is away from that dead-end of dull stagnation of spirit, out into a thoroughfare that goes somewhere with thrill and enthusiasm, out of the center of indifference, as Carlyle would say, into *the everlasting yea*.

[20] Goethe's song of the "Earth Spirit" in *Faust*, written in a period of confusion and disaster, strikes the right note for the present situation:

> Thou hast destroyed it,
> The beautiful world,
> With powerful fist:
> In ruin 'tis hurled
> By the blow of a demigod shattered!
> The scattered
> Fragments into the void we carry,
> Deploring

> The beauty perished beyond restoring.
> Mightier
> For the children of men,
> Brightlier
> Build it again,
> In thine own bosom build it anew!

21 If we do not learn how to rebuild our own inner life, we shall only partially succeed in rebuilding our depressed world. The deepest issues of life in this crucial moment are concerned with man's soul. We shall not be able to rebuild our shattered world until we recover our faith in eternal realities, and we shall not do that until we discover something spiritual within ourselves.

22 Somebody has humorously said that the doctrine of relativity means that there isn't any "hitching post" anywhere in the universe. Well, "relativity" notwithstanding, there *is* a "hitching post." It may be taken as settled that there can be "relativity" only in reference to something that is not relative, *something that abides.* We are very familiar with the words *process, change, flux,* the "flow" of all things. But the notion of *permanence* is just as essential for science or philosophy or religion as *fluency* is. One of the greatest of our hymns strikes both the essential notes of life:

> Change and decay in all around I see;
> O Thou who changest not, abide with me.

23 It comes back once more to this central issue of the soul. The discovery of that abiding Reality must be made by each man for himself. It must not be dogmatically asserted; it becomes real only when it is a personal experience which we have for ourselves. If men have lost their faith in God, it is because they have first lost their expectant faith in themselves. If the universe seems to be devoid of a living Spirit and a Heart that cares, it is because we have not sufficiently discovered a spiritual quality at the center of our own lives.

24 We have been floundering about for a generation over the question whether man is a high-grade simian, escaped from the jungle, though still partly in it, or whether he is a child of God; whether we are curious biological products, or whether we partake of a spiritual world of transcendent meaning. This is the real battle line of our time. There is no ready-made answer. It is an issue which each person must face for himself.

25 In any case it will not be settled altogether in biological classrooms, or by studying orangoutangs in the Zoo. We must give more time to the business of *restoring* our own souls and of discovering that they may be centers of revelation of spiritual reality, what Thomas Traherne, in the seventeenth century, called "centers of eternity." That is the place to begin our rebuilding. We need to get "a new heaven" before we can get "a new earth." We must have a new mental sky, new windows for the soul, new dimensions upward, truer conceptions of God, deeper assurance of his life in our lives, before we can remake our cities or transform our political life.

[26] You cannot make a new world by schemes of human betterment that ignore basic spiritual laws of the universe. You cannot get a golden age by merely reshuffling old leaden human units. There is no patent pill that will calm the earthquake when the seismograph is working overtime. The "acids of modernity" have eaten under many "quick" schemes to rehabilitate the sick old world. We must face our tasks with a new faith in the infinite worth and the infinite preciousness of the human soul, and in its high destiny as something kin to God Himself. No one, I am sure, will suppose that I think that a religious experience is a substitute for a sound economic or social or financial or political solution of the world's troubles. I only mean that we must deepen the quality of life and enlarge our faith in the scope of human destiny before any of the fine schemes on hand will work.

Your Unknown Self

Is thy servant a dog?—II Kings 8:13

WALKING one summer day along the historic Cumberland Road, high upon the summit of the Alleghenies, I saw in the midst of a field, in the shadow of venerable pine trees, a mountain grave. I left the road and crossed the field to see whose lonely grave this might be. As I drew near, I read upon the wooden marker the name MAJOR GENERAL EDWARD BRADDOCK. At once my mind ran back a century and a half, and I saw the long procession of red-coated regulars, blue-coated colonials, and lumbering wagons pass down that mountain highway until they were lost in the recesses of the primeval forest. After the disastrous defeat at the fords of the Monongahela, Braddock, mortally wounded, had been borne along in the retreat as far as this spot where now he lies buried. After his grave had been filled, the artillery carriages and wagon trains were driven over to hide the body from the profaning hands of the savages. Just before he died, Braddock, reclining in the arms of Washington, looking up into the faces of his officers and past them to the calm heavens, exclaimed, "Who would have thought it!" Who would have thought that the British general who had won renown on the fields of Europe would have been defeated by a handful of French and Indian allies in the midst of the American bush?

2 Who would have thought it! It is an expression which comes to mind when we think, not only of military disasters, but of those crushing moral disasters and ambushes which suddenly overwhelm the souls of men.

3 The story from which our text is taken is a case to hand. Benhadad, the king of Syria and inveterate enemy of Israel, lay on his royal bed desperately ill. But while there is life, there is hope. Like any brave man, Benhadad did not want to die until he had to; he was a soldier to the last. When he learned that the man of God, Elisha, had come to Damascus, there was a flutter of hope in his heart. "Perhaps," thought the stricken monarch, "Elisha can cure me of this illness. At least he can tell me if I am going to die." Summoning his prime minister, Hazael, the king sent him to Elisha to ask if he would recover from his sickness. The answer of the prophet was: "Go, say unto him, Thou mayest certainly recover; howbeit, the Lord hath shewed me that he shall surely die." So far as his illness was concerned, the king would

From *The American Pulpit Series*, Book X (New York and Nashville, 1946). By permission of Abingdon-Cokesbury Press.

recover; it was not fatal. Nevertheless, he was to die, for Hazael purposed in his heart to kill him and take his throne. When he had said this, Elisha fastened his eyes steadfastly upon Hazael until Hazael winced beneath their searching gaze, and the man of God wept. Disturbed at his tears, Hazael exclaimed, "Why weepest my lord?" "Because," said Elisha, "I know the evil that thou wilt do unto the children of Israel: their strongholds wilt thou set on fire, and their young men wilt thou slay with the sword, and wilt dash their children, and rip up their women with child." "Monster, dost thou wonder that I weep?" Elisha might have added.

At this prophecy of a king assassinated upon his sickbed, a scepter seized by treachery, smoking cities, devastated houses, ravished women, and murdered children, Hazael drew back with unaffected horror. "What, is thy servant a dog, that he should do this great thing?" To this the prophet answered briefly, "The Lord hath shewed me that thou shalt be king over Syria."

4 When Hazael came back to the palace, the sick monarch eagerly asked him what Elisha had said. Hazael answered, "He told me that thou shouldest surely recover." The rest of the answer he hid. His mind now free from anxiety, Benhadad fell into a deep sleep, and out of that sleep he would have awakened to new life and health. But on the morrow, while he still slept, Hazael slipped into his chamber and, taking a towel, dipped it in water, wrung it out, and then spread it tightly over the face of the king. A few convulsive struggles and Benhadad was dead, and "Hazael reigned in his stead." As he went out from the chamber to inaugurate a reign of crime and violence which outdid the prophet's sketch, was it from the still lips of the murdered king or from the hidden recesses of his own conscience that there sounded those words which but yesterday he had uttered to Elisha, "Is thy servant a dog, that he should do this great thing?"

5 I. *Ignorance of Our Own Selves.* The incident is an alarming comment upon human nature, teaching us first how ignorant we may be of our own hearts, and how evil may thrive and expand in the heart and we be ignorant of it, until the evil thing is done. Then in sad and bitter recollection, the man cries out, "How could I have done it?" And others exclaim, "Who would have thought it!" "Who can know himself and the multitude of subtle influences which act upon him?"

6 When the prophet sketched his future for him, Hazael drew back with horror and detestation, and exclaimed, "Am I a dog, that I should do this thing?" So you would say if one were to suggest, not bloody crimes like these of the Syrian satrap, but many of the common transgressions which stain and darken human character. This, you say, you might be tempted to do; but that you should ever commit, or even be tempted to commit, such and such an evil—that, you say, is unthinkable, impossible! How do you know? Are you sure? You may be as ignorant of your heart as Hazael was of his when he protested that he could never do what Elisha foretold for him. The Bible says that a man's heart "is deceitful above all things" and "he that trusteth in his own heart is a fool." Whatever opinion you may hold about the Bible, the fact is that what the Bible has to say about human

225

nature receives striking and sometimes appalling confirmation as men live out their allotted span upon the earth. The humanity of the Bible needs no revision.

⁷ Mere personal disinclination is no guarantee against any evil that men have done. The great doers of evil were the men who thought they could never do it. As a youth, Napoleon wrote an essay for the Lyons Academy on "The Dangers of Ambition." "Would that this hand had never learned to write!" exclaimed Nero when asked to sign his first death warrant. The same Robespierre who during the Reign of Terror sent thousands to the guillotine resigned his office as a provincial judge because he could not bring himself to pronounce sentence of death upon a man convicted of capital crime. Tell the young King David that he will live to darken the closing days of his reign with murder and adultery, and he too would have said, "Is thy servant a dog!" Tell Solomon as he kneels that holy night on Gibeon's sacred slope, asking God for wisdom to discern between good and evil to judge his people, that he will forsake his father's God and bend his aged knees to heathen deities and follow after strange women, and he would have said, "Is thy servant a dog!" Tell Peter on that fateful night, as he boasts of his fidelity to Jesus, that before the sacramental wine is dry upon his lips he will have denied his Lord with an oath, and he would have said it. Clothe yourself with power to discern the secrets of men's hearts and foresee their actions, and tell this man and this woman of the offences which they will one day commit, and they too will rise up to denounce you as an impostor and to exclaim against such a possibility. But in many a life your prophecy may be fulfilled, yea, more than fulfilled. How often the tears of Elisha would be our tears, had we his power to search men's hearts. "Who can understand his errors?"

II. *There Is a Man of Evil Within Us, Ready to Act When He Has the Opportunity*

⁸ Speaking of the moral breakdown of a relative, a man of great promise and unusual advantages and opportunities, a friend said to me, "How, with all this back of him, can you account for it?" As for secondary causes we may be ignorant, but in that man's fall, in that of any other man, the final explanation is that we have within us an evil person, who will declare himself if he can. He is there beneath the breast of the ripest saint and beneath the breast of the worst criminal. It was this discovery that Paul made when he took that great venture into the depths of his own personality. He said that he discovered two Pauls, a law of the mind and a law of sin—one Paul who hated the evil and desired to do the good, and the other Paul who hated the good and wished to do evil. When Paul thus described himself, did he not describe you also, and me?

⁹ In an art museum I once saw a piece of statuary by Carpenter illustrating the words of Victor Hugo, "I feel two men struggling within me." Out of a block of marble two figures are emerging. One is bestial, fierce, cruel,

sensual; the other, desperately striving to get free, is refined, noble, spiritual, intellectual. It is a study for which any one of us might sit as a model.

¹⁰ I know that this is not very complimentary to human nature. But it is not our purpose now to praise human nature. A missionary preacher, commencing his sermon before Louis XIV and his court at Versailles, said, "Sire, I have not come here to praise you. I find no grounds for doing so in the gospels." You may at first resent this sketch of your heart, but if you reflect for a moment, you will see that we all proceed upon such an assumption. A burglary has been committed in your home, and you summon the police and a detective. They go carefully over the ground and conclude that the thief entered here, went yonder, and that this or that was his purpose and plan. The detective puts himself into the place of the thief. How can he do that? Only because in him too there is a possible thief. Or think of a man who is on trial for murder. The attorney for the commonwealth describes his crime and declares that he acted through this or that motive—envy, jealousy, hate, greed. How does he know under what motive a man acts when he commits a murder? Only because in him too there is a possible murderer. If that were not so, the attorney could not prosecute, nor the jurors decide, nor the judge declare sentence. It is because you and I share with one another the common nature of man that we are warned to take nothing for granted but ever to be on our guard. Every man has his own ladder down to hell.

III. *How Desire and Imagination Lead to Evil Deeds*

¹¹ Hazael must have been thinking about the possibilities of becoming king. Elijah had earlier predicted that he would become ruler over Syria. Elisha, looking into the face of Hazael and knowing the desire that was in his heart, saw the shadow and reflection of evil deeds which as yet were abhorrent to Hazael. He wanted to be king, and now the sole obstacle to the fulfillment of his ambition lay there, weak and sick, upon his bed! Only a towel dipped in water, wrung out, and stretched over the face of the sleeping monarch —and Hazael would be king!

¹² The dangerous thing about any repressed desire that may be evil is that the opportunity to gratify it may suddenly arise, and then the thing to be grasped at is the great thing, and the way of securing it is the secondary thing. What in the distance may seem unthinkable and detestable takes on a far different appearance when our desire and our opportunity suddenly and unexpectedly meet each other in our life's experience.

> How oft the sight of means to do ill deeds
> Makes deeds ill done!

¹³ I was told some time ago of a Shakespearean scholar who said that several times in the year he reads through *Macbeth*, not for scholastic purposes or literary investigations, but because the reading did him good, warning him and instructing him, because it showed the danger of ambition and the

227

menace which lurks in the secret pool of imagination and desire. In that respect Macbeth is an illustration of all that I have been saying: the evil man in us, the loosing of him through the meeting of evil desire and opportunity. As that loyal soldier is returning from the wars in Norway, the spirits salute him as thane of Glamis, thane of Cawdor, and then as the future king. "All hail, Macbeth! that shalt be king hereafter." The spirits have hardly left him when messengers arrive to tell him that he has been elevated to the rank of thane of Cawdor. Why should not the final prophecy be fulfilled also? His companion warns the excited Macbeth against even entertaining such a desire:

> And oftentimes, to win us to our harm,
> The instruments of darkness tell us truths,
> Win us with honest trifles, to betray 's
> In deepest consequence.

14 Then he would scorn the slightest suggestion that he gain his ambition by treason or murder. But when he reaches his home, he finds that the king is to visit him. In that moment his own ambition and the opportunity to fulfill it are married, and the issue of that marriage was crime and sin.

IV. How Men Fall Slowly and How Moral Deterioration May Proceed Without Being Observed

15 Tramping through the woods on an autumn day, you have set your foot upon the trunk of a fallen tree. The moment your weight came upon the bark it gave way, and your foot crashed through to the rotten heart of the log. That final collapse was sudden, but the rotting and decomposition of the tree was not sudden. It was the process of months and years, the rains of summer, the snows of winter.

16 There are men whose hearts are like that fallen trunk; they are simply waiting for the pressure of the iron heel of temptation before they give way. When they go down, the newspapers herald it in flaming colors, or agonized friends weep over it at night. Men say, "How sudden! Who would have thought it!" But it was not sudden at all. It was the last stage in a long process of corruption and deterioration. "Search me, O God, and know my heart: try me, and know my thoughts: and see if there be any wicked way in me."

Conclusions

17 In view of this solemn and piercing truth, there are several conclusions which press upon us for our good and our safety.

18 Accept with fear and trembling the Bible's account of the heart of men—your own heart. Look upon it as deceitful and evil, as needing a keeper and a Saviour. In that powerful book *The Silence of Dean Maitland* when, after long efforts to hide his sin, the dean made his final confession, he said: "I fell because I deemed myself above temptation." See to it that you do not fall for a like reason. If you do go down, let it not be because you were so foolish as to think yourself above temptation. "Let him that thinketh he standeth take heed lest he fall."

¹⁹ Set a watch over your thoughts and imaginations. Because they regard a thing which is flashed upon them as impossible, men feel it safe to admit it in thought. That is the first step in their downfall. (A man allows himself unrestrained thoughts of revenge, violence, dishonesty, pride, covetousness, or impurity, and before he realizes it, these thoughts flower into evil deeds.) Each man is tempted by his own desire. Then the desire, when it hath conceived, "bringeth forth sin; and sin, when it is finished, bringeth forth death"—always death.

²⁰ Examine your life and test your heart. As the physicians have certain tests for the physical health, so there are tests for the moral and spiritual health of a man. Test your life by the reaction of your mind to the preaching of redemptive truth in Jesus Christ. Is it distasteful to you to hear that man is a sinner, and that he can be forgiven only through faith in the atoning death of Jesus Christ on the cross? If so, beware! You are not in moral or spiritual health. Examine yourself and see if you can mark any decline in moral sensitiveness. Are there things that you can now do without the least compunction of conscience, but which a year or five years ago would have cost you many a pang and deep unhappiness? If so, beware! Test yourself and see what your weak side is, where the enemy is most likely to break through. Find out what your most easily besetting sin is, for you may be sure that you have one. You can find out what it is if you wish to. What are the thoughts that embarrass you when you think of Jesus, when your soul aspires to go higher? What is the sin that rises up to cover you with confusion when you come to the Communion table? A fearless, honest answer to these questions may be of tremendous advantage for you.

²¹ Have Christ in your heart. That internal defense is better than any wall of habit or bastion of resolution. With him you are safe. Jesus said that the devil came and found nothing in him, no possible place of contact or lodgment. The trouble with you and me is that when he comes—as come he will—he finds so many things in us, so many places of contact. If a spark falls on ice, nothing happens. If it falls on water, nothing happens. If it falls on marble, nothing happens. But if it falls on the powder magazine, there is explosion and disaster and death. Temptation finds the Christ-filled heart as the spark finds the ice, the water, the marble. But the Christless, careless heart it finds as the spark finds the powder. In Christ is your safety. Pray that he may dwell in your heart. If all your resolutions and struggles and fightings have proved unavailing, try Christ, fall back upon the Everlasting Arms.

²² But should the day ever come to you, as come it has for not a few already, when you discover that Satan has sifted you as wheat, that you have done not only what you would not have done, but what you thought you could not have done, when your heart is sick with failure and shame and self-reproach and fear, remember that this same Jesus who sets you his own

great example and warns you and instructs you is also your Saviour. Seek his forgiveness, and ask him to restore you and give you another chance and a new start. For he is "able to keep you from falling, and to present you faultless before the presence of his glory with exceeding joy."

23 "The Son of man is come to seek and to save that which was lost." Oh, wondrous Love! Take him for your guide and safety, and take him for your Redeemer from the guilt and power of sin.

Thanks Be unto God for His Unspeakable Gift!

Thanks be unto God for his unspeakable gift!
—II Cor. 9:15

MAY the Christmas grace of giving glory to God in the highest, the inner peace granted at Bethlehem, and the Christ-child's good will toward our fellow-men be and remain with every one of you today and always!

² As I extend these greetings to you, not only in behalf of myself but also in the name of a hundred workers associated with me in this radio mission for Christ, I remind you that, while we are now gathered from coast to coast for this afternoon's glorification of the Christ-child, Christmas is almost ended in Bethlehem. The hush of midnight has drawn its silent curtain over the little town with its seven thousand inhabitants and the many visitors who crowd its time-grooved streets. On the other side of the world, westward in the blue Pacific, in this very moment Christmas is still young. On many of the coral islands eager children and happy parents are meeting for Christmas worship in their little palm-thatched churches amid the fragrance and beauty of a tropical December. Should it not be so,—Christmas ending, yet always beginning,—Christmas everywhere, Christmas for every one?

³ Incomparably more personal and blessed than the widespread and continued Christmas rejoicing is the benediction of the Christ-child in our own lives. Before this busy, blessed day of the Savior's birth draws to its close, let us remind ourselves of the glorious gift with which God would enrich every one of us today. It is the most precious and blessed bestowal that you can ever receive, even though you may be showered with costly and lavish remembrances, almost without number. It is the priceless gift, more valuable than all the mountain of earthly presents and honors that you may accumulate during the rest of your life, including Nobel prizes, Rhodes fellowships, Congressional awards, royal grants, extra dividends, and lavish bonuses. Ranking high among the most costly manuscripts in the world is the Sinai Codex, a Bible manuscript written in the fourth century. British children

From *The Radio from Coast to Coast* (St. Louis, 1940). By permission of T[cordia Press.

saved their pennies and finally purchased the parchment from the Soviet government for $500,000. If you have a New Testament and believe it, particularly the 263 simple words of Saint Luke's Christmas-story, you have a treasure which in the sight of God far exceeds $500,000.

⁴ Among the most valuable paintings in all the art galleries of the world is Raphael's glorification of the Christ-child and His mother. Five million dollars, we are told, could not purchase this picture. If you receive and believe God's Christmas-gift, and have Christ imprinted in the fibers of your heart, you have a blessing that makes five million dollars seem paltry. One of the most costly pieces of property in the world is the site of the Church of the Nativity in Bethlehem. No amount of money could purchase this reputed spot of our Savior's birth; streams of blood have flown from ten thousand wounds as many have tried to seize or to protect this place. Yet if you have God's Christmas-gift, and kneel in spirit at the Christ-child's manger, even if you are out of work, out of funds, out of supplies, you are richer than if you held the title to that church at Bethlehem; for when Christ is born in your hearts, you have a living, victorious assurance that can never come from any disputed traditional spot of the Savior's birth.

⁵ What is it, we may well ask, then, that gives this incomparable greatness to Christmas, and how are we to reflect its inestimable glory? As you in the East begin to light your Christmas-trees at the approach of evening darkness, and you in the West rise from your holiday dinners, let me show you before another Christmas has passed all too quickly into the irrevocable gulf of the past, that the joy of this day is much more definite than a mere hazy feeling of good will, a sense of material happiness through good times, good business, good friends. Above the sparkle of the Christmas lights, the fragrance of the Christmas greens, the brightness of the Christmas colors, the echo of the carols, the heaped gifts, there must be, if this day is to bring its blessings to you and to your home, that Christ-directed faith, that Christ-centered joy, that Christ-focused confidence, which makes us join in that eight-word yet all-comprehensive Christmas hymn intoned by the apostle: "Thanks be unto God for his Unspeakable Gift!"

I. *The Unspeakable Gift and Its Blessings*

⁶ When St. Paul calls Christ God's "Unspeakable Gift," he is not toying with exaggerated superlatives, polishing his style with impressive phraseology. The blessing of the Savior's Gospel was as inexplicable to him as it must be to us. The apostle uses a term here which means: one "cannot bring out" or "express" the blessing, the fulness, the glory, the riches, the value of this divine gift. If Saint Paul, acknowledged even by the Christless world as a master of logic, expression, and rhetoric, asserts that God's Christmas-gift to the world defies all description, where shall we find words or pictures, poetry or painting, that can reproduce in full majesty the limitless love of our Lord Jesus? No sacred oratorio, not even the unforgettable strains of Handel's *Messiah*, and its climax in the stirring "Hallelujah Chorus," or the artistry of Bach's *Christmas Oratorio,* can be classed with the angel chorus reechoing over

232

Bethlehem; and even those angel voices could not sing the full glory of Christ. All the hands of genius painting nativity scenes, the fifty-six Madonnas of Raphael, or an art gallery graced with the masterpieces of the ages that have depicted the Christ-child, cannot truly delineate the personal blessings of Bethlehem. No poetry, not even the sacred lines of our hymnals, the measured stateliness of any nativity ode, not even the ancient psalms of inspired prophecy, can fully express the height and depth of God's love in Christ. The heart of Christmas remains unspeakable in its beauty, immeasurable in its power, unutterable in its glory.

⁷ All other gifts, from the festively decorated packages beneath your Christmas-trees to the most elaborate grants ever recorded in history, can be measured and valued. A crowned churchman once drew a line through North and South America and presented the eastern section of this hemisphere to one country, and the entire West, today consisting of dozens of nations, multiplied millions of black-skinned, red-skinned, white-skinned men, to another country. Surveyors and assessors can describe in voluminous detail the contents, the value, the extent, of this grant, perhaps the greatest gift in all history; yet not all the corps of experts and the intricacies of higher mathematics can provide a gage to mark the extent of Christ's blessing in individual hearts and in the history of nations. Even in an age where billions are common figures of high finance, the Christ of Christmas remains incomputable. Study the nativity Gospel from whatever angle you wish, and you will repeat Saint Paul's "unspeakable." Reason falters, logic fails, orators stammer, and authors grope for words when confronted by the "unspeakable" mystery of Christmas, the Incarnation of God, God made man; the divine mortal; the Creator a creature; the Son of God the Son of the virgin; the King of Heaven's throne a Babe of Bethlehem's stall. No scientific treatises can explain the unfathomable miracle concealed behind Saint John's simple summary of the Christmas evangel, "The Word was made flesh and dwelt among us; and we beheld His glory, the glory as of the Only-begotten of the Father." No master minds can discover any deeper truth concerning the Incarnation of Christ than the confidence which has enriched the simple trust of millions, the assurance that the Son of Mary is the "Son of the Highest," that, as the angels caroled, the Babe "wrapped in swaddling-clothes," is "Christ, the Lord." His birth, which brought heaven to earth, remains the unspeakable mystery before which, humbled and awe-struck, mighty intellects have worshipped with joy and childlike trust.

⁸ While the Christmas mystery of God manifest in the flesh transcends our poor powers of analysis, its truth remains as unchangeable as heaven itself. Even if unbelief and denial combine, as they do today across the waters in the strongholds of atheism, and in our own country, to shower harsh words of blasphemous attacks on the Holy Child; even if doubt and skepticism unite to shrug shoulders in suspicion, and question the Christmas Gospel; even if infidelity and apostasy join hands and voices in churches which a century ago exalted the Incarnation of God in the Christ-child, but which today are trying to palm off an all-too-human Jesus as the true son of Joseph instead of

233

the true Son of God, as the Christ of Bethlehem, but not of heaven;—if you value your soul, if you think thoughts of eternity and weigh the alternatives of endless living with Christ or endless dying without Him, do not let any influences on earth or in hell move your trust from that basic conviction of Christmas faith in which you declare, "I believe that Jesus Christ, true God, born of the Father from eternity, and also true Man, born of the Virgin Mary, is my Lord." Don't say, "Explain the birth of Christ, and I will accept it"! This, the apostle reminds us, belongs to the "unspeakable" glory of Christmas; and instead of probing into these mysteries, we are to trust them; instead of questioning, to affirm them; instead of debating, to declare them. If we take the word of man for a thousand mysteries of life, why not take God at His word for this supreme mystery of our faith, and, beholding the Child born unto us and the Son given to us, crown Him—and I pray you will—"the mighty God"?

⁹ Equally "unspeakable" is the mercy granted to us in the birth of Jesus. It has been the custom to remember with our gifts today those who are near and dear to us, to whom we are bound by ties of friendship or indebted by obligation. The great gift of Christ is granted not to God's friends, but to His enemies, to those who in their sins have risen up against God and declared war against the Almighty. To every one of us, suffering, as we and our world are, under the destructive powers of sin, God offers His gift of "unspeakable" grace. Christmas does not offer rejoicing to a selected few; it cries out, "Joy to the world!" We stand before that supreme and saving truth, the holy of holies of our Christian faith, the blessed assurance that "Christ Jesus came into the world," not to build big and costly churches, not to give His followers earthly power and rule, but—and this is why the angels sang their praise—"to save sinners." He came, not to establish social service, social consciousness, social justice, but first and foremost He came to seal our salvation. No wonder that the apostle calls the mercy of God as shown by the gift of Christ "unspeakable"; it goes beyond the limit of human speech. Just as beholding the glare of the sun, men lose their power of vision, so raising our eyes to the brilliance of Jesus, the Sun of Righteousness, we are blinded by the splendor of the greatest Gift that God Himself could bestow. Christ came to save—blessed assurance! But more: He came to "save . . . to the uttermost," so that no sin is too great, no sinner too vile, to be blessed, when penitent and believing, by this Gift. Christ came to save; but more: He came to save freely. No conditions are attached to this gift of God in Christ; nor is it offered to those who have earned or deserved it. It is the free, gracious, unearned, unmerited gift of God to those who with the humility of the shepherds and the reverence of the Magi believe with a personal and trusting faith that Jesus is the Ransom of their souls and that He "shall save His people from their sins." Christ came to save; but more: He came to bring with His salvation positive, doubt-destroying conviction. The gift of His grace is not a matter of speculation, not a theory of conjecture. It is the absolute and final truth, which does not leave men in suspense, in question, or in doubt as to their salvation. It does more than teach men to

yearn and pray and hope for their deliverance from sin; it gives them that exultant conviction by which nothing in life or death itself "shall be able to separate us from the love of God which is in Christ Jesus."

[10] Christ, our Christmas-gift, is "unspeakable" because of His everlasting triumph and eternal blessing. All other gifts decay and perish; all other love, even the most deep-rooted devotion that binds husband and wife, parents and children, must end; but the love with which Christ loved us never weakens, never changes, never ends. Octavius, whom we usually refer to as Augustus, ruled the world when Christ was born at Bethlehem; today only a few statues, some crumbling columns of broken temples, remain as the tottering evidence of his departed glory. The helpless Babe in the manger, crowded out of the inn, hunted by Herod, exiled from His homeland, towers over the wrecks of time. That Child changed our calendar, our race, our world, because He changed the hearts and lives of millions as He displaced fear with confidence, despair with hope, doubt with trust, punishment with pardon, terror with peace, hell with heaven, and death with eternal life,—all the rich blessings of our "unspeakable Gift."

II. *The Unspeakable Gift and Our Thanks*

[11] Need we wonder, then, that the great apostle, contemplating the mystery of our Savior's advent into the flesh, breaks forth in this heart-deep "Thanks be unto God"? Who today, having refused to desecrate the birthday of our King by drunkenness, gluttony, or gross sin, knowing what Christmas truly means, will not reecho this hymn of gratitude for Christ, our Christmas-gift, "Thanks be unto God"? Only the smug and self-satisfied who boast that they need no Savior; only blatant sinners who raise their clenched fists against God and resolve to continue in sin; only the blasé, the spiritually dying, and the dead whose greedy hearts and covetous eyes have been focused on the treasures and trinkets of the season, the dollars and cents of Christmas profit or loss,—can refrain from joining the chorus of gratitude raised by hundreds of millions of Christians today: "Thanks be unto God!"

[12] This gratitude must not be restricted to words. You who have now heard the blessed essence of Christmas must show your thanks. No praise means so much in the sight of our heavenly Father as your trusting acceptance of the "unspeakable Gift"; and it is my prayer on this Christmas, a day divinely appointed to call men to Christ and His salvation, that many of you will make His historical birthday your spiritual birthday and blend your hearts and voices in this Christmas *Te Deum.*

[13] To this end I ask you, Have you received this "unspeakable Gift"? Have you thanked God for the first Christmas and its ageless blessing to you? I know that some of you may feel like asking me, "How can I give thanks when I have so many reverses and hardships in my life; when I have no Christmas bonuses and dividends, as hundreds and thousands of others have; when, at best, I have received only a few straggling gifts?" To you Christmas comes with a personally-directed message of hope, and teaches you the blessings of compensation in Christ; for if you are His and He is yours, you

are unspeakably rich. Then the apostle reminds you, "Ye know the grace of our Lord Jesus Christ that, though He was rich, yet for your sakes He became poor, that ye through His poverty might be rich." Your Christ is a sympathetic Savior, who was poor, too, so poor that, though the earth and its fulness are His, the first moments of His life were lived in a manger and the last on a crude, gory cross. Clinging to Christ, you can draw on the resources of heaven and find the peace that men of fabulous wealth who have rejected His atoning love can never purchase. If you have Christ, you can behold this "unspeakable Gift" and exult: "He that spared not His own Son, but delivered Him up for us all, how shall He not with Him also freely give us all things?"—believing that the God who gave the greater gift, His Son, will in His way and at His time grant you the incomparably smaller gifts required for the support of your body, your home, your family.

[14] With Christ you know that all these sorrows serve a remedial, purifying, building purpose. I recently read an account of the 1864 Christmas in the Confederate States. The price on flour on that Christmas was $600 a barrel, sugar $30 a pound, beef $40 a pound; a ham cost $300. The vegetables for a Christmas dinner,—cabbage, potatoes, and hominy,—represented an outlay of $100. There was no dessert in this typical plantation dinner; instead, black molasses, which cost $60 a gallon. Yet out of that harrowing war and privation there emerged, as you on the other side of the Mason-Dixon Line personally realize, a better and happier South. In a much higher degree God often checks our ambitions, reverses our plans, destroys our programs, so that we may be saved for the everlasting blessings.

[15] Perhaps some of you have greeted this Christmas morning on sick-beds; and you who are wasting away in wearying illness, let me bring you a special Christmas comfort by stressing the fact that Jesus, too, suffered, bore agonies that no man can endure, the punishment for all sin, that we might look with Him to the homeland, where there shall be no suffering. Some years ago a young man of only twenty-three years, recovering from a siege of sickness, thought of Christ and, subduing his impatience, penned the lines that many of you will sing, even on sick-beds:

> As with gladness men of old
> Did the guiding star behold;
> As with joy they hailed its light,
> Leading onward, beaming bright,
> So, most gracious Lord, may we
> Evermore be led to Thee.

That was William Chatterton Dix, born just a hundred years ago. May your pain thus help to bring you closer to Christ!

[16] Some of you are lonesome on this Christmas Day, separated by great distances from your loved ones; and some of you are misunderstood, oppressed. Take heart, however, as you recall that the beginning of our Savior's life was marked by Herod's brutal murder and its end with the cruelty of the crucifixion. During the ravages of the Thirty Years' War Paul Gerhardt, one

of the greatest hymn-writers of the Church, met with harsh opposition and hatred. Yet when Christmas came, he could sing:

> All my heart this night rejoices,
> As I hear, far and near,
> Sweetest angel voices;
> "Christ is born," their choirs are singing,
> Till the air, everywhere,
> Now with joy is ringing.

God grant that with Christ born in you again today you will experience His sacred companionship even through heartaches and heart-breaks, sorrow and loneliness, misunderstanding and family quarrels.

17 Since the "unspeakable Gift" was freely given for all, the appeal that surges up in our hearts now calls, "O come, let us adore Him!" Fathers should understand that Christmas is the most appropriate Father's Day, revealing as it does the fatherhood of God with His divine love for wayward children; mothers should remember that Christmas, with its unequaled exaltation of motherhood, is the best and truest Mother's Day. Let the aged rejoice that the Christmas truth enables them to shake off the uncertainty of life and the fear of death to join aged Simeon in his psalm of everlasting praise, "Lord, now lettest Thou Thy servant depart in peace, . . . for mine eyes have seen Thy Salvation"; and let children be happy on Christmas, which as no other day brings the full glory of childhood, since the Savior of mankind, the true Son of God, becomes a wee, small Babe. The rich, the learned, and the mighty, who can follow the star of faith and, like the Wise Men from the distant East, find in the service of Christ the goal toward which their money, time, talents, influence, but above all their faith must be devoted; the great masses in America, the common working people, for whom Christmas always brings a special blessing, since we recall that the first Nativity message was proclaimed not to kings but to commoners, not to aristocrats but to working-men, not to princes of finance but to shepherds who were guarding their flocks,—all to whom this gift of all ages, all mercy, all blessing, has been freely granted on this day, come now!

18 It is not too late. Your sins are not too numerous and not too grievous. You need bring no gift to win the favor of the Christ-child, for He loved you before you were. Come now, and as you attune your faith to the angelic song, "Glory to God in the highest," repeat with me this resolute promise of your Christmas gratitude in hovels and mansions, in darkened sick-rooms and radiant sitting-rooms, in dingy basements and towering apartments, in old folks' homes and orphanages, in asylums and prisons, on land, on the sea, and in the air, in crowded cities and snowbound villages, the strong in courage and the weak in faith, those who have always known Christ and those in whose hearts even now the first flickering flame of faith begins to banish darkness,—O shout it from Maine to California, from Canada to Mexico, this chorus of Christ-centered praise, "Thanks be unto God for His unspeakable Gift!" God grant you this Christmas gratitude for Jesus' sake. Amen.

Reconciliation

Be ye reconciled to God.—II Cor. 5:20

SOME words seem large enough to hold all our thoughts, all that we have felt and hoped and dreamed about life. Of such a word Keats said in one of his finest lines, it is like a bell that gives a tongue to time and a voice to eternity, revealing God. Thus, when we would utter our deepest thought about life and what it means, about God and what He is, there is one word that leaps to our lips—love. It is like a magic chalice into which we pour all that we have learned here, all that we hope for hereafter; like a seashell in which we hear the voices of many waters that drift and sing. Another such word is the Amen that follows after prayer, the mighty answer of the heart to the will of God, the ineffable homeward sigh of the soul, breathing out the unutterable longings no tongue can tell.

² Just so St. Paul, in the great passage from which the text is taken, sums up the secret of religion, the heart of it, the height and depth of it, in one word—Reconciliation. It is the whole of theology in one revealing word, as a noble thinker, now gone to his reward, has recently shown us,[1] leaving his exposition of it as a legacy to the church. The mighty yearning of God, the deep need of man, the life and death of Jesus, the redeeming ministry of the church, the prophetic meaning of song, sacrament and symbol—all find focus in this profound, far-reaching word. The power of God is in it, His passion, His purpose, and the prophecy of the final harmony of all souls in His fellowship. Such a word has in it a thousand sermons, too many to be preached in a lifetime; and so we can deal with only one facet of it.

³ First of all, let us put out of our minds forever the idea that it is God who is angry and alienated, and who needs to be reconciled to man, as if He could not forgive until He had been placated and appeased. Such a suggestion should have died in the first breath that uttered it. Not so St. Paul, who tells us that God is revealing himself in Christ, and beseeching us to be reconciled in Him. God is love, and love beareth all things, believeth all things, hopeth all things, seeking to reconcile and to redeem; and love never faileth. The vision of God in Christ makes the dark theology of olden time not only

---

[1] James Denney, *The Christian Doctrine of Reconciliation* (New York: Doran, 1918)—EDITOR.

From *The Angel in the Soul* (New York, 1932). By permission of Harper & Brothers.

obsolete, but intolerable. Nor is it the primary turning of the soul to God in repentance and forgiveness that St. Paul has in mind. Wonderful is that first awakening of the soul, more wonderful than the discovery of a new star out on the edge of the sky; but the apostle is thinking of something more difficult to attain.

⁴ Consider to whom these words were written, and it will be plain that they "speak to our condition," as George Fox would say, bringing the whole problem and process of life before us. They were not addressed to wicked men walking in evil ways, forgetful or defiant of God, but "to the church of God which is in Corinth, with all the saints which are in all Achaia." The apostle is writing to men and women who had confessed their sins, had accepted Christ as their Lord and Leader, and who were trying to follow Him—imperfectly, no doubt, but faithfully; and it is to such as these that he says, "Be ye reconciled to God." Clearly it is one thing to accept God in Christ, and another thing to reconcile ourselves to the mysterious and awful order of the world. What we call conversion is only the beginning, only the alphabet, so to speak, of a school of discipline in which we learn to spell out here a word and there a line of a book of hieroglyphics. Beyond the first joy of the surrender of the soul to God lies the long, hard way of the trial and perfecting of our faith, and what this means we know when we open the Catechism of Facts.

⁵ Let each one ask himself the question, "Am I yet fully reconciled to God?" At times we are. There are hours of insight, moments of vision when we can see afar, mounts of transfiguration where the rivers seem like threadlets of silver in the valley. But there is a coming down again, and at the foot of the mount we hear the cry of pain and the turbid ebb and flow of human misery, to say nothing of the shadow that darkens the world today. If we have moods of lucid joy, there are also days of peevishness, of restless self-regard, of actual atheism, of bitter distrust or cold suspicion of the worth of life. Which one of us can say that he is reconciled to God in the way in which He is managing his life? When that disappointment fell upon us, crushing our hopes, how was it? When God came into the sick chamber in our home, and said to us, "Make this a schoolroom, make your sufferings a sacrifice of praise," were we reconciled? Who can say that he is reconciled to God? All of us are atheists at times and in spots, depending upon the Grace of God to decrease the number and size of those dark blots of God-blindness. No man must lecture another upon this topic; let each search his own heart.

⁶ It was the habit of sweet Margaret Fuller to exclaim in her eager, happy, heroic manner, "I accept the universe." When this was told to Carlyle, the old man remarked, sardonically, "Gad! she'd better!" William James, who tells the story, makes use of it to emphasize the fact that at bottom the whole concern of morality and religion is with the manner of our acceptance of the universe. And he goes on to ask these questions, to which those who knew him are not in doubt as to what answers he himself would give: "Do we accept it only in part and grudgingly, or heartily and altogether? Shall our

protests against certain things in it be real, radical, and unforgiving, or shall we think that, even with evil, there are ways of living that must lead to good? If we accept the whole, shall we do so as if stunned into submission, as Carlyle would have us—or shall we do so with enthusiastic assent?" Three ways, three attitudes are open to us, and the joy of life depends on which we take—Rebellion, Resignation, and Reconciliation.

⁷ Perhaps we do not realize that all round about us innumerable lives are lived out in sullen bitterness, in daily, hourly refusal to "accept the universe." For multitudes of our race life is irking, vexing, maddening, and it would surprise us to know how many deem it a farce, a foolishness, or at best a rather stupid jest. The very conditions of existence, its limitations, its hardships, its handicaps, its senseless triviality, fret them, at times, to fury. Macaulay applied to Byron the fable with which the Duchess of Orleans used to illustrate the character of her son. All the fairies, save one, were bidden to his birth, each bringing a gift, until he seemed dowered with all the treasures of genius and fame. But the uninvited elf came last and so mixed with the profuse offerings of her sisters her malignant gift that every blessing became a curse. Hence a man with the genius of an angel, but awry with himself, angry with life, and railing against fate. Restless, resentful, "impatient of the intolerable patience of God," he blew the silver bugle of revolt against everything, and our hearts applauded. Nearly all of us have passed through such a period. Like his own Lucifer, we shook our fists in the face of Fate defiantly. When pain nags, when sorrow stabs, when hopes fade and plans go awry, that mood is apt to recur even today, filling us with the old rage or a new cynicism. Such is the way of rebellion, and if it does not end in "the worm, the canker, and the grief," as it did with Byron, its fruit is futility and folly.

⁸ Some one said that the sum of the religion of Carlyle is, "Close your Byron, open your Goethe"; that is, lay down the flag of revolt and learn a large, serene, wise resignation. It is sane advice, and here the wise ones of olden time, and especially the Stoics, have much to teach us. Lucretius, Virgil, Aurelius testify to the deep peace that comes to those who bow to the inevitable, not bitterly, but in benign submission. They found that the way of wisdom is not to resist nature, not to triumph over it, much less to pervert it, but to realize our orginal unity with it. They learned that, after all, the external is nothing, and the inner life is all. Stern, strong, austere, they accepted the universe, and they attained to something akin to saintliness, or at least to a bright, gem-like beauty of spirit which we see in the lonely, lovely soul of Aurelius, in whom courage was continual and culture a habit. Yet how devoid of passion, how bereft of joy and color! Not hopeless but unhopeful; if this way did not lead to victory, it defied defeat, as we may read in the challenging lines of Henley:

> Out of the night that covers me,
>   Black as the pit from pole to pole,
> I thank whatever gods may be,
>   For my unconquerable soul.

In the fell clutch of circumstance
I have not winced or cried aloud.
Under the bludgeonings of chance
My head is bloody, but unbowed.

⁹ But there is another way, if haply we may find it, whereby grim resignation passes into glad reconciliation, and life is lifted into joy and love and victory. It is the Christian way which receives life, not as a decree of Fate, but as an opportunity, a discipline, a gift from the Father of men, "in whose will is our peace." It does not simply endure life, as Epictetus did, because he saw no honorable way to get out of it, holding the fort, awaiting a signal for retreat. Nor does it divide life in two, as Dostoevsky did, accepting God but refusing to accept His world with its senseless suffering. No; it accepts life—the whole of it, black as well as bright—with all its ills, its weariness, its woes, as a school wherein to learn a truth that transcends and transfigures it. Such is the way of Jesus, and those who walk in it testify that if it seems hard at first, in fact its yoke is easy, its burden light, and it becomes a singing way further on; even though it lead into a Valley of Shadow. If one were to sum up this better wisdom, it would be to say, "Close your Goethe, and open your Browning"; that is, learn that God is Love, and that a thread of all-sustaining purpose runs through the often strange medley of things:

The world's no blot for us,
Nor blank; it means intensely, and means good:
To find its meaning is my meat and drink.

¹⁰ Now, the glad, grateful, heroic reconciliation to which Jesus leads us is much more than the feeble quietism which says that whatever is, is right; which may be only another name for sloth. Much more, indeed. Jesus accepted the dark tragedy of his Cross as the loving will of God, but he did not accept it too soon and all at once. No, there was his bitter battle in the Garden of Sorrow, in which his quivering sensibility struggled with his faith, until it became clear that he must either accept the Cross or betray his ideal. Once that was plain, he did not hesitate to accept the inevitable, not as mere fate, but as the holy will of his Father. "The cup which my *Father* giveth me, shall I not drink it?" So it must be with us, albeit no sorrow of ours is for a moment to be put alongside that profound tragedy. God forbid! Yet here is a truth to take to heart, and it is sorely needed. Sin, disease, and death exist by the will of God, yet we must not submit and let them have their way, but must resist them to the utmost, and by so doing discover and fulfill his higher will.

¹¹ Just so, when we look out over the world today we must not lose faith and rail at a blind, brutal fate, much as we may be tempted to do so. Truly there is much to dismay us, much to fill us with horror, and we often feel as the writer of the seventy-third Psalm did in his day. He saw the sufferings of the innocent, the downfall of the righteous, and the sleek prosperity of

the wicked, and he thought about it until his head ached, without finding a clue. Indeed, he slipped and well nigh lost his faith, until he went into the sanctuary. There, in the stillness of the Presence, amid the sound of haunting Amens, he learned that the purpose of God may be something other and greater than he had ever dreamed, much less grasped; and that the injustices which had hurt him and shaken his faith are not outside its sweep, but may, indeed, be necessary to it. At any rate, he was taught of God to trust a truth deeper than his doubt, and his rebel mood was melted into the reconciling wonder of worship.

¹² Nor must we forget the plain words of Jesus, telling us that if we would be reconciled to God, our Father, we must first be reconciled with man, our brother. If we bring our gift to the altar, and remember that we have aught against a brother man, it is better to leave the gift unoffered—it will keep—and go and make amends, or seek forgiveness, lest we be not forgiven. No one ought ever to use the brief, grand prayer which Jesus taught us to pray, if he has hate or bitterness in his heart. For in that prayer we actually ask God to make our forgiveness the measure of His own: "Forgive us as we forgive those who have sinned against us." That is, until we act toward man as a brother, God will not—cannot—act toward us as a Father. It is not an edict, but a law, almost terrifying in its implications, if we know what we mean by the words we use. What wonder that our prayers do not rise to heaven, but fall like lead upon our own souls, bringing no blessings? How can we know the love of God—save as a remote rumor or a vague theory— if we harbor hate in our hearts? It is spiritually impossible. As Bojer said in one of his great stories: "I went and sowed seed in my enemy's field *that God might exist!*" Because God is love, we know Him only by love, for love is both revelation and reconciliation.

¹³ One of the most striking of modern stories is *The Bridge of San Luis Rey*, by Thornton Wilder, so unique in its plot, so exquisite in its art. A famous bridge falls and five people are lost—why those five and no others? It is the very question which we ask when some one near to us is smitten with some awful ill, filling us with mingled pity and dismay. The old monk who tried to keep books, in the effort to solve the riddle, failed sadly, since no one can keep books for God. Yet, as the writer tells the story of each of those five lives, leading up to and ending in the accident—if it was an accident—we are left with the feeling that some merciful divine motive may have been at work in the tragedy. At least, we know that if we knew all, much would be clearer, and perhaps all would be explained. It is all summed up in one last shining sentence: "There is a land of the living and a land of the dead and the bridge is love, the only survival, the only meaning." It is a haunting line, telling us what our hearts know to be true, that all God will keep and value when He sorts out the strange medley of our days and years is the love of our lives, with which we anointed our fellow men; "the only survival, the only meaning."

¹⁴ My friends, "be ye reconciled to God." Remember that His will is wider than we know, wiser than we can dream, and must include many things which

242

we can never hope to fathom on earth. Our task is not to understand the Eternal Will, but to learn what it is in respect to our own lives, and do it. Jesus, by facing the bitter worst, found the best, and if he did not lose faith we have no right to do so. Take counsel of him, trust the spirit which he evokes in your heart, and follow where it leads. Make friends with those who have walked in his way; with St. Paul, who won his victory not without agony and tears, by reason of his pride and his intrepid ambition; with the goodly company of those who, having failings like our own, mastered them by his grace. At last, slowly, the sky will become sunny overhead, and the road plain to your feet, and you will learn, what all the mystics have known, the peace, the power, the incredible joy of the surrendered life. Such is the way of reconciliation, even the way of Eternal Life.

> Have Thine own way, Lord! Have Thine own way!
> Thou art the Potter; I am the clay.
> Mold me and make me after Thy will,
> While I am waiting, yielded and still.
>
> Have Thine own way, Lord! Have Thine own way!
> Hold o'er my being absolute sway!
> Fill with Thy Spirit, till all shall see
> Christ only, always, living in me! [2]

Maundy Thursday

For as often as ye eat this bread, and drink this cup,
ye do shew the Lord's death till he come. —I Cor. 11:26

O N THE eve of that Good Friday on which three crosses were erected on
Golgotha, our Lord and Saviour gathered about himself his more intimate circle of disciples—the later apostles—for the last Paschal meal, for that
remembrance meal through which God's people of the old covenant recalled the wonderful rescue from the Egyptian bondage. In accordance with
the customary celebration of the festival, they ate the Paschal lamb, drank
the cup of thanksgiving, and sang together the great hymn of praise. Now
the celebration is finished and the disciples await the evening departure to the
usual lodging house outside the city, on the Mount of Olives. But Jesus makes
no move to get ready to leave, but rather joins to the just-finished Paschal
meal a second solemn act. He takes the bread, which is still lying on the
table at which they had eaten, breaks it in pieces, and gives it to the disciples
with the words: "Take, eat: this is my body, which is broken for you: this
do in remembrance of me." Thereafter he took the cup, which was still
standing before him after the Paschal meal, passed it to his friends, and
said, "This cup is the new testament in my blood; this do ye, as oft as ye
drink of it, in remembrance of me."

² At first, in their astonishment, the Twelve presumably did not know
what was happening. But one thing they could not fail to hear, even in
their first amazement: the Lord spoke here to them about his death. His body
is broken like the bread that he distributes to them; his blood is shed like
the draught of wine that He has given them to drink. His earthly life's
work, hardly begun according to human reckoning, is finished; their Master
takes leave from them.

³ According to what the Evangelists have recorded for us, this was not
the first time Jesus spoke to his disciples about his impending death; but
we always read, in connection with the preceding announcements of the
coming sufferings, that they did not understand him. Jesus spoke to them
in riddles when he said that his death was a divine necessity. They hoped for
the inauguration of the Kingdom of God announced by him, they waited for
the time when their Master would appear before the world as ruler and judge

From *Dachau Sermons*, tr. Robert H. Pfeiffer (New York, 1946). By permission of
Harper & Brothers.

in order to usher in a new Golden Age. But now such a misunderstanding is no longer possible: all these dreams are at an end. One of the Twelve goes forth to betray his Lord, the others will be scattered, and the most loyal of them will deny that he had anything to do with this man. The whole thing is a catastrophe, an utter collapse!

⁴ Since that evening almost two thousand years have passed, and still now, and always, the disciples of Jesus gather again on the evening of Maundy Thursday around his table to partake of the meal to which the Lord invites them. Thereby they think of that hour in which Jesus ordered the disciples to observe this holy command. "This do in remembrance of me." Here one asks naturally—and who among us has never raised this question?—"Fundamentally what is it that gives to this celebration its unparalleled power over the human heart? How does it happen that in spite of all theological disputations and schisms, which have flared up again and again, particularly about this sacrament, the Christian community continues to break the bread and partake of the cup as if all this strife did not concern it at all?"

⁵ Yes, my friends, it really does not concern the Christians at all. The Lord Jesus has given us no doctrines about this Holy Supper of his, nor did he wish to give us any such doctrines at all. All doctrines by which we try to assert something about God's activity are subject to the law of aging and changing. What interested mightily the ancient Greeks, in their pious curiosity, namely, the question of how a Man could be at the same time Son of God, involved theological disputations for centuries. They fought about it back and forth with arguments and counterarguments. Today this no longer interests us in the least; not because we have become so much more indifferent about religion, but because we know that this is not a question which is connected with and rooted in the spirit of the New Testament and therefore in our Christian faith. Later periods have racked their brains trying to find out how it is possible that God, for the sake of Jesus, forgives the sins of those who believe in Him. How can He, if He is the holy and just God, place our sins upon another? Nowadays only some very learned theologians are accurately informed about these theories and mental exercises, while the Christian community has long since understood that a miracle cannot be explained, and consequently it is better to abstain from the attempt.

⁶ And in regard to the disputed questions about the Holy Supper the situation is not radically different. How can bread and wine be the body and blood of Jesus Christ? The great division in the Reformation Church springs in a considerable measure from the different answers to this question. Luther taught differently from Zwingli in the matter, and the latter differently from Calvin; all of them united only in the rejection of the medieval Roman Catholic doctrine of transubstantiation. At present these theological differences have become so subtle that one must be a philosopher with a better-than-average education in order to recognize them in their variety of types. If our salvation depended upon such a recognition, then the Kingdom of

245

Heaven would be accessible only to learned thinkers—which is obviously contrary to the conception held by Jesus himself, and to his own words.

⁷ No, what matters in the Holy Supper is something essentially different, something which the shrewdest cannot conceive with all his shrewdness, but which the most simple-minded can well grasp and comprehend. The Lord Jesus announces in this meal his own death, and thus he draws the veil from the mystery of his life's conclusion. And what he himself said at the time about the significance of his death became for his apostles and then for his Church the actual core of the Christian faith and of the Christian message; and it has remained so until this day. When Paul wished to condense the contents of his missionary preaching into a single sentence, he wrote: "I determined not to know anything [namely, in the field of religion] among you, save Jesus Christ and him crucified." And when the Christian Church wishes to give to its faith the shortest and yet the most unmistakable expression, it uses the symbol of the cross. The cross stands over the altars in our churches, greets us on the paths of our homeland, it is the sign of hope on the graves of our beloved. We know only one comfort and one assurance, Jesus Christ the crucified.

⁸ The interpretation of his death which the Lord Jesus gives his disciples in the Holy Supper is extremely plain. To understand it there is no need of any philosophy nor of any Biblical learning, but only of an open heart which is ready to see what is here happening, and to hear what is here being said.

⁹ The Lord himself breaks the bread; he himself passes the cup: he himself gives up his body and blood. There is therefore no basis to what may have appeared true to a casual bystander, namely, that his life was taken from him against his will. No, he gives it up voluntarily, as a saying of the Lord states in the Gospel of John: "No man taketh it [i.e., my life] from me, but I lay it down of myself." But he does not cast it from himself, as may happen in other cases, as something good for nothing, for which one has no further use. He gives the bread and the wine to his disciples to eat and to drink, that they may live thereby. So his death is a gift that should be of advantage to them. Finally, however, there arises from this eating and drinking a new kind of communion, the communion of those to whom the Lord grants a share in his self-sacrifice—the eucharistic community. This much the action per se, as we see it taking place before our eyes, tells us.

¹⁰ The Lord Christ, however, adds to the action his explaining words. These words are not transmitted identically in the various accounts, but on the whole the meaning is the same. According to these accounts, as Jesus broke and distributed the bread, he said, "Take, eat; this is my body, which is given for you"; and in passing the cup: "Take and drink all of it; this cup is the new testament in my blood, which will be shed for you and for many for the remission of sins." And both times he added as a conclusion, "This do in remembrance of me."

¹¹ We are therefore told here that the Lord does not withdraw from us by his death, especially not if we accept his gift. On the contrary, here he

would become entirely united with us, here he gives himself fully to us, his body and his blood belong to us—"for you." Nay, in this "for you" lies the real and effective mystery of his death on the cross. For it does not merely say that Jesus dies for his own friends, like a soldier for his people and country, or like the saver of a life who snatches another from the flames or from the waves and perishes himself. He says so: "For you for the remission of sins." This is the unparalleled feature of his death, that he dies in our place, the Just for the unjust, the holy one for the sinners. And now we stand in his place: freed of all guilt and through him and on his account beloved children of God.

[12] This is the end of the old covenant, in which the relation between God and us was regulated according to the principle of reward and punishment. With the death of Jesus for us, the new covenant, which rests on the forgiveness of sins, has been established, and it removes terror from our own death, because another has already allowed our punishment to be executed upon himself. Now the saying is, "Where there is forgiveness of sins, there is also life and bliss."

[13] This interpretation which Jesus himself gives of his death is, as we noted, plain; but in its wonderfulness incomprehensible and in its depth unfathomable: with brain work we get nowhere here. But where a human heart is in distress because it longs for the assurance of a merciful God, where a conscience is afraid under the pressure of guilt, there the message of the cross and death of the Lord Christ becomes tidings of joy: "For you for the remission of sins." This is no human mental invention, he himself has so said it. And he has given us, his congregation, the covenant meal in order that we may not only hear, but also "taste and see that the Lord is good."

[14] "This do in remembrance of me." Thus we celebrate with the Christian Church of all times the meal of the Lord in remembrance of his death, and we hear at the same time his voice, which allots to us his death: "For you —for the remission of sins." And we eat of the bread and drink of the cup and listen to the words, "My body given for you, my blood shed for you." This message does not age, does not lose any of its living strength with the passage of time. For in its need for God and in its longing for him the human heart remains ever the same. And when all the dead are once forgotten, the death of the Lord Jesus Christ will ever be preached and confessed by his church because there flows the source of its life, and the church will continue to gather around his table and confess thereby its crucified Lord in repentance for its transgression, in gratitude for his love, and in the praise of God for His inconceivable loving-kindness, until—yes, until its Lord will come at the end of time, and with him that Kingdom of God in which all patchwork ceases. There we see him as he is, and there we shall be with him forever.

[15] To this great community of those who proclaim the death of their Lord as a message of joy belong this evening also we, who come here to his table. A small company, everyone of us torn away from his earthly

home and from the circle of his dear ones, all of us robbed of freedom and ever uncertain about what the following day or even the following hour will bring. But, despite all this, we are at home. We eat and drink at the table of our heavenly Father and we may be comforted. There is nothing that could tear us away and separate us from Him, since our Lord and Master gave his life for us and for many, indeed even for both of the friends who have gone away from our circle and whom we remember in our intercession, even for our dear ones far away or out there at the fronts, for whom we are anxious. For them also did the Lord die, and with him they and we are well protected.

> We are people washed up by the stream of time on the earth-isle,
> Full of mishaps and full of heartache, 'till home brings us the Saviour.
> The father-home is ever near, though changeable be fates;
> It is the Cross on Golgotha, the home for the homeless.
>
> Amen.

An Angel in the Sun

And I saw an angel standing in the sun.—Rev. 19:17

ALTHOUGH seeming to border on the sensational, this subject is taken directly from the Bible. In the book of Revelation, the nineteenth chapter and the seventeenth verse, we read: "And I saw an angel standing in the sun."

² The book of Revelation was written when Christianity was fighting for its life. Christians were enduring as severe a period of persecution as has ever been their lot. Imperial Rome had a tolerant attitude toward the various religions within her borders. One notable exception was Christianity; another Judaism. The Christians were singled out for harsh treatment because, like the Jews and unlike the other religious sects, they were strict monotheists who refused to worship the Roman emperor. They were therefore suspected by Rome of disloyalty and even of treason, and they paid the price as victims of unrelenting persecution.

³ The author of the book of Revelation was a prisoner on the Isle of Patmos. He was writing to encourage his fellow Christians. But, fearing lest his message to them should fall into the hands of the Roman authorities, he had to write in cryptic language, language which only he and they could understand. This accounts for the strange and at times even weird symbols of the book. The Roman authorities would not know that by "the beast" he meant Rome nor that "the false prophet" meant the imperial priesthood; nor would they understand the other symbols.

⁴ Some of these symbols we have been able to decode; to others of them, like the one under consideration, we have no key. "And I saw an angel standing in the sun." We do not know what the original idea underlying this phrase may have been. And yet we are justified, it seems to me, in taking this symbol and considering what it means to us. For, you see, the book of Revelation is not to be taken literally. It is much closer to being drama than history. It was written by a man of superb imagination and great faith. This is why it is so wrong for literalists, prosaic folk devoid of imagination, to use this book as though it were a cosmic timetable of world events. In trying to force its glorious imagery within the literalistic concepts of our matter-of-fact minds we rob the book of its meaning. There is a truth in

From *The American Pulpit Series,* Book I (New York and Nashville, 1945). By permission of Abingdon-Cokesbury Press.

poetry which is lost when we try to treat poetry as though it were history. Here, for example, is how the poet J. G. Holland once described a sunset. He said that the sun

> ... threw his weary arms far up the sky,
> And, with vermillion-tinted fingers,
> Toyed with the long tresses of the evening star.

Would it not be too bad to treat that as though it were literal fact! So with our text: it is not to be taken as literal fact. But truth is much bigger than fact. What, then, is the truth in this poetic symbol?

[5] I. For one thing, the symbol of an angel standing in the sun suggests that we should always try to see the spiritual in the material. You will recall the striking experience of Moses when he was called of God to be the deliverer of the children of Israel. This is the way the Bible describes it: "And the angel of the Lord appeared unto him in a flame of fire out of the midst of a bush: and he looked, and, behold, the bush burned with fire, and the bush was not consumed." Elizabeth Barrett Browning has immortalized this incident in a few lines of verse which are very familiar:

> Earth's crammed with heaven,
> And every common bush afire with God;
> But only he who sees takes off his shoes,
> The rest sit 'round it and pluck blackberries.

[6] A somewhat similar incident that shows how men have seen the spiritual in the material occurs in the Gospel of John. Jesus had been praying. After his prayer a voice was heard. Some, upon hearing the voice, "said that it thundered: others said, An angel spake to him." From that day to this there have been two schools of thought as to the ultimate source of this voice that speaks to us out of the material universe. On the one hand there are those who insist that the voice that speaks to us out of the universe is merely the sound of thunder, the operation of physical laws that grind themselves out mechanically, blindly, unconsciously, without any knowledge of their own existence and therefore without plan or purpose. Bertrand Russell is perchance a typical exponent of this point of view. He wrote a small book years ago entitled *A Free Man's Worship*, a classic in its way. In it he writes: "Blind to good and evil, reckless of destruction, omnipotent matter rolls on its relentless way." In such a world he pictures man standing "proudly defiant of the irresistible forces," sustaining alone "the world that his own ideals have fashioned despite the trampling march of unconscious power."

[7] This philosophy of materialism is losing ground today. It is not too much to say that an increasing number of serious-minded people are beginning to see "an angel standing in the sun," the spiritual in the material. They are beginning to see within and behind this vast material universe something that is not material, and to hear in the voice that comes out of this universe something more than the purposeless rumblings of unconscious power.

⁸ For this philosophy which sees only the sun, beholds only a material universe utterly bankrupt of any spiritual leaven, is not alone an utterly hopeless philosophy but a quite inadequate one. Our materialists have yet to explain how a universe of blind force and omnipotent matter, an unconscious mechanical universe, has been able to produce the mind and spirit of man. To ask us to believe that unconscious matter has produced the plays of Shakespeare, the art of Rembrandt, the music of Tschaikovsky, or the character of Jesus, is to ask us to believe the incredible. It takes faith to see an angel in the sun. It takes faith to believe that back of this material universe, the vastness of which staggers our imagination, stands God, who created it and is immanent in it. But the alternative belief takes more than faith. It takes credulity. Blessed is the man, then, who with the seer of Patmos sees an angel in the sun—the spiritual in the material.

⁹ II. In the second place, this symbol suggests that we look for the divine in the human. If it is the leaven of spirituality that gives meaning to the material world, it is the spark of divinity that gives significance to human life. The Scriptures leave us little doubt that there is something divine in man. The Epistle to the Hebrews tells us that man was made "a little lower than the angels." The creation story says, "God created man in his own image, in the image of God created he him." Although man has terribly defaced the image of God, he has not succeeded in quite destroying it. However, it is unfortunately true that we more readily see the devilish in others than the angelic. If you and I were perfectly honest with ourselves, we should have to admit that at times we take a strange delight in dwelling upon the unattractive, base, and sinful characteristics of each other. We often put the faults of others so much in the foreground of our thinking that we never see their virtues. That was wise and salutary advice Paul once gave when he said: "Whatsoever things are true, whatsoever things are honest, . . . whatsoever things are lovely, whatsoever things are of good report; if there be any virtue, and if there be any praise, think on these things."

¹⁰ Now let us be realistic here. I do not mean that we should be blind to the sins and shortcomings in our fellows any more than in ourselves. I am advocating no such Pollyanna attitude. Some of us can never be sufficiently grateful to those trusted friends whose kindly, constructive criticisms have spurred us on to better living. Yet there are two ways of seeing the faults in others—one through the eyes of cold, hard criticism; the other through the eyes of faith and love.

¹¹ Perhaps the kind of attitude I have in mind is the one Jesus had. No one ever saw so clearly the evils in man, yet no one has ever had such faith in humankind. Jesus was not blind to the sins and shortcomings of his fellows. He was terribly honest and frank in dealing with them. He called one of his closest disciples "Satan." He told the Pharisees that they were a "generation of vipers." He confronted the woman of Samaria with her moral weakness. He told a rich man who saw nothing in life but the amassing of wealth that he was a fool. But Jesus saw more than

251

this in people. He saw an angel in the sun, the divine in the human. In the forefront of his mind he placed not the faults of people but their virtues, not their actualities but their possibilities. When he thought of a person, his first reaction was not, "How bad he is, how awful! What objectionable traits he possesses!" He saw and knew all this, to be sure, but he did not stop there. He looked beyond this, as one might look beyond an unattractive city dump to the landscape in the distance. Despite all the deviltry in men, he looked for the angel, the good, in them. Sometimes the good was only potential; like the grain of mustard seed, it appeared quite small. Yet the possibilities of good always seemed bigger to him and more significant than the actualities of evil.

[12] Think of Jesus' attitude toward Peter. He knew the faults of Peter, yet he said in substance to him: "Peter, I know you are weak, vacillating, unreliable. I know you are going to deny me. You are Simon, but you *shall be* Peter. I am going to make you as strong as a rock. You are—but you shall be." Psychologically Jesus was right. For, you see, his purpose was to change men, to redeem life; and the redemptive forces work better in the atmosphere of appreciation than in that of condemnation. How true this is with each of us! Every one of us at times faces a moral crisis in his life, some choice he must make, some stand he must take. Will it be with honor or dishonor? In the interests of our better selves or our worse selves? The people who in such a crisis help us to make the wise choice are not they who only blame and condemn, but those who, despite our faults, love us, trust us, believe in us. Ah, how could we ever fail them! How could we let them down! "For their sakes I sanctify myself," said the Master—"for the sake of these people who trust me, believe in me, depend on me."

[13] One of the classic examples of this truth is found in Victor Hugo's *Les Miserables*. Jean Valjean is an escaped convict. "It would be difficult," writes Hugo, "to meet a wayfarer of more wretched appearance." So miserable-looking is he that nobody will give him shelter. Finally a bishop admits him to his home. He repays the bishop's hospitality by walking off with his silver plate. Yet the bishop sees the angel in Valjean. He says to him, "Jean Valjean, my brother, you no longer belong to evil, but to good. I have bought your soul of you. I withdraw it from black thoughts and the spirit of perdition, and give it to God." One fancies that thereafter the thought of this good man who trusted him must have had a redemptive influence on Valjean. Paul writes, "The love of Christ constraineth us"— not the condemnation of Christ, not the judgment of Christ, but the love of Christ. Christ condemned poeple, he criticized people, he judged people. But he also saw the angel in people, the divine in the human; and on that he built. For he came to redeem us, to save us; and it is in the atmosphere of trust, of faith, of appreciation, of love, that the redemptive forces work.

[14] Let us remember, then, that the way to conquer evil is not by always thinking about it and talking about it, but by discovering and nurturing the good until it comes to glorious growth. I am not, of course, saying that this method always succeeds. It does not. Judas lived in this very

atmosphere of appreciation, trust, and love; yet he betrayed Jesus. Peter was very near to the Master, yet he denied him. This much, however, is certain: if this method fails, nothing will succeed. "Be not overcome of evil, but overcome evil with good."

15 III. In the third place, this symbol of an angel standing in the sun suggests not only that we should look for the spiritual in the material and the divine in the human, but that we should look for the constructive elements in every destructive experience. This last suggestion is certainly the most difficult to practice.

16 The sun is a ball of fire. Nothing can live on it. Everything is burned up. One wonders how an angel could ever be in a place like that! Have not you and I at times passed through the fires? How many people have had experiences which have seemed to consume, to burn up, all their fairest hopes and plans and turn their choicest dreams into ugly nightmares?

17 A woman who had passed through severe afflictions once came to Robertson of Brighton, the great English preacher of another generation, to seek help. In speaking to him about her grief she used such words as "withered" and "blighting," truly descriptive words. We sometimes pass through experiences that have the same effect upon our lives that a bomb has on a building. After the explosion all that remains is a heap of rubble. To ask a man to look even in that for the face of an angel is to ask much. Yet the angel is there—must be there—for so many brave souls have found possibilities in every calamity, have rescued out of tragedy something that has permanently enriched, strengthened, or beautified their characters.

18 Booker T. Washington had a great phrase. He spoke of "the advantage of disadvantages." How well he knew the disadvantages of life! As another has said of him, "Born a Negro slave, allowed to carry the books of his white master's children to the schoolhouse door but never to enter, shut out from the areas of privilege he craved most, the advantage of his disadvantages was far from obvious." But he found it. He was able to see an angel in the sun. Out of his calamities he had the insight to see and lay hold of certain constructive elements which lifted him above the ruins. Others have done the same thing. Victor Hugo, in speaking of the bishop, wrote: "He did not try to efface grief by oblivion, but to aggrandize and dignify it by hope. . . . He knew that belief is healthy and he sought to . . . transform the grief that gazes at a grave by showing it the grief that looks at a star."

19 Seldom has this earth of ours been so grief-stricken as today. Suffering and tragedy have been immeasurably increased as the dark, deep shadows of affliction have fallen upon millions and millions of hearts and homes across this war-torn world. This is true not only of the war-torn world. "The heart knoweth his own bitterness." How can we keep the sting of grief from poisoning our spirits? How can we keep the weight of sorrow from so flattening our hearts as to rob them of the expansive spirit of gratitude and praise? The answer of the Christian religion is that through the grace of God we are able to see an angel in the sun, to see what Victor Hugo called a "star" shining through the low-hanging clouds which so often veil our

sky. There is hardly a more profound Christian conviction than that God is in all the experiences of life, even those which may be caused by our own ignorance or sin, and that if we bring them within the light of his presence and power he is able to turn them to our good. It was out of the depth of his own experience that Isaiah wrote: "In all their affliction he was afflicted, and the angel of his presence saved them." And Paul testified: "All things work together for good to them that love God." Such is our faith.

²⁰ When John Milton lost his sight, he wrote a "letter to a foreign friend." In it he said: "I do not even complain of my want of sight; in the night with which I am surrounded the light of the divine presence shines with a more brilliant lustre. . . . I am under the shadow of the divine wings which have enveloped me with this darkness." Milton was able to see an angel in the sun.

²¹ It may be that not only in our personal calamities but even in a world tragedy there is, as Shakespeare has said,

> . . . some soul of goodness in things evil,
> Would men observingly distil it out.

During the last war we spoke loudly and long of the reconstruction period. We were going to rebuild the broken world on new and more enduring foundations. That was the divine light illumining the awful tragedy of the first World War. But while we made wonderful plans on paper, we did not renounce a single one of the policies which had been our undoing; and so the light failed. A second World War has come. Once more we see the divine possibility, namely, the possibility of taking this broken world and refashioning it—making it more nearly the kind of world God intends. This is the only bright spot in the encompassing darkness. If we can lay the foundations of the new world in righteousness and justice, the appalling cost will not have been wholy in vain. Shall we, when the guns have ceased to roar, keep before us the face of the angel, keep steadily in view this God-given opportunity; or shall we lose it again in the dark clouds of revenge or of the self-defeating policies of discredited imperialism and bigoted nationalism? It seems incredible that this could be so.

²² All that I have been saying comes down to this: that to live in a Christian sense is to adopt a positive attitude toward life. This was the supreme mark of Jesus' character. There was little that was negative about his life or message. Life, to him, was always one grand affirmation. He took a positive view of the material universe. He saw the spiritual in the material, the glory of God in the lilies of the field, the providence of God in a sparrow. Nature revealed God to his sensitive soul. He took the positive view of man. Seeing plainly the evil in man, he chose to put the emphasis on the good in him. He sought to discover and develop that. Of weak, sinning man he said, "Greater works than these shall he do." He even went so far as to utter those astonishing words, "Be ye therefore perfect, even as your Father which is in heaven is perfect." What amazing faith!

254

²³ He also took the positive attitude toward trouble. We read of him that he "for the joy that was set before him endured the cross." Imagine finding joy in a cross! But he did! He saw the angel in the sun, the "soul of goodness in things evil." He handled his life's major tragedy so heroically and constructively that the cross, which was a symbol of defeat, disgrace, and death, has become the symbol of life's rarest and choicest values. God give us grace that, like Christ, we too may see the angel in the sun.

Vandalism or Faith?

They broke open the roof just over his head.
—Mark 2:4 (Goodspeed)

JOHN A. HUTTON, editor of *The British Weekly*, recently had this penetrating observation in a sprightly leader:

"What makes the Bible inspired, infallible, the word of God and the supreme standard of faith and practice is that it is all directed against us. When the Bible fails to take the feet from under us it has ceased to be for us the Word of God. When we are no longer aware of a steady eye looking at us, when we are content to make comfortable observations about its make-up, approving of this in it, but not approving quite so heartily of that, and protesting that we are frankly shocked at something else—by that time the Bible has become a mere story-book, a book of ghost-stories and fairy-tales."

² That, it appears to us, is essential common sense and piety. And in the story that provides us our meditation today, in a situation itself quite extraordinary and rich with many of those elements that enliven human nature, we have a fine illustration of Doctor Hutton's point.

³ There are elements in the story of the paralytic borne of four that have long supplied the materials for the construction of dogma. The prerogatives of forgiveness; the priority of the need of physical over spiritual healing, or vice versa, according to one's established prejudices—for both have a suggestion and support in the story; the adroitness of Jesus in turning the criticism of the cynical scribes and Pharisees back upon themselves; all these matters have engaged the attention of those who have found dogmatics of primary concern. And yet, by the wide margin by which dogma is apt to miss most of us, the story itself may—in the language just quoted—"fail to take the feet from under us." We "make comfortable observations about its make-up, approving of this in it, but not approving quite so heartily of that, protesting that we are frankly shocked at something else." We even fabricate doctrines out of it, and in that very act deflect the force or cushion the impact which in itself—did we but dare stand up to it—would threaten to take our feet from under us.

⁴ For here we have four desperate men upon whom a most uncommon cir-

From *Jesus and the Liberal Mind* (Philadelphia, 1934). By permission of The Judson Press.

cumstance turns. They do something which if generally practiced would violate every property right that ages of social experiment have established among us. In their desperation they destroyed a man's property under the assumption that the end justified the means. What endless debates have stormed about that phrase. Mankind might very glibly be divided into two categories on the basis of the two conventional responses to the idea. Those who agree that the end justifies the means and those who deny it, would be clearly and finally divided. "Stand thou on that side, for on this am I."

5 Jesuits, some would uncritically and invidiously call the assenters; Kantians would perhaps describe the others, due to the fairly general knowledge that Kant set at the center of his moral philosophy the unequivocal proposition that a man must never be regarded as a means to an end. Surely our attitude toward the academic question is reflected in our moral conduct. But it is quite possible that we have clouded some situations by demanding and getting a categorical answer where a realistic compromise might have yielded more secure results. It is no settlement of the moral issue in general to asseverate that the end *never* justifies the means or that it *always* does. Moral absolutism of that sort is hard to live with. It is no sagging of the support of our moral ideals that says, "Sometimes yes; sometimes no."

6 However, we did not set out to settle that matter. It might destroy somewhat the zest of the moral conflict that keeps us morally in condition if the argument could be finally adjourned. What we are interested to point out is that here in this familiar story the question jumps out at us, and by drawing us to an attitude about it, in that way, and to that extent, authenticates *this* story as "inspired, infallible, the word of God, and the supreme standard of faith and practice," to quote again. Was the act of these four men vandalism, or was it faith? It is likely that upon our answer to that question will rest the inspiration of this segment of the sacred scriptural arc. Surely, in this situation we are aware of a steady Eye looking at us.

7 Consider the incident. For the most part we have concentrated on the man Jesus cured. How utterly helpless he was. And, if inferences are allowed, what a wretch he must have been. For Jesus, though aware of his paralytic immobility and the completeness of his physical distress, seems to quite overlook it in diagnosing his spiritual condition. "Son, your sins are forgiven," is a cruel word to a stricken invalid unless the sinner secretly approved it, knowing his sinfulness. But whether sinner or not, the fact is that his cure was categorical—sin and paralysis disappeared before the therapeutics of this amazing Healer.

8 Or we have attended with delight to the discomfiture of the scribes; the rhetorical question about the relative ease of shriving and healing, and Jesus' quick act as they demur, fumbling for an answer. But most assuredly that point at which this story begins to gather the momentum that finally knocks us off our feet is beyond the limits of the record. It starts when the four men initiate the plan to bring their stricken friend within range of the extraordinary power that was visiting their village. There the determination takes rise that before long has taken four men on to the roof of a house and

suspended a fifth through a gaping hole, in the execution of a daring plan for securing the healer's attention.

⁹ There is an atmosphere of urgency about it that excites interest. The street was narrow, and most likely the main thoroughfare of the little town. The regular pedestrian traffic; hawkers with wares to sell and advertise noisily; donkeys burdened with heavy loads, unmercifully belabored as the bulging crowd at the door of the house retards their advance; the curious filling the street and the expectant hurrying toward the place where report has it a free clinic is in progress; dust, heat, noise, disease, rudeness, jostling, abuse, crowding—it is not difficult to picture the disorder of the scene. Meanwhile within a dark and low-ceiled dwelling stands a man who is the picture of industry and imperturbability, healing all who come within reach of his hands.

¹⁰ And then, up the narrow street come four men, struggling under a litter, carrying a man, prone and motionless. The crowd has dammed the stream of traffic, and about the door of the house there is a pressing jam of importunate folk. It looks bad for the silent paralytic who lies where the four friends have rested his bed as they mop perspiration from their faces and confer hurriedly as to a plan of procedure. Never mind what they say. It is enough that they act decisively and without delay. Their cause is an emergency, for only an emergency would warrant their trespass. Police or firemen might presume to invade and destroy property in the interests of peace or security, but such presumption in others should call for sharp rebuke. Perhaps they got it. As they worked around to the side of the crowd and by dint of much pushing and heaving arrived on top of the house, it is possible that someone called out an inquiry or shouted a warning. It did not, we judge, deter them. They rested on the roof long enough to catch their breath. Then they proceeded to demolish the roof—not a mere crack, but a hole half the size of the squat structure, big enough indeed for a bed supporting a recumbent invalid to be comfortably lowered into the darkness below. The consternation of the owner is unrecorded. Perhaps he saw the need and yielded graciously and thereby deserves to be anonymously canonized. Jesus, who was arrested in his care of those who thronged about him by the noise of tiles being pulled up and by the falling dust, as the labor began to yield results, looked up approvingly. Whatever the determined men may have appeared to be to the others who shared the incident—whether they were reckless, or rash, or vandals—to Jesus they were men of compelling faith. "And when he saw *their* faith he said to the sick man, Son, your sins are forgiven." Clearly, it was not vandalism but faith, to one who knew that rare thing when he saw it; and a faith that brought its peculiar blessing to a whole mob of astonished onlookers.

¹¹ That's the story, a real story. If it were left there it would deposit its permanent good in our spirits. For, as is the case with all good stories, everything turned out well; the man was healed, Jesus was pleased, the friends won the reward they sought (and immortality of remembrance), the scribes —villains of so many Gospel stories—were completely discredited, and every-

body lived happily ever afterward. As a story it is interesting; but as a story it would hardly take our feet from under us, or discomfit us like the roving focus of a searching eye. We must press on therefore to matters that make it authoritative for us in the area of personal religious faith.

12 And here is the way that aspect may be summarized: "There was a need for getting into immediate touch with Jesus. It was not enough simply to reach the neighborhood where he was. And that enlarges itself to one of the aspects of true liberalism. Liberalism on its intellectual side is the mood that is restive unless it can feel itself ever pressing inward toward the centers of power and reality. And though this genuine liberal mood is mistaken by many for vandalism, it is, on the contrary, the temper of all authentic and puissant faith.

13 An ism, more often than not, is the structure housing a dynamic idea. This is due to a tendency that undertakes to protect naked truth with a garment of words or a house of substantive materials. Stark, unadorned reality is likely to dazzle with its sheer brilliance or confuse with its reflections. The sun blinds one who looks at it, but the light that suffuses the landscape is beneficent and healing. Yet light is not sun. So it happens that the great hypotheses upon which life rests can be gazed on only by geniuses who seem endowed with eyes that are not beclouded or dazzled by a fixed, steady beam.

14 This may be illustrated by reference to what we may call the secondary hypotheses of life—those ideas that support life in certain forms or places, but which do not create life. Communism is such an idea. It assumes sharing as the heart of the social complex. But communism is housed in a structure, vast and terrifying, which few have yet the hardihood to enter. We shiver with fear as we come into its neighborhood. Nazi-ism is another idea about which much the same could be said. So also capitalism.

15 On the drill ground of pure ideas, theism, deism, atheism, absolutism, naturalism, and a whole regiment of similar words march by us, each with a measure of essential validity or plausibility, but so caparisoned in splendor or rags—according to our fixed views—that we see less of the soldier than of his uniform.

16 Now it is inescapable that reality should be treated thus. Most of us will have to be satisfied with its broad, general approximations. It will comfort us if we can always be found in the suburbs of truth. In ethics, in social theory, in philosophy, in religion, yes, in what is popularly called science, we will trust our fortunes to approximations. Yet contentment with such a state —whether individual or corporate—is often purchased at too dear a figure. For as the light is not the sun, neither are rules of behavior ethics; nor are social amenities the essential quality of society; nor is common sense philosophy; nor is creed religion. Reality is not skin deep. Some there must always be who will search the nethermost depths to lay hold on it, or soar to empyrean heights to see its burning clarity. . . .

17 But we must get back to our story. Here were four men whose necessity was such that nothing except breaking through to the Master's presence

259

could satisfy them. To be in the neighborhood, or in the street, or to see someone who had been suddenly restored and was hilariously announcing his cure—that would be interesting, but inadequate. At any cost they must press past the crowds and through barriers and lay their burden at his feet. I have heard it told of at least two different French skeptics, that when asked if they knew God, they replied, "We salute, but we do not speak." These four Palestinian villagers were determined on no such superficial contact.

[18] It therefore strikes us that there is something relevant in all this to our concern for religious vitality in the present age—that is to say, this experience takes the feet out from under us if we face it squarely. For call it what you will—conservatism, indolence, or fear—the fact is we find our Christian dynamic measurably weakened because we have drawn the transmission lines too far away from the center of power. Jesus is today, as in our story, still surrounded by crowds. Those who boast of such matters can present statistical tables showing exactly how many there are milling about, and how many were added last year. And what is perhaps more disquieting, they can point approvingly to those whose church rosters have swelled most with new names as the most potent witnesses among us of the manifold grace of God. We cannot be critical of this unless such so-called progress leaves these good folk forever just a part of the crowd, or stands in the way of those urgent spirits who, pressing forward to Christ's feet, find their advance checked by the very crowds that surround Him. We greatly fear that most of us are content to be in His neighborhood. Church membership may be the aim of enlistment programs, and, strangely, be the death of the Christian enterprise. Our nicely erected, fabricated and argument-proof barriers that protect Jesus from precipitate folk who would unceremoniously press through to Him have tended to destroy that greatest of Christian impulses, the incurable quest for the real and the true. And yet those in whom this priceless impulse is dead are standing contentedly in the neighborhood, satisfied with proximity. Coleridge saw this peril and put it in memorable language: "The man who begins by loving Christianity more than truth will soon love his particular sect more than Christianity, and finally come to love himself more than his sect."

[19] It immediately follows that such persons, though remote by ever so little from Him, are skeptical to that extent of the power of His spirit. What would the paralytic ever have known of healing or forgiveness if his friends had dropped him in the alley and departed? It is because we Christians of the good, conventional type are not at Jesus that the powers of the living Christ are not released into our flagging and distressed spirits.

[20] And yet, the efforts of the occasional intrepid and unconventional soul to destroy barriers are condemned as impious. What have we made of Jesus' word, "Blessed are they that hunger and thirst after righteousness?" We have made it read: "Blessed are they who rather like an ice-cream soda of righteousness between meals." So, when some avid soul, with an insatiable hunger for religious reality, voices skepticism of milling crowds, or begins demolishing the structures within which Jesus has been immured for centuries, the

cry of "Vandal!" is raised. There was a time when they were treated as criminals. Alas, many a man upon whom Jesus would have looked fondly and to whom he would have said, "Great is thy faith," has been the victim of cruel torture and bitter death at the hands of the Christian brotherhood. The record of the Christian movement discloses the paradoxical fact that the Church has been most relentless toward those who have taken the obligations of the Christian life most seriously.

21 There has been vandalism in religion; but it has been exceedingly rare. Philosophy does not raise the cry or march to resist a new idea that threatens to destroy some prevailing surmise of the soul. Scientists may pause and turn a startled ear toward a new effort to go more deeply into fact and theory, but they rarely cry "Vandal!" And so it is unlikely that there has been much considered effort to destroy Christianity by students of religion. Certainly what has for a long time been called "destructive criticism" has been inspired by the same sort of faith that urged the four friends up on to the roof. A man who out of a mean or perverse heart would seek to destroy religion would immediately create suspicion as to his sanity. Voltaire, Thomas Paine, Renan, Weiss and Schweitzer are not the names of destroyers, but of pioneers; and as they have dared the displeasure of crowds and torn up roofs that time had made sacred, they have done so in obedience to a faith within them that drove them on with an irresistible power. Religion, often afraid of such radiant spirits, has really less to fear from them than from many in the orderly crowd who seem to have slight inclination to move ever closer to the feet of Jesus.

22 What then can we say if the efforts of some advocates of religion seem to be tearing up the roof in order to get to Jesus? Shall we order them to withhold their impious hands, or specify what they shall find once they have the tiles removed and have exposed him to light from above?

23 It has been well put in the language of poetry:

> Friend, you are grieved that I should go
> Unhoused, unsheltered, gaunt and free,
> My cloak for armor—for my tent
>   The roadside tree;
> And I—I know not how you bear
> A roof betwixt you and the blue;
> Brother, the creed would stifle me
>   That shelters you.
> Yet that same light that floods at dawn
> Your cloistered room, your cryptic stair,
> Wakes me too—sleeping by the hedge—
>   To morning prayer.[1]

To some that may be the voice of a vandal; to others that of a vagabond; to us it is the word of faith.

24 You see how this story is a searching Eye. I for one am increasingly im-

[1] Karle Wilson Baker, "Creeds." Used by permission of the author.

pressed that the weakness of much current Christianity is that it lacks the courage and faith, and the sense of need for what Jesus can give this generation, to tear up the roof of the building in which the ages have imprisoned Him—if that be necessary. We fear that faith will be mistaken for vandalism. We may reassure ourselves, however, for Jesus knew faith when He saw it.

²⁵ There is a final word. Perhaps it needs reemphasis, the matter of faith's being the inspiration of this trespass. At least Jesus called it that. And that makes it crucial. Much of the theological tinkering, and most of the sophistication that parades as enlightenment, but which frequently turns out the light in order to denounce the dark, are far from faith. It is only when we discover that the marauders on our roofs are serious truth-questers that we welcome their mild iconoclasm; so that we can say what Holmes said of Emerson, "You remove our idols so gently that it seems to us an act of worship."

²⁶ Even this may be a prudence born of fear of religious stagnation. We have already indicated that in our story the roof-demolishing worked out to the advantage of all concerned. If we are deeply concerned over the future of our holy religion we must look about us. There is no little indication that in certain ranges of religious thought and practice we must choose today between keeping our roofs intact or curing our paralysis. That may be more bluntly put by saying that some matters for centuries regarded as inviolably orthodox must be modified if the hurt of the world is to be ministered to. Paralysis is all about us. What a fully restored Church could do, pushing through to the feet of Christ and feeling the surge of His power, is beyond imagination, but not beyond hope. We temporize because our roofs are sacred. And so we remain stricken. But when courage and faith can mount to levels which will undertake to do anything that will restore us to life again, then we shall be able to bring our invalids to Him, and He will tell them to get up, take their beds and be off!

²⁷ That's the story, and the way it has directed itself at us validates its inspiration. There is an imaginary epilogue, apocryphal and fallible, but not, perhaps, totally lacking in inspiration. Here it is:

²⁸ The next day after Jesus had healed the crowds in the low-ceiled house, a man came briskly down the street, looking for a door. His step was elastic and his whole appearance suggested the vigor and eagerness of youth. He paused before a door, and looked within. On a scaffold, precariously poised, a lone workman was plastering the ceiling. The floor and doorway were cluttered with debris. The young man greeted the plasterer:—

²⁹ "Good morning, neighbor; what are you doing?" There was a slight delay as the workman looked toward the doorway before answering pleasantly: "O ho; have you not heard about the excitement here yesterday? There was a young man, a healer from Galilee. The place was jammed with people who came to be cured, and He used this house for His ministry. Scribes were here, too, and they didn't seem to like some of the things He said. But the big excitement was when four fellows brought a poor palsied wretch, and being unable to crowd into the room, tore open this roof here,

and lowered the sick man right down in front of the healer. He seemed pleased by it, cured the paralytic, and commended his friends."

[30] "Yes," observed the young man with an inflection that indicated amusement.

"Who may you be, if I may ask," went on the workman, "and how happens it that you have not heard this strange story?" There was a pause before the answer came.

"I'm the palsied wretch," he said, smiling.

"Indeed! And how do you feel?"

"Why, I feel great. By the way, whose house is this? I thought I'd come round and offer to repair the damage my friends caused."

The workman laughed quietly, carefully descended from the scaffolding, straightened up stiffly, and proudly answered:

"I'm the owner, and you owe me nothing. As a matter of fact," he went on, stooping as he talked to pour more water into the mixture of mortar and straw, "I've been thinking for some time that my roof was in pretty bad shape and needed attention. I have a new one now, and we're all lots better off, it seems. But I'll confess I never thought it would come about in any such way as this."

The Victory of God in the
Disasters of Life

*And Joseph said, Fear not, for am I in the place of God?
But as for you, ye thought evil against me, but God meant
it unto good, to bring to pass, as it is this day, to save much
people alive.*   —Gen. 50:19-20

Fʀᴏᴍ his youth upwards we recognize in Joseph a man with a great soul.
He has all the marks of it. He never falls beneath his best. He is always
the same, whether you meet him in a prison or in a palace. His circumstances,
whatever they may be, become a background for his qualities, as the night
becomes a background for the stars. In a moment of blinding temptation he is
the soul of chivalry. In a prison, where he is kept for years, his greatness
makes its mark, and he comes to the front. In the national crisis in Egypt,
when they are faced with famine, he takes the situation in hand and saves
the country. The stiffest test of a really great soul is the hour of prosperity.
"It takes a steady hand to carry a full cup." Perhaps that is why God often
sends with the success something to humble us, to steady us, to keep us
alive to Him. In any case prosperity emphasizes the sterling quality of
Joseph. In this hour that our story describes, his greatness outshines itself.
It outshines itself, and reveals, behind him and through him, the face of God.

² It might have been a tempting moment for many another man. His
brothers were absolutely in his power. His father, for whom he had a
tremendous affection, was dead, and no longer there to protect them or appeal
for tenderness. They had come back from the funeral wondering how it was
going to be with them now. They came cringing to Joseph, whining for
kindly treatment. It takes a great man to forget the wrongs of youth when
the iron has entered into the soul, yet Joseph did it. It takes a greater man
to confess to those who have wronged him that the injury has turned out
to his advantage, yet Joseph did that. "As for you, ye thought evil against
me, but God meant it unto good, to save much people alive."

³ Two motives toward magnanimity are suggested here, two things that
helped Joseph to forgive, and it is well that in days like these we should
get hold of them. For magnanimity today, as then, may be the pivot on
which our future turns, and a day like this the background against which

From *The Victory of God* (New York, 1933). By permission of Harper & Bros.

God is giving us the chance to reveal our souls. One of these motives was that God was at work upon those who had injured him. "Am I in place of God, that I should take revenge?" It was as if he said, "This work of punishment is none of my business." It is a perilous position for any man to take that he is the instrument of the judgment of God. There are crimes far too big for us to assess. God is working out there beyond us, in the hearts of those who have wronged us as well in our own. His mills are grinding out resistlessly the judgments of righteousness. The justice of God is a net from which no evil-doer can escape. George Eliot in *Romola* gives us a terrible picture of a man tracked down by his sin. The father he had wronged becomes possessed by a passion of hate, whose haunting persistence turns the blood cold.

⁴ It is a terrible thing to fall in the hands of a hate like that. There is only one thing more terrible; that is to be the hater. Hate desolates both wronged and wrong-doer. But the justice of God is far more sure and unerring, for it is the justice of love, a love that will not let men go, but follows them through all the mazes of their flight, till it brings them face to face with sin, that it may bring them to redemption. This vision of God behind the scenes calms the heart, and takes away the heat of rancour and revenge. When a man is sure of God, and of the love that is justice, his soul is swept clean of all bitterness. Has not the time come for us to think of our late foes with Joseph's spirit? Reparation is right and just, but is not the craving to make Germany suffer another form of faithlessness towards God and the moral forces of life? When we remember Edith Cavell's heroism it is well to remember her magnanimity: "Standing before God and eternity, we must have no hatred or bitterness toward anyone." That is where Joseph stood—before God and eternity, seeing the mighty sweep of the moral forces which are the nature of things. Because he saw God working in and through things, he was able to forget the past and put it behind him: "Fear not; am I in the place of God?"

⁵ Another thing made it easy for him to rise above the pettiness of a puny revenge. He had seen how God had handled the wrongs he had suffered, to make them work together for good. He had been cruelly treated by his brothers, taken a helpless youth and sold into slavery, but that wrong did not stand alone in his mind. It had become the vital link in a chain of events which had made him Prime Minister of Egypt. He saw again through the mist of years his father's broken heart as he bowed his head to the inevitable and looked into a grave. But that picture did not stand alone. The mysterious fate that had snatched away Jacob's son swung back in his old age to rescue him from starvation, and bring him to the proudest day of his life. God was working ceaselessly, taking the savage wrongs and building them into the structure of a mighty purpose for Joseph and for the world. Can you wonder that his soul was lit with gratitude and worship which swept all bitterness clean out of his life? It did not abate in his mind one jot of his brothers' sin. They had done it and done it deliberately. They were no puppets in the hands of a master who made them dance to his tune. They were no mere

265

helpless tools in the giant grip of God. They thought out their sin and deliberately carried out their design. It was not God's will that they should wrong their brother for his good. They sinned against their brother and they sinned against God. But God took the wrong and used it for His purpose, adapting it to His great design. Against the background of their treachery there shone out a victorious love, riding upon the storm and triumphing through the catastrophe. "Ye meant evil unto me, but God meant it unto good, to bring to pass, as it is this day, to save much people alive."

⁶ Does not this experience of Joseph throw a wonderful light upon the darkness which shrouds many a life today? There is a problem which is ever with us, the problem of the evil of the world and the goodness of God. Sometimes it sleeps for a while but again and again it awakens and tears at the vitals of some sensitive soul. How can the evil of our life be reconciled with the goodness of God? Why has He permitted this wrong, this sickness, this accident, this savage crime, which has broken into our happiness? There is a whole host of problems here which are too deep for us. But there is light in this word of Joseph. The root of the trouble for many people is a wrong view of Providence. We think of Providence as a power of love which looks after us as a mother looks after her toddling child, and keeps it out of harm's way. We forget that we are not children any more, but men and women whom God is training to play a big part somewhere, and training to give Him back a love which shall be strong and independent and worthy of Him. That means a hard school and a long schooling. What a tremendous thing is this love of His—a thing so wonderful that it will use every kind of means to make us what we are able to be, even the graving tool of pain and the hammer blows of misfortune—a love which can adapt anything in the world to its great designs!

⁷ One thing too we must be clearer about; that is God's relation to the evil that happens to us. Many people have the fixed idea that God is directly behind all that comes to them. "God took him" they say when their child dies through accident or disease. They either resign themselves to the will of God, in a resignation that brings peace, or else they become bitter and pettish, thinking hard thoughts of God, as if He need not have done this if He had had a little more love or had been a little more attentive to their case. There is a half-truth when a mother says of her dead boy, "God took him." God took him, but only when death released him. This is not to say that God engineered the cause which killed him. Calamities come in many ways. Sometimes they come through sheer accident—a storm at sea, a passing sickness, and the like. But when we look into these things, what are they? They are just the other side of the privilege and the joy of living in such a world as this. If there were no spice of risk there would be no zest of adventure. It is a glorious world we live in, and the sickness, the risk, and the calamities which happen by land or sea, are the price we pay for the privilege of vital living.

⁸ And there is evil which comes through the sin and malice of others, or their callousness and neglect. Are we going to make God responsible for

266

these? If a nurse is careless of her patient, shall we blame God for his death? If a surgeon's hand is unsteady, shall we accuse God of callousness? If a nation forgets the duty of neighbourliness, grows big with power, and fills the air with poison gas, and wrecks the earth with high explosives, shall we call it an act of God? When Joseph's brethren sold him into slavery, was it God's doing or God's will? The injury others have the power to do us is the price we pay for those social relationships which make the world fragrant when they are sweet and loving, but poison it with bitterness when they break down. When these things are done you may be sure that they are done in defiance of God's will. They are not God's original way. They are not God's plan. They are done in spite of the pleading voices and the guiding light within, by which God seeks to win men to the higher way. When they are done they are part of the Cross which God carries in His heart, the Cross of love resisted, of righteousness defied, of truth dishonoured. They are the currents of human passion which run athwart God's gracious will, and threaten shipwreck to His creation. And God's load is big enough to carry without adding to it our reproach or our complaints. If only we could grasp that, would it not awaken a new desire to come to God's side, to help Him with what strength we have, against the foes that darken His universe?

⁹ There is another thing we need to grasp, that God is not helpless amid the wreckage of His plans. The world is no derelict ship. Our broken lives are not lost, though they have been driven from their course. God is working still; He comes in and takes the calamity that came, no matter how, and uses it victoriously, working out His wonderful plan of love. That is God's victory. He is always master of the situation. There are no second bests with God for the man who puts his broken life in His hands. There is infinite resourcefulness in the Almighty love. There is a divine ingenuity in the grace of God. "Ye thought evil against me, but God meant it unto good, to bring it to pass as it is this day."

¹⁰ History is full of examples of this very miracle of victorious Love. How many lives have been redeemed from failure into a splendid success! Here is a woman whose life has been crippled by sorrow, and she becomes the foundress of a hospital. Here is a man whose career is blasted by blindness, and he gives himself up to work for the blind as if he had been equipped for this very work. Sir Arthur Pearson has written a fascinating book which he calls *Victory over Blindness*. His work is indeed a victory, not only for thousands whom he has lifted from despair into a new life, but also for himself, and behind all, for God. Could any other man have done the work he has done? Could he have lived to such purpose if he had kept the divine gift of eyesight? Who can tell? No one will dare to say that the calamity was predestined, but things being as they were, God took the situation in hand. The result is nothing less than a victory of God, shaping a calamity into an equipment, opening out a cul-de-sac, a dead-end, into a field of glorious service, and setting the man into it wonderfully gifted with sympathy and appeal. Or here is Paul, taken by cruel hands, which would have crushed

267

him as they would have crushed a fly, and flung into a prison at Rome. He makes that prison a pulpit from which his words resound through Europe. It was not God who shut him in that prison. But it was God who used that prison.

11 And there is the supreme example, the Cross of Christ Himself. At a camp meeting where questions were invited on religious problems, a man immediately spoke up. It was the old question: "How is it the Bible tells us that Judas betrayed Christ, and condemned him for betraying Christ, and yet the Bible also says that Christ in dying fulfilled the plan of salvation? Was Judas a mere tool?—then why was he condemned? Or was he a deliberate treacherous sinner?—then how could his treachery be in the plan of God?" You see the difficulty. Joseph found out the answer long ago. It is the victory of love. That love of God took up the treachery of Judas and the cruelty of men defying love, and made them the means of a sacrifice by which love conquers the world. They meant it for evil against Him. It was not God's will that they should do it. It was God's agony. It was God's crucifixion; but God meant it, shaped it, redeemed it unto good to save much people alive.

12 There is a final point that we must notice. This victory of God does not always happen. It is not inevitable. Before you can understand it you must think of Joseph and see the kind of man he was. If he had got bitter, if he had said to himself when he was wronged that it was useless trying to do anything with his life which had been so shamefully marred, he would have ended his days as a slave. There are people who are the sport of trouble, who have gone under just because they have taken the bitter and pettish attitude to life, or have lost heart, or have given up trying to make anything out of it. There are plenty of rocks around for a ship whose captain has left the bridge because he has been driven out of his course. But Joseph stood up to his trouble, and kept his faith clear, and his life clean towards God. He kept himself in touch with the almighty love, linked himself up with the almighty will, and looked for chances of helping out the purpose he was sure God still had for him. That alertness, that faith, that willingness to co-öperate with God, and to make the best of every situation, because he knew that God could help him make the best of it, were the means by which God's love at last made him what he became. If God is to be victorious through our broken lives, we must help Him all we can. We must put ourselves into His hands. We must rise to the call of His purpose at every turn that offers. We must, in fact, take everything as if it came from Him, and see in everything the workings of His love.

13 Everything does become the working of love when we put life into the hands of God. Everything that comes to us becomes mighty for love's own designs in the hands of God. That outlook changes everything. It changes the effect of trouble upon ourselves, and makes it beautiful. Someone said to a man whose body had been crippled by a disease of childhood, "Affliction does so colour the life." "Yes," he replied, "but I propose to choose the colour." That is the point. It is ours to choose the colour; or rather, it is

ours to choose the Artist, and He chooses the colour. Wonderful beyond description is the beauty which the genius of Christ brings forth in us by the tools of calamity and sorrow, when we put life into His hands.

14 Do I speak to any who are weighed down by some load of grief, or handicapped by some trial, who see nothing before them but the slow numbing which the years will bring, or the final release of death from a world which is all upset? Your one hope is in linking up your life with this almighty will of love revealed in Christ. The key to this victory is loyalty—loyalty to the victorious and redeeming will of love. As Clutton Brock puts it, "Salvation is seeing that the universe is good, and becoming a part of that goodness." As Paul puts it, "All things work together for good to them that love God." In other words, those who accept the purpose of God in Christ and give themselves to it in loyal faith and service find there the secret of a continual victory—a victory in which life with all it holds of joy or woe becomes subdued to the mighty mastery of love. "This is the victory that overcometh the world."

Protestantism: Its Liabilities and Assets

> *Ye are a chosen generation, a royal priesthood, an holy*
> *nation, [not your own but God's]; that ye should shew*
> *forth the praises of him who hath called you out of dark-*
> *ness into his marvellous light.*   —I Pet. 2:9

So DID Peter write in the first epistle that bears his name, the second chapter at the ninth verse, to the scattered Christians of Asia Minor. It was their time of troubles, and he wanted them to know that neither they nor their troubles were accidental. They stood within the charmed circle at the very center of God's providence, a chosen people, holy, not their own, called out of the darkness of a pagan world into the light of a new era, a coming age that somehow had already arrived.

² I am wondering if very much the same thing could not be said about the Protestant church: except that perhaps we have grown more or less accustomed to the light and so have forgotten that the darkness can come again! Many a "royal priesthood," caught up once for God's possession, has found that out. And it worries me. I have no mind at all to keep alive prejudices which have already outlived their usefulness. None of us have. Yet I hardly see how it's possible for any of us in days like these not to be freshly and profoundly concerned about that within the framework of the Christian religion which seems to be our original and peculiar charge, without which the years to come would be indescribably poorer, and which, if ever it should be lost, would have to be beaten out again in the fire and on the anvil of still another Huss or Luther or Calvin or Knox. We should be fools and blind to forfeit it, or by carelessness and indifference simply to let it slip. Yet that precisely is our peril. What we have in our hands to administer is something more than relevant: it's decisive. Of that I'm convinced. What we have done with it may well be on the point of plunging us into a heresy as great as any from which we broke away, and a bondage even worse.

³ I. The subject then is "Protestantism: Its Liabilities and Assets." I would not have you think that these are simply the two opposite faces of a single coin: they are the opposing hosts on the battlefield of the twentieth century! Not parallel columns, red and black, marching down a page; they are the

---

By arrangement with the author.

clash of tragedy and triumph which is itself the history of our Western civilization!

⁴ When the apostles began preaching the gospel of Jesus Christ back there in the days of the New Testament, they had to do really just what we have to do: they had to address an order of life that prided itself on its culture, and justly so; but it was on its last legs for all that. It had come to the end of its resources, as we have. Man had made up his mind again that history was about *him*. I saw an account of some sermon not long ago which defined history as what man thinks of himself, what he thinks of his fellows, and what he thinks of God. The outline emphasized a good deal of skill but much less insight. There is another Thinker in the universe! And He matters more! So it was that two thousands years ago the picture was falling to pieces. That always happens when we get in front! Such religion as was left in the world could no longer hold things together. Philosophy couldn't. Government couldn't. Force couldn't. Another chapter was done, and God, with a deep sigh, turned over a new leaf!

⁵ Suddenly out of the ruins—it took two or three centuries; but never mind: that's sudden, as time goes!—out of the ruins, from under the very heels of an invading barbarism, something altogether different appeared. The ancient culture of the Hebrews had fused with the culture of Greece and of Rome at the white-hot point of the Christian gospel: and the history of the West had begun! Here was the creative impulse which gave to our unlettered European ancestors that meaningful outlook on human experience which for a thousand years *became* their history—that dynamic sense of spiritual unity which more than anything else characterized the Middle Ages. It was the richest legacy to which mankind has ever fallen heir.

⁶ And four centuries ago it split wide open (at the last)! The mystery is that in spite of everything it has kept us going this long, even after it was torn apart. We still owe it all the best of what we are, though it shows signs now of being spent, unmistakable signs—the Greco-Roman side of it, in the high tradition of the Renaissance, man-centered and world-bent, marching off down the years at a tempo that keeps on accelerating, while it worries its head less and less about God; the Hebrew-Christian side of it, in the Reformation, sin-shaped and God-haunted, hoping against hope that way to save its heady other half from going haywire and committing suicide, swinging its weight over toward a Word that was to stand up again stark and free, and the soul of a man, bound now only by the terrible compulsion of that truth, and Christ gazing at it long and steadily trying to love it out of all its poor ways into His! This is actually the cleavage in our own minds, between the secular and the religious, natural and supernatural, as if God's universe were two. We are ourselves the Reformation and the Renaissance.

⁷ But a good many of the bridges have gone under the water since then, and queer things have happened. Little by little the generations that would not be bound by the pope decided in an ecstasy of freedom not to be bound by anything! From believing too much they took to believing too little.

271

Maybe nothing was true, except that the mind was a sort of twitching in matter and all of us lived together in mindless space, circling aimlessly on a fifth-rate planet around a third-rate sun, with fewer and fewer morals, but always with more and more of something "just as good"—everybody quite objective about it, whittled down to something a little less than human by everything he had found out, yet thinking very well of himself indeed! I don't know just how he figured it, but he figured! Almost any book on sociology you pick up wants to begin with him as a base; while it insists on winding up with him, after two hundred pages, at the center of the sun, with man in Utopia! History was by no means a religious drama. It was nothing but the pull and thrust of automatic and self-adjusting forces. Man himself would undertake to manipulate them insofar as possible and build his own world. It would be real, and it would be decent! You'd see! Let religion be for those that needed it. He would rather be practical. I like now to rub in that word! We have been—practical! We are standing on the edge of an abyss.

[8] "A chosen generation." Sure enough? "A royal priesthood. What do you mean? "An holy nation." Is that right? "Not your own but God's." Who says so?

[9] I understand that the blame for all this is not solely ours, but just let me point out one significant fact. There is no manner of doubt about it. Protestantism has proved to be far and away the most active religious leaven in the development of the West. For one reason or another over the last four centuries the power of our expanding civilization ceased to flow through the Roman church. If then the upshot of it is a culture which seems to have grown progressively more and more important and self-destructive, where both the Christian community and the state have tended steadily to slip away from the functioning center of human life toward the circumference, where right and wrong no longer have the roots in eternity and man is already well along the road to moral anarchy, where the gospel in a thousand pulpits across the land is reduced to the level of good Christian manners, with Christ referred to as "the gentleman on the cross"—I say if that is the upshot of an era during which, within the whole pattern of the Christian faith, Protestantism has provided the major dynamic, isn't it obvious that we this day, preeminently *we*, must stand before the bar of God and of human history to give an account of our stewardship? Whatever it is that has happened, and whatever part we have played in it, it has made the world sick, totally so for the vomit. God pity us if like dogs we go back to it! All that is needed for a first-class funeral is that we should go on as we've been going!

[10] II. There is one side of the ledger, the debit side. Now for the other. What about the assets? Let me submit to you that we have them, and that they are not without their relevance. We have something to say that in all soberness nobody else is going to say for us. We would do well to start saying it and saying it together. Not pugnaciously against those who differ from us. There are times when all that we seem competent to ask is: How best can we find something about somebody? What should we watch? Whom should

we fear? And this in spite of the fact that once more, as in the sixteenth century, the common enemy, more deadly both to ourselves and to Rome than either to the other, is a world that keeps flatly refusing to know anything beyond or above itself. Under such circumstances controversy is not likely to prove either useful or impressive. We made that mistake in the years which followed immediately on the Reformation, and both of us lost! Do we have to make it again? The only way to say what we have to say and get it to stick is to use it. We shall not find any other. We have to recover something, instead of commemorating it.

11 For one thing, the immediacy of that encounter, as Dr. Brunner calls it, in which a man, fully to be a man, finds himself before the face of the living God, with nothing between. No political makeshift, no hierarchy of saints, not any collectivism "that has no face," whether inside of the church or outside of it. No doctrine that with us becomes an end in itself, no way of looking at life, or trying to disentangle its knots. We are confronting God!

12 How relevant that is to our present dilemma you may judge for yourselves. What seems to be clearer today than ever is that *we* are irrelevant without it! Entangle it with blood and soil, obscure it, let it be nudged over to one side in favor of the state, and humanity inch by inch loses its stature. In that relationship and in no other stands the final sanction of your very being. It is the first lie of our modern world that values somehow or other begin down here—whether they reach up there or not is supposed to be more or less beside the point. "I think," said Descartes, "therefore I am." Rather is it that God thinks, therefore you are. The values begin up there! That is what the Middle Ages had lost. The reformers got hold of it again. The Roman church is not clear about it yet. Neither, I am afraid, are we. There is no end of glib talk about the dignity of the human soul. How many of us understand where that dignity roots? It roots in God. Tear many of us away from our roots, as Nazism tried to do, as Communism wants to do still, and see what happens to our dignity! It is the immediacy of this encounter that Protestantism at its best has always underscored. Without it the agelong quest for meaning which is human history and human civilization becomes itself meaningless!

13 But there is more. The core of that relationship is nothing that *we* do. The core of it is something that *God* does—about *what we do*. That too is part of our Protestant inheritance. And nobody will ever say it for us.

14 You might think that what we are would be an open secret by this time. There is plenty of evidence around. There is a good deal of evidence at home. I have wrestled with it, and you have. It is no stranger to anybody, that war in your members. It was no stranger to Paul. "The good that I would, I do not: but the evil which I would not, that I do." If there is no answer to this, there is no answer to anything! The problem is not how it happened. The priest of Apollo and his two sons in the Laocoön group being choked and bitten to death by serpents aren't leafing through the pages of a best book on zoology to discover the origin of snakes.

The problem is what can be done about it. Luther, in those years before the Reformation, scourged himself and fasted and made his pilgrimage to Rome, and nothing was of any use. He wanted what we all want in the loneliest places of our life; he wanted peace. And nobody could remember where it was!

15 That is near enough the focus of our human tragedy to keep it from being blurred! And Protestantism, whenever it speaks its lines, says that *nothing* can be done about it—unless an act of faith starts up, not between me and a book, nor between me and a church, but between me and the God who in Jesus Christ has already done something about it! What chance is there of having anybody else see this for us when we quit? In a world that on Monday, Tuesday, and Wednesday goes romantic and insists there are no snakes, while on Thursday, Friday, and Saturday it is altogether intent on working out its own salvation, a bundle at a time? Running off on Sunday perhaps with these demonic drives in human nature, either to a priest in the morning or more likely to a psychiatrist in the afternoon, or get the reins straightened out and back again!

16 What renewal comes will not come by way of some belief that the Almighty has borne what only the Almighty can bear. You don't piece together anything very creative out of that with a few charitable if somewhat bewildered impulses thrown in. It will come of sheer trust and gallantry like a flame in the human soul, touched off by Christ's compassion —until a man is somehow himself again, clean and eager, back in the turbulent thick of the world, to have his try there with God under the shadow of a cross at the shaping of human history.

17 And still another thing. Consider now if you will that in no context except in this does Christian conduct become ultimately meaningful. The ground of what a man ought to do as a Christian is not the natural law, written on the tables of the heart, nor even the divine law, that "naked obligation" laid on us by the holy will of God. The ground of the Christian conduct is the Christian gospel. Not the imperative of the Word thundered at us from Sinai, but the constraint of a Life that died on Calvary. We may talk all we like about freedom of conscience and the right of private judgment. Nobody else will. But they amount to little or nothing of them-selves. They belong against the background of God's saving deed in Jesus of Nazareth, that work of rescue which *is* the Christian gospel. Anywhere else they either cannot hold their own and become impotent, or they run wild and turn into brigands or freebooters.

18 The Reformation was no revolt against *that* authority. It was a revolt against the kind of authority that wanted to handcuff a man: tell him what he could think and what he could do, set him at tasks by which he could earn the forgiveness of his sins, order his life from the cradle to the grave, and lock him even in his grave with the keys of the hereafter. Rome had done a far more thorough job of regimentation than even Hitler did in Nazi Germany, and with the same motive. It sprang out of the deep distrust of human nature and human conduct, which is actually quite Christian in

274

its character, but which for the church of the Middle Ages as for the Führer had turned into an ultimate pessimism from which there was no way out but to put the Gestapo in charge!

¹⁹ May I add that there is no other way out to this day? unless we can somehow thrust this life of ours back where it belongs, under the only authority that can possibly maintain itself: the authority of a God who came down from Mount Sinai and climbed to Golgotha! Your conscience and mine are altogether *too* free, our judgments far and away *too* private, until they get there—before the face of One whose idea of morality is not compliance but courage to set your course bleak against the wind as His was set—until it isn't His teaching anymore that you need first, nor His example; you need *Him*, working in you both to will and to do! It is not that you want to save your own skin now. You don't care to rest and have peace. The world is like that, and you are this much like Him: you have to get into it.

²⁰ Here, then, is our commitment. These are the things that of all things always need most to be said. And nobody is going to say them for us when we quit. *Thou*, and *I*, that we may be one in *Christ*. Paul calls it "the glorious liberty of the children of God."

²¹ But we don't have it in order to squander it, divide it among ourselves, parcel it out here a little, there a little. The time for that is passed, if ever there was a time for it. Milton Mayer some time ago in the columns of *The Progressive* listed a dozen different people and organizations, representing almost every possible shade of political and economic opinion, all of them out now unanimously for world government—from the CIO to the National Association of Manufacturers—with only this caustic and devastating comment at the bottom: "The atom bomb has blown some very strange fellows to bed."

²² Well, bed is not exactly what I am talking about. I am talking about the strange fellows. There are a good many of us in Protestantism; and we had better find out soon that we have been blown together! We shall move now pretty much side by side toward the dawn of a global fellowship or toward the doom of a global battlefield. Never mind uniformity. Who cares about or wants that? Wherever these denominations of ours preserve an effective witness to some particular aspect of the Christian gospel, let them. But for God's sake and humanity's, to say nothing of our own, why not bear it at long last each as his eager contribution to the wealth of the total tradition to the sum of Christ's varied kingdom? Tolerance does not involve laxity. The wiping out of convictions marks no advance toward anything but chaos. What we have to understand is that there is a unity which already binds us. It is the work of God's Spirit. You cannot deny it. You can only betray it. I believe there is enough of it for us to begin living some of it! A torn church has no mandate for a torn world.

²³ And with that I am through. What we mean to do about all this is decisive beyond any thought we have had. You cannot deplete human existence morally and spiritually as the last four centuries have depleted it, to the

point not of high tragedy but of dismal triviality and farce, and then expect to transform it with a United Nations. You cannot transform it with anything less than a faith that has a Cross in the middle, and the kind of people gathered round that God Himself will underwrite!

[24] "Ye are a chosen generation, a royal priesthood, an holy nation, [not your own but God's]: that ye should show forth the praises of him who hath called you out of darkness into his marvellous light."

The Way of Faith

Lord, I believe; help thou mine unbelief.—Mark 9:24

THERE are people in the world for whom faith is a lifelong conflict. They are so constituted that it is difficult for them to believe. Many times religion seems to them so utterly unreal and unreasonable. There is no rational basis for faith and they cannot grasp its worth. They do not boast of their unbelief; they rather regret it; they wish it might be otherwise. They are perfectly willing to admit that one hundred million people can't be wrong, but say what you will, they cannot believe and they are determined to be honest. What has religion to say to those for whom faith is a lifelong conflict and who find it difficult to believe?

² One day Jesus of Nazareth met up with a man like that. With three intimate friends He had lived through the all-glorious vision on the Mount of Transfiguration. When the vision had passed, Jesus came down the mountain to go back to the work of the world. As He came to the foot of the Galilean hill there met Him a motley crowd of people shouting and heckling. When some semblance of order and quiet had been restored, a man stepped out of the crowd to ask Jesus to heal his paralytic boy. There followed the usual questions: What is his name? What is the ailment? How long has he been ill? When the answers had been given, Jesus said, "If thou canst believe, all things are possible," to which the man replied: "Lord, I believe; help Thou mine unbelief." Then in the very next sentence it is recorded that Jesus healed the son of the man who did not believe.

³ It is strange that Jesus should select a man who did not believe for this miracle of healing. One would suppose, if He had been disposed to heal, He might have selected one who believed implicitly. At any rate, if this man were known as an unbeliever, Jesus might have done it rather quietly and avoided the publicity of the occasion. If it does not matter to Him whether we believe or no, why should it matter to us? If it is no issue with Him whether we accept or reject Him, then why should we struggle so hard for our convictions? And yet, as you read the narrative you become impressed with the fact that Jesus held this man in high esteem and loved him. Why was that so?

⁴ I. He was honest. Indeed, he was honest to his own hurt. This unnamed

From *The Way of Faith* (New York, 1935). By permission of Harper & Brothers.

father is one of the most honest men who walk through the New Testament. There was but one deep desire in his heart. Days unending he prayed that his boy might be made whole again. The one unfulfilled wish of his spirit was to see his child in normal health and strength. And now he faced at last one who could heal him. Can't you imagine his neighbors and friends pulling him to one side with the admonition, "Say nothing about your unbelief. This is your chance for the boy." Or perhaps they advise, "Promise anything. Don't stand on your own opinions too much, for, after all, they may be only idiosyncrasies. Don't stand too much on your own convictions. Tell this man what He wants to hear, so only your son is made well again."

⁵ But he was honest. He was no "yes man." He was willing to believe some things, but he drew a line about his faith beyond which he would not go. He did not propose to live by any false pretense. Some things he was willing to accept about Christ, but other things he was compelled to reject. He was glad to make affirmation, but he was also compelled to express denials. Though it involved the well-being of his boy, he did not want what he was not entitled to. And Jesus never lost patience with such a man. He never turned a deaf ear to any honest doubt. When Thomas, a little later, could not accept the evidences of the Resurrection, Jesus did not lose patience with him. He came back a week later with further incontestable proofs, which convinced Thomas. In this age of the "yes man," of ready-to-wear clothing, of predigested breakfast foods and philosophies, it is good to look into the face of a man who was honest to his hurt. I wonder what we would have done in his place. Let us pray God that we may never be called to face such a dilemma. One does not have to leave his inquiring mind in the vestibule to worship God. Christianity is not a questionable religion, but Christianity is a religion that lets you ask questions. Always it comes to those who doubt, saying: "Come, let us reason together."

⁶ II. But Jesus was drawn to this man for reasons deeper than his honesty. That does not tell the whole truth. The romance of the story does not turn on what the man did not believe, but on what he did believe. He saw very quickly that the things he could accept were of infinitely greater consequence and importance than the things he could not accept. Faith in things he could see was of more importance than doubt concerning the things he could not accept. He rejected more than he accepted, but however tiny or frail that faith was, he lived by it. The man soon discovered that having unbelief and living by unbelief are two different things. He did not cultivate his doubt; he did not try to pamper and pet his unbelief. He expressed regret for it. He was ashamed of it and asked forgiveness for all his doubt. He did not hire a hall and charge one dollar admission to tell people that he could not believe. He did not tramp across a college campus with his head swathed in a halo of degrees staggering the minds of his students by the brilliancy of his negations. He lived in the area of belief, rather than in the area of unbelief.

. .⁷ What a challenge this unnamed father is to our day and age! All too often those who have doubt are satisfied to live in it. We are so apt to emphasize what is not there rather than what is there; to proclaim what we

278

reject rather than what we abide by. There is so often an ugly and regrettable temper about human nature which causes it to see what does not exist rather than what does exist. We not only have our doubts, but we live in them. Take it in the realm of literature. One day you read a book and when you have come to the end you close it and walk away from it. When asked to express an opinion about it you only see the faulty development of one of the characters, the want of style in certain chapters, and a shortcoming in the portrayal of one of the minor figures. You will not let that book speak to you. You emphasize what is not there rather than what is there. One day you go to an art gallery to see a new picture. As you walk away from it you only think of the want of contrast in colors, the lack of balance or a faulty delineation in some minor detail. You will not let the picture speak to you. You only see what is not there rather than what is there. One day you go to a symphony and as you leave the concert-hall you think only of the one string that was out of tune or the one measure that was faultily played. You have not permitted the symphony to surge through your soul with the up-welling of new hope and joy. You hear plans projected for a new world. Mankind has come to a bend in the road and has resolved upon a new way of life in the years that lie ahead. But you only see the imperfections of the plan or the want of poise in an occasional leader, and you will have nothing to do with it. You emphasize what does not exist rather than what does exist.

⁸ What is true in those everyday relationships of life is especially true in religion. There are in us all areas of unbelief. Most people, when it comes to faith, draw the line somewhere, and beyond it they will not go. That experience is inevitable to us all. Not only is it inevitable, but it is also the inherent right of the sons of men. Independence of personal judgment is a heritage of which we may well be proud. It is the very essence of Protestant Christianity. It may be that there is place for regimentation in the economic order, but man will never goose step in the pilgrimage of the spirit. But what is so regrettable about this unbelief is not that we should hold it, but that we should cultivate it. We are always in danger of fondling and petting the things that we deny. It is all too common to live by negations rather than by positive convictions. We make it the basis of life, sail ships by it, and hold it as the philosophy of the universe. One must stand dismayed before those contemporaneous thinkers who not only express their unbelief, but cultivate it.

⁹ Now I confess that I have never been greatly disturbed by those who boast about their unbelief. I remember in a recent crossing of the Atlantic walking at noon into the smoking-room where the log had been posted to find what had been the run for the day. As I was walking to the bulletin board I passed four men sitting at a table, playing poker—at least that is what they said it was. One of them was in the midst of a furious tirade against religion in general, Christianity in particular, and foreign missions specifically. I heard what he said, but it did not greatly disturb me because I could not believe that a man under those circumstances at such a moment was an adequate authority on religious matters. A buzzing horsefly on the

padded back of an elephant may disturb, but cannot hurt the animal. I have lived long enough to know that some dear old spinster knows more about raising children than a mother of five; that a man who has never been able to save a nickel knows better how to invest money than a banker; that one who is not even able to control his own temper knows better than government how to rule people. I would rather commit my soul to the keeping of the humble pilgrims of the road who through dawn and dusk, summer and winter, in tears and in joys, in defeat and in victory, meet life cheerfully and hopefully because their daily litany is "Lord, Thou hast been our dwelling place throughout all generations," than to put myself in the keeping of some quasi-intellectual fly-by-night theorist whose only purpose in life is to smear religion and laugh at the faiths of men. I, for one, would rather drink fresh spring water out of a rusted dipper than vinegar out of a gold chalice.

¹⁰ What is so tragic about these men is not that they have doubt, but that they live in their doubt. They are more susceptible to error than to truth. They always see first what is not there rather than what is there. It reveals a tragic flaw in character and a moral defeat in their being. Francis Bacon pointedly remarked, "Behind spiritual uncertainty is moral decay." The Pharisees of old were such men. With a sneer upon their faces and with their lips curling in scorn, they call out cynically: "Can any good thing come out of Nazareth?" In that very scornful question they write themselves down as men who love a false note more than a true note, who are more moved by flaws than by perfection, who are more attracted by shortcomings than accomplishments. They thought they condemned Christ, when in reality they condemned themselves.

¹¹ The Christian attitude calls man to live by what he can accept rather than by what he cannot accept. Concern yourself with what you can believe rather than with what you cannot believe. All faith is a growth. Your brittle belief may be only the cloud the size of a man's hand, but one day it may overcast the whole sky; it may be only a seed, but one day it may come to a glorious harvest; it may be only a star, but it may lead you to the Christ of Bethlehem. Nothing so blinds life as to complain about the things that do not exist rather than to live cheerfully in the things that do exist. Supposing we would count our blessings and for one brief hour think of the friends who are still true, the health that we still enjoy, the homes that are still unbroken, the books that are still worth reading, and say of them: "Thanks be to God." I tell you that for most people the whole of life would be altered and their outlook upon the universe transformed.

¹² Take it in the matter of health. Many there are who carry about frail bodies. Much of the day is spent in struggling against physical weakness, until actually they come to enjoy poor health. They emphasize what they have not, rather than the measure of health they still enjoy. In so doing they only increase their own misery and that of others. Live with the health that you still have. Take it in the matter of adversity. For multitudes the savings of a lifetime have been swept away. All that they have worked for in the

years gone by has suddenly turned to ashes. But the pity of it is that they are forever rehearsing their adversity and reminding the world of what they no longer have. They seemingly forget that many things are still left to us: the sun still rises at its appointed time; the tides of the sea still run in ebb and flow; there is still brilliance in the stars, blue in the sky and color in the rose. Live by what you have, rather than by what you do not have.

13 So it is in the realm of religion. Take it in our attitude to the Bible. All too often we close the Book because we cannot accept this statement or that story or some other episode. Tales of the Old Testament are laughed into oblivion and the prophecy of the New Testament is ridiculed. But the question arises, "What do you believe about the Bible?" You reply, "It is the most glorious portrayal of the human soul. It holds the noblest love story in literature, and portrays the character of the truest man who ever lived." Very well! Live by what you can accept of it rather than by what you cannot accept of it and one day the horizons will lift and this Book will again become the lamp unto your feet, the light unto your path. Lincoln was right when he said, "Accept all you can of the Bible by reason, and the rest by faith, and you will live and die a better man!"

14 Take it in one's attitude to God. A young student walked into a New England university in utter denial of that conception of God by which multitudes have lived. The only thing he could accept about God was the sense of right. Everything else he rejected. But he was honest and lived by what he could accept rather than by what he could not accept. He gave his life to following this sense of right, and years afterward Horace Bushnell walked through New England as a torch-bearer lighting the road that leads to God and became one of the great Christian prophets of our American civilization.

15 So it is also with our conception of Christ. There are those who cannot see eye to eye with what Christ is to untold multitudes throughout the world. They can only think of Him as a noble teacher, a wholesome humanitarian, and a rare, good man. Everything else about Him they deny. To all such there comes the voice of Christian faith, "Live by what you can accept rather than by what you cannot accept, and as sure as there is a God in heaven the committal of life to Him in these terms of your own experience will crowd back the foothills, blaze trails through fogs and misunderstandings, until at last a new horizon breaks and you cry out with Thomas, 'My Lord and my God.'"

16 There is hope for a person who lives by faith, however brittle or broken, but there is no hope for the one who lives by his unbelief. There is hope for the man who holds the door ajar, but there is no hope for the man who shuts the door. There is hope for the one who says "maybe," but there is no hope for the one who says "never." There is hope for those who say "perhaps," but there is no hope for those who call out "We know it can never be." The temper which forces men to live by what they cannot accept has no chance for improvement. It is not a sign of wisdom, but of folly, to live in

unbelief. The man who thinks fish do not swim in rivers will never find out by nursing his pet prejudice sitting before a coal stove in carpet slippers.

[17] There is a tragedy in a sentence of the New Testament about Jesus of Nazareth: "He could do no mighty work there because of their unbelief." Christ was utterly helpless in the face of those who nursed a denial of faith. God can do nothing for the man who lives in his unbelief. Treasure your faith, however frail; guard the flame of faith, however feeble; cling hopefully to the things you can accept in the universe; take this broken and battered trust of yours and build on it. "Lord, I believe; help Thou mine unbelief."

Through Jesus Christ Our Lord

A GOOD many years ago a Hebrew lad was learning to read his sacred Scriptures. He struggled through the sentences, picking out one by one the words in the ancient characters. By and by he would come to a word of four letters, and, boy-like, he would begin to spell. "No," his father would say, "do not say that. That word is not said. Say *Adonai*," which means "the Lord." For centuries the Jew has never said that name of four letters, but always "the Lord."

² This Jewish lad grew up. He studied to be a rabbi. In the midst of his student days there appeared in Jerusalem a revolutionary sect. They were the followers of one Jesus of Nazareth, who had been crucified as a blasphemer but who, according to his disciples' claims, had risen from the dead. This sect so angered the rabbinical student, whose name was Saul, that he tried to stamp it out. But his persecutions failed to fire the followers of Jesus into hatred or to dampen their faith. Saul saw one of them, a man named Stephen, as he was being stoned to death; and he saw Stephen lift up his eyes and say with a beautiful smile, "I see the heavens opened, and the Son of man standing on the right hand of God."

³ Saul's mind was haunted by the strange power of this Jesus. What secret did he possess which enabled him to give his followers peace and joy in the midst of pain and death? Saul could not escape the hounding pursuit of this thought. At last it caught up with him on the Damascus road, and Saul surrendered himself to the will of Christ, thereby being transformed from a hater to a follower of Jesus.

⁴ Then it became Paul's turn to be hounded and persecuted. His family turned from him in sorrow. His life became one long series of sufferings and trials. And yet out of all these harrowing experiences a conviction was being formed in his mind that at last One had appeared worthy to bear the name of the Lord, the word which stood for those four letters too sacred for him to pronounce as a Jew. Thus Paul's letters came to be filled with references to the Lord Jesus Christ.

⁵ Nineteen centuries have passed since Paul's day. Men have pondered this tangled skein of experience called life. The world in which we live wears an enigmatic face—a face as ugly as sin and as beautiful as an angel, as cruel as a sea in storm and as tender as a woman in love. It is a world of snakes and stars,

From *Now to Live* (New York and Nashville, 1946). By permission of Abingdon-Cokesbury Press.

of laughter and tears, a world of contradictions and confusion. Some have said this world's life is "a tale told by an idiot." But better judgment has contended that this medley of events has behind it a Creator with a purpose and a program.

⁶ And out of this confusing sequence of history, centuries of seasoned thought have selected one flaming section as the key of the whole book of life. It is the brief biography of Jesus, that strange man on the cross, who from his blood-stained throne has so ruled the hearts of men that they, like Paul, say, "the Lord Jesus Christ." In his character we see the highest we know or can imagine, and therefore we too believe that in beholding him we see the Father also. In his life of love we see the most heavenly revelation of life's possibilities. Therefore we conclude that God must be like him. And so we begin our Apostles' Creed with the statement, "I believe in God the Father Almighty, Maker of heaven and earth; and in Jesus Christ his only Son, our Lord." And the prayers which we repeat in our rituals we conclude with the words, "through Jesus Christ our Lord."

⁷ What does it do for our prayers to conclude them with the words, "through Jesus Christ our Lord"?

⁸ I. First of all, when we pray "through Jesus Christ our Lord," the words give us an invitation to pray.

⁹ Does it ever seem to you that prayer is a rather presumptuous thing on our part? Here is God with a whole world on his hand, a world of some two billion souls. Moreover, he has millions of other heavenly planets in his universe. Why should I presume to bother him with my little personal problems? When we think of the Creator with his innumerable concerns, we feel perhaps as did the little boy who said, "God is like my father; he is too busy to listen." Is it not presumptuous for us to take our affairs to God in prayer?

¹⁰ Furthermore, is not prayer a sign of weakness on my part? Here am I, an adult person. Ought I not to handle my own affairs and not childishly carry them to God for his help? A minister some years ago said that the only person in the community who can talk about God without causing something of a sensation is the preacher. If, for instance, at a directors' meeting in a business office the president of the board should say, "Let us ask God's guidance," the suspicion would spread that the business must be heading for the rocks. Yes, for us to stop and pray in the midst of a business meeting or a social gathering would create a mild sensation—an awkward pause, to say the least. Some of us blush to be caught at prayers. To many it seems presumptuous, or weak, or pious.

¹¹ But not when we pray "through Jesus Christ our Lord." Christ invites us to pray. He makes it as natural as a child's turning to a father. He teaches us to pray, saying, "Our Father." When we close our eyes in prayer, of what or of whom do we think? Dale Carnegie has said that one reason why we do not better remember the names of the persons we meet is that when we meet them we are thinking of ourselves rather than of them. Perhaps that is one trouble with our praying. When we meet God in prayer we are

thinking of ourselves. But Christ taught us when we pray to say "Our Father," and to think of God and not of ourselves.

¹² And when we do think of God, how do we behold him? I confess frankly that God becomes vivid and personal to me only as I think of him in the image and spirit of Christ. When I see God "through Jesus Christ our Lord," I see a God who cares—cares as did the father of the prodigal who longed for his boy's return. I see not only a God who cares but one who also knows me. A college student once said to her professor of religion, "What I really want to know is this: Does God know my name?" Well, our gospel says that the very hairs of our head are all numbered. The God who notes the sparrow's fall takes notice of us, for we are of more value than many sparrows. When I pray, I am not pleading my case before an implacable judge in a cold court of justice; I am talking to a Heavenly Father who knows and understands.

¹³ Moreover, he is a Father who believes in me, even when my faith is too thin to believe in him. In A. J. Cronin's book *The Keys of the Kingdom*, which was a best seller some years ago, there is a conversation between a young Scottish physician and a Roman Catholic priest. The young doctor was an agnostic. He could never be quite convinced by theological arguments that God exists. But he went out to China to help cure the plague which was raging. In his efforts to heal he contracted the disease and lay dying. As he gasps his last breaths he says to the priest, "I still can't believe in God." The priest tenderly replies, "Does that matter now? He believes in you."

¹⁴ Yes, when we pray "through Jesus Christ our Lord," we see a God who cares and knows and understands and believes in us. Thus Christ makes prayer inviting.

¹⁵ II. Secondly, when we pray through Jesus Christ our Lord, we have a test for our praying.

¹⁶ We read that in the wilderness Jesus fasted and prayed. In Gethsemane, Jesus sweat great drops of blood. Prayer, as Jesus taught it, means surrendering our wills to God's will, and that means more than relaxing the muscles and stretching out the body. It means saying, "Not my will but thine be done," and that's a pretty hard struggle sometimes.

¹⁷ So much of the current talk about prayer leaves Christ out of the process. Prayer is treated as a power after the analogy of the radio. Here God's power pervades the universe as the ether waves penetrate the air. Just tune in. Just desire hard enough, and you can get anything you want. Well now, suppose we could. Suppose that each of us could by wishing strongly enough, and invoking God hard enough, receive anything we wanted. What a confusion we would have! It makes me think of what a man said to me in Washington after our entrance into World War II. The man said whimsically, "We hope Washington will not be bombed because it would disturb the confusion!" Yes, what a confusion we should have if we could all lobby the Heavenly Throne with our personal interests!

¹⁸ But when we pray "through Jesus Christ our Lord," we cannot ask for just anything our hearts desire. Christ said, "Whatsoever ye shall ask in my

name, that will I do." Not everything can be asked for in Christ's name, can it? I can pray for help in my business problem "through Jesus Christ our Lord" provided my business is designed to further the good of men and the program of Christ on earth. I can pray for health "through Jesus Christ our Lord" provided I desire that strength not merely to prolong my own self-indulgence, but to serve my fellow men. I could pray for victory in war "through Jesus Christ our Lord" provided I believe that the victory will further the reign of righteousness and good will on the earth. I could pray "through Jesus Christ our Lord" for the safety of my boy or girl provided I am not selfishly thinking of my own family's welfare and forgetting the welfare of other parents' sons and daughters. When we pray "through Jesus Christ our Lord," it sifts the selfish motives from our petitions.

¹⁹ More than that, it lifts the sights of our prayers. When we pray in the name of Christ, our horizons are enlarged toward the unattainable. His perfection makes us aim at the impossible. He said: "Be ye therefore perfect even as your Father which is in heaven is perfect." Of course, we cannot be perfect in this life, but we can pray and strive toward perfection. He taught us to pray, "Thy kingdom come. Thy will be done in earth, as it is in heaven." Of course, God's Kingdom will not come fully here on this earth. But if we stop striving for it, what happens? The paradox of life is this, that unless we strive for the impossible, we never realize the possible. Recall King David. He desired to conquer the enemies of his people, to establish his capital at Jerusalem, to unite his nation, and to build a worthy temple to his God. David never built the temple, but because he strove for that which was beyond him he was enabled to achieve that which was within his reach. Great lives are never self-contained.

²⁰ When we pray "through Jesus Christ our Lord," our reach exceeds our grasp, but that is what heaven is for. And that is what will make earth more and more like heaven. We need Christ to sift our prayers and lift their sights toward perfection.

²¹ III. Thirdly, when we pray "through Jesus Christ our Lord," we get power in our praying. For one thing, we get the strength which comes through confidence in the rightness of Christ. If you have ever had the experience of being lost in a strange region, you know how much difference it makes to feel that your guide knows the way. If you have confidence in your guide, a strength comes into your limbs to keep you going. But if you doubt your guide's knowledge, then you lose heart and weariness overtakes you. However bewildered we are by the confusion of our world, we at least know that Christ is right. He is our Lord, the Son of God. Other leaders may falter and change, but Jesus Christ is "the same yesterday, today, and for ever." Men may think him wrong. They do so in every generation. A generation ago Nietzsche, the German philosopher, said that to follow Christ would make slaves of any nation. So he persuaded the German people to repudiate the principles of the Christ. And what happened? Germany turned to militarism and was beaten, while Nietzsche himself died in a madhouse. Every generation has those who call Christ a foolish dreamer, but eventually

men wake up to find that it was they who were dreaming while Christ saw the truth. One generation turns from Christ, but the force of circumstances pulls their children back to him as the one hope.

22 Moreover, Christ gives us power not only through his own rightness but also by imparting to us a faith that we too can reach toward his rightness. Dr. Harold Walker, of Oklahoma City, says that his own father once gave him a glimpse into the meaning of Christ's redemptive love. In his boyhood he had taken piano lessons. His teacher was giving a program with her pupils as the participants. He himself was to play a few chords and swing into a little piece entitled "Moonlight on the Waters." He sat down to the piano. In his fright he struck the chords in rather miserable fashion. He looked over at his father, whose face was glum, and at his mother, who was on the verge of tears. His performance was pretty bad, and he finished with a feeling of mortification. On the way home his father said to him, "Son, I know you can play those chords in 'Moonlight on the Waters,' and as long as we know it, what do we care about anybody else?"

23 What that father said to his son is somewhat like what Christ interprets God as saying to us. God knows what we can do, and he makes us feel that if he knows it and we know it, why worry about what others think or say?

24 When we pray "through Jesus Christ our Lord," we feel ourselves in the presence of a heavenly Father who believes in us, who banks on us, who so loved us "that he gave his only begotten Son, that whosoever believeth in him should not perish, but have everlasting life." In that feeling we can do all things through Him who strengthens us. A modern novel makes a devoted wife say to her faithless husband: "We will face this thing together, you and I, until we win over it." That is what Jesus Christ our Lord says to us.

The Lord God Omnipotent Reigneth

Alleluia: for the Lord God omnipotent reigneth.
—Rev. 19:6

WHAT is the biggest fact in life to you at this moment? What is the real centre of your universe? "The biggest fact in life?" replies one man. "Well, I reckon it is my home. That, for me, is the centre of everything." A very noble thing to be able to say! "The main fact in life to me," says a second, "is, without any shadow of doubt, my work. If you take that away from me, you take just everything." "The central thing for me," declares a third, "is health and happiness. As long as I have that, I am quite content. I can't bear to be unhappy." But what is your own answer?

² I know what Jesus' answer was. Was it home? No—though none has ever hallowed home-life as Jesus hallowed it. Work, then? No—though none has toiled so terribly as the Son of God. Health and happiness? No—though none has been responsible for nearly so much clean happiness and mental and physical health as Jesus. The central fact in life to Jesus was none of these things. It was this—"the Lord God omnipotent reigneth!"

³ Is that your answer? More blessed than home, unspeakably blessed as home may be; more crucial than work, be that work never so urgent; more vital than health and happiness, though sometimes, especially when you lose them, happiness and health seem to be the only things that matter—greater and higher and deeper and more paramount than them all—the fact of God! The power behind every thought of your brain and every beat of your heart and every breath of your body—God! The element in which you live and move and have your being—God! The final, irreducible, and inescapable denominator of your universe—God! That was the conviction on which Christ staked His life and marched to Calvary; that is the conviction which has inspired the breed of the saints; and that is the conviction which can turn very ordinary people like ourselves into men and women of whom Christ and the saints will not need to be ashamed; this conviction, strong as steel, firm as a rock, and stirring as a battle-cry: "The Lord God omnipotent reigneth!"

⁴ Now that cardinal conviction will be found, when you explore and examine it, to lead to three results. It involves three tremendous consequences,

From *The Gates of New Life* (New York, 1940). By permission of Charles Scribner's Sons.

and as these concern us all most intimately, I would ask you to think of them now.

⁵ I. It means, first, *the liberation of life*. It means a sense of absolute release. Release from what?

⁶ Release from petty worries, to begin with. Every one knows how sometimes things which are comparatively unimportant can obsess the mind and blot out all the sunshine. Here, let us say, is a man to whom some slight or some injustice has been administered, and he cannot get it out of his mind; he has not the grace to perform a surgical operation on that rankling thing, to cut it out and eradicate it; but he keeps on brooding and brooding about it, and with his mind continually coming back to it, and going round it in wearisome circles—until the last vestige of peace of soul has been destroyed, his whole outlook on life warped, and all his sky obliterated by the mists and murky fogs of what is, from any spiritual standpoint, a wretched, insignificant triviality. Run and tell him, "The Lord God omnipotent reigneth!" Tell him to bring his worry into the light of that great truth, and just see how the fretting thing will fade and die. This, mark you, is not fancy nor hyperbole; it is proved experience, and the grace of the Lord Jesus Christ is in it.

⁷ The fact of the matter is, as Robert Browning said succinctly, " 'Tis looking downward that makes one dizzy." The man who has his gaze riveted on the narrow little circle of his own experience, obsessed (like the poor creature in Bunyan's dream) with the sticks and straws and dust of the floor, never thinking of the stars and the crown, cannot see life in true perspective. Oh, if only he would look away from all that—one long look into the face of the Lord God Almighty, if only he would take even five minutes in the morning to stabilize his soul by remembering Christ, how that would reinforce and liberate him! Yes, it is release—this great conviction—from the worries of life.

⁸ Notice, further, that it means release from the fears of life, and especially from the fear of tasks that seem too great for us. Life is forever trying to make us lose our nerve and turn away from new responsibilities, saying like Jeremiah, "I can't do this! You must let me off: I am not the man for it. Please, God, get some one else!" Do you know what it means, when you have some particularly difficult duty confronting you, to lie awake through the night, revolving your anxious fears? You have that dreadful three-o'clock-in-the-morning feeling, "I'll never get through this! I'll never be able for it." But if religion cannot help us there, there is something wrong.

⁹ I remember Dr. John Mott telling some of us of a conversation which he had had with Dr. Cheng, the great Christian leader in China. "Would it not be a great thing," said Dr. Cheng, "for all of us Christians in China to unite, and go out and double the number of Protestant Church Christians within the next five years?" Dr. Mott asked, "How many are there now?" "Four hundred and thirty-five thousand," was the answer. "Well," said Dr. Mott, "it has taken over a hundred years to build in China a Christian Church of these dimensions, and do you now suggest the practicability of doubling

that number in five years?" And Mott said that never would he forget the answer. "Why not?" exclaimed that gallant Chinese leader. "Why not?" And indeed, when a man has seen God—*why not?* "Impossible?" cried Richard Cobden when they had been criticizing as wild and fanciful and quite unfeasible his agitation for the repeal of the Corn Laws, "Impossible? If that is all that is the matter, I move we go ahead!" And again—why not, if "the Lord God omnipotent reigneth"? It is release from the fears of life.

¹⁰ Moreover, it is release from self-contempt. One fact which modern psychology has been driving home to our minds is this, that there are multitudes of people to-day who are losing half the happiness which God intended them to have, and are being made quite unnecessarily miserable by inward repressions and conflicts and self-contemnings with which they do not know how to deal. And all the time there lies in religion (I am thinking, mark you, not of religion of the unbalanced, over-emotional, unduly introspective type, for that may easily do more harm than good, but of the sane, healthy, objective religion of Jesus of Nazareth) the power to end the conflict and to set the prisoned soul free. What is the key with which Christ's religion unlocks the prison door? What but this, "The Lord God omnipotent reigneth"? "There," declares Jesus, "is the Father of whom you—even you—are a son. Son of man, stand upon your feet! Son of the omnipotent God, lift up your head and be free!"

¹¹ Release from worry, release from fear, release from self-contempt—all that is bound up with this great central conviction of the faith. It means the liberation of life.

¹² II. But that is not all. Notice now, in the second place, that it means *the doom of sin.* It proclaims the ultimate defeat of evil in every shape and form.

¹³ Take this book of Revelation. You know the historic background of the book. It is the background of blood and smoke and martyrdom and reckless cynical laughter. Here you have the Rome of the Cæsars and the Church of the Galilean locked in the death-grapple. Here you have the mailed fist of Nero and Domitian smashing its way through the hopes and dreams of the saints. Here you have, in the words of an old psalmist, "the kings of the earth taking counsel together against the Lord, and against His Anointed, saying, 'Let us break their bands asunder, and cast away their cords from us!'" Here you have the second Babylon, mother of all the abominations of the earth, drunk with the blood of the friends of Jesus, laughing in the intoxication of her triumph, shrieking with laughter to see the poor, pathetic Body of Christ being crushed and mangled and battered out of existence. That is the background when this man takes up his pen to write. And you and I look over his shoulder, wondering what his message is going to be. What can it be, we think, but an elegy and a lament? "The battle is lost! Our cause is ruined. There is nothing left but to sue for mercy." Is that what we see him writing? No! But this—flinging defiance at all the facts, and with the ring of iron in it and the shout of the saints behind it—"Hallelujah! Babylon

is fallen, is fallen!" And why? What made the man write like that? It was because at the back of the visible world, at the back of Caesar and all his pomp and pride, he had seen something which Caesar never saw, something which spelt the doom of Caesar and of all sin like Caesar's for ever: a throne upreared above the earth, and on the throne the Lord God omnipotent reigning!

14 We sometimes talk pessimistically about the future of Christianity. We find ourselves wondering what will be the ultimate issue in the warfare between good and evil. Is it not possible that force and injustice may prevail, and that the Jesus whom we love may go down at last before powers that are too strong for Him? But to any one who has seen what this writer of Revelation saw, that is no longer an open question. Evil is done for—already. "Well," some one may say incredulously, "it certainly does not look like it. Look at the international scene. Look at our current literature. Look at the chaos in morals. See how evil flaunts itself in the open, how it strikes its roots deeper and still deeper." Yes, I know. But I know also this, that if God is on the throne of the universe, then evil is doomed, never has been anything else but doomed, doomed from the foundation of the world!

15 Now no one was ever so sure of this as Jesus. There was a day when the seventy followers whom He had sent out into the surrounding villages to preach and to heal returned to Him, with their faces eager and glowing and triumphant. "Master," they cried excitedly, "Master, it works—this new power that has been given to us—it really works! We have proved it. The darkest, foulest, most stubborn spirits are subject to us through Thy name!" Whereupon, says the evangelist, Jesus, hearing that glad news, and realizing its deeper significance, which even they could not quite fathom, had a sudden vision. "I beheld Satan," He exclaimed, "as lightning fall from heaven!" as though to say—"This message which you have brought settles and confirms and ratifies My hope. The power of darkness is broken, snapped, done for; and henceforth the initiative is with God!"

16 Or take the amazing scene which meets you at the end. Have you not gazed in wonder at the sight of Christ before His judges? How calm and self-possessed He was, far more self-possessed than Caiaphas, or Pilate, or Herod, or any of the other actors on that tragic stage! What was the secret of it? Was it just His innate heroism asserting itself? Was it just Christ's way of steeling His heart to be brave? Was it only a reckless contempt of death? No. It was the open vision that behind Caiaphas, and behind Pilate, and behind Herod, there was Someone else; and that it was not they nor any earthly governor who reigned in Jerusalem that night, but that Other, that watching, brooding figure among the shadows—God! And Caiaphas, Pilate, Herod—who or what were they? Less than the dust beneath time's chariot-wheels. The Lord God omnipotent reigneth!

17 Such was the source of Jesus' heroism. And such, in the face of all the evils of the world, has been the source of the blessed optimism of the saints in every age. God is on the throne; therefore evil is doomed. "Here on this

Rock," said Jesus once, "I will build my Church, and the gates of hell shall not prevail against it." Here on the Rock! That sudden cry of Christ, echoing down into the world of darkness, must have shaken that world to its foundations—like the thunderous chant of a great marching host, fair as the moon, clear as the sun, terrible as an army with banners. Francis Xavier, four hundred years ago, said a magnificent thing about the Christian mission to the Far East. "You may be very sure of one thing," he declared, "the devil will be tremendously sorry to see the Company of the Name of Jesus enter China." And then he went on—"Just imagine! A thing so vile as I am to bring down such a vast reputation as the devil's! What great glory to God!" Do you ask what is the mainspring of Christian hope and courage? It is the certainty that we are not fighting a losing battle; that evil, flaunt itself as it may, carries the seal of its own doom upon it; and that the real pull of the universe is on the side of the man who goes out for righteousness.

[18] Fight on, then, you who have lost heart because your own conflict is so difficult, your tempter so strong and dogged and subtle. Fight on! It is your battle, not his. For the Lord God omnipotent reigneth.

[19] III. We have seen, then, two decisive consequences bound up with our text: the liberation of life, and the doom of sin. I ask you, finally, to observe that we have here *the comfort of sorrow.*

[20] The man who wrote the twenty-ninth psalm, which we were reading today, had a marvelous sense of the dramatic. Do you remember how he sums up the great old story of the Flood in Genesis? He is looking back across the ages, and in imagination he can see the horror of the encroaching waters, rolling their waves higher and still higher, creeping up with slow, inexorable destruction and death, beating down all fragile human defences built against them—until men and women, staring at those mounting waters, felt terror clutching at their throats, for the end of the world seemed nigh. All that, the psalmist sees; but he sees something else as well. "The Lord," he cries, "sat as King at the Flood." Then, like a great shout—"Yea, the Lord sitteth King for ever!"

[21] And what of the floods of life? What shall we say of the days which every soul must know when, as Jesus put it, "the rain descends, and the floods come, and the winds blow and beat upon the house," until your whole structure of things, all your philosophy of life, is threatening to come toppling down? What about the happiness you build for yourself—the plans you lay, the dreams you dream, the hopes you cherish, and the heart's desires you yearn for—and then, thundering and rolling mountain-high come the waves and the breakers, crashing down on that shore of dreams, leaving only some poor bits of wreckage behind? What then? What then, blessed be God, the Lord sits as King at the flood, the Lord sitteth King for ever! Which simply means that the heartbreaking things of life have meaning and purpose and grace in them, for the Lord God omnipotent reigneth.

[22] There was a terrible night out on the Galilean Lake when the sudden whirlwind blew, and the sea was lashed to fury, and the boat struggled in

292

the troughs of the waves, and the disciples were telling themselves—"Our last hour has come: this is the end!" And there was Jesus, sleeping through it all. "Master, Master, carest Thou not that we perish?" But that night they learned by the grace of God this lesson—there is something higher in human experience than life's waves and storms: there is a Christ who rules the waves! Have we discovered that? It is a great thing, when the floods begin and the desolation of sorrow comes beating down, to hear the divine *sursum corda*—up with your heart!—for the Lord sits King at the flood, your flood, and the Lord God omnipotent reigneth!

23 Did not Chesterton, in one of his most vivid poems, preach the same victory of the soul?

> Though giant rains put out the sun,
>   Here stand I for a sign.
> Though Earth be filled with waters dark,
>   My cup is filled with wine.
> Tell to the trembling priests that here
>   Under the deluge rod,
> One nameless, tattered, broken man
>   Stood up and drank to God.[1]

24 There was once a flood called Calvary. And all the bitterness and ugliness, all the shame and sorrow of life, entered into that flood, and came beating around the brave soul of Jesus, sweeping Him down at last to the barbarity and infamy of the death of the cross. "What can God have been doing?" we want to ask. "Was He asleep? Or on a journey? Or was He dead?" No! The Lord was sitting as King at the flood, that surging flood of Calvary; and out of that grim cross He has brought the salvation of the world. Tell me—if God did that with the cross of Jesus, do you think that your cross can be too difficult for Him to deal with, and to transfigure? He can make it shine with glory.

25 Do you believe it? My friend, here is surely the final victory of faith—to be able to say, "The Lord God omnipotent reigneth," to cry it aloud, not only when life is kind and tender and smiling, and the time of the singing of birds is come and the flowers appear on the earth, but even more when the night is dark, and you are far from home, and the proud waters are going over your soul; to cry it then, not weakly nor diffidently nor uncertainly, but vehemently and passionately and with the ring of faith in every syllable in it—"The Lord God omnipotent reigneth. Hallelujah!"

26 This is the Lord God who has come again to the gate of your life and mine to-day. This is the Lord God who claims the right to reign, and from whose patient, haunting pursuit we can never in this world get free. Behold, He stands at the door, and knocks. While the sands of time are running out, and the hurrying days mould our destiny, He stands at the door and

[1] From "The Deluge" in *Collected Poems of G. K. Chesterton*. Used by permission of Dodd, Mead & Co.

knocks. Tenderer than the kiss of a little child, mightier than the flashing lightnings of Heaven, He stands at the door and knocks. What will your answer be? "You, out there at the door, you who have been haunting and troubling me all these years—begone, and leave me in peace!" Is that it? Or is it not rather this? "Blessed and glorious Lord Almighty, dear loving Christ of God—come! Come now. My life is yours. See, here is the throne. Oh, Christ, take your power—and reign!"

Why People Do Go to Church

WE HEAR a great deal of complaint in these days that people don't go to church, and in the preceding sermon I discussed some reasons for this. Let us look now at the reasons for which people *do* go to church.

2 Half a century ago it might have been true to say that many people went to church because it was the conventional thing to do. The men put on terrible frock coats and top hats, and the ladies were appropriately garbed— I will not attempt a fuller description of their dress—and they would have been shocked at the very thought of not attending church at least once on a Sunday. That is certainly not true now. I don't suppose there are many persons today who attend church from a purely conventional motive. There may be one or two reluctant husbands dragged by their wives, but that kind of compulsion doesn't account for much churchgoing these days. The truth is that those who now attend, though fewer in number, are of more sincere motive. They are truly seeking something or Someone, even if the goal of their quest is a little uncertain even to themselves. Let us ask ourselves why we attend, for if we are clear about what we are seeking, we are much more likely to find it.

3 Here, then, are four reasons why people go to church:

1. The first—and by far the most important—is that you go to worship God. You do not, I trust, go to hear a preacher, or hear lovely music, save as both do what they are meant to do, help you to worship God. And what does worshiping God mean? It means all that prayer means—adoration, thanksgiving, confession, petition, intercession, meditation, dedication—and we cannot, of course, discuss them all now. But I do feel very sorry for a person who has excluded God from his life, who neither in joy nor in sorrow has any sense of "otherness" about his life, who as he wakes up after a night's refreshing sleep and finds himself healthy in body and mind has no one to thank. I pity even more a person who in the depths of sorrow has no one to offer him comfort, and still more the person who, crushed beneath a burden of sin and self-loathing, has no one to whom he can turn, no philosophy of life except a bleak humanism, no resources of strength save his own. One of my friends was driven to a belief in God by the sheer intolerableness of supposing that man was alone in the universe with no outside help whatever and with no hopes at all save those which arise from man's self-born striving.

From *The Significance of Silence* (New York & Nashville, 1946). By permission of Abingdon-Cokesbury Press.

⁴ I came across two sentences in my reading lately which express that forlorn attitude. Here is the first: "Man is a low form of cellular life on his way to the manure heap." Here is the second: "Man is fighting a lone fight against a vast indifference."

⁵ I believe that you go to church, in spite of all the alluring voices calling you elsewhere, because you believe in Someone, strong, loving, serene, and holy, who is the personification of all those qualities which you believe matter most to man. They are of priceless *worth*, and I need not remind you that the word "worship," the word "worth," and the word "worthy" all come from the same root. As you look up from your humanity to God, your spirit is already climbing up to realize that in him there are, and that in you there may be increasingly, those qualities in life which are of greatest *worth*.

⁶ It is not my intention to go into that vexed question as to whether God is so self-sufficient that he does not *need* our worship at all. I think, if I were pressed, I should say that, of his own ordaining, he has decreed that his entire perfection lacks something if it is denied human response. But I cannot, at any rate, escape the belief that God is *pleased* with our worship. Suppose that you had enough money and time to make a very lovely garden. You would set it about with trees and lawns, flower beds and shady pools, and you would welcome into it little children. It would be true to say that every flower in the garden was already yours. But if some little child whom you loved plucked a flower and brought it to you and said, "I picked this for you," would you not be pleased? You would not say, "They are all mine, anyhow." Of course they are all yours, but if you loved the child, it would give you joy to think that he picked something that was beautiful and gave it to you. You would be delighted that his little mind linked up together the beauty of something and the desirability and suitability of giving it to you. God has made a lively spiritual garden in which are thoughts and feelings and acts, as well as the translation of his thoughts into the things we see and hear and touch. All are his already. But if you go into this garden of thinking and feeling and willing and offer him your little blossom of worship, saying, "I have brought this to you," he will not say, "I need it not." The offering will bring him joy, and, if the figure of speech may be pressed, he will wear your flower in his bosom. Said Tennyson, "Our wills are ours to make them thine." So are our thoughts and feelings and every power of our personality.

⁷ But apart from that, apart from what worship may mean to God, I am quite sure that it can mean something very important to us; and it is because of that that we do go to church. Our minds lay hold on those qualities which we believe he not only possesses but *is*, and as our minds lay hold on the thought of what he is, to some tiny extent we become like that ourselves. "As he thinketh in his heart, so is he." I suppose the psychology of it runs somewhat thus: Whenever you express an emotion, you strengthen the emotion. When, therefore, you express the emotion of admiration for those things which God is—and worship is partly such an expression—admiration for the qualities concerned is increased, and it is a commonplace to say that we tend to become what we admire. In a more profound sense than perhaps the words

have sometimes meant to us, man is made in the image of God. The man who looks up to God in worship is constantly being *remade* in the image of God. The sneer has often been uttered that man makes God in his own image, and I admit the danger and comparative truth in that sneer; but in worship, as our hearts go up to him in adoration, God remakes us in his own image. To some tiny extent we become like the God we worship. Even, therefore, if a man goes to church in a bad mood, the music, the hush, the beauty of the building, the grandeur of the hymns, the majesty of God's word, and the message of the preacher may so remind him of the things of God in whose image he is made that, as it were, he will put out the hands of his spirit and draw down into himself something which his best self has always admired, and he will strengthen, not only the emotion of admiration, but the will to possess the admired quality. That, then, is our first point. People go to church to worship God.

8 2. People also go to church to find forgiveness. Don't be shocked if I say that nine times out of ten that doesn't make sense at all. They don't find pardon, because they don't seek it. They have such a faint sense of sin. How many people ever notice the petition in the monotoned Lord's Prayer, "Forgive us our trespasses"? It is no good pretending. We just let the petition slide over us. Unless we have a real sense of sin, felt either as a personal burden or a share in the corporate guilt for the evils in the world, we find no reality in the offer of forgiveness. And the truth is that, more and more, the modern man tends to give sin a more attractive title. It is not *sin;* it is his inhibitions or complexes or perversions. It is his heredity or environment or the treatment of his nurse in infant days. It is moral disease, for which, it is said, he is no more to be blamed than for measles. It is due to evolution, the legacy of the jungle for which he cannot be held responsible. A friend wrote me recently of a girl for whose illegitimate baby he wanted me to find parents. The father was unknown. The girl wanted to be rid of the baby. But, in the writer's view, the girl hadn't sinned. She had, in his phrase, "slipped up." She had been "unlucky." It was a mere peccadillo, a youthful adventure that turned out badly. There was no thought of a little life pushed out into the world with neither father nor mother, of a holy thing made cheap and shameful—no case needing forgiveness. There was no sense of sin.

9 If there is not even a sense of guilt in regard to the gross sins, when will men wake up to a sense of sin in regard to the evils Jesus condemned, such as unkindness, spiritual pride, the unforgiving spirit, gossip, failure to do our duty to those who pay us to do it, the neglect of the suffering of others, and causing the weak to stumble? Forgiveness is unreal because, in the main, the sense of sin is weak, and, even where it exists, God is thought of as a sentimental indulgent father who will pat us on the back and say, "There, there, I'm sure you didn't mean it."

10 But sometimes there steals into the place of worship some burdened spirit, some depressed heart, some crushed soul, writhing sometimes in a torment of agony and self-loathing; and then what has been a truth of the intellect becomes what Shelley called "a truth of the emotions." A truth to

which the reason assented becomes a truth that burns in the heart like a living flame. We might use the illustration of the automobile and say that the energy expressing itself in the revolving flywheel suddenly becomes geared in so that the car moves forward. Something that has always been true becomes a power to drive and to satisfy. When that happens, we are caught up into that unity with God which is one of the most amazing experiences we can know. I am not talking now to anyone who has no sense of sin at all, who is not burdened in that way—though I would in parenthesis suggest that truly to look upon the spotless purity of God would, if we let it do so, produce a deep and healthy sense of sin. I am talking to the one who feels unworthy, overburdened, sick of himself; and I am offering in the name of Christ that miracle, much more amazing to me than many of the miracles in the Gospels, by which we can be rid of the burden. It really can fall off our shoulders. We can reach that unity of God which the birds, who have never known sin, express; which the flowers, that worship in unblemished splendor, reveal; which the stars, shining in a majesty unassailed by evil, manifest—a unity deeper than they can ever know, the unity of the sons of God. We can be caught up joyously, gladly, volitionally, into that perfect harmony with God. There is no greater experience in the world than that. You may have "known" all your life that God forgives sins, and then in a time of worship "know" it in a completely different sense. I am aware that you may find this pardon outside the church, but every part of the worship of the church is there to remind you of God and of the endless offer of his forgiveness.

11 I remember this happening to me during the last war. I wasn't a chaplain then, but a staff officer riding from one Arab sheik to another on government business. I had not been able to attend a service for weeks. One Easter Sunday night I remember going into a crowded Y.M.C.A. tent to a service. I cannot remember a word of the sermon or who preached it, but we sang that great hymn "Christ the Lord is risen today," and suddenly his presence became a fact. His forgiving love became real. I think I felt something of what John Wesley felt when, having *known* the fact of forgiveness for years, having preached about forgiveness, having gone as a missionary to Georgia and offered forgiveness to others, he afterward sat in a little room in Aldersgate Street and *experienced* forgiveness for himself. "I *knew*," he wrote, "that Christ had forgiven my sins, even mine, and saved me from the law of sin and death."

12 The rapture of this experience no one knows until he has had it. It was of this that Masefield was writing when he made Saul Kane say:

> O glory of the lighted mind,
> How dead I'd been, how dumb, how blind.
> The station brook, to my new eyes,
> Was babbling out of Paradise;
> The waters rushing from the rain
> Were singing, "Christ has risen again."
> I thought all earthly creatures knelt
> From rapture of the joy I felt.

The narrow station wall's brick ledge,
The wild hop withering in the hedge,
The lights in huntsman's upper story,
Were parts of an eternal glory,
Were God's eternal garden flowers.
I stood in bliss at this for hours.[1]

[13] Our second point, then, is that people go to church to restore a broken relationship, to find forgiveness of God, and that they should go out, whatever they may have done in the past, looking up into the face of God and saying to him, "There is nothing between us now."

[14] 3. Men go to church to find fellowship. One of the things that used to please me most about the City Temple in the days when great crowds thronged it was the fact that people would write again and again—not only our own members and regular worshipers, but visitors—to say something like this: "As soon as I crossed the threshold I felt that I was among friends." If we church members pray more and love more, if we gossip less and find fault less, eager, not to see where others are wrong, but to see and draw out their best, if we go to church determined not only to get good for ourselves but to make it easier for others to find God and to find love and friendship, then even strangers and wayfarers will find something worth coming to seek. I am quite sure that the synagogue at Capernaum was quite different when Jesus was present. I do not mean when he was preaching or reading the Scriptures, but when he was worshiping there. If we go to church in the right spirit to pour out our hearts in prayer and intercession, to ask God to unite us with all others present and give us loving thoughts about them, then the whole service can become a unity of fellowship, so that the downhearted and unhappy, the lonely and the sad, the mentally tortured and the spiritually dead, will be caught up into fellowship and thus into the life of God.

[15] I have been rather disturbed in my correspondence lately because so many people have talked about taking their own lives. I know that my correspondence is unusual and that I am therefore liable to get a distorted view of life, which for the great majority is probably still happy. I know that I spend most of my time with people who are ill in either body or mind or else unhappy and in some kind of distress. The war has something to do with it, not because the war can destroy the Christian faith, but because so often it proves that we have no real hold on the Christian faith, that what we thought was faith was merely assent, or else faith in something false. But, insanity and nervous illness apart, people would never talk about taking their lives if they had the security that comes from belonging to a fellowship in which one is loved. One can be desperately unhappy, worried, and restless, but a fellowship should be strong enough to hold one, however great the individual agony. I think the suicide is the person who, at the dread moment, believes that nobody cares or that nobody cares enough. The Christian church should offer a fellowship that goes down underneath that tendency

[1] "The Everlasting Mercy," *Poems*. By permission of The Macmillan Co.

toward disintegration, as though to say, "We love you, and we will hold on to you."

[16] I believe that the very memory of what Christian fellowship can mean can become a strong factor in a man's life. A man I know had been a victim of sex temptation and had successfully resisted it over a long number of years. Only his very best friends knew what a battle this particular problem was for him. One evening he found himself on business in Berlin with time on his hands. As he strolled down the Friedrichstrasse, his attention was caught by a large framed photograph of nude women. You can guess the kind of place that was thus advertised. He was greatly tempted to go in. No one would have known. His character would not have been damaged in the eyes of his friends. His respectability would have been unsoiled at home. Then suddenly, with great resolution, he walked away. A hundred yards from the place he had an immense sense of relief and spiritual power. When asked how he had found strength to make that great decision, he answered without hesitation, "My church at home." Even the memory of the fellowship, even the thought that he belonged to a company who loved him and who, with him, were seeking together the high and the lovely and the true and the beautiful things, strengthened him in the hour of temptation.

[17] But the fellowship of the church involves not merely "my church at home." It is a fellowship that goes right across the world into all lands, where men are worshiping in jungle villages, in desert towns, in ice-bound solitudes, in tropical forests. It is a fellowship that goes back throughout all the centuries, a line of witnessing in an unbroken chain, so that as we imagine it we note that the last man in the chain has his hand in the hand of Christ in a little upper room at Jerusalem. It is a fellowship indeed that goes not only across the world and back through the centuries but up into the unseen. "Therefore with angels and archangels, and with all the company of heaven, we laud and magnify thy glorious name, evermore praising thee, and saying: Holy, Holy, Holy."

Our third point, then, is that men come to church to find fellowship.

[18] 4. Lastly, people come to church to find power—spiritual power for this difficult task of living. Here again I suppose the psychology of it is this: power is released in the will through the emotions whenever the mind takes hold on truth. I would ask you to ponder that statement. Whenever the mind is really possessed by truth to such an extent that we *feel* it to be true as well as give it our intellectual assent, then power is released in the will. The will alone is not enough. The feeling alone is not enough. One might risk the illustration that feeling is to the will what gasoline is to the machinery of an automobile.

[19] It is all very well for people to tell us that everything depends on will power. I was reminded, by a sermon of Dr. Fosdick, of the following hymn:

> Awake, my soul, stretch every nerve,
> And press with vigor on;
> A heavenly race demands thy zeal,
> And an immortal crown.

Philip Doddridge wrote five hundred hymns, including "O God of Bethel," but "Awake, My Soul" is not one of his best. Certainly when he wrote it he was not in any deep trouble. I can imagine very few situations in which I should wish it to be my message. The people I talk to are not much interested in an immortal crown. They are wondering whether they can get through today and tomorrow without defeat, and I for one would not dare to say to say to anyone, "Stretch every nerve." The people I deal with have their nerves stretched to the breaking point.

20 I know a young woman who wanted very badly to be a surgeon. She took the long and arduous medical course necessary, passed with distinction in surgery, and was ready to set out on that grand career. But in a bomb explosion glass was flung in her face, and for a long time it seemed as though all hope of her ever being able to see had gone. She has had thirty-five operations, and there is left to her only the glimmer of sight in one eye. Shall I say to her, "Stretch every nerve, and press with vigor on"?

21 In a family of my acquaintance there are two daughters, one fifteen and one twenty. The girl of fifteen is what a girl should be at that age, healthy, happy, full of life. But what shall I say about a lovely girl of twenty, at the very threshold of life, whose brain has been infected by germs which have destroyed her controls so that she cannot be left day or night? I have consulted a specialist on her behalf, and his opinion is that there is no hope whatever. Twice she has tried to take her own life, and there always exists the danger of her attacking others. The sentence of the most eminent medical opinion is that she must remain in a mental hospital for the rest of her life. That may be fifty years. Yet for periods she is entirely sane and pleads to be taken home. Shall I say to her and to her stricken family, "Stretch every nerve, and press with vigor on"?

22 I will not harrow your feelings by talking thus. If you and I were meeting in a little room, you would say to me, "Yes, I know a case where. . ." and I would only have to open my own diary at any week in the year to tell you of case after case of deep human need, so deep that no human resourcefulness is an adequate reply. All last winter, when the horror of bombing went on night after night, I found it almost unbearable to listen to some new story each day. There are many people to whom I minister who have lost their boys, lost their home, lost their business, lost everything except their faith. I would not like to ask them to say to themselves:

> Awake, my soul, stretch every nerve,
> And press with vigor on.

I would not presume to offer them the petty shallowness of any word of human wisdom, the pagan triviality of being told to endure, the irritating irrelevance that others suffer similarly, the heartless torture which falsely teaches that all suffering is punishment for sin.

23 But I think I know why such people go to church. Those people go to church because the only comfort for them is God—not God explaining him-

self in arguments, for no explanation I have ever met satisfies the need of the mind, let alone the hunger of the heart; not God remote and far away; but God coming down into human life and into human suffering; God who is himself crucified and who still remains serene, calm, loving. That God, who doesn't try to answer our questions, answers our need; and I believe in a God who brings his children through their dread sufferings with finally nothing lost, but with something gained which is of immortal worth.

[24] Since I have criticized one hymn, let me offer you another:

> See, from his head, his hands, his feet,
> Sorrow and love flow mingled down:
> Did e'er such love and sorrow meet,
> Or thorns compose so rich a crown?

[25] Those who go to church and find the real God answer for themselves the question with which we started, "Why do men go to church?" They go to worship; they go to find pardon; they go to enter a fellowship; they go to get power. No! No! We need not divide it thus. They go to find all their deepest longings satisfied when they find God himself. He is the goal toward which our spirits move. He is the reality behind all men's dreams. He is the answer to all our prayers. Jesus, who was the supreme Master of the art of living, could not live without God. Can you?

APPENDIX

Appendix A

A Work Sheet: *How to Study a Sermon*

First find out if anyone has written a biography of the preacher. Go through it with care. Do the same with his lectures on the subject, if he has delivered such a series. Then take up his printed sermons. Gain a working knowledge of these books. Study a few sermons that show him at his best. Single out one discourse that grips your soul. Follow the plan below, but only as a way to open up the subject. Soon you will be going out into by-paths of your own choosing. Live with this sermon so that you will know it as a friend for the rest of your life.

Two books will help in this kind of study. *The Principles of Preaching* (University of Chicago Press, 1929), by Ozora S. Davis, consists of eight sermons, with a teaching method like the one now in view. *The Art of Plain Talk* (Harper and Brothers, 1946), by Rudolf Flesch, tells how to use the King's English with clarity and force, rather than beauty. This latter book deals with other matters, not with religion. But the author can teach one how to write and speak so as to grip the reader or hearer. With some such guide take up one sermon after another. Make it your own, part by part. Thus you can learn how to preach today.

A Sample Work Sheet

AIM: Appeal mainly to the intellect, the feelings, or the will? Chiefly textual, topical, expository? Largely doctrinal, ethical, evangelistic, pastoral? (Such labels overlap. Use them with imagination.)

TEXT: Familiar? Short? Clear? Interesting? Appeal to the eye? Correctly interpreted? Often repeated? Echoed? Influence over the sermon?

TOPIC: Relation to text? Length of topic? Religious? Clear? Interesting? Accurate? Rhythmical? Repeated often? Echoed? Influence over sermon?

INTRODUCTION: Textual? Topical? Problem approach? A life situation? Some other kind? Length? Interest? Discuss opening sentence. Any theme, or key sentence (proposition)?

MATERIALS: Wealth? Variety? Biblical? Which parts of Bible? From theology? Church history? Biography? Literature? Personal thinking? Other sources? Sermon factual or abstract?

PLAN: Outline the sermon. Unity? Order? Symmetry? Progress? Climax? Divisions announced? Parallelism in stating headings? Plan memorable?

CONCLUSION: Content? Fitness? Length? Beauty? Force? Use of pronouns? Discuss last few sentences. Conclusion fulfill aim of sermon?

ILLUSTRATIONS: Number? Variety? Sources? Length of each? Clear? Interesting? Beautiful? Effective? ("Materials" enter into the walls of the house; illustrations serve as windows.)

LITERARY STYLE: Clear? Interesting? Beautiful? Varied? Forceful? The work of an artist, or an artisan? Mark passages you wish to remember.

PARAGRAPHS: Number? Length? Unity? Use of connectives? Discuss the opening sentences, closing sentences. Work of a skilled craftsman?

SENTENCES: Long? Simple? Balanced? Periodic? Varied? Clear? Rhythmical? Marks of skill and care? (See *The Art of Plain Talk.*)

WORDS: Anglo-Saxon? Latin? Length? Accuracy? Range? Beauty? Facts, or abstractions? (See *The Art of Plain Talk*.)

SPECIAL MARKS: Use of the interrogative? Direct address (speaking to hearer)? Direct discourse (using exact words of another)? Humor? Pathos? Use of quotations? Hypothetical cases? Personification? Any other quality that stands out?

IMAGINATION: As a whole and in its parts does the sermon show the use of the creative, the constructive, or the descriptive imagination? [1] (Imagination here means ability to see, and put things together, as an artist sees and then paints his picture.)

[1] See "The Interpreter's Imagination," chap. xii in my *Preaching from the Bible* (New York and Nashville: Abingdon-Cokesbury Press, 1941).

Appendix B

Bibliography: *Books for Study in This Field*

Books like the ones below stand on the shelves of a seminary library. Most of these works do not belong in a pastor's study. They tell more about a master preacher's life than about his sermons. Thus far scholars have delved into the pulpit work of the early fathers, but not much into that of Protestant divines. In the list that follows the asterisks point to books for the student who wishes to start on a quest that may last all his days. If he is wise he will study books of sermons and not books about sermons.

Abbott, Lyman, et al. *Prophets of the Christian Faith.* New York, 1896.
———. *Silhouettes of My Contemporaries.* New York, 1922.
Addison, Daniel D. *The Clergy in American Life and Letters.* London, 1900.
Bacon, Leonard. *The Genesis of the New England Churches.* New York, 1874.
*Blackwood, Andrew W. *Preaching in Time of Reconstruction.* Great Neck, New York, 1945.
Blaikie, W. Garden. *The Preachers of Scotland from the Sixth to the Nineteenth Century.* Edinburgh, 1888.
Booth, John N. *The Quest for Preaching Power.* New York, 1943.
Boreham, Frank W. *A Bunch of Everlastings.* New York, 1920.
———. *A Casket of Cameos,* New York, 1924.
———. *Faggot of Torches.* New York, 1926.
Brastow, Lewis O. *The Modern Pulpit.* New York, 1906.
———. *Representative Modern Preachers.* New York, 1904.
Broadus, John A. *Lectures on the History of Preaching.* New York, 1907.
Brown, Charles R. *They Were Giants.* New York, 1934.
Brown, John. *Puritan Preaching in England.* New York, 1900.
Buckham, John W. *Progressive Religious Thought in America.* Boston, 1912.
Burns, James. *Revivals, Their Laws and Their Leaders.* London, 1909.
Cadman, S. Parkes. *Ambassadors of God.* New York, 1923. Chap. II.
———. *The Three Religious Leaders of Oxford and Their Movements.* New York, 1916.
Cambridge History of English Literature. New York, 1916. Chap. III, "The Growth of Liberal Theology."
Carpenter, William B. *Prophets of Christendom.* London, 1884.
Chrisman, Lewis H. *The Message of the American Pulpit.* New York, 1930.
Clark, Henry W. *History of English Nonconformity.* 2 vols. London, 1911, 1913.
Cornish, Francis W. *The English Church in the Nineteenth Century.* London, 1910.
Currier, Albert H. *Nine Great Preachers.* Boston, 1912.
*Dargan, Edwin C. *A History of Preaching.* Two vols., New York, 1905, 1912.
Dargan, Edwin C. *The Art of Preaching in the Light of Its History.* New York, 1922.
Davies, George J. *Successful Preachers.* London, 1883.

Dictionary of National Biography. Ed. Sidney Lee. New York, 1896.

Dix, J. R. *Pulpit Portraits.* Boston, 1854.

Edwards, John. *Nineteenth Century Preachers.* London, 1902.

Eliot, Samuel A., ed. *Heralds of a Liberal Faith.* Three vols., New York, 1910.

Fish, Henry C., ed. *Masterpieces of Pulpit Eloquence,* Two vols., New York, 1877.

Fish, Henry C., ed. *Pulpit Eloquence of the Nineteenth Century.* New York, 1875.

Fosdick, Harry E. "What Is the Matter with Preaching?" *Harper's Magazine,* July, 1928.

Gammie, Alexander. *Preachers I Have Heard.* London, 1945.

*Garvie, Alfred E. *The Christian Preacher.* New York, 1921, Part I, "The History of Preaching."

Gray, Joseph M. M. *Prophets of the Soul.* New York, 1936.

Hall, Thomas C. *The Religious Background of American Culture.* Boston, 1930.

Harris, Muriel. *Prophets and Preachers.* London, 1935.

Hood, E. Paxton. *The Throne of Eloquence.* New York, 1888.

Hood, E. Paxton. *The Vocation of the Pastor.* New York, 1888.

Hoppin, James M. *Homiletics.* New York, 1883. Pp. 13-242, "The History of Preaching."

Horne, C. Silvester. *A Popular History of the Free Churches.* London, 1903.

*———. *The Romance of Preaching.* London, 1914.

*Howard, Harry C. *Princes of the Christian Pulpit and Pastorate.* Two series, Nashville, 1927, 1928.

Hoyt, Arthur S. *The Pulpit and American Life.* New York, 1921.

Hutchinson, Paul. *Men Who Made the Churches.* Nashville, 1930.

Jeffs, Ernest H. *Princes of the Modern Pulpit.* London, n.d.

Jones, Edgar D. *American Preachers of Today.* Indianapolis, 1933.

Kempe, John, ed. *The Classic Preachers of the English Church.* Two series, London, 1877, 1878.

Ker, John. *Lectures on the History of Preaching.* London, 1888.

*Latourette, Kenneth S. *A History of the Expansion of Christianity.* Seven vols., New York, 1937-45.

Levy, Babette L. *Preaching in the First Half Century of New England History.* Hartford, Conn., 1945.

Macartney, Clarence E. *Six Kings of the American Pulpit.* Philadelphia, 1942.

———. *Sons of Thunder.* New York, 1928.

McComb, Samuel. *Preaching in Theory and in Practice.* New York, 1926.

McKail, John Wm. *Studies in Humanism.* New York, 1938.

Mitchell, W. Fraser. *English Pulpit Oratory from Andrewes to Tillotson, a Study of Its Literary Aspects.* New York, 1938.

Newton, Joseph Fort. *If I Had Only One Sermon to Prepare.* New York, 1932.

———. *Some Living Masters of the Pulpit.* New York, 1923.

*Nicoll, William Robertson. *Princes of the Church.* London, 1921.

Paniel, Karl F. *Pragmatische Geschichte der christlichen Beredsamkeit und der Homiletik.* Leipsic, 1939.

Pattison, T. Harwood. *The History of Christian Preaching.* Philadelphia, 1909.

Powell, Lyman P. *Heavenly Heretics.* New York, 1909.

Russell, G. W. E., et al. *Leaders of the Church.* London, 1905.

Ryle, John C. *The Christian Leaders of the Last Century.* London, 1869.

Sears, Lorenzo. *History of Oratory.* Chicago, 1896.

Shepherd, William G. *Great Preachers as Seen by a Journalist.* New York, 1924.

Simpson, James G. *Preachers and Teachers.* London, 1910.

Sinclair, W. M. *Leaders of Thought in the English Church.* London, 1896.

Sprague, William B. *Annals of the American Pulpit.* Nine vols., New York, 1857-69.

Sweet, William W. *Religion in Colonial America.* New York, 1942.

———. *The Story of Religions in America.* New York, 1939.

Taylor, William M. *The Scottish Pulpit.* New York, 1887.

Thompson, Ernest T. *Changing Emphases in American Preaching.* Philadelphia, 1943.

Trumbull, H. Clay. *My Four Religious Teachers.* Philadelphia, 1903.

Vinet, Alexandre. *Histoire de la predication parmi les réformés de France au dix-septième siècle.* Paris, 1860.

Von Oosterzee, J. J. *Practical Theology* (trans.). Pp. 62-165, "History and Literature" (of homiletics). London, 1878.

Walker, Williston. *Ten New England Leaders.* New York, 1901.

Wilkinson, William C. *Modern Masters of Pulpit Discourse.* New York, 1905.

Biographical Index of Authors

BARTH (bärt), KARL: Born at Basel, Switzerland, 1886. Educated at Bern Univ., Berlin Univ., Tübingen Univ., Marburg Univ. Reformed Church. Originally a Ritschlian. Pastor in Switzerland twelve years. There he found his preaching message in the Epistle to the Romans. Prof. theology, Goettingen, 1921-25; Munich, 1925-30; Bern, 1930-35; Basel, since 1935. Author of famous books, including *The Epistle to the Romans* (1919), *The Word of God and the Word of Man* (1923), *The Resurrection of the Dead* (1924), *Prolegomena to Christian Dogmatics* (first vol., 1932), *Credo* (1935). Sermons in collaboration with Eduard Thurneysen: *Come, Holy Spirit* (1933), *God's Search for Man* (1935). (Dates above refer to English translations.) He interprets the Scriptures in his own way; stresses doctrine, not duty; delights in paradox; appeals to conscience, and sounds the note of urgency. He has won many disciples, and aroused strong opposition. He has influenced preaching all over Europe and America.

Repentance 173

BEECHER, HENRY WARD: Born at Litchfield, Conn., 1813. Died at Brooklyn, 1887. The son of a well-known preacher, and a member of a brilliant family. A Congregationalist. Henry Ward became famous as a pulpit orator. At Plymouth Church, Brooklyn, 1847-87, he showed the power of a preaching personality. A lover of God and man, a student of life in town and field, a master of humor and pathos, a consummate actor with a voice like an organ, he did for hosts indoors what Whitefield had done in the open air. By voice and pen, as preacher and editor, as well as reformer and lecturer, Beecher helped to change the religious climate of his day, and of our own. His three series of *Yale Lectures on Preaching*, especially the first (1872), ought to be known by every student of the art. Biography recommended: *Henry Ward Beecher*, by Lyman Abbott (1903).

The God of Comfort 86

BOREHAM (bōr'am), FRANK WILLIAM: Born at Tunbridge Wells, England, 1871. Educated there and at Metropolitan Col., London. Early experience as a journalist. A Wesleyan pastor in New Zealand, Tasmania, and Victoria, Australia. A voluminous author of sermonic essays, especially ones about texts that have moved well-known persons. During the years after World War I his writings went around the world. They show how to secure interest, mainly by illustration. His many books include these: *A Handful of Stars* (1922), *A Casket of Cameos* (1924), *A Faggot of Torches* (1926), *A Tuft of Camel's Hair* (1926), and *A Bunch of Everlastings* (1920). What a way to describe texts from Holy Writ!

David Livingstone's Text 164

BROOKS, PHILLIPS: Born at Boston, 1835. Died there, 1893. Educated at Harvard Univ. and the Divinity School in Alexandria, Va. An Episcopalian. Held two pastorates in Philadelphia, 1859-69, where he wrote the Christmas hymn "O little town of Bethlehem." In 1869 he became the rector of Trinity Church, Boston, and in 1891 was chosen bishop of Massachusetts. As a Christian humanist, in Boston and at Harvard, as in England, he won a wide hearing for evangelical Christianity. In 1877 he delivered the *Yale Lectures on Preaching*, a series never surpassed, if ever equaled. He described preaching as "the bringing of truth through personality." His personality appears in ten volumes of sermons, still on sale, and in the standard biography, *The Life and Letters of Phillips Brooks*, by A. V. G. Allen (1901).

The Fire and the Calf 129

BUNYAN, JOHN: Born at Elstow, a mile from Bedford, England, 1628. Died at Bedford, 1688. A Baptist. A preacher to the common people. Imprisoned because of insistence on preaching the gospel. During twelve years in Bedford jail he became a writer. His best-known books include his spiritual autobiography, *Grace Abounding to the Chief of Sinners* (1666), and two allegories, *The Pilgrim's Progress* (1678-84) and *The Holy War* (1682). His sermons now extant do not show Bunyan at his best. The present volume substitutes the beginning and the ending of his famous allegory. By his simple words, quiet rhythm, and doctrine set to music Bunyan shows the meaning of Bushnell's phrase "Our Gospel a Gift to the Imagination." Standard biography: *John Bunyan*, by John Brown, of Bedford (1885).

From *The Pilgrim's Progress* 21

BUTTRICK, GEORGE ARTHUR: Born at Seaham Harbor, England, 1892. Educated at Lancaster Col., Manchester, and Victoria Univ. A Presbyterian. A pastor in Quincy, Ill.; Rutland, Vt.; Buffalo, N.Y.; Madison Avenue Presbyterian Church, New York City, since 1927. Associate prof. practical theology, Union Theol. Sem. Lyman Beecher Lectures at Yale: *Jesus Came Preaching* (1931). Former president, Federal Council of Churches. Editor in chief, the forthcoming *Interpreter's Bible*. In demand as a lecturer at Bible conferences and ministerial assemblies, and as a preacher at universities and colleges. Dr. Buttrick has become in many circles "the preacher's preacher," but he has yet to publish his first volume of sermons. Author: *The Parables of Jesus* (1928), *The Christian Fact and Modern Doubt* (1934), *Prayer* (1942), *Christ and Man's Dilemma* (1946).

The Sound of Silence 180

BUSHNELL (boosh'nel), HORACE: Born near Litchfield, Conn., 1802. Died at Hartford, 1876. Educated at Yale Univ., in the arts, in law, and in divinity. A Congregationalist. Only one pastorate, at the North Church, Hartford, 1833-59. An original thinker, an impressive speaker, a moving writer, a versatile man of affairs—including civic government, study of good roads, and education, both religious and secular. Best known as a writer of theological works and of sermons. His *Christian Nurture* (1847) has largely dominated Christian education for a hundred years. Three volumes of his sermons used to stand on the shelves of almost every manse in Scotland: *Sermons for the New Life* (1858), *Christ and His Salvation* (1864), and *Sermons on Living Subjects* (1872). Every student of preaching should also know his essays, notably *Building Eras* (1881). The biography, *Life and Letters*, by his daughter, Mary Bushnell Cheney (1880-1903), prepares the way for *Horace Bushnell, Theologian and Preacher*, by T. T. Munger (1899).

Every Man's Life a Plan of God 75

CHALMERS (chä'mers), THOMAS: Born at Anstruther, Fifeshire, Scotland, 1780. Died at Edinburgh, 1847. Educated at St. Andrews Univ., where he taught mathematics. A Presbyterian. In 1803 he became pastor at rural Kilmany. After seven years of fruitlessness he experienced a change of heart. Afterward he spoke with holy passion, often with "blazing force." In each discourse he stressed a single idea, which he repeated often, with amazing variety and growing intensity. Despite bondage to the manuscript, and use of long sentences, he became known afar for "that voice, that face, those great, simple, living thoughts, those floods of resistless eloquence, that piercing, shattering voice." Chalmers excelled as a pastor, a seminary professor, and a churchman. He has become the patron saint of many Presbyterians. His sermons appear in various forms. Standard biography: *Memoirs*, 4 vols., by his son-in-law, William Hanna (1849-52).

The Expulsive Power of a New Affection 50

CHANNING, WILLIAM ELLERY: Born at Newport, R. I., 1780. Died at Bennington, Vt., 1842. Educated at Harvard Univ. A Unitarian. He spent his ministerial life in Boston. There he represented Unitarianism at its best. He believed in the pre-existence of our Lord, in His miracles, and in His resurrection. But Channing stressed the subordination of the Son to the Father. The Boston divine deplored controversy. He preferred to speak and write about the bearing of historic Christianity on education and other circles of life. As a man of culture and a writer with charm he drew from the poet Coleridge this tribute: "He has the love of wisdom and the wisdom of love." His *Works,* 10 vols. (1849), show versatility and strength. Biography recommended: *The Memoir,* by William H. Channing (1880).

The Character of Christ 63

CHAPPELL (chap'pel), CLOVIS GILLHAM: Born at Flatwood, Tenn., 1882. Educated at Duke Univ. and Harvard Univ. A Methodist. A pastor successively in leading congregations of the South; now at First Methodist Church, Charlotte, N.C. Beginning with *The Village Tragedy* (1921), he has issued a volume of sermons almost every year. Their popular appeal springs partly from simplicity and human interest. A lover of people, he deals with Bible characters as though they lived down the street. His recent volumes include *The Road to Certainty* (1940), *Faces About the Cross* (1941), *Familiar Faces* (1942), *Sermons from Revelation* (1943), *Living Zestfully* (1944), *If I Were Young* (1945), *And the Prophets* (1946). Someday his epitaph may read: "The common people heard him gladly."

The Forks of the Road—Moses 185

CLOW (klō), WILLIAM McCALLUM: Born at Glasgow, Scotland, 1853. Educated there. Died there, 1930. A Presbyterian. Pastor successively in five congregations of the United Free Church. In 1911 became prof. practical training and Christian ethics at the United Free Church Col. (divinity school), Glasgow; and in 1921 the principal. His published sermons are evangelical in content, devotional in spirit, pleasing in form: *The Cross in Christian Experience* (1908), *The Day of the Cross* (1910), *The Secret of the Lord* (1910), and *The Evangel of the Strait Gate* (1916).

The Cross and the Memory of Sin 152

EDWARDS, JONATHAN: Born at East (now South) Windsor, Conn., 1703. Died at Princeton, N.J., 1758. Educated at Yale Univ. A Congregationalist. Pastor at Northampton, Mass., 1727-49. There he led in a community revival, and later in the nation-wide Great Awakening. Pastor at Stockbridge, Mass., and missionary to the Indians, 1750-57. President for six weeks in 1757 of what is now Princeton Univ. Known at home and abroad as a philosopher, a theologian, an author, and a preacher. His famous sermon "Sinners in the Hands of an Angry God" shows one side of his nature. His heart appears in *A Treatise Concerning the Religious Affections* (1746). Recent biographies by Arthur C. McGiffert, Jr. (1932), Ola Elizabeth Winslow (1940).

The Christian Pilgrim 40

FOSDICK, HARRY EMERSON: Born at Buffalo, N.Y., 1878. Educated at Colgate Univ., Union Theol. Sem., Columbia Univ. A Baptist. Pastor, First Baptist Church, Montclair, N.J., 1904-15; Riverside Church, New York City, 1926-46. Instructor in homiletics, Union Theol. Sem., 1908-15; prof. practical theology from 1915 until retirement. Lyman Beecher Lectures at Yale: *The Modern Use of the Bible* (1924). Over the nation-wide radio Dr. Fosdick has spoken to hosts of admirers, who regard him as a skillful exponent of evangelical liberalism. As a writer he seems never to send out a hasty or a careless line. In addition to other works he has written these books of sermons: *The Hope of the World* (1933), *The Secret of Victorious Living* (1934), *The Power to See It Through* (1935), *Successful Christian Living* (1937), *Living Under Tension* (1941), *A Great Time to Be Alive* (1944), and *On Being Fit to Live With* (1946). Note the stress on living.

Forgiveness of Sins 191

GOSSIP, ARTHUR JOHN: Born at Glasgow, 1873. Educated at Edinburgh Univ. A Presbyterian. Pastor successively in Liverpool, Farfar, Glasgow, and Aberdeen. Chaplain at the front in World War I. Prof. practical theology and Christian ethics, Trinity Col., Glasgow, 1928-39; in Glasgow Univ. since 1939. Warrack Lectures on Preaching: *In*

Christ's Stead (1925). Author of sermons in the series "Scholar as Preacher": *From the Edge of the Crowd* (1924), *The Galilean Accent* (1926), *The Hero in Thy Soul* (1928), and *Experience Worketh Hope* (1944). Dr. Gossip did his best pulpit work while a pastor. His theory appears in the Warrack Lectures: "Preaching resembles music in this respect, that for a real success three things are required—a message worth hearing, a sufficient instrument, and a master whose deft touch can draw from both what his soul finds in them." Recent book: *In the Secret Place of the Most High: Studies in Prayer* (1947).

But When Life Tumbles In, What Then? 198

HORTON, DOUGLAS: Born at Brooklyn, N.Y., 1891. A Congregationalist. Educated at Princeton Univ.; New Col., Edinburgh; Mansfield Col., Oxford; Tübingen Univ., Germany; and Hartford Theol. Sem. Pastor at First Church of Christ, Middletown, Conn.; Leyden Congregational Church, Brooklyn; United Church (Congl.–Presb.), Hyde Park, Chicago, 1931-38. General secretary of Congregational Christian Churches since 1938. Chaplain, U. S. Navy, 1918-19. Dr. Horton has taught at Andover Newton, Chicago Theol. Sem., and Union Theol. Sem. After World War II he served on the commission of churchmen to visit Japan. He has written these books: *Out into Life* (1925), *A Legend of the Grail* (1926), *Taking a City* (1931), and *The Art of Living Together* (1935). He has translated from the German *The Word of God and the Word of Man* (1928), by Karl Barth, and has edited *The Basic Formula for Church Union* (1937).

Taking a City 205

JONES, EDGAR DeWITT: Born at Hearne, Tex., 1876. Educated at Missouri Univ. and Transylvania Univ. He gave up the practice of law to become a Disciples of Christ clergyman. A pastor at Erlangen, Ky.; Cleveland, Ohio; Bloomington, Ill.; Central Church, Detroit, Mich., 1920-26; Central Woodward Church, 1927-46. Exchange preacher to Scotland, 1932. Frequent contributor to the *Christian Century* and other religious journals. Former president, Federal Council of Churches. Dr. Jones has made a special study of Americana. In 1939 he won a prize for the best sermon about Lincoln. His published works include *What Jesus Wrote on the Ground* (1924), *American Preachers of Today* (1933), *The Pulpit Stairs* (1934), *This Great Business of Preaching* (1936), *Lords of Speech* (1937), *This Great Business of Being a Christian* (1938), and *A Man Stood Up to Preach* (1944).

The Light on the Lord's Face 211

JONES, RUFUS MATTHEW: Born at South China, Me., 1863. Educated at Haverford Col., Heidelberg Univ., Univ. of Pennsylvania, Harvard Univ., Oxford Univ., and Marburg Univ. Teacher at Haverford Col. since 1893; prof. of philosophy after 1904; emeritus since 1934. A Quaker. Editor of Friends' church papers. Speaker and preacher at many colleges and universities. Author of more than fifty books, including, from recent years: *The Testimony of the Soul* (1936), *Some Problems of Life* (1937), *The Eternal Gospel* (1938), *The Flowering of Mysticism* (1939), *Small Town Boy* (1941), *The Spirit in Man* (1941), *and New Eyes for Invisibles* (1943). By voice and pen Dr. Jones has commended Christian mysticism among both scholars and men of affairs.

The Heart of Christianity 218

JOWETT, JOHN HENRY: Born at Halifax, Yorkshire, England, 1864. Died at London, 1923. Educated at Edinburgh Univ. and Mansfield Col., Oxford. A Congregationalist. Pastor at Newcastle-on-Tyne; Carr's Lane Chapel, Birmingham; Fifth Avenue Presbyterian Church, New York City, 1911-18; and Westminster Chapel, London, 1918-22. Lyman Beecher Lectures at Yale: *The Preacher, His Life and Work* (1912). Because of his devotional spirit, care about words, and pleasing delivery, Dr. Jowett became widely popular among evangelical churchgoers on both sides of the Atlantic. His published sermons include *Apostolic Optimism* (n.d.), *The School of Calvary* (1910), *The Transfigured Church* (1910), *The Whole Armour of God* (1916), and *God, Our Contem-*

porary (1922). An excellent biography: *John Henry Jowett,* by Arthur Porritt (1929). The Magnetism of the Uplifted Lord 147

LUTHER, MARTIN: Born at Eisleben, Germany, 1483. Died there, 1546. Founder of Lutheranism. A lover of music, a writer of hymns, translator of the Bible into noble prose, a writer of commentaries, and a protagonist for the Protestant faith—Luther thought of himself as a preacher to the common people. In his *Table Talk* he declares that a preacher must be able to "teach systematically." He should "remain by the text, and deliver that which he has before him, that the people may well understand it." "He must define, describe, and show what it is." "Cursed are all preachers that aim at high and hard things, and neglecting the saving health of the poor, unlearned people, seek their own honor and praise." Unfortunately, as with Calvin, Luther's sermons have received little attention, especially in the United States. Biographies in English by J. Köstlin (1875), Henry E. Jacobs (1898), et al.
Justification by Faith 13

MACARTNEY, CLARENCE EDWARD: Born at Northwood, Ohio, 1879. Educated at Wisconsin Univ., Princeton Univ., and Princeton Theol. Sem. A Presbyterian. Pastor successively in downtown churches: Paterson, N.J.; Arch St., Philadelphia; and First Church, Pittsburgh, since 1927. Stone Lectures at Princeton Sem.: *Sons of Thunder* (1928). Smyth Lectures at Columbia Sem., Georgia: *Six Kings of the American Pulpit* (1939). A student of homiletics and of American history, especially the time of Lincoln. A champion of the older orthodoxy. Dr. Macartney attracts throngs, especially at night. With endless variety of biblical themes, dramatic presentation of familiar truths, and abundance of illustrations, he searches the conscience and moves the will. His many books include these volumes of sermons: *Things Most Surely Believed* (1931), *Sermons from Life* (1932), *Peter and His Lord* (1937), *The Greatest Men of the Bible* (1941), *Great Nights of the Bible* (1943), *Great Interviews of Jesus* (1945), and *Trials of Great Men of the Bible* (1946).
Your Unknown Self 224

MACLAREN (or McLaren), ALEXANDER: Born at Glasgow, Scotland, 1826. Died at Manchester, 1910. A Baptist. Educated at Glasgow Univ. and Stepney Col. (divinity school), London. After a humble pastorate in Southampton he became pastor of Union Chapel, Manchester, 1858-1903. In that educational center he excelled as a pulpit teacher. Though he spoke ex tempore, his style charmed cultured hearers. His published works include the *Expositions,* uneven in value; commentaries, notably on the Psalms; and sermons, of which these are among the best: *The Secret of Power* (1882), *A Year's Ministry,* 2 series (1884, 1885), *The Holy of Holies* (1890), and *Sermons Preached in Manchester,* 3 series (1891-93). Maclaren has become known as "the prince of expositors." A mediocre biography: *Alexander McLaren of Manchester,* by Miss E. T. McLaren (1912).
Love and Forgiveness 107

MAIER (mī'yer), WALTER ARTHUR: Born at Boston, 1893. A Lutheran. Educated at Boston Univ., Concordia Theol. Sem., and Harvard Univ. (Ph.D. 1929). Prof. Semitic languages and Old Testament interpretation, Concordia Sem., since 1922. Editor, *Walther League Messenger,* since 1920. Speaker on the Lutheran Hour over national stations since 1930; heard by millions. Dr. Maier speaks from the heart to the heart. His appeal shows what many conservative folk like to hear. These are some of his recent published sermons: *The Cross from Coast to Coast* (1940), *The Radio for Christ* (1940), *Peace Through Christ* (1940), *Courage in Christ* (1941), *For Christ and Country* (1942), *Victory Through Christ* (1943), *America, Turn to Christ* (1944), *Jesus Christ, Our Hope* (1946), and *Rebuilding with Christ* (1947). Note the stress on Christ.
Thanks Be unto God for His Unspeakable Gift! 231

MOODY, DWIGHT LYMAN: Born, East Northfield, Mass., 1837. Died there, 1899. A self-made man with little schooling. He turned aside from a successful business career to enter full-time Christian service as a Congregational lay evangelist. In 1870 he joined in evangelistic work with Ira D. Sankey, a song leader. They journeyed over this country, and made three tours of England, notably the first, 1873-75. At home and abroad they attracted hosts of hearers, won countless friends, and secured many converts. Moody relied largely on biblical preaching, simple diction, abundant illustrations, and plain horse sense. He received vast sums of money, which he used to establish and promote institutions: the Northfield Bible Conference, the East Northfield School for Girls, the Mount Hermon School for Boys, and the Moody Bible Institute. Standard biography by his son, William R. Moody (rev. ed. 1930).

What Think Ye of Christ? 138

NEWTON, JOSEPH FORT: Born at Decatur, Tex., 1880. Educated at Hardy Institute, Southern Baptist Theol. Sem., Louisville, Ky. An Episcopalian. Pastor in Paris, Tex.; St. Louis, Mo.; Dixon, Ill.; Cedar Rapids, Ia.; City Temple, London; Church of the Divine Paternity, New York City; Church of St. Luke and St. James, Philadelphia, since 1938. Dr. Newton has changed his style in recent times, because of eleven years' experience as a writer of syndicated articles for the daily press. The flood of mail showed him "the actual enemies that human beings have to fight day in and day out." He has issued many books on varied themes. These are representative works: Some Living Masters of the Pulpit (1922), Altar Stairs: A Little Book of Prayers (1928), The New Preaching (1929), The Stuff of Life (1939), His Cross and Ours (1940), Living Up to Life (1941), Live, Love, and Learn (1943). Autobiography: River of Years (1946).

Reconciliation 238

NIEMÖLLER (ně'mûl-er), MARTIN: Born in 1892 in Germany. A Lutheran. During World War I he served as captain of a U-boat. Afterward he became a parish minister at Dahlen, a suburb of Berlin. There he sent out books that later appeared in English translations: From U-Boat to Pulpit (1937), Here Stand I (1937), and God Is My Führer (1941). Even before the Nazis took control he opposed the movement. In 1937 he was arrested, tried in secret, and sent to solitary confinement for four years. Then he was held at the infamous Dachau camp for another four years. "Amidst the horrors of those days," he says, "the Gospel remained alive for us as the power of God. It remains even now our only hope." He preached the sermon contained in this book to fellow captives shortly before his release by United States forces in May, 1945. Recent works: Dachau Sermons (1946), Of Guilt and Hope (1947).

Maundy Thursday 244

PHILLIPS, HAROLD COOKE: Born at Westmoreland, Jamaica, B.W.I., 1892. A Baptist. Educated at Denison Univ., Columbia Univ., Union Theol. Sem. Pastor in Mount Vernon, N.Y.; First Church, Cleveland, since 1928. A popular speaker and preacher at colleges and universities, as well as Bible conferences and ministerial assemblies. Always an evangelical preacher, in recent years Dr. Phillips has become more pronounced in setting forth the central realities of evangelical Christianity. Author: Life That Is Life Indeed (1928), Seeing the Invisible (1932), Sails and Anchors (1934), Life's Unanswered Questions (1944), and In the Light of the Cross (1947).

An Angel in the Sun 249

POTEAT (po-tēt'), EDWIN McNEILL: Born at New Haven, Conn., 1892. A Baptist. Educated at Furman Univ., Southern Baptist Theol. Sem. Traveling secretary, Student Volunteer Movement, 1916-17. Missionary, Southern Baptist Foreign Mission Board, China, 1917-26. Associate prof. philosophy and ethics, Shanghai Univ., 1926-29. Pastor, Raleigh, N.C.; Euclid Avenue Church, Cleveland, Ohio, 1937-44. President, Colgate-Rochester Theol. Sem. since 1944. Writer of poetry and hymns. In demand as a preacher and lecturer because of original thought, gifts of expression, and persuasive presentation of evangelical liberalism. Author: Coming to Terms with the Universe (1931), Jesus and the Liberal Mind (1932), Rev. John Doe (1934), Thunder over Sinai (1936), The So-

cial Manifesto of Jesus (1937), *These Shared His Passion* (1938), *These Shared His Cross* (1939), *These Shared His Power* (1941), *Four Freedoms and God* (1943), *Last Reprieve* (1946).
Vandalism or Faith? 256

REID (rēd), JAMES: Born at Leven, Fifeshire, Scotland, 1877. A Presbyterian. Educated at Edinburgh Univ. and New Col., Edinburgh. Pastor at Oban; Paisley; St. Andrew's Church, Eastbourne, England, 1915-46; now retired. President, Free Church Council of England and Wales, 1932-33. Moderator, Presbyterian Church of England, 1935. Warrack Lectures: *In Quest of Reality* (1924). A staff contributor to the *British Weekly*. With a strong sense of structure, a wide range of knowledge, and a mastery of speech, Dr. Reid has influenced pulpit work on both sides of the Atlantic. Author: *The Victory of God* (1933), *The Springs of Life* (1933), *The Key to the Kingdom* (1934), *Making Friends with Life* (1936), *The Temple in the Heart* (1937), *In Touch with Christ* (1938), *Facing Life with Christ* (1940), and *Where the New World Begins* (1947).
The Victory of God in the Disasters of Life 264

ROBERTSON, FREDERICK WILLIAM: Born in London, 1816. Died at Brighton, 1853. Church of England. During his brief lifetime he made little stir; afterward his published sermons brought him fame. In England he became known as "the preacher's preacher." The majority of his extant sermons, ninety-three in number, have recently become available in a single volume. This book affords the young clergyman a rich field for the study of his art. However, he ought to remember what the compiler wrote about these discourses: "They are not notes previously prepared, nor are they Sermons written before delivery. They are simply 'Recollections:' sometimes dictated by the Preacher himself to the younger members of a family in which he was interested, at their urgent entreaty; sometimes written out by himself for them when they were at a distance and unable to attend his ministry." What a series of special providences! Standard biography: *Life and Letters*, 2 vols., Stopford A. Brooke (1865). Also *The Soul of Frederick W. Robertson*, by James R. Blackwood (1947).
The Loneliness of Christ 99

SCHERER (shĕr'er), PAUL EHRMAN: Born at Mount Holly, Pa., 1892. A Lutheran. Educated at Col. of Charleston, S.C., and Lutheran Theol. Sem., Mount Airy, Pa. Instructor, Mount Airy Sem., 1919-29. Pastor of Holy Trinity Church, New York City, 1929-45. Associate prof. practical theology, Union Theol. Sem., since 1945. Radio preacher, national broadcast, Sunday Vespers, since 1932. Lyman Beecher Lectures at Yale: *For We Have This Treasure* (1943). Preacher and lecturer at many colleges and universities, Bible conferences, and ministerial assemblies. Associate editor of forthcoming *Interpreter's Bible*. A thoughtful interpreter of books and of life, a master of the King's English, Dr. Scherer appeals to the thoughtful and cultured. Books of sermons: *When God Hides* (1934), *Facts That Undergird Life* (1938), *The Place Where Thou Standest* (1942), and *Event in Eternity* (1945).
Protestantism: Its Liabilities and Assets 270

SIZOO (sī-zō'), JOSEPH RICHARD: Born in the Netherlands, 1884. Reformed Church in America. Educated at Hope Col., New Brunswick Theol. Sem., Columbia Univ. Missionary in southern India, 1911-17. Pastor in Walden, N.Y.; Somerville, N.J.; New York Avenue Presbyterian Church, Washington, D.C.; St. Nicholas Collegiate Church, New York City, 1936-46. President, New Brunswick Theol. Sem., since 1946. Chaplain, U. S. Army, World War I. An admirer of Lincoln and William J. Bryan. An indefatigable worker, a student of affairs, an intense speaker, and an irrepressible optimist. Sermonic writings: *The Kingdom Cometh* (1930), *The Way of Faith* (1935), *Make Life Worth Living* (1937), *Not Alone* (1940), and *On Guard* (1940).
The Way of Faith 277

SOCKMAN, RALPH WASHINGTON: Born at Mount Vernon, Ohio, 1889. A Methodist. Educated at Ohio Wesleyan Univ., Columbia Univ. (Ph.D. 1917), Union Theol. Sem. Intercollegiate secretary, Y.M.C.A., 1911-13. Pastor of Madison Avenue Church (now Christ Church) since 1915. Lyman Beecher Lectures at Yale: *The Highway of God* (1942). Radio preacher over national network. A deep, melodious voice, a wide range of human interests, and a command of virile English make him popular as a preacher and lecturer in New York City, as in colleges and universities. Author: *Suburbs of Christianity and Other Sermons* (1924), *Men of the Mysteries* (1927), *Morals of Tomorrow* (1931), *The Unemployed Carpenter* (1933), *The Paradoxes of Jesus* (1936), *Recoveries in Religion* (1937), *Live for Tomorrow* (1939), *Date with Destiny* (1944), and *Now to Live* (radio sermons, 1946).

Through Jesus Christ Our Lord 283

SPURGEON, CHARLES HADDON: Born at Kelvedon, Essex, England, 1834. Died 1892. A Baptist. A self-made preacher, with little schooling. Began to preach when sixteen years of age. Four years later went to London, where he built up a vast congregation at what became the Metropolitan Tabernacle. He brought to the pulpit manifold gifts, including a vivid imagination, a pleasing rhythm, and a marvelous voice, with simple diction, quaint humor, and rare pathos. Like Beecher, Spurgeon was almost a genius. Unlike the other, Spurgeon preached as well at twenty-two as ever after. He became the foremost modern herald of the old evangelical faith. His published writings include sixty-three volumes of sermons, and many other works, all religious. He built up an orphans' home and a pastors' college. His *Autobiography*, in four large volumes, was compiled by his widow and his secretary (1897-1900), abridged by D. O. Fuller (1947). Also, biographies by Fullerton, Carlile, Pike, et al.

Songs in the Night 114

STEWART, JAMES STUART: Born at Dundee, Scotland, 1896. A Presbyterian. Educated at St. Andrews Univ., Edinburgh; Bonn Univ., Germany. Pastor at Auchterarder; Aberdeen; North Morningside Church, Edinburgh, 1936-46. Invited to succeed H. R. Mackintosh as prof. theology at Edinburgh, 1936. Became prof. New Testament at Edinburgh, 1946. With H. R. Mackintosh co-editor of Schleiermacher's *The Christian Faith* (1928). Cunningham Lectures: *A Man in Christ* (1934). Warrack Lectures: *Heralds of God* (1946). Dr. Stewart attracts throngs of university men, as well as city folk. His two books of sermons show skill in the popular use of doctrine, felicity in phrasing, and range of illustrative materials. Author: *The Life and Times of Jesus Christ* (1933), *The Gates of New Life* (1937), *The Strong Name* (1940). The last two belong in the series "Scholar as Preacher."

The Lord God Omnipotent Reigneth 288

SUNDAY, WILLIAM ASHLEY: Born at Ames, Ia., 1863. Died at Winona Lake, Ind., 1935. A converted baseball player. A Presbyterian lay evangelist. With a team of experts "Billy" Sunday held meetings in most American cities. In a vast tabernacle he would reach more people than Moody, enroll more converts, and receive more money. Sunday appears to have done more lasting good in cities like Omaha, Neb., and Trenton, N.J., than in centers like New York and Boston. He attracted crowds by tireless energy, platform acrobatics, and attacks on public evils, notably the liquor traffic. He strove to preach the old gospel as he saw it. He won admiration and provoked opposition. Friends and critics agree that his type of mass evangelism has practically disappeared. A friendly biography: *Billy Sunday, the Man and His Message*, by William T. Ellis (1914). The other side emerges in *River of Years*, by Joseph F. Newton, pp. 99-100.

Heaven 144

TRUETT (troo'et), GEORGE WASHINGTON: Born in Clay County, North Carolina, 1867. Died at Dallas, Tex., 1944. A Baptist. Pastor at Waco, Tex.; and First Church, Dallas, 1897-1944. He led in making the First Church probably the largest Protestant congregation in America. He became the leading religious figure in the city and the state, if not in the South. President of the Southern Baptist Convention, and of the Baptist World Alliance, 1934-39. His pulpit work was both evangelistic and pastoral, as well as simple. Author of sermons: *Follow Thou Me* (1932), *God's Call to America* (1924), *A Quest for Souls* (1917), and *We Would See Jesus* (1919). A biography: *George W. Truett* (rev. ed. 1945), by his son-in-law, Powhatan W. James.

The Conquest of Fear 158

WEATHERHEAD, LESLIE DIXON: Born at London, 1893. Educated at London Univ., Manchester Univ., Richmond Hill Theol. Col. A Wesleyan. A special student of psychology. In World War I an officer of the line, later a chaplain. Pastor in the English Methodist Church, Madras, India; Manchester, England; Leeds; City Temple, London, since 1936. He is said to be the only clergyman who can draw a capacity crowd anywhere in England at any hour of the week. Author: *Psychology in the Service of the Soul* (1930), *Psychology and Life* (1934), *The Mastery of Sex through Psychology and Religion* (1931). Among his many sermonic and devotional writings these are recent: *The Eternal Voice* (1940), *This Is the Victory* (1941), *Personalities of the Passion* (1943), *In Quest of a Kingdom* (1944), *A Plain Man Looks at the Cross* (1945), and *The Significance of Silence* (1946).

Why People Do Go to Church 295

WESLEY, JOHN: Born at Epworth rectory, 1703. Died in London, 1791. Educated at Charterhouse (school for boys) and Oxford Univ. Founder of Methodism. A classical scholar, a writer of hymns, and the author of thirty books. "The evidences of a mind steeped in classical culture, and keenly alive to the thought of his day, appear on almost every page. . . . When this man preached, the world knew that the hour of battle had been sounded." His immediate work was that of an itinerant evangelist. As an ecclesiastical statesman he was laying the foundations for world-wide Methodism. In England as a social reformer he seems indirectly to have averted a counterpart of the French Revolution. His sermon on "The Grand Assize" has long been widely known. The message that appears in this volume seems to have been another of his favorites. Standard biography: *The Life and Times of John Wesley*, 3 vols., by L. Tyerman (1880). More popular in form: *Life of John Wesley*, by Caleb T. Winchester (1906).

The Scripture Way of Salvation 23

WHITEFIELD (whit'fēld), GEORGE: Born at a tavern in Gloucester, England, 1714. Died at Newburyport, Mass., 1770. A Wesleyan. An associate of John and Charles Wesley. Whitefield won renown as an open-air preacher. In England and in the American Colonies he owed almost hypnotic powers to his histrionic gifts and his voice, which was "like an organ, a flute, a harp, all in one." According to the historian Lecky, Whitefield moved vast concourses by "a large command of vivid, homely, and picturesque English, and an extraordinary measure of the tact which enables a practiced orator to adapt himself to the character and disposition of his audience." With John Wesley the other might have said: "I look on the world as my parish. . . . In whatsoever part of it I am, I judge it meet, right, and my bounden duty to declare unto all that are willing to hear, the glad tidings of salvation." Unlike John Wesley, Whitefield worked largely alone, whereas the older man resembled Paul in being a builder of the Christian Church. Standard biography by L. Tyerman, in 2 vols. (1876-77).

The Burning Bush 32